National Law in WTO Law

This book examines how national law is treated in WTO law – both in the WTO treaty and dispute settlement cases. The WTO treaty contains a set of far-reaching obligations establishing a systemic and constitutional framework of interaction between WTO law and national law. WTO dispute settlement operates as an international layer of judicial review of national laws and administrative, judicial or quasi-judicial measures. Consequently, many of the WTO dispute settlement decisions and rulings relate in different ways to Members' national laws. Yet, there is no systematic analysis of this vastly important subject. This book provides the first thorough map of an increasingly complex field. In doing so, it extends the enquiry beyond well known formulas and combines practical analysis with principled discussion of how the treatment of national law in international law can – and indeed should – ensure effectiveness of international rules and promote good governance within nation-states.

SHARIF BHUIYAN is an Advocate of the Supreme Court of Bangladesh, a Partner at the law firm, Dr. Kamal Hossain & Associates, and Director of the South Asian Institute of Advanced Legal and Human Rights Studies (SAILS). He received LL.B. (Hons.) and LL.M. degrees from Dhaka University and LL.M. and Ph.D. degrees from Cambridge University.

National Law in WTO Law

Effectiveness and Good Governance in the World Trading System

Sharif Bhuiyan

CAMBRIDGE
UNIVERSITY PRESS

CAMBRIDGE UNIVERSITY PRESS
Cambridge, New York, Melbourne, Madrid, Cape Town,
Singapore, São Paulo, Delhi, Tokyo, Mexico City

Cambridge University Press
The Edinburgh Building, Cambridge CB2 8RU, UK

Published in the United States of America by Cambridge University Press, New York

www.cambridge.org
Information on this title: www.cambridge.org/9780521175340

First published 2007
First paperback edition 2011

A catalogue record for this publication is available from the British Library

ISBN 978-0-521-87531-8 Hardback
ISBN 978-0-521-17534-0 Paperback

In memory of my father Sharafat Ullah Bhuiyan and to my mother Nur Jahan

Contents

Acknowledgements

This book has its origin in a Ph.D. thesis submitted to Cambridge University in September 2004. My greatest debts, respectively, for the thesis and the book are to Daniel Bethlehem and James Crawford. Daniel was my Ph.D. supervisor and without his support, encouragement and advice nothing would have been possible. His sharp comments and criticisms, which combined his wealth of knowledge, academic acumen and practical experience in different branches of public international law, have always been useful. The Ph.D. thesis could not have metamorphosed into a book without the encouragement and guidance of James Crawford. I had the good fortune of being able to rely on James's support and to discuss both research and pastoral matters with him during my Ph.D. years as well. James was my examiner for the Certificate of Postgraduate Legal Studies course and in that capacity he read and commented on the paper that I submitted for that course. An abridged and updated version of the Certificate paper forms Chapter 8 of this book. Later, as I embarked on revising the thesis for publication, James made valuable suggestions and read, commented on and corrected various drafts of the concluding chapter.

I am indebted to my Ph.D. examiners, Dan Sarooshi and Guglielmo Verdirame, anonymous reviewers for Cambridge University Press and Joost Pauwelyn, who all made helpful, acute and provocative suggestions and criticisms. Many of their suggestions and criticisms have been taken into account in the final product. I thank John Barratt and Barbara von Tigerstrom for reading and commenting on earlier versions of Chapters 7 and 8. I had spent the autumn of 2002 with the Legal Affairs Division (LAD) of the WTO Secretariat, which gave me the opportunity to interact with the WTO's excellent legal team. I thank all staff and lawyers of the LAD for their warmth and cordiality and would like to mention in particular María Pereyra-Friedrichsen and Bruce Wilson. While at the WTO, I was able to discuss the research project with Lothar Ehring, Jeffrey Gertler, Reto Malacrida, Gabrielle Marceau and Ernst-Ulrich Petersmann, to all of whom I extend my sincere thanks.

I am grateful to the Commonwealth Scholarship Commission at the Association of Commonwealth Universities and Trinity College, Cambridge, for their generous financial support, without which neither the Ph.D. nor this book would have been possible. Thanks are due to the Lauterpacht Research Centre for International Law and its excellent international law community for their kind invitation and generosity, which made possible a visit to the Centre for purposes of revising the manuscript. At Cambridge University Press, many thanks to Finola O'Sullivan, Brenda Burke, Leigh Mueller and Richard Woodham. This is an opportunity also to thank the staff of the British Council, Commonwealth Scholarship Commission, Faculty of Law in Cambridge, Lauterpacht Research Centre, Squire Law Library and Trinity College.

At a personal level, there is an endless list of people to whom I am deeply indebted. Grae Worster has always listened with patience and kindness to various difficulties that I confronted and provided invaluable help, support and encouragement to cope with them. I received similar support and encouragement from my supervisor and James Crawford. I owe a very special debt to Kamal Hossain, for his affectionate advice, guidance, encouragement, relentless help over the years and, especially, for the example of his scholarship. I am indebted to Mizanur Rahman for an enjoyable introduction to international law and to Salahuddin Ahmad for his guidance during my transition from a student to a lawyer. I express thanks to my friends M. M. Akbar, Tanjib-ul Alam, John and Hilary Barratt, Mudasser Chowdhury, Lesley Dingle, Zakir Hafez, Manzoor Hasan, Sara Hossain and Shah Jahan for their support and encouragement. I am grateful to my former in-laws, particularly my parents-in-law, for their kindness and affection. Last but not least, I have always recognized the love and affection of my parents, brother and sisters to be my greatest good fortune. It is because of them that everything seems achievable and enjoyable and they deserve many thanks for that.

Abbreviations

AB	(WTO) Appellate Body
ADA	(WTO) Agreement on Implementation of Article VI of the General Agreement on Tariffs and Trade 1994 (commonly referred to as the "Anti-Dumping Agreement")
Agriculture Agreement	(WTO) Agreement on Agriculture
AJIL	*American Journal of International Law*
ARO	(WTO) Agreement on Rules of Origin
ASCM	(WTO) Agreement on Subsidies and Countervailing Measures
ATC	(WTO) Agreement on Textiles and Clothing
Berne Convention	Berne Convention for the Protection of Literary and Artistic Works 1971
BYIL	*British Year Book of International Law*
Customs Valuation Agreement	(WTO) Agreement on Implementation of Article VII of the General Agreement on Tariffs and Trade 1994
DSB	(WTO) Dispute Settlement Body
DSU	(WTO) Understanding on Rules and Procedures Governing the Settlement of Disputes (commonly referred to as the "Dispute Settlement Understanding")
EC	European Communities

EC Treaty	Treaty Establishing the European Community, March 25, 1957; consolidated version, November 10, 1997
ECHR	European Court of Human Rights
ECJ	Court of Justice of the European Communities
EHR Convention	Convention for the Protection of Human Rights and Fundamental Freedoms 1950
EJIL	*European Journal of International Law*
EU	European Union
GATS	(WTO) General Agreement on Trade in Services
GATT 1947	General Agreement on Tariffs and Trade 1947
GATT 1994	(WTO) General Agreement on Tariffs and Trade 1994
GPA	(WTO) Agreement on Government Procurement
ICJ	International Court of Justice
ILC	International Law Commission
IPRs	intellectual property rights
ITLOS	International Tribunal for the Law of the Sea
JIEL	*Journal of International Economic Law*
JWT	*Journal of World Trade*
Licensing Agreement	(WTO) Agreement on Import Licensing Procedures
MFN	most-favored nation
NAFTA	North American Free Trade Agreement
PCIJ	Permanent Court of International Justice
PSI Agreement	(WTO) Agreement on Preshipment Inspection
Safeguards Agreement	(WTO) Agreement on Safeguards
SPS Agreement	(WTO) Agreement on the Application of Sanitary and Phytosanitary Measures

TBT Agreement	(WTO) Agreement on Technical Barriers to Trade
TPRM	(WTO) Trade Policy Review Mechanism
TRIMS Agreement	(WTO) Agreement on Trade-Related Investment Measures
TRIPS Agreement	(WTO) Agreement on Trade-Related Aspects of Intellectual Property Rights
UNCLOS	United Nations Convention on the Law of the Sea
UR	Uruguay Round of Multilateral Trade Negotiations
VCLT	Vienna Convention on the Law of Treaties 1969
WTO Agreement	Marrakesh Agreement Establishing the World Trade Organization

Table of GATT cases

Short title	Full case title and citation
Belgian Family Allowances	*Belgian Family Allowances* Working Party Report, adopted November 7, 1952, BISD 1S/59 246
Belgium – Tax Legislation	*Income Tax Practices Maintained by Belgium* Panel Report, adopted December 7–8, 1981, BISD 23S/127 138
Brazil – Milk Powder	*Brazil – Imposition of Provisional and Definitive Countervailing Duties on Milk Powder and Certain Types of Milk from the European Economic Community* Panel Report, adopted April 28, 1994, GATT Doc. SCM/179 153, 159
Brazilian Internal Taxes	*Brazilian Internal Taxes* Working Party Report, adopted June 30, 1949, BISD II/181 247
Canada – Alcohol I	*Canada – Import, Distribution and Sale of Alcoholic Drinks by Canadian Provincial Marketing Agencies* Panel Report, adopted March 22, 1988, BISD 35S/37 64, 246
Canada – Alcohol II	*Canada – Import, Distribution and Sale of Certain Alcoholic Drinks by Provincial Marketing Agencies* Panel Report, adopted February 18, 1992, BISD 39S/27 64, 65, 246

These cases are referred to in the text by the short title given in the left-hand column. While most of the GATT panel reports are published in GATT's *Basic Instruments and Selected Documents* (BISD), these reports, as well as the ones that are not so published, are also available from the WTO website at www.wto.org/english/tratop_e/dispu_e/gt47ds_e.htm.

(cont.)

Short title	Full case title and citation
Canada – FIRA	*Canada – Administration of the Foreign Investment Review Act* Panel Report, adopted February 7, 1984, BISD 30S/140 219
Canada – Grain Corn	*Canadian Countervailing Duties on Grain Corn from the United States* Panel Report, adopted March 26, 1992, BISD 39S/411 153, 159
EEC – Parts and Components	*EEC – Regulation on Imports of Parts and Components* Panel Report, adopted May 16, 1990, BISD 37S/132 102, 136, 137, 248, 262
Existing Measures	*Notifications of Existing Measures and Procedural Questions* Working Party Report, adopted August 10, 1949, BISD II/49 245
France – Tax Legislation	*Income Tax Practices Maintained by France* Panel Report, adopted December 7–8, 1981, BISD 23S/114 138
German Import Restrictions I	*Import Restrictions of the Federal Republic of Germany* Working Party Report, adopted November 30, 1957, BISD 6S/55 246
German Import Restrictions II	*Import Restrictions Maintained by the Federal Republic of Germany* Working Party Report, adopted May 2, 1958, BISD 7S/99 246
Japan – Agricultural Products I	*Japan – Restrictions on Imports of Certain Agricultural Products* Panel Report, adopted March 22, 1988, BISD 35S/163 101
Japan – Alcohol I	*Japan – Customs Duties, Taxes and Labelling Practices on Imported Wines and Alcoholic Beverages* Panel Report, adopted November 10, 1987, BISD 34S/83 46
Japan – Semi-Conductors	*Japan – Trade in Semi-Conductors* Panel Report, adopted May 4, 1988, BISD 35S/116 101
Korea – Polyacetal Resins	*Korea – Anti-Dumping Duties on Imports of Polyacetal Resins from the United States* Panel Report, adopted April 27, 1993, BISD 40S/205 153, 159

Short title	Full case title and citation
Netherlands – Tax Legislation	*Income Tax Practices Maintained by the Netherlands* Panel Report, adopted December 7–8, 1981, BISD 23S/137 138
New Zealand – Transformers	*New Zealand – Imports of Electrical Transformers from Finland* Panel Report, adopted July 18, 1985, BISD 32S/55 153
Norway – Apples	*Norway – Restrictions on Imports of Apples and Pears* Panel Report, adopted June 22, 1989, BISD 36S/306 246
Swedish Anti-Dumping Duties	*Swedish Anti-Dumping Duties* Panel Report, adopted February 26, 1955, BISD 3S/81 153, 158
Thai – Cigarettes	*Thailand – Restrictions on Importation of and Internal Taxes on Cigarettes* Panel Report, adopted November 7, 1990, BISD 37S/200 49, 101, 171, 246, 248
Uruguayan Recourse	*Uruguayan Recourse to Article XXIII* Panel Report, adopted November 16, 1962, BISD 11S/95 99
US – Cement	*United States – Anti-Dumping Duties on Gray Portland Cement and Cement Clinker from Mexico* Panel Report, September 7, 1992, unadopted, GATT Doc. ADP/82 21
US – DISC	*United States Tax Legislation (DISC)* Panel Report, adopted December 7–8, 1981, BISD 23S/98 38, 138
US – Fur Hats	*Withdrawal by the United States of a Tariff Concession under Article XIX of the General Agreement on Tariffs and Trade* Working Party Report, adopted October 22, 1951, GATT/CP.6/SR.19, Sales No. GATT/1951–3 153, 159
US – Malt Beverages	*United States – Measures Affecting Alcoholic and Malt Beverages* Panel Report, adopted June 19, 1992, BISD 39S/206 101, 171, 219, 246, 248
US – Manufacturing Clause	*United States Manufacturing Clause* Panel Report, adopted May 15–16, 1984, BISD 31S/74 38, 64, 246

(*cont.*)

Table of WTO cases

Short title	Full case title and citation
Argentina – Ceramic Tiles	*Argentina – Definitive Anti-Dumping Measures on Imports of Ceramic Floor Tiles from Italy* Panel Report, WT/DS189/R, DSR 2001: XII, 6241 (September 28, 2001) 185
Argentina – Footwear	*Argentina – Safeguard Measures on Imports of Footwear* Panel Report, WT/DS121/R, DSR 2000: II, 575 (June 25, 1999) Appellate Body Report, WT/DS121/AB/R, DSR 2000: I, 515 (December 14, 1999) 65, 188
Argentina – Hides and Leather	*Argentina – Measures Affecting the Export of Bovine Hides and the Import of Finished Leather* Panel Report, WT/DS155/R, DSR 2001: V, 1779 (December 19, 2000) 69, 76, 77, 78, 101
Argentina – Peaches	*Argentina – Definitive Safeguard Measure on Imports of Preserved Peaches* Panel Report, WT/DS238/R, DSR 2003: III, 1037 (February 14, 2003) 188
Argentina – Poultry	*Argentina – Definitive Anti-Dumping Duties on Poultry from Brazil* Panel Report, WT/DS241/R, DSR 2003: V, 1727 (April 22, 2003) 145, 146, 185

These cases are referred to in the text by the short title given in the left-hand column. All WTO panel and Appellate Body reports and arbitration awards (including those cited herein) are available through the Dispute Settlement Gateway of the WTO website at www.wto.org/english/tratop_e/dispu_e/dispu_e.htm.

(*cont.*)

Short title	Full case title and citation
Argentina – Textiles	*Argentina – Measures Affecting Imports of Footwear, Textiles, Apparel and Other Items* Panel Report, WT/DS56/R, DSR 1998: III, 1033 (November 25, 1997) Appellate Body Report, WT/DS56/AB/R, DSR 1998: III, 1003 (March 27, 1998) 22, 93, 101, 219, 254
Australia – Leather 21.5	*Australia – Subsidies Provided to Producers and Exporters of Automotive Leather, Recourse to Article 21.5 of the DSU by the United States* Panel Report, WT/DS126/RW, DSR 2000: III, 1189 (January 21, 2000) 109
Australia – Salmon	*Australia – Measures Affecting Importation of Salmon* Panel Report, WT/DS18/R, DSR 1998: VIII, 3407 (June 12, 1998) Appellate Body Report, WT/DS18/AB/R, DSR 1998: VIII, 3327 (October 20, 1998) 160, 170, 201, 239, 240
Australia – Salmon 21.5	*Australia – Measures Affecting Importation of Salmon, Recourse to Article 21.5 by Canada* Panel Report, WT/DS18/RW, DSR 2000: IV, 2031 (February 18, 2000) 170
Brazil – Aircraft 21.5 II	*Brazil – Export Financing Programme for Aircraft, Second Recourse by Canada to Article 21.5 of the DSU* Panel Report, WT/DS46/RW/2, DSR 2001: XI, 5481 (July 26, 2001) 259
Brazil – Aircraft 22.6	*Brazil – Export Financing Programme for Aircraft, Recourse to Arbitration by Brazil under Article 22.6 of the DSU and Article 4.11 of the SCM Agreement* Decision by the Arbitrators, WT/DS46/ARB, DSR 2002: I, 19 (August 28, 2000) 115
Canada – Aircraft	*Canada – Measures Affecting the Export of Civilian Aircraft* Panel Report, WT/DS70/R, DSR 1999: IV, 1443 (April 14, 1999) Appellate Body Report, WT/DS70/AB/R, DSR 1999: III, 1377 (August 2, 1999) 102, 254
Canada – Autos	*Canada – Certain Measures Affecting the Automotive Industry* Panel Report, WT/DS139/R, WT/DS142/R, DSR 2000: VII, 3043 (February 11, 2000) Appellate Body Report, WT/DS139/AB/R, WT/DS142/AB/R, DSR 2000: VI, 2985 (May 31, 2000) 46, 135, 136

(*cont.*)

Short title	Full case title and citation
	Award of the Arbitrator, WT/DS207/13, DSR 2003: III, 1237 (March 17, 2003) 113
Chile – Alcohol	*Chile – Taxes on Alcoholic Beverages* Panel Report, WT/DS87/R, WT/DS110/R, DSR 2000: I, 303 (June 15, 1999) Appellate Body Report, WT/DS87/AB/R, WT/DS110/AB/R, DSR 2000: I, 281 (December 13, 1999) 227, 228–9
Chile – Alcohol 21.3(c)	*Chile – Taxes on Alcoholic Beverages, Arbitration under Article 21.3(c) of the DSU* Award of the Arbitrator, WT/DS87/15, WT/DS110/14, DSR 2000: V, 2583 (May 23, 2000) 113
Dominican Republic – Cigarettes	*Dominican Republic – Measures Affecting the Importation and Internal Sale of Cigarettes* Panel Report, WT/DS302/R (November 26, 2004) Appellate Body Report, WT/DS302/AB/R (April 25, 2005) 79, 88, 100, 201, 210
EC – Asbestos	*European Communities – Measures Affecting Asbestos and Asbestos-Containing Products* Panel Report, WT/DS135/R, DSR 2001: VIII, 3305 (September 18, 2000) Appellate Body Report, WT/DS135/AB/R, DSR 2001: VII, 3243 (March 12, 2001) 49, 99, 136, 171, 196, 197, 198, 201, 219
EC – Bananas	*European Communities – Regime for the Importation, Sale and Distribution of Bananas* Panel Reports, WT/DS27/R/ECU, DSR 1997: III, 3 (Complaint by Ecuador), WT/DS27/R/GTM, WT/DS27/R/HND, DSR 1997: II, 695 (Complaint by Guatemala and Honduras), WT/DS27/R/MEX, DSR 1997: II, 803 (Complaint by Mexico), WT/DS27/R/USA, DSR 1997: II, 943 (Complaint by the United States) (May 22, 1997) Appellate Body Report, WT/DS27/AB/R, DSR 1997: II, 589 (September 9, 1997) 46, 61, 75–7, 78, 116, 136, 223
EC – Bananas 21.3(c)	*European Communities – Regime for the Importation, Sale and Distribution of Bananas, Arbitration under Article 21.3(c) of the DSU* Award of the Arbitrator, WT/DS27/15, DSR 1998: I, 3 (January 7, 1998) 113

Short title	Full case title and citation
EC – Bananas 22.6	*European Communities – Regime for the Importation, Sale and Distribution of Bananas, Recourse to Arbitration by the European Communities under Article 22.6 of the DSU* Decision by the Arbitrators, WT/DS27/ARB, DSR 1999: II, 725 (April 9, 1999) 47, 115
EC – Bananas (Ecuador) 22.6	*European Communities – Regime for the Importation, Sale and Distribution of Bananas, Recourse to Arbitration by the European Communities under Article 22.6 of the DSU* Decision by the Arbitrators, WT/DS27/ARB/ECU, DSR 2000: V, 2237 (March 24, 2000) 115
EC – Bed Linen	*European Communities – Anti-Dumping Duties on Imports of Cotton-Type Bed Linen from India* Panel Report, WT/DS141/R, DSR 2001: VI, 2077 (October 30, 2000) Appellate Body Report, WT/DS141/AB/R, DSR 2001: V, 2049 (March 1, 2001) 146, 160, 177, 179, 185
EC – Bed Linen 21.5	*European Communities – Anti-Dumping Duties on Imports of Cotton-Type Bed Linen from India, Recourse to Article 21.5 of the DSU by India* Panel Report, WT/DS141/RW, DSR 2003: IV, 1269 (November 29, 2002) Appellate Body Report, WT/DS141/AB/RW, DSR 2003: III, 965 (April 8, 2003) 179, 201
EC – Chicken Cuts 21.3(c)	*European Communities – Customs Classification of Frozen Boneless Chicken Cuts, Arbitration under Article 21.3(c) of the DSU* Award of the Arbitrator, WT/DS269/13, WT/DS286/15 (February 20, 2006) 113
EC – Customs Matters	*European Communities – Selected Customs Matters* Panel Report, WT/DS315/R (June 16, 2006) Appellate Body Report, WT/DS315/AB/R (November 13, 2006) 68, 77, 79, 80

(cont.)

Short title	Full case title and citation
EC – Export Subsidies on Sugar 21.3(c)	*European Communities – Export Subsidies on Sugar, Arbitration under Article 21.3(c) of the DSU* Award of the Arbitrator, WT/DS265/33, WT/DS266/33, WT/DS283/14 (October 28, 2005) 113
EC – Hormones I	*EC – Measures Concerning Meat and Meat Products (Hormones)*, Complaint by the United States Panel Report, WT/DS26/R/USA, DSR 1998: III, 698 (August 18, 1997) Appellate Body Report, WT/DS26/AB/R, WT/DS48/AB/R, DSR 1998: I, 135 (January 16, 1998) 62, 106, 116, 122, 136, 156–7, 158–63, 168, 179, 184, 198, 201, 226, 227, 239
EC – Hormones II	*EC – Measures Concerning Meat and Meat Products (Hormones)*, Complaint by Canada Panel Report, WT/DS48/R/CAN, DSR 1998: II, 235 (August 18, 1997) Appellate Body Report, WT/DS26/AB/R, WT/DS48/AB/R, DSR 1998: I, 135 (January 16, 1998) 62, 106, 116, 122, 136, 156–7, 158–63, 168, 179, 184, 198, 201, 226, 227, 229
EC – Hormones I 22.6	*European Communities – Measures Concerning Meat and Meat Products (Hormones), Original Complaint by the United States, Recourse to Arbitration by the European Communities under Article 22.6 of the DSU* Decision by the Arbitrators, WT/DS26/ARB, DSR 1999: III, 1105 (July 12, 1999) 88, 115
EC – Hormones II 22.6	*European Communities – Measures Concerning Meat and Meat Products (Hormones), Original Complaint by Canada, Recourse to Arbitration by the European Communities under Article 22.6 of the DSU* Decision by the Arbitrators, WT/DS48/ARB, DSR 1999: III, 1135 (July 12, 1999) 88, 115
EC – Hormones 21.3(c)	*EC – Measures Concerning Meat and Meat Products (Hormones), Arbitration under Article 21.3(c) of the DSU* Award of the Arbitrator, WT/DS26/15, WT/DS48/13, DSR 1998: V, 1833 (May 29, 1998) 113
EC – Pipe Fittings	*European Communities – Anti-Dumping Duties on Malleable Cast Iron Tube or Pipe Fittings from Brazil* Panel Report, WT/DS219/R, DSR 2003: VII, 2701 (March 7, 2003) Appellate Body Report, WT/DS219/AB/R, DSR 2003: VI, 2613 (July 22, 2003) 146, 185

Short title	Full case title and citation
EC – Poultry	*European Communities – Measures Affecting the Importation of Certain Poultry Products* Panel Report, WT/DS69/R, DSR 1998: V, 2089 (March 12, 1998) Appellate Body Report, WT/DS69/AB/R, DSR 1998: V, 2031 (July 13, 1998) 76, 93, 239, 240
EC – Sardines	*European Communities – Trade Description of Sardines* Panel Report, WT/DS231/R, DSR 2002: VIII, 3451 (May 29, 2002) Appellate Body Report, WT/DS231/AB/R, DSR 2002: VIII, 3359 (September 26, 2002) 136, 201
EC – Tariff Preferences	*European Communities – Conditions for the Granting of Tariff Preferences to Developing Countries* Panel Report, WT/DS246/R, DSR 2004: III, 1037 (December 1, 2003) Appellate Body Report, WT/DS246/AB/R, DSR 2004: III, 951 (April 7, 2004) 38, 47
EC – Tariff Preferences 21.3(c)	*European Communities – Conditions for the Granting of Tariff Preferences to Developing Countries, Arbitration under Article 21.3(c) of the DSU* Award of the Arbitrator, WT/DS246/14, DSR 2004: IX, 4313 (September 20, 2004) 88, 113
Egypt – Rebar	*Egypt – Definitive Anti-Dumping Measures on Steel Rebar from Turkey* Panel Report, WT/DS211/R, DSR 2002: VII, 2667 (August 8, 2002) 145, 185, 219
Guatemala – Cement I	*Guatemala – Anti-Dumping Investigation Regarding Portland Cement from Mexico* Panel Report, WT/DS60/R, DSR 1998: IX, 3797 (June 19, 1998) Appellate Body Report, WT/DS60/AB/R, DSR 1998: IX, 3767 (November 2, 1998) 64
Guatemala – Cement II	*Guatemala – Definitive Anti-Dumping Measures on Grey Portland Cement from Mexico* Panel Report, WT/DS156/R, DSR 2000: XI, 5295 (October 24, 2000) 145, 185
India – Autos	*India – Measures Affecting the Automotive Sector* Panel Report, WT/DS146/R, WT/DS175/R, DSR 2002: V, 1827 (December 21, 2001) Appellate Body Report, WT/DS146/AB/R, WT/DS175/AB/R, DSR 2002: V, 1821 (March 19, 2002) 259

(cont.)

Short title	Full case title and citation
Japan – Apples	*Japan – Measures Affecting the Importation of Apples* Panel Report, WT/DS245/R, DSR 2003: IX, 4481 (July 15, 2003) Appellate Body Report, WT/DS245/AB/R, DSR 2003: IX, 4391 (November 26, 2003) 38, 88, 160, 171–2, 201
Japan – Film	*Japan – Measures Affecting Consumer Photographic Film and Paper* Panel Report, WT/DS44/R, DSR 1998: IV, 1179 (March 31, 1998) 99, 101, 211–12. 277
Korea – Alcohol	*Korea – Taxes on Alcoholic Beverages* Panel Report, WT/DS75/R, WT/DS84/R, DSR 1999: I, 44 (September 17, 1998) Appellate Body Report, WT/DS75/AB/R, WT/DS84/AB/R, DSR 1999: I, 3 (January 18, 1999) 113, 160, 201, 239, 240
Korea – Alcohol 21.3(c)	*Korea – Taxes on Alcoholic Beverages, Arbitration under Article 21.3(c) of the DSU* Award of the Arbitrator, WT/DS75/16, WT/DS84/14, DSR 1999: II, 937 (June 4, 1999) 113
Korea – Beef	*Korea – Measures Affecting Imports of Fresh, Chilled and Frozen Beef* Panel Report, WT/DS161/R, WT/DS169/R, DSR 2001: I, 59 (July 31, 2000) Appellate Body Report, WT/DS161/AB/R, WT/DS169/AB/R, DSR 2001: I, 5 (December 11, 2000) 49, 101, 171, 197
Korea – Commercial Vessels	*Korea – Measures Affecting Trade in Commercial Vessels* Panel Report, WT/DS273/R (March 7, 2005) 259
Korea – Dairy	*Korea – Definitive Safeguard Measure on Imports of Certain Dairy Products* Panel Report, WT/DS98/R, DSR 2000: I, 49 (June 21, 1999) Appellate Body Report, WT/DS98/AB/R, DSR 2000: I, 3 (December 14, 1999) 65, 188
Korea – Procurement	*Korea – Measures Affecting Government Procurement* Panel Report, WT/DS163/R, DSR 2000: VIII, 3541 (May 1, 2000) 99
Mexico – HFCS	*Mexico – Anti-Dumping Investigation of High Fructose Corn Syrup (HFCS) from the United States* Panel Report, WT/DS132/R, DSR 2000: III, 1345 (January 28, 2000) 145, 185

(cont.)

Short title	Full case title and citation
	Decision by the Arbitrators, WT/DS136/ARB, DSR 2004: IX, 4269 (February 24, 2004) 115
US – 1916 Act 21.3(c)	*United States – Anti-Dumping Act of 1916, Arbitration under Article 21.3(c) of the DSU* Award of the Arbitrator, WT/DS136/11, WT/DS162/14, DSR 2001: V, 2017 (February 28, 2001) 113
US – Carbon Steel	*United States – Countervailing Duties on Certain Corrosion-Resistant Carbon Steel Flat Products from Germany* Panel Report, WT/DS213/R, DSR 2002: IX, 3835 (July 3, 2002) Appellate Body Report, WT/DS213/AB/R, DSR 2002: IX, 3781 (November 28, 2002) 62, 88, 201, 210, 259
US – Certain Products	*United States – Import Measures on Certain Products from the European Communities* Panel Report, WT/DS165/R, DSR 2001: II, 413 (July 17, 2000) Appellate Body Report, WT/DS165/AB/R, DSR 2001: I, 373 (December 11, 2000) 109
US – Copyright Act	*United States – Section 110(5) of the US Copyright Act* Panel Report, WT/DS160/R, DSR 2000: VIII, 3769 (June 15, 2000) 25, 38, 88, 211, 223, 226, 262
US – Copyright Act 21.3(c)	*United States – Section 110(5) of the US Copyright Act, Arbitration under Article 21.3(c) of the DSU* Award of the Arbitrator, WT/DS160/12, DSR 2001: II, 657 (January 15, 2001) 113
US – Copyright Act 25	*United States – Section 110(5) of the US Copyright Act, Recourse to Arbitration under Article 25 of the DSU* Award of the Arbitrators, WT/DS160/ARB25/1, DSR 2001: II, 667 (November 9, 2001) 91, 192
US – Cotton Yarn	*United States – Transitional Safeguard Measure on Combed Cotton Yarn from Pakistan* Panel Report, WT/DS192/R, DSR 2001: XII, 6067 (May 31, 2001) Appellate Body Report, WT/DS192/AB/R, DSR 2001: XII, 6027 (October 8, 2001) 160, 172, 187–8, 189, 198

(cont.)

Short title	Full case title and citation
US – FSC 21.5 II	*United States – Tax Treatment for "Foreign Sales Corporations" Second recourse to Article 21.5 of the DSU by the European Communities* Panel Report, WT/DS108/RW2 (September 30, 2005) Appellate Body Report, WT/DS108/AB/RW2 (February 13, 2006) 38, 88, 114, 139
US – FSC 22.6	*United States – Tax Treatment for "Foreign Sales Corporations," Recourse to Arbitration by the United States under Article 22.6 of the DSU and Article 4.11 of the SCM Agreement* Decision of the Arbitrator, WT/DS108/ARB, DSR 2002: VI, 2517 (August 30, 2002) 15
US – Gambling Services	*United States – Measures Affecting the Cross-Border Supply of Gambling and Betting Services* Panel Report, WT/DS285/R (November 10, 2004) Appellate Body Report, WT/DS285/AB/R (April 7, 2005) 38, 201
US – Gambling Services 21.3(c)	*United States – Measures Affecting the Cross-Border Supply of Gambling and Betting Services, Arbitration under Article 21.3(c) of the DSU* Award of the Arbitrator, WT/DS285/13 (August 19, 2005) 75, 8, 113
US – Gasoline	*United States – Standards for Reformulated and Conventional Gasoline* Panel Report, WT/DS2/R, DSR 1996: I, 29 (January 29, 1996) Appellate Body Report, WT/DS2/AB/R, DSR 1996: I, 3 (April 29, 1996) 65, 88, 93, 97, 173, 184–5
US – Hot-Rolled Steel	*United States – Anti-Dumping Measures on Certain Hot-Rolled Steel Products from Japan* Panel Report, WT/DS184/R, DSR 2001: X, 4769 (February 28, 2001) Appellate Body Report, WT/DS184/AB/R, DSR 2001: X, 4697 (July 24, 2001) 61, 64, 78, 88, 145, 146, 177, 178, 185, 186, 220, 231, 232, 259
US – Hot-Rolled Steel 21.3(c)	*United States – Anti-Dumping Measures on Certain Hot-Rolled Steel Products from Japan, Arbitration under Article 21.3(c) of the DSU* Award of the Arbitrator, WT/DS184/13, DSR 2002: IV, 1389 (February 19, 2002) 113

(cont.)

Short title	Full case title and citation
US – Lamb	*United States – Safeguard Measures on Imports of Fresh, Chilled or Frozen Lamb Meat from New Zealand and Australia* Panel Report, WT/DS177/R, WT/DS178/R, DSR 2001: IX, 4107 (December 21, 2000) Appellate Body Report, WT/DS177/AB/R, WT/DS178/AB/R, DSR 2001: IX, 4051 (May 1, 2001) 160, 188, 198
US – Lead and Bismuth	*United States – Imposition of Countervailing Duties on Certain Hot-Rolled Lead and Bismuth Carbon Steel Products Originating in the United Kingdom* Panel Report, WT/DS138/R, DSR 2000: VI, 2623 (December 23, 1999) Appellate Body Report, WT/DS138/AB/R, DSR 2000: V, 2595 (May 10, 2000) 155
US – Line Pipe	*United States – Definitive Safeguard Measures on Imports of Circular Welded Carbon Quality Line Pipe from Korea* Panel Report, WT/DS202/R, DSR 2002: IV, 1473 (October 29, 2001) Appellate Body Report, WT/DS202/AB/R, DSR 2002: IV, 1403 (February 15, 2002) 172, 188, 198
US – OCTG Sunset Reviews	*United States – Sunset Reviews of Anti-Dumping Measures on Oil Country Tubular Goods from Argentina* Panel Report, WT/DS268/R, DSR 2004: VIII, 3421 (July 16, 2004) Appellate Body Report, WT/DS268/AB/R, DSR 2004: VII, 3341 (November 29, 2004) 77, 201
US – Offset Act	*United States – Continued Dumping and Subsidy Offset Act of 2000* Panel Report, WT/DS217/R, WT/DS234/R, DSR 2003: II, 489 (September 16, 2002) Appellate Body Report, WT/DS217/AB/R, WT/DS234/AB/R, DSR 2003: I, 375 (January 16, 2003) 38, 61, 77, 88, 99, 192, 220, 226, 227, 229–30, 231, 259
US – Offset Act 21.3(c)	*United States – Continued Dumping and Subsidy Offset Act of 2000, Arbitration under Article 21.3(c) of the DSU* Award of the Arbitrator, WT/DS217/14, WT/DS234/22, DSR 2003: III, 1163 (June 13, 2003) 113
US – Rules of Origin	*United States – Rules of Origin for Textiles and Apparel Products* Panel Report, WT/DS243/R, DSR 2003: VI, 2309 (June 20, 2003) 88

Short title	Full case title and citation
US – Section 129	*United States – Section 129(c)(1) of the Uruguay Round Agreements Act* Panel Report, WT/DS221/R, DSR 2002: VII, 2581 (July 15, 2002) 62, 88, 104, 192, 215, 219, 220–27, 229, 231, 232, 241–2, 259
US – Section 211	*United States – Section 211 Omnibus Appropriations Act of 1998* Panel Report, WT/DS176/R, DSR 2002: II, 683 (August 6, 2001) Appellate Body Report, WT/DS176/AB/R, DSR 2002: II, 589 (January 2, 2002) 22, 38, 80, 83, 88, 192, 219, 220, 223, 231, 236, 237, 240–1, 259
US – Section 301	*United States – Sections 301–310 of the Trade Act of 1974* Panel Report, WT/DS152/R, DSR 2000: II, 815 (December 22, 1999) 38, 61, 62, 88, 102, 160, 176, 194, 217, 219, 220, 222, 223, 235, 236–7, 238, 254–7, 260, 261, 262, 263, 264, 265, 266, 267, 268, 269
US – Shirts and Blouses	*United States – Measure Affecting Imports of Woven Wool Shirts and Blouses from India* Panel Report, WT/DS33/R, DSR 1997: I, 343 (January 6, 1997) Appellate Body Report, WT/DS33/AB/R, DSR 1997: I, 323 (April 25, 1997) 156, 157, 210, 211
US – Shrimp	*United States – Import Prohibition of Certain Shrimp and Shrimp Products* Panel Report, WT/DS58/R, DSR 1998: VII, 2821 (May 15, 1998) Appellate Body Report, WT/DS58/AB/R, DSR 1998: VII, 2755 (October 12, 1998) 19, 88, 136, 171, 172, 195, 197, 205, 225, 226, 227, 228, 230
US – Shrimp 21.5	*United States – Import Prohibition of Certain Shrimp and Shrimp Products, Recourse to Article 21.5 by Malaysia* Panel Report, WT/DS58/RW, DSR 2001: XIII, 6529 (June 15, 2001) Appellate Body Report, WT/DS58/AB/RW, DSR 2001: XIII, 6481 (October 22, 2001) 22, 88, 223, 224–5
US – Softwood Lumber III	*United States – Preliminary Determinations with Respect to Certain Softwood Lumber from Canada* Panel Report, WT/DS236/R, DSR 2002: IX, 3597 (September 27, 2002) 62, 88, 259

(cont.)

Short title	Full case title and citation
US – Softwood Lumber IV	*United States – Final Countervailing Duty Determination with Respect to Certain Softwood Lumber from Canada* Panel Report, WT/DS257/R, DSR 2004: II, 659 (August 29, 2003) Appellate Body Report, WT/DS257/AB/R, DSR 2004: II, 587 (January 19, 2004) 134, 140
US – Softwood Lumber V	*United States – Final Dumping Determination on Softwood Lumber from Canada* Panel Report, WT/DS264/R, DSR 2004: V, 1981 (April 13, 2004) Appellate Body Report, WT/DS264/AB/R, DSR 2004: V, 1917 (August 11, 2004) 179
US – Softwood Lumber V 21.5	*United States – Final Dumping Determination on Softwood Lumber from Canada, Recourse to Article 21.5 of the DSU by Canada* Panel Report, WT/DS264/RW (April 3, 2006) Appellate Body Report, WT/DS264/AB/RW (August 15, 2006) 179
US – Softwood Lumber VI 21.5	*United States – Investigation of the International Trade Commission in Softwood Lumber from Canada, Recourse to Article 21.5 of the DSU by Canada* Panel Report, WT/DS277/RW (November 15, 2005) Appellate Body Report, WT/DS277/AB/RW (April 13, 2006) 160, 179, 190, 191, 195, 201–2
US – Stainless Steel	*United States – Anti-Dumping Measures on Stainless Steel Plate in Coils and Stainless Steel Sheet and Strip from Korea* Panel Report, WT/DS179/R, DSR 2001: IV, 1295 (December 22, 2000) 78, 145, 146, 176–7, 185
US – Steel Plate	*United States – Anti-Dumping and Countervailing Measures on Steel Plate from India* Panel Report, WT/DS206/R, DSR 2002: VI, 2073 (June 28, 2002) 145, 146, 252, 259
US – Steel Safeguards	*United States – Definitive Safeguard Measures on Imports of Certain Steel Products* Panel Report, WT/DS248/R, WT/DS249/R, WT/DS251/R, WT/DS252/R, WT/DS253/R, WT/DS254/R, WT/DS258/R, WT/DS259/R, DSR 2003: VIII, 3273 (July 11, 2003)

Short title	Full case title and citation
	Appellate Body Report, WT/DS248/AB/R, WT/DS249/AB/R, WT/DS251/AB/R, WT/DS252/AB/R, WT/DS253/AB/R, WT/DS254/AB/R, WT/DS258/AB/R, WT/DS259/AB/R, DSR 2003: VII, 3117 (November 10, 2003) 187, 188, 189, 198
US – Underwear	*United States – Restrictions on Imports of Cotton and Man-made Fibre Underwear* Panel Report, WT/DS24/R, DSR 1997: I, 31 (November 8, 1996) Appellate Body Report, WT/DS24/AB/R, DSR 1997: I, 11 (February 10, 1997) 70, 85, 156, 157, 189
US – Upland Cotton	*United States – Subsidies on Upland Cotton* Panel Report, WT/DS267/R (September 8, 2004) Appellate Body Report, WT/DS267/AB/R (March 3, 2005) 201, 259
US – Wheat Gluten	*United States – Definitive Safeguard Measures on Imports of Wheat Gluten from the European Communities* Panel Report, WT/DS166/R, DSR 2001: III, 779 (July 31, 2000) Appellate Body Report, WT/DS166/AB/R, DSR 2001: II, 717 (December 22, 2000) 160, 188, 201
US – Zeroing	*United States – Laws, Regulations and Methodology for Calculating Dumping Margins (''Zeroing'')* Panel Report, WT/DS294/R (October 31, 2005) Appellate Body Report, WT/DS294/AB/R (April 18, 2006) 62, 179, 259

Table of other cases

1 Introduction

1 The WTO and its coverage

The coming into being of the World Trade Organization (WTO) on January 1, 1995 has been described as "a watershed moment for the institutions of world economic relations"[1] and the international agreement that gave birth to this international organization has been viewed as "the most important event in recent world economic history."[2] The creation of the WTO lay in a trade negotiating round, namely the Uruguay Round of Multilateral Trade Negotiations (UR), that, in turn, has been described as "the largest and most complex negotiation concerning international economics in history" or even as "the largest and most complex negotiation ever."[3] None of these remarks may appear to be an overstatement if seen in the light of the WTO legal and institutional framework, which consists of about 30,000 pages of rules and concessions.[4]

The Uruguay Round was launched in 1986 by the Contracting Parties of the General Agreement on Tariffs and Trade (GATT), the rather modest predecessor of the WTO, and, after eight years of negotiations by more than 120 nations, culminated in the signing of the Final Act embodying the results of the UR negotiations on April 15, 1994. The Final Act comprises the Marrakesh Agreement Establishing the World Trade Organization (WTO Agreement) and various Ministerial Decisions and Declarations. Set out in the WTO Agreement are the purposes and objectives of the WTO and its institutional framework. Numerous

[1] Jackson 1998, 1. [2] Bierman *et al.* 1996, 845.

[3] Jackson 1997a, 1. On the UR negotiating history see: T.P. Stewart 1993; and (for a concise "non-technical" account) Croome 1999.

[4] See Bacchus 2003, 8.

other agreements and legal instruments, covering a very broad and diverse range of subject-matters and establishing a multifaceted normative framework – consisting of substantive, institutional and implementation aspects – are set out in three annexes to the WTO Agreement that form integral parts of the WTO Agreement and are binding on all Members.[5] All of these entered into force when the WTO came into existence in 1995 with seventy-six Members, i.e. the countries that had ratified the WTO agreements by that time. The number of Members has rapidly increased since then and is 150 at present, with many other nations engaged in negotiations for accession.

Much has happened in the world of international trade since the completion of the Uruguay Round and the coming into being of the WTO. In the third WTO Ministerial Conference[6] held in Seattle in 1999 the international trade community witnessed the failure and breakdown of efforts to launch a new round of trade negotiations. However, a new round was launched at the next WTO Ministerial held in Doha in 2001. In terms of market access or new disciplines, the goals originally set for the Doha Round were no less, perhaps even more, ambitious than the Uruguay Round.[7] In addition, for the first time in history, a trade negotiation round was expressly linked to development by designating the new round as the Doha Development Agenda. The Doha Round has seen many ups and downs in subsequent Ministerials at Cancún and Hong Kong, at the WTO headquarters in Geneva and in various capitals of the world. Most recently, in July 2006, the round was suspended because gaps between the key negotiating WTO Members have remained too wide even after five years of negotiations.

At the time this book went to press, Doha negotiations were yet to be resumed.[8] The cost of a failure of the Doha Round would certainly be huge, but it would not unravel the established multilateral trading

[5] WTO Agreement, Article II:2. There is also a fourth annex that sets out four agreements known as Plurilateral Trade Agreements, which are binding on those Members that have accepted them (see Article II:3, WTO Agreement). (Two plurilateral agreements have since been terminated.) Throughout this book the Marrakesh Agreement Establishing the World Trade Organization, without its annexes, is referred to as the "WTO Agreement" and the WTO Agreement together with the annexed agreements and associated legal instruments are collectively referred to as the "WTO agreements" or "WTO treaty."

[6] The Ministerial Conference is the highest-level decision-making body of the WTO.

[7] Lamy 2006.

[8] Latest information on the Doha Round can be found through the Doha Agenda Gateway of the WTO website at www.wto.org/english/tratop_e/dda_e/dda_e.htm.

system. The existing agreements under the umbrella of the WTO will remain well in place and so will the highly successful WTO dispute settlement mechanism. This book is devoted to an analysis of the state of the relationship between WTO law and national law. If eventually there is a successful outcome to the Doha negotiations, the analysis contained herein will be relevant in understanding the relation between national law and the new subjects, disciplines and market access commitments that the negotiations will bring under the WTO umbrella. In the unhappy event of a failure of the Doha Round, the analysis would continue to be relevant for the existing multilateral trading system.

As some readers may not be familiar with the coverage of the WTO, it is worth pointing out the subject areas and matters dealt with under the current WTO agreements. The basic legal texts of the WTO (i.e. the WTO agreements exclusive of schedules of tariff, services trade and other concessions) alone take more than 500 pages;[9] and the coverage is as extensive. While the predecessor, GATT, dealt only with trade in goods (that too with some significant exceptions, e.g. agricultural trade was de facto excluded from the scope of the GATT), through the WTO international discipline was extended for the first time to trade in services[10] and to trade-related aspects of intellectual property rights.[11] In addition, in the goods sector many new innovations and improvements were introduced.[12] The principal agreement concerning trade in goods is the GATT 1994, which consists of the provisions in the GATT 1947 and a number of protocols, decisions and understandings that either entered into force under the GATT 1947 or were agreed upon during the UR.[13] In addition, twelve new agreements were introduced dealing with two particular sectors of trade, namely agriculture[14] and textiles,[15] and addressing substantive subjects as diverse as sanitary and phytosanitary measures,[16]

[9] See World Trade Organization 1994. [10] See GATS, WTO Agreement, Annex 1B.

[11] See TRIPS Agreement, WTO Agreement, Annex 1C.

[12] See the Multilateral Agreements on Trade in Goods set out in Annex 1A of the WTO Agreement.

[13] See para. 1 of the GATT 1994. Throughout this book the expression "GATT 1994" is used to refer to the General Agreement on Tariffs and Trade 1994 as contained in Annex 1A of the WTO Agreement, while the expression "GATT 1947" is used to refer to the General Agreement on Tariffs and Trade, opened for signature October 30, 1947, 55 UNTS 194. The acronym "GATT" is used to refer to the de facto institution that came into being under the auspices of the GATT 1947.

[14] See Agriculture Agreement, WTO Agreement, Annex 1A.

[15] See ATC, WTO Agreement, Annex 1A.

[16] See SPS Agreement, WTO Agreement, Annex 1A.

technical standards,[17] trade-related investment measures,[18] customs valuation,[19] preshipment inspection,[20] rules of origin,[21] import licensing,[22] dumping,[23] subsidies[24] and safeguards.[25] On the institutional and implementation side, in addition to the WTO Agreement, two more agreements were introduced: one of them provided for a new set of dispute settlement procedures[26] and the other established a mechanism for periodic review of Members' trade policies.[27]

2 Aims, objects and relevance of the study

The complexities of the WTO legal framework is such that Professor Jackson, a leading scholar in the field, on the basis of his interviews with WTO officials and Uruguay Round negotiators, has observed that: "the WTO Agreement, including all its elaborate Annexes, is probably fully understood by no nation that has accepted it, including some of the richest and most powerful trading nations that are members."[28] Thus it is no wonder that since its inception the WTO has attracted a considerable amount of attention from all quarters: governments, academics and professionals (coming from a range of disciplines – legal, socio-political, economic and so on) and, of course, from the public at large. Commensurately with this increased attention, the scrutiny and analysis of the international trading system has also increased. For instance, two foremost academic publishing houses in England have commenced publication of two newly established journals devoted, largely, to WTO-related legal issues.[29] Leading legal periodicals published from Europe, North America and elsewhere have already devoted thousands of pages to research and analysis concerning the WTO system. The number of books on WTO and international trade topics that have been published

[17] See TBT Agreement, WTO Agreement, Annex 1A.
[18] See TRIMS Agreement, WTO Agreement, Annex 1A.
[19] See Customs Valuation Agreement, WTO Agreement, Annex 1A.
[20] See PSI Agreement, WTO Agreement, Annex 1A.
[21] See ARO, WTO Agreement, Annex 1A.
[22] See Licensing Agreement, WTO Agreement, Annex 1A.
[23] See ADA, WTO Agreement, Annex 1A. [24] See ASCM, WTO Agreement, Annex 1A.
[25] See Safeguards Agreement, WTO Agreement, Annex 1A.
[26] See DSU, WTO Agreement, Annex 2. [27] See TPRM, WTO Agreement, Annex 3.
[28] Jackson 1998, 1.
[29] These are the *Journal of International Economic Law* from Oxford University Press, established in 1998 under the editorship of Professor Jackson and with a multinational editorial board, and the *World Trade Review* from Cambridge University Press, established in 2002 on the initiative of the WTO itself.

since the completion of the Uruguay Round is equally remarkable.[30] So far as legal scholarship is concerned, many conceivable aspects and implications of the WTO – covering constitutional and substantive issues, dispute settlement, implications of the WTO for "non-WTO subjects" such as environment, labor, competition, investment and so on – have been subjected to extensive and rigorous research and analysis.

Nonetheless, given the complex and multifaceted labyrinth of the WTO legal framework it is unconvincing to argue, as former Director-General of the WTO Mike Moore has put it, "that there is ever enough research and analysis."[31] The aim of this book is to attempt to bring into proper focus an aspect of the WTO legal order that as yet remains relatively less explored.

One of the many topics that the establishment of the WTO has generated interest in is the relationship between WTO law and national law.[32] There are two different aspects of this relationship, namely, (i) the relation in a domestic context, and (ii) the relation in WTO law. There already exists an enormous amount of scholarly research and vibrant analysis devoted to many important issues that arise in the former context.[33] Thus much has been written – to note just a few selected issues – on various matters concerning implementation of WTO obligations in the domestic laws of Member countries (including the contentious question of giving or denying self-executing or direct effect to WTO norms), the procedures under national law to enable private businesses to take advantage of the international trade discipline or the lack of such procedures, the question of interpretation of WTO agreements by national courts, the doctrine of consistent interpretation (i.e. construing

[30] For lists of selected titles see JIEL book surveys in: 1(3) JIEL 492 (1998); 4(1) JIEL 261 (2001); 5(1) JIEL 245 (2002); 6(1) JIEL 263 (2003); 7(1) JIEL 183 (2004); 8(1) JIEL 245 (2005); 9(1) JIEL 237 (2006); and 10(1) JIEL 181 (2007).

[31] M. Moore 2002.

[32] Since the EC itself is a Member of the WTO, for purposes of this work, the expression "national law" should be understood as including, where appropriate, EC/EU law. Similarly, references to national governments, legislative bodies or courts should be understood as including relevant EU institutions.

[33] The following is a list of only a very few representative materials: Jackson & Sykes 1997 (this publication surveys the position in a number of domestic jurisdictions including those of the richest and most powerful trading countries); Hilf & Petersmann 1993; Applebaum & Schlitt 1995; T.P. Stewart 1996; Eeckhout 1997 and 2002; Hilf 1997; Schaefer 1997 and 2000; Cottier & Schefer 1998; Yamane 1998; Bourgeois 2000a; Griller 2000; Iwasawa 2000; Lauwaars 2000; Louis 2000; S.N. Lester 2001; and Zhang 2003. As regards the wider issue of the effects of international treaties in domestic law see Jacobs & Roberts 1987; Jackson 1992; Eisenmann 1996; and Henkin 1996, 198–211.

national law in accordance with WTO obligations), etc. In marked contrast, the question of how national law is treated in WTO law, important as it is, has not received the necessary critical attention.[34] Although recently one or two discrete issues that can be viewed as specific facets of this question have started to gain prominence,[35] as yet no study has been undertaken that looks at the matter in a more comprehensive manner. The purpose of this book is to begin this wider analysis by drawing together and underscoring the significance of the vital issues concerning national law that exist or arise at the WTO level.

However, apart from the above, there are other important systemic and policy reasons for undertaking a project such as the present one. Compared to any other contemporary international treaty, the WTO agreements make it much more common for international and national legal norms to have endless points of contact between them. There are a number of reasons for this. First, the WTO treaty establishes rules and discipline for the conduct of international trade, which as a subject-matter is more heavily legislated by national legislatures than most other subjects. In addition, WTO rules and discipline cover, and either regulate or hinge on, a very wide array of matters relating to trade (some of which have already been referred to[36]), ranging from customs, tax and fiscal matters to dumping and subsidies, product standards, environment, health, national security and so on (perhaps almost anything under the sun that can affect and hamper movement of goods or services or the protection of intellectual property rights). Thus it is only natural for every WTO Member to have an enormous amount of laws, regulations and other instruments that address the same subject-matters as the WTO agreements. As a result, there are innumerable points of contact between WTO norms and national laws. Second, such contacts become all the more frequent because of the level of detail at which the massive WTO treaty, in its more than 500 pages of legal texts, seeks to regulate various conducts and relations.

One should also be mindful of the value of the economic activities covered by the WTO treaty,[37] which surpasses, by far, the economic value

[34] Cottier & Schefer 1998 briefly notes this aspect of the relationship (three and a half pages) before turning to issues that arise at the national level.

[35] The problem of standard of review that forms the subject-matter of Chapter 6 below is an example of such a topic.

[36] See text at nn. 10–27 above.

[37] For instance, in 2006 the value of world merchandise trade was US $11.76 trillion and that of commercial services was US $2.71 trillion: see WTO Press Release, Press/472.

represented by most other international treaties. The enormity of economic interest at stake makes it all the more common to have conflicts of interest or disputes between WTO Members.[38] Such disputes are almost inevitably animated by the disputing parties' perception of the relevant WTO norms and the national trade and "trade-related" laws and policies that may be in question. Thus disputes play a vital role in making the interaction between WTO law and national law more explicit.

Accordingly, the process that makes the interaction highly prominent at the WTO level – not to mention much more prominent than under any other international treaty or before any other international forum – is the WTO's unique dispute settlement system. While some of the aspects and threads of that system relevant for purposes of the present study are discussed later in Chapter 4, a few general but salient features may be mentioned here. Put succinctly, WTO dispute settlement is at once "compulsory," "exclusive" and "automatic." The first of these characteristics does not require much elaboration: it means that the jurisdiction of various dispute settlement organs of the WTO is compulsory[39] and any Member can unilaterally trigger against another Member any of the various procedures set out in the WTO text on dispute settlement, namely, the Dispute Settlement Understanding (DSU). Because all of the 150 Members of the WTO are bound by the DSU, it is, as has been rightly noted, "the most extensive network of compulsory dispute settlement obligations in contemporary international law."[40] So much so that seasoned commentators have suspected that the WTO procedures are destined to "exert a gravitational pull, drawing into the WTO system disputes that could not easily find a forum elsewhere, and recasting them as 'trade' disputes."[41]

(April 12, 2007). Although exact data regarding trade among WTO Members are not readily available, as regards merchandise trade it can be estimated that about 95 percent of the stated trade of US $11.76 trillion was among WTO Members and, as such, was done under the WTO rules and discipline: see, e.g., World Trade Organization 2006, 28–29.

38 The word "dispute" or "conflict" should not be understood as having a negative connotation. In any legal system disputes or conflicts do serve a very useful and positive role of accommodating the interests of every one of the actors through necessary adjustments of their relationship. On this theme see Collier & Lowe 1999, 1–2.

39 Cf. the jurisdiction of the International Court of Justice (ICJ) with regard to a state that makes a declaration under Article 36(2) of the Court's Statute accepting, in relation to any other states making similar declarations, the jurisdiction of the ICJ "as compulsory *ipso facto* and without special agreement."

40 Collier & Lowe 1999, 104.

41 Ibid.

The system is "exclusive" in the sense that with regard to disputes concerning matters provided for in the WTO agreements Members are required to have recourse to the DSU procedures *to the exclusion of any other procedure or system.*[42] The standard procedure under the DSU comprises ad hoc panels and a standing Appellate Body (hereinafter also AB). Thus, a dispute is referred in the first instance to an ad hoc panel and from its decision an appeal can be made to the standing Appellate Body. In addition, the DSU envisages arbitration for certain disputes concerning implementation of recommendations and rulings issued through the panel and appeal procedure.[43] The only alternative to the standard panel process is "arbitration *within the WTO*" under Article 25 of the DSU.[44] However, such arbitrations are subject to multilateral control in that any agreement to arbitrate must be notified to all Members and the award must be notified to the Dispute Settlement Body (which is a plenary organ representing all Members) as well as to any relevant council or committee where Members may raise any point relating to it.[45] Thus the WTO, or, more specifically, various dispute settlement organs established under the DSU taken together, is the "exclusive forum" for the adjudication of all "trade-related" disputes among Members.

The words "automatic" and "automaticity" have been coined to describe the binding nature and timeliness of the WTO dispute settlement system.[46] Once the dispute settlement mechanism is set in motion by a complainant, various procedural steps envisaged in the DSU – for instance, establishment of a panel and its terms of reference, selection of panelists, circulation and adoption of panel and Appellate Body reports, taking retaliatory measures, etc. – are triggered "automatically" in accordance with a strict time-frame set out in the DSU. Thus the respondent government can neither block nor delay the proceedings at any stage.

The above characteristics of the WTO dispute settlement system, coupled with the broad substantive coverage of the WTO agreements, have

42 See Article 23.1 of the DSU which provides as follows: "When Members seek the redress of a violation of obligations or other nullification or impairment of benefits under the covered agreements or an impediment to the attainment of any objective of the covered agreements, they shall have recourse to, and abide by, the rules and procedures of this Understanding." See also Panel Report, *US – Section 301*, para. 7.43 (describing Article 23.1 as an "exclusive dispute resolution clause"); and Jackson 1997a, 124.

43 See further, Chapter 4, pp. 112–14.

44 Until now Article 25 arbitration has been used only once. See further, Chapter 4, p. 91.

45 See DSU Article 25. See also Article 3.6, which requires mutually agreed solutions to be similarly notified.

46 See, e.g., Jackson 1998, 76.

resulted in its extensive use.[47] Beginning from its inception in 1995 until now, 363 cases have been initiated and 136 panel reports, 81 Appellate Body reports and 38 arbitration awards – in total more than 48,000 pages of reports and awards – have been issued.[48] This huge body of jurisprudence has already been seen as reflecting the emergence of "a distinct WTO legal system."[49]

In terms of length, breadth of the substantive coverage, value of the economic interest represented and number of states parties, the treaty that, at least to an extent, can be compared to the WTO treaty is the United Nations Convention on the Law of the Sea of 1982 (UNCLOS).[50] However, the dispute settlement mechanism provided in UNCLOS is neither as exclusive nor as compulsory as that of the DSU.[51] More importantly, the states parties to UNCLOS are not finding it necessary to make an extensive use of that mechanism. Thus, for instance, until now a total of only thirteen cases have been brought before the International Tribunal for the Law of the Sea – the central dispute settlement forum established by UNCLOS.[52]

It may also not be beside the point to say a few words about two other international (or more accurately "regional") treaty regimes that have,

47 See Bacchus 2002, 1025–26.

48 For a recent statistical analysis of the WTO dispute settlement see Leitner & Lester 2007.

49 McRae 2004, 5.

50 In a single treaty (of about 200 pages) UNCLOS provides a universal and comprehensive legal framework to regulate all ocean space, its uses and resources – including management and conservation of resources, protection of the marine environment, marine scientific research, development and transfer of marine technology, etc.: see United Nations 1983. There are currently 153 states parties to UNCLOS.

51 Under UNCLOS states have the right to settle any dispute between them by peaceful means of their own choosing (see Articles 279–82); and the "compulsory procedures" set out in the Convention come into play only if settlement is not possible by means chosen by the parties to the dispute (Article 286). Again, the parties are free to choose between four different "compulsory procedures": the International Tribunal for the Law of the Sea (ITLOS); the International Court of Justice; arbitration (under Annex VII of UNCLOS); and special arbitration (under Annex VIII of UNCLOS) (see Article 287). Finally, the obligation to submit disputes to any of these procedures is subject to certain limitations *ratione materiae* (see Articles 297–98). For an overview of the dispute settlement provisions of UNCLOS see Collier & Lowe 1999, 84–95, and Sands *et al.* 1999, 39–61 (the latter work also provides a useful bibliography).

52 ITLOS is of similar age to the WTO dispute settlement system. While UNCLOS entered into force on November 16, 1994, ITLOS was established on August 1, 1996, and first judges of the Tribunal were sworn in on October 18, 1996. Information about UNCLOS and its dispute settlement can be found on the UN Law of the Sea web site, www.un.org/Depts/los/; and copies of the judgments and orders of the Tribunal can be obtained from the ITLOS web site, www.itlos.org.

in terms of both subject-matters and details, a substantive coverage similar – indeed even wider – to the WTO agreements. These are the European Communities or the European Union (EC/EU) and the North American Free Trade Agreement (NAFTA), both of which are trade liberalization regimes and, as such, in respect of many substantive matters share with the WTO "a common legal vocabulary."[53] There are also well-developed and compulsory dispute settlement systems established under the EC Treaty and the NAFTA. However, both the EC/EU and NAFTA have a very limited number of member states or states parties, respectively. The EU used to comprise fifteen developed countries of Western Europe until the recent enlargement that took place in May 2004, when ten other European nations joined the group. NAFTA has only three states parties – two developed countries (Canada and the United States) and a developing country (Mexico).

Thus, WTO dispute settlement organs stand out for their nearly universal compulsory jurisdiction and for having such jurisdiction over a set of international obligations that is truly extensive. As discussed in greater detail in Chapter 4 below, the disputes before the WTO are about the WTO-compatibility of national measures, i.e. national laws and other governmental (administrative, judicial or quasi-judicial) acts. As a result, WTO adjudicative bodies confront issues of national law on a rather regular basis: obviously, they do so in cases where they are called upon to review the WTO-compatibility of national *laws*; but issues of national law can also be important in cases where the review concerns other national measures such as administrative or judicial *decisions*, because such decisions are often taken in pursuance of a *law*. Thus, much of the more than 48,000 pages of WTO jurisprudence relates in different ways to Members' national laws.

Another notable aspect of the WTO legal regime is that the WTO treaty imposes certain obligations on Members regarding their national laws that are not only far-reaching but are also "systemic" in character. As discussed in Chapter 3 below, broadly, there are four categories of such obligations: obligations to implement WTO commitments in domestic laws and to ensure conformity of such laws with the WTO agreements; obligations to ensure transparency in respect of national laws through their publication and notification to the WTO; obligations to administer national laws in a certain (e.g. in a uniform, impartial, reasonable, consistent, neutral, fair, equitable, objective) manner; and obligations to

[53] J. H. H. Weiler 2000a, 1.

make available under national laws specified procedures and remedies (e.g. procedures for judicial review of administrative acts).

The treatment of national law in WTO law – both in the WTO treaty and in dispute settlement cases – has important implications for the proper allocation of power between national and international levels. That is to say, WTO obligations concerning national law as well as determination of national law issues in dispute settlement cases have important consequences for the legislative competence (some would say "sovereignty") of national parliaments and also for the competence of other domestic constituencies that may be engaged in the interpretation and application of national laws, e.g. domestic courts, administrative agencies, etc. Indeed, the question of proper allocation of power is a recurring theme throughout this work, and it also usefully highlights that a study of how national law is treated in WTO law may not be a futile exercise from a systemic or policy point of view.

3 Organization of the study

Turning now to the organization of the present study, it is divided in two parts. Part I opens with Chapter 2 on how national law is treated in international law in general. While throughout this work efforts are made to put the analysis of WTO law against the wider international legal context, Chapter 2 is motivated by the assumption that as a starting point it is necessary to note certain key principles that underpin the approach of international law towards national law. The next chapter, i.e. Chapter 3, examines four groups of WTO obligations concerning national law that have been referred to above as "systemic" in character. Chapter 4 looks at the jurisdiction and competence of the WTO dispute settlement organs vis-à-vis Members' national laws. It also addresses other relevant aspects of the WTO dispute settlement mechanism, for example WTO remedies are discussed with a view to explaining whether an adverse WTO ruling can effectively lead to changes in national measures including laws. From the perspective of the relation between WTO law and national law both Chapters 3 and 4 are important on their own, because they clarify, respectively, obligations concerning national law and competence of dispute settlement organs over national law. In addition, they provide, like Chapter 2, a necessary background for Part II of this study, which takes up national law issues that arise in the context of adjudication of disputes by the WTO dispute settlement organs. Part II comprises Chapters 5 through 8. All of these chapters relate in different ways to WTO dispute settlement organs' review of the legality, i.e. WTO-compatibility, of national laws.

In some measure, the review of national laws by WTO bodies resembles the review of constitutionality of national laws by national supreme or constitutional courts.[54] As is well known, under national legal systems it is not uncommon for a supreme or constitutional court to possess and exercise the power to review the constitutionality of laws enacted by the legislature.[55] Such review by domestic courts is intended to ensure that constitutional norms and guarantees are not transgressed by the legislature, whether intentionally or by mere accident. Of course, the review of national laws by WTO bodies is not intended to check their constitutionality under national constitutions. Rather, the purpose of this review is to determine whether a contested national law transgresses the limits set by the WTO treaty. Nonetheless, the similarity between review by a domestic supreme or constitutional court and review by a WTO adjudicative organ lies in the fact that in both instances a judicial body reviews whether a law violates some superior legal norms – constitutional in one case and international in another.[56]

Thematically, the work develops two different but related strands. Firstly, it explains and critically evaluates the treatment of national law in the WTO treaty and by the WTO dispute settlement organs. Secondly, it analyses WTO dispute settlement organs' review of the legality, i.e. WTO-compatibility, of national laws: Part I elucidates the foundational aspect of this review, by explaining the approach of international courts and tribunals in general to national law (Chapter 2), the nature of the WTO obligations regarding national law (Chapter 3) and the key features of the WTO dispute settlement mechanism (Chapter 4). Part II then examines different dimensions of the actual process of review of the legality of national laws by the WTO dispute settlement bodies (Chapters 5 through 8). Because all four chapters of Part II relate in different ways to dispute settlement, their basic features, as well as the

[54] See below, Chapter 4, pp. 86–87, and Chapter 9, pp. 271–73.

[55] It may be mentioned parenthetically that in a domestic context, in addition to legislative measures, the power of judicial review is exercised in respect of administrative measures. The grounds of review are often wider in respect of administrative measures, which can be reviewed for constitutionality as well as for the violation of basic principles of justice. For obvious reasons, the present comparison is with judicial review of legislative measures.

[56] See below, Chapter 4, pp. 86–87 Cf., however, Chapter 6, pp. 161–62 below (pointing out that, as far as *specific* techniques or criteria of review are concerned, international and national methods of review can, should and do vary in important respects).

interrelation between them, are noted below in Chapter 4 in the course of the discussion of the dispute settlement process.[57]

4 Organizing principles: effectiveness and good governance

The policy objectives of effectiveness of international rules and supervision and good governance at the domestic level have both a constitutive and an evaluative role in respect of the relationship between WTO law and national law. However, before explaining these issues, it may be in order to say a few words about other broad policy issues that feature in the present study.

As already noted, the treatment of national law in the WTO treaty and in dispute settlement cases has implications for the proper allocation of power between national and international levels. By setting out standards of treatment for goods, services and intellectual property rights originating abroad, the WTO treaty delineates the scope of lawful national conduct. The substantive provisions concerning standards of treatment are then supplemented by systemic provisions. The latter includes provisions requiring WTO Members to ensure the conformity of their national laws with the WTO treaty; to ensure transparency and fairness in the adoption, implementation and administration of domestic laws and regulations relating to international trade; and to establish and maintain domestic legal procedures for the review and modification or reversal of actions of domestic administrative authorities on matters covered by the WTO treaty and for the enforcement of private rights by individuals under the TRIPS Agreement.[58] A fundamental objective of these systemic obligations is to ensure the effectiveness of the substantive provisions that set out limits on national regulatory conduct. Likewise, the purpose of the WTO's extraordinarily powerful dispute settlement system is to ensure the effectiveness of the substantive obligations. Accordingly, in the WTO treaty it is stated in lapidary language that "the dispute settlement system of the WTO is a central element in providing security and predictability to the multilateral trading system."[59]

Thus, nation states' regulatory decision-making powers are subject to real and effective limits under the WTO treaty. Whether fully appreciated or not, the parameters of these limits are, at least theoretically,

[57] See below, Chapter 4, p. 105. [58] See, further, Chapter 3 below.
[59] DSU, Article 3.2.

agreed to by each WTO Member at the time of joining the Organization. However, as a practical matter, an international treaty dealing with subjects as diverse as those dealt with under the WTO treaty can neither anticipate nor seek to address specifically all the precise issues of allocation of decision-making power between domestic and international levels. Consequently, in policing national regulatory conduct the WTO dispute settlement organs must make their reasoned judgments on a case by case basis. Yet it is certain that, through their acceptance of the WTO treaty and its dispute settlement mechanism, WTO Members have parted with some of their "sovereign" decision-making power and thereby agreed to a reallocation of power between domestic and international levels.

The question of proper allocation of power between national and international levels is closely associated with the "sovereignty debate" that occurs relentlessly in political forums, scholarly journals and treatises, popular media and elsewhere. The arguments that one hears not so infrequently about the WTO or its dispute settlement decisions infringing upon "national sovereignty" in essence mean that, in respect of the (health, environment or other) policy issues that are at stake, the decision-making power should be exercised at the national level rather than the WTO level. Indeed, an eminent international trade law scholar, Professor John Jackson, has written extensively and incisively on this, emphasizing the need to "decompose" the concept of sovereignty. He has pointed out quite perceptively that "sovereignty," as used in current policy debates, refers most of the time to "questions about the allocation of . . . government decision-making power."[60] A seasoned pragmatist,[61] Professor Jackson has long since underscored the "operational functions" of international rules and institutions.[62] Thus, in the context of economic behavior, international-level power allocation is necessary for "coordination benefits."[63] Without the "predictability or stability" of coordination under international rules and institutions, trade or investment flows might be more risky and inhibited than otherwise.[64]

Like Professor Jackson, this work proceeds from the understanding that it is scarcely possible to manage the present-day global economic interdependence without centralized institutions, which have vital roles to play. However, it is equally important that there is no overreaching

[60] Jackson 2003, 790. See also Jackson 1997c, 2002 and 2006.
[61] See D. Kennedy 1994. [62] See, e.g., Jackson 1997a, 27–28.
[63] Jackson 2003, 791–92. [64] Jackson 1997a, 28.

by an international institution as powerful as the WTO. Yet all issues of proper allocation of power between national and international levels are not settled in the WTO treaty once and for all. Accordingly, in resolving disputes, a major, and sometimes arduous, task of the WTO adjudicative organs is to strike an appropriate balance between WTO obligations and national regulatory competence.

This study will highlight that a number of other values are closely related to the value of proper allocation of power, such as deference to national authorities, flexibility and effectiveness of international rules and supervision. Throughout this book repeated references are made to the value of deference to national authorities, in preserving national regulatory competence.[65] The importance of flexibility in accommodating the diverse points of view of various nations in the dispute settlement process is also discussed.[66] Effectiveness is important because proper allocation of power, on the one hand, entails that there should not be a usurpation of legitimate national authority by an international tribunal; on the other hand, it requires that the effectiveness of both the international rules and the associated mechanism – if there is one – of international supervision is ensured.[67]

Turning now to the constitutive and evaluative roles of the policy objectives of effectiveness and good governance, these policy objectives are constitutive because they are a vital constituent part of the WTO legal framework. They are evaluative because one of them (effectiveness) represents a standard or level of review against which the WTO-compatibility of national measures and laws is evaluated or tested by WTO adjudicative organs, and the other (good governance) represents a significant criterion of such review. For absolute clarity it needs to be mentioned that in the present context the relevant aspect of good governance is good governance *within the nation-state*. There is, of course, an additional dimension of good governance, i.e. good governance *at the WTO*. Some of the practical issues concerning the latter are ensuring transparency at the WTO including access to WTO meetings and documents; guaranteeing non-asymmetric bargaining positions of developed and developing countries in WTO negotiations; having necessary mechanisms and safeguards for "civil society" groups' or non-governmental organizations' participation in the WTO; having proper procedures for submission, screening, acceptance or rejection of *amicus* briefs in WTO dispute settlement, etc. This aspect, unlike the

[65] Cf. Chapter 9, pp. 280–81 below. [66] Cf. Chapter 9, pp. 281–82 below.
[67] Cf. Chapter 9, pp. 282–83 below.

first-mentioned aspect, is dealt with extensively in existing literature.[68] This book, however, evaluates the first-mentioned aspect during the course of its analysis of how the WTO legal system and the related mechanism of "judicial review" can - and indeed do - promote good governance within the nation-state.

4.1 *Constitutive function of effectiveness*

As discussed in greater detail in the next chapter, a fundamental international law principle regarding the relationship between national and international law is that national laws cannot be relied upon to avoid international obligations. The object of this principle is to prevent evasion of international obligations by means of domestic legislation and, as such, it is a sine qua non for the effectiveness of international law. Through its systemic obligations regarding national law and its powerful dispute settlement system, the WTO treaty, however, goes much further than this general international law principle in ensuring effectiveness of the WTO obligations. Chapters 3 and 4 - devoted, respectively, to systemic obligations and dispute settlement - explore this aspect of the WTO legal framework.

4.2 *Evaluative function of effectiveness*

Chapter 6 explains that, whether explicitly articulated or not by WTO panels and the AB, the policy objective of effectiveness of WTO rules and dispute settlement has a crucial - and perhaps even dispositive - role in the context of review of national laws and measures. For instance, in *EC - Hormones* the Appellate Body expressly excluded the possibility of a *de novo* standard of review, yet it did not overturn the Panel's factual finding with respect to risk assessment, which came quite close to *de novo* review.[69] Such an outcome was due to the fact that in the circumstances of that case applying a more limited standard of review would have rendered the WTO obligation in question ineffective. The problem of characterization discussed in Chapter 5 also highlights the evaluative function of effectiveness: WTO panels or the AB are unlikely to accede to the domestic law characterization of a rule of domestic law, if thereby the relevant WTO rules would become ineffective. Indeed, it is common for panels and the AB to tailor the benchmark of review - be

[68] See, e.g., Krajewski 2001; Beviglia Zampetti 2003; Bacchus 2004; Bhagwati 2004, ch. 4; Lacarte 2004; Shaffer 2004; Sutherland *et el.* 2004; Durling & Hardin 2005; Finger 2005; Odell 2005; Van den Bossche & Alexovicová 2005; Wolfe 2005; and Esty 2006.

[69] This aspect of the case is discussed in detail in Chapter 6, pp. 161–62 below.

it in the context of characterization, applying standards of review, determining the content of national law and so forth – so as to ensure the effectiveness of the WTO treaty provisions.

4.3 *Constitutive function of good governance*

The constitutive function of good governance needs to be understood from a number of different perspectives. First, a key object of different systemic obligations to which references have been made earlier is to promote good governance within national legal systems. In this context it is worth recalling once again that such obligations include those requiring transparency and fairness in the adoption, implementation and administration of domestic laws and regulations or those obliging Members to make available domestic legal procedures for the review, modification and reversal of actions of domestic administrative authorities and for the enforcement of private rights by individuals.[70]

Second, various substantive obligations also promote good governance in important ways. To note but a few examples, the non-discrimination principles of most-favored nation (MFN) and national treatment (principles which lie at the heart of the substantive WTO obligations) promote good governance by (i) guaranteeing some protection for the commercial interests of foreign states, who have little or no representation in the political life of a state enacting or implementing a trade or trade-related law or measure; and (ii) ensuring that national trade policy is not unjustifiably biased in favor of one domestic constituency (e.g., exporters, producers) at the expense of another domestic constituency (e.g., importers, consumers). The requirements under different WTO agreements[71] that health protection, environmental, sanitary and phytosanitary, and technical laws and measures should not be arbitrary, discriminatory or more trade-restrictive than necessary promote good governance by outlawing arbitrariness, unjustifiable discrimination and disproportionality.[72] The Agreement on Government Procurement (GPA)[73] is an instance of a "good governance-spirited" text that seeks to increase accountability and prevent corruption in public procurement

[70] See, further, Chapter 3, sections 4–6.

[71] See, e.g., GATT 1994, Article XX; GATS, Article XIV; SPS Agreement, Article 5.6; and TBT Agreement, Article 2.2.

[72] See, further, Chapter 3, section 2; and Chapter 6, section 3.2.

[73] WTO Agreement, Annex 4. Because the GPA is a plurilateral agreement, not all WTO Members are parties to it. Currently there are thirty-eight parties to this agreement, mostly from the developed world.

through its elaborate provisions on non-discrimination, bidding procedures, transparency, etc.[74]

Third, WTO dispute settlement, which (as noted a few pages ago and discussed in detail in Chapters 4 and 9) often operates as a further layer of judicial review of national laws and administrative measures, has important good governance ramifications. Genuine access to fair and impartial judicial review is widely considered to be an important element in ensuring good governance, because it acts as a check on legislative and administrative bodies. WTO dispute settlement organs' review of the legality, i.e. WTO-compatibility, of national laws and administrative measures also acts as a check on national legislators and executives.

4.4 *Evaluative function of good governance*

Deliberative, rational and transparent decision- and rule-making is an essential ingredient of good governance.[75] In the context of the "judicial review" of national laws and measures, there is a tendency on the part of the WTO panels and the AB to show greater deference to a contested law or measure if it is adopted through a deliberative, rational and transparent process. Thus, good governance has an important evaluative function in respect of the assessment of the legality of national laws and measures.

Chapter 6 discusses the point that in certain circumstances panels and the AB apply a two-pronged standard of review: they examine whether the contested measure is adopted after evaluating *all relevant facts or factors* and whether a *reasoned and adequate explanation* is provided by the national authority as to how those facts/factors support the contested measure.[76] A national measure that does not duly take into account the interests of all relevant stakeholders – both foreign and domestic – may well fall short of the first element of this standard of review. A deliberative decision- or rule-making process that gives stakeholders the opportunity to be heard is more likely to take into account "all relevant facts or factors" than a secretive, non-participatory process. Accordingly, the first element may in effect lead to greater deference to measures based on adequate *public deliberation*. The second element directly promotes rational and transparent decision- and rule-making as it tests whether a contested measure is explicitly supported by sufficiently reasoned analysis. It also has implications for deliberative decision-making,

[74] Cf. McCrudden & Gross 2006, 161.
[75] Cf. Habermas 1984 and 1996.
[76] See, further, Chapter 6, pp. 187–90.

because the competing interests of various stakeholders must presumably be addressed – and resolved – as part of the reasoned and adequate explanation for adopting a measure.

Transparency in the adoption, application and administration of national laws and measures can also be a discrete and overt criterion of review. For instance, in the *India – Patent* cases the lack of transparency in adopting certain "instructions" by the Indian administration was one of the main reasons that led to findings of violations of WTO obligations by India.[77]

As explained fully in Chapter 6, there are a number of variables that have bearings on the standard of review.[78] One such variable is the WTO provision/s concerned, i.e. provision/s under which the legality of the contested national measure is assessed. It may be recalled from the discussion of the constitutive function of good governance that many WTO provisions promote good governance in important ways. Whenever the legality of a national measure is determined under such a provision, "good governance" becomes an essential evaluative tool of review. For instance, in the *US – Shrimp* case, the AB found that there was "arbitrary discrimination" within the meaning of Article XX of the GATT 1994, because the US authorities, in their certification process for shrimp imports, did not comply with the fundamental requirements of transparency, fairness and due process with regard to notice, the gathering of evidence, and the opportunity to be heard.[79] The AB, quite innovatively, also went much further than the text of Article XX in promoting deliberative decision- and rule-making by deciding that the failure of the United States to *negotiate seriously* with some of the affected countries amounted to "unjustifiable discrimination" under Article XX.[80]

5 Related issues

As a final introductory matter, it may be in order to note briefly two issues that seemingly have a certain affinity with the subject-matter of this book, but that are not discussed in the chapters that follow. These are the exhaustion of local remedies rule and the question of the relevance of general principles of national law as a source of international law, or, for present purposes, of WTO law. Generally, these represent two

[77] This aspect of the *India – Patent* cases is discussed in Chapter 6, pp. 194–95, and Chapter 7, pp. 233–34 below.

[78] See Chapter 6, pp. 191–98 below.

[79] See AB Report, *US – Shrimp*, paras. 180–83.

[80] See ibid., para. 166.

rather obvious situations in which national laws can be relevant before international courts and tribunals. As a consequence, it is necessary to explain the reasons for not canvassing these two issues in greater detail, and the next few paragraphs aim to do so.

5.1 *The exhaustion of local remedies rule*

The exhaustion of local remedies rule, as is well known, is a rule of customary international law.[81] According to this rule, a state cannot exercise its right of diplomatic protection, i.e. present a claim on behalf of one of its nationals (individual or corporate), unless the injured national has exhausted any effective remedies available under the legal system of the state responsible for the injury.[82] If this rule is pleaded before an international court or tribunal, it becomes essential for that court or tribunal to examine the relevant laws of the respondent state with a view to ascertain what remedies are available under the legal system of that state, and to determine other related matters, for instance whether the remedies available are effective in redressing the injury.[83] The application of the rule is, however, strictly limited to cases of diplomatic protection where the injury complained of is "indirect" to the claimant state, caused by an injury to one of its nationals; and the rule has no relevance in cases concerning injuries caused directly to the state itself.

Although earlier analyses of the issue were perplexed with its ambivalence at a theoretical level, as a matter of practice it is now more than clear that in the WTO there is no requirement for exhaustion of local remedies. Turning first to the theoretical aspect, the difficulties in this regard resulted from the fact that neither the WTO treaty, nor its predecessor the GATT 1947, contains any clear statement either endorsing or excluding the applicability of the rule. In the *ELSI* case a Chamber of the International Court of Justice expressed the view that, because it is an important principle of customary international law, the local remedies rule cannot be "tacitly dispensed with, in the absence of any words making clear an intention to do so."[84] In the light of this observation some commentators – albeit writing just after the conclusion of the UR and

[81] See, e.g., *Interhandel* case, ICJ Rep. 6 (1959) at 27; and *Elettronica Sicula S.p.A. (ELSI)*, ICJ Rep. 15 (1989) at 42 (para. 50).

[82] See, generally, Brownlie 1998, 496–506; Collier & Lowe 1999, 195–98; Crawford 2002, 264–65; and Amerasinghe 2004.

[83] See, e.g., *Panevezys-Saldutiskis Railway* case, PCIJ Ser. A/B No. 76 (1939); and *ELSI* case, above, n. 81.

[84] ICJ Rep. 15 (1989) at 42 (para. 50).

thus without the aid of the WTO dispute settlement jurisprudence[85] – considered that the silence of the WTO treaty on the matter meant that the rule remained applicable in WTO dispute settlement.[86]

Of course, if the above view were correct, the rule would have applied only in respect of those WTO claims that are in the nature of diplomatic protection. But it is difficult to find such claims. Theoretical analyses commonly focused on claims concerning a limited number of WTO obligations. Thus, in respect of anti-dumping, countervailing and safeguard measures, it was suggested that, because the ultimate aim of these measures is to protect domestic products against imports from identifiable foreign producers, claims in these areas should be subject to the local remedies rule.[87] The new WTO obligations in the area of trade in services and protection of intellectual property rights (IPRs) were also thought to fall in the same category, given that they provide for the protection of the rights of individuals as "service suppliers"[88] or as owners of IPRs.[89] Finally, the group of WTO provisions that require Members to put in place under their national laws specified judicial and administrative procedures and remedies[90] was considered as lending support to the applicability of the local remedies rule.[91]

However, on a closer look it does not seem plausible that the three groups of obligations noted above could in fact lead to diplomatic protection of individuals. First, WTO obligations including the ones noted above are intended to protect the interests of the Members themselves rather than their nationals and, accordingly, the main object of those obligations are the goods, services or the IPRs themselves rather than the individuals who may be involved in goods or services trade or may be the owners of IPRs. Second (and this flows from the previous factor), WTO claims are always presented as claims of the claimant Member itself rather than as espousal of a claim of one or more of its nationals. In addition, there are many other specific factors that make it evident that the local remedies rule does not apply in the WTO. Thus, for instance, the WTO dispute settlement procedures can be invoked

[85] However, there were a number of panel decisions rendered under the auspices of the predecessor GATT that rejected the applicability of the rule in respect of GATT dispute settlement: see, e.g., Panel Reports, *US – Cement*, para. 5.9; *US – Norwegian Salmon I*, paras. 33–59, 348; and *US – Norwegian Salmon II*, paras. 22–41, 217.

[86] See, e.g., Kuyper 1994, 233–38; and Martha 1996.

[87] See, e.g., Kuyper 1994, 238.

[88] See, GATS, Articles II and XXVIII(g).

[89] See, e.g., Martha 1996, 119–21.

[90] As already noted, these provisions are discussed in Chapter 3 below.

[91] See, e.g., Martha 1996, 121–23.

against an anti-dumping measure *as soon as* it is imposed by the administrative branch,[92] which, in effect, means that having recourse to or waiting for the completion of any available domestic judicial review procedures is not necessary. And yet more importantly, WTO procedures can be invoked not only against "final" anti-dumping measures, but also against "provisional" anti-dumping measures that are imposed pending the completion of the relevant domestic (administrative) procedures.[93] Finally, in respect of the obligations to make available under national laws specified procedures and remedies, it may be mentioned that it is one thing to require Members to put in place certain procedures so that, if necessary, an affected individual can have recourse to those procedures, and it is an entirely different thing to say that a WTO Member cannot pursue its own claim unless one or more of its nationals have had recourse to available domestic procedures. The WTO treaty, of course, does not envisage the latter.[94]

So much for the theoretical aspect of the matter, as far as practice is concerned, as respondents, WTO Members have shown a complete and astonishing reluctance to raise objections on the ground of non-exhaustion of local remedies.[95] And there is not a single instance in which exhaustion of local remedies was considered by a panel or the Appellate Body to be a pre-requisite for the dispute to be properly brought before the panel or the AB. But rather, there are numerous instances in which WTO dispute settlement procedures were pursued in parallel with domestic legal proceedings.[96] Thus, the dispute settlement practice makes it evident that the local remedies rule does not have a place in the WTO; and this is also recognized in more recent academic works.[97]

[92] See ADA, Article 17.4. [93] See ibid.

[94] See, e.g., Panel Report, *US – Section 211*, para. 8.95, footnote 131.

[95] Cf., however, the *Argentina – Textiles* case, where a somewhat similar objection was raised but was rejected by the Panel. In this case Argentina argued that the availability of procedures under its domestic laws to successfully challenge the WTO-compatibility of any Argentine measure meant that Argentina did not and would not violate its WTO obligations by the measure that was at issue before the Panel. The Panel rejected this argument on the ground that an inconsistent measure violates WTO obligations "regardless of whether [the] Member provides a remedy for such violation in its domestic legal system": Panel Report, *Argentina – Textiles*, para. 6.68. This, no doubt, can be viewed as an indirect rejection of the applicability of the local remedies rule: see, e.g., Waincymer 2002, 203.

[96] See, e.g., Panel Report, *US – Shrimp 21.5*, para. 5.109; and AB Report, *US – Shrimp 21.5*, para. 95.

[97] See, e.g., Petersmann 1997a, 240–44; Bourgeois 1998, 264–66; Davey 2001, 103–4; and Waincymer 2002, 202–5.

Because of this lack of practical significance, the local remedies rule is not treated further in the present work.[98] It is, however, worth pointing out that the non-applicability of this rule in WTO dispute settlement has implications for the effectiveness of the WTO legal system in general and its dispute settlement in particular. If the rule were applicable, speedy recourse to WTO dispute settlement would have been seriously hampered; and, accordingly, the WTO legal system and its dispute settlement could have been less effective. Thus, the total lack of interest on the part of the WTO Members in raising objections on the ground of non-exhaustion of local remedies perhaps shows a corresponding interest on their part in having an effective WTO dispute settlement system.

5.2 *General principles of national law as a source of international and WTO law*

As regards the issue of general principles of national law as a source of WTO law, first it is necessary to direct attention to Article 38(1)(c) of the Statute of the International Court of Justice. In this Article, as is well known, "the general principles of law recognized by civilized nations" are set out as one of the three primary sources of international law (the other two being treaties and international custom). While standard textbooks on international law note various instances in which both the PCIJ and the ICJ, as well as other international courts, have had recourse to general principles of national law as authority on particular points,[99] it is commonly acknowledged that, as a source, such principles by no means have the same significance as treaties or custom.[100] Indeed, often, general principles of national law become relevant as a source only for purposes of filling gaps in the law that might otherwise be left

[98] It may be mentioned parenthetically that there is also no prospect for Members to introduce changes in the WTO treaty, or, specifically, in the DSU, with a view to requiring exhaustion of local remedies – the reason being that it would lead to a considerable amount of delay in having recourse to the WTO procedures, which would be unacceptable to most Members. For instance, rather than introducing delay, many proposals for reform put forward by Members in the context of the ongoing Doha negotiations call for making the already expeditious WTO dispute settlement procedures even more speedy: see the WTO document series, TN/DS/W*, available at http://docsonline.wto.org.

[99] See, e.g., Jennings & Watts 1992, 36–40; Shaw 1997, 77–82; Brownlie 1998, 15–18; Harris 1998, 47–53; and Cassese 2001, 155–59.

[100] See, e.g., Jennings & Watts 1992, 36 (noting that "custom and treaties are in practice the principal sources of international law").

by the operation of treaty and custom (or, put differently, to avoid a *non liquet*).[101]

Thus, in the nineteenth and early twentieth century, general principles of national law had a certain usefulness as a reservoir for filling legal gaps and thereby "developing the then rather rudimentary and incomplete body of international law."[102] But as international law gradually evolved into its present state comprising a whole network of treaties and numerous customary rules, recourse by international courts and tribunals to general principles of national law as a source declined correspondingly.[103] This, however, does not mean that it would no longer be necessary to have recourse to general principles of national law as a source of international law. Certainly, there can still be circumstances where a solution may not be found on the basis of customary and treaty law and, accordingly, it may be necessary to refer to general principles of national law. This would particularly be the case in new areas of international law where gaps and lacunae in legal regulation may not be uncommon. An obvious example is international criminal law, which as a body of law is still in an evolving stage and is replete with lacunae.[104] Consequently, on various occasions, the newly established ad hoc international criminal tribunals[105] have found it useful to refer to the general principles of criminal law recognized in the major legal systems of the world.[106]

However, given that recourse is made to general principles of national law only as a "gap-filler," there is not much scope for optimism about the role that national law can play as a source of WTO law, consisting of extensive treaty texts supplemented by legal interpretations developed in the ever-increasing dispute settlement jurisprudence. In addition, it is argued by commentators that in certain circumstances non-WTO public international law rules – both customary and treaty-based – may apply

[101] See, e.g., ibid. 40; Shaw 1997, 77–78; and Cassese 2001, 155.

[102] Cassese 2001, 156. For a detailed account of the role that general principles of law played in international adjudication during the nineteenth and early twentieth century, see Cheng 1987. It is notable that many principles of national law discussed by Cheng have since become either general principles of international law or rules of customary international law.

[103] Cassese 2001, 157. [104] Ibid. 158.

[105] I.e., the International Criminal Tribunal for the Former Yugoslavia (ICTY) and the International Criminal Tribunal for Rwanda (ICTR).

[106] See, for instance, the cases cited by Cassese 2001, 158. Cf. also the Rome Statute of the International Criminal Court 1998, Article 21(1)(c) (envisaging that, if necessary, the permanent International Criminal Court may have recourse to general principles of national law).

in the WTO.[107] Thus, should there be gaps in the WTO treaty, recourse may first be had to non-WTO international law rather than to principles of national law.[108]

Yet, the above is not the all-important reason for not treating in detail the issue of general principles of national law. Rather, it is not so treated because the present study is not about the sources of WTO law. This study, as already underscored, aims to examine WTO obligations concerning national law and, more importantly, national law issues that arise in the context of the WTO dispute settlement organs' *review* of national measures including laws. Needless to say, the process of inducting from national laws principles that may be applied as rules of WTO law does not involve the kind of "judicial review" issues with which this study is concerned. Accordingly, a more detailed analysis of the matter is postponed for another occasion.

107 See, further, Chapter 4, pp. 92–97, and the works cited there.

108 There are hardly any examples in which a panel or the AB spelled out a rule of WTO law on the basis of general principles of national law: in *US – Countervailing Measures* the Panel rejected the US argument that the distinction made in national corporate laws between a company and its shareholders was relevant for purposes of interpreting the ASCM (see Panel Report, para. 7.50). In *US – Copyright Act* state practice as reflected in the national copyrights laws of States parties to the Berne Convention for the Protection of Literary and Artistic Works 1971 (available at www.wipo.int/treaties/en/ip/berne/index.html) and of WTO Members was said to *confirm* the Panel's conclusion that "minor exceptions" to copyright protection are permissible (see Panel Report, para. 6.55). (The Berne Convention is incorporated into the WTO TRIPS Agreement by its Article 9.1.) As is apparent, in this instance the reference was not to general principles of national law but to the *state practice* as reflected in national laws; furthermore, such reference was made simply to *confirm* a conclusion that the Panel had already reached on the basis of the relevant provisions of the Berne Convention. In *US – FSC 21.5 I* the AB, in interpreting a provision of the ASCM, sought to derive assistance from certain "widely recognized principles which many States generally apply in the field of taxation." However, the principles concerned were those of international tax law as reflected in bilateral or multilateral tax treaties or in model tax conventions, rather than those of national law (see AB Report, paras. 141–45).

Part I

2 National law in international law

1 Introduction: dualism and monism

It is a customary practice to commence any discussion about the relationship between international and national law by reference to the theoretical debate known as the dualist-monist controversy.[1] While there are a number of different aspects of both doctrines, they derive their appellations – dualism and monism – from their respective viewpoint on the question as to whether international law and national law belong to two separate legal orders or to the same legal order. Dualist doctrine points to differences between national and international law, such as: the subjects of the former are individuals while the subjects of the latter are states; or, while the source of the former is the will of a particular state, that of the latter is the common will of states; or, the fundamental principle that underpins the national system of law is that legislation is to be obeyed, while that of international law is the principle of *pacta sunt servanda*.[2] For dualists these differences mean that international law and national law are two entirely distinct legal orders existing independently of one another.

By contrast, monist doctrine regards all law – national or international – as part of one single legal structure. This doctrine is put forward either on formalistic logical grounds or from an ethical perspective to assert the supremacy of international law as the best way to protect

[1] See, for instance, the treatment of the subject in any of the following standard textbooks on international law: Jennings & Watts 1992, 53–54; Shearer 1994, 63–67; Shaw 1997, 100–2; Brownlie 1998, 31–34; Harris 1998, 68–71; and Cassese 2001, 162–66.

[2] The German and the Italian positivist writers Heinrich Triepel and Dionisio Anzilotti were the two principal proponents of the dualist doctrine. Their views are usefully summarized in Starke 1936, 70–74; and Gaja 1992. See also the works cited in n. 1 above.

human rights. From the former perspective it is argued that the same definition of law – as norms that lay down patterns of behavior that ought to be followed – is applicable to both national and international law, and accordingly they cannot but be part of a unified legal structure.[3] The other monist strand proceeds from distrust for "sovereign" states as vehicles for guaranteeing human rights. International law is believed to be the best guarantor of human rights; and as such it is concerned, like national law, with the conduct and welfare of individuals. Furthermore, the supremacy of international law is asserted even within the municipal sphere, such that the entire monistic legal architecture is imbued with a moral purpose founded upon respect for human rights.[4]

Much of the dualist–monist controversy turns on whether – and if so, on what basis – one system of law can be said to be superior to or supreme over the other. For dualists the rules of national and international systems of law are so fundamentally different that it is not possible for the rules of one system to have an effect on, or overrule, the rules of the other. When national law provides for the application of international law within the national jurisdiction, rules of international law are adopted or transformed as rules of national law: thus rather than being a detraction, it is an example of the supreme authority of national law within the national jurisdiction. Monists, on the other hand, often tend to argue, either on the basis of abstract logic or because of the importance of international guarantees for the protection of human rights, that international law is superior to municipal law.

Fitzmaurice has critiqued the entire dualist–monist controversy, including the debate about supremacy, as being "unreal, artificial and strictly beside the point."[5] He points out that both doctrines assume that there is a common field in which the international and municipal legal orders operate simultaneously in respect of the same set of relations and transactions. Because in reality there is no such common field, the entire controversy is as sterile as a controversy as to whether English law is superior to French law or vice versa. Just as French law is supreme in France and English law in England, international law is supreme in the international field and national law in the national field. And in neither case does the supremacy result from the content or any inherent character of the law, but rather from the respective fields of operation.[6] While Fitzmaurice emphasizes that his view is neither dualist nor monist, it

[3] See Kelsen 1949, 328–88, and 1966, 551–88. [4] See Lauterpacht 1975, 547–50, and 1950.
[5] Fitzmaurice 1957, 71. [6] Ibid. 70–74.

can certainly be regarded as a modified dualist position, because on the one hand it rests, like the traditional dualist doctrine, upon the distinctness of the two legal orders, and on the other hand it avoids, unlike the traditional dualist doctrine, the question of supremacy of one system of law over the other.

But in any case, the points raised by Fitzmaurice have much practical significance. Despite their intellectual or ideological appeal, theories indeed are not terribly helpful in understanding the actual process of interaction between national and international law. The tremendous growth of international law during the second half of the twentieth century has increasingly made the relationship between national and international law less clear and more complex than it was during the nineteenth and the first half of the twentieth century, when both the dualist and the monist doctrines were put forward.

The gradual emergence of individuals as subjects of international law in such areas as human rights, investment, international administrative law, or international criminal law has thwarted one of the basic premises of the dualist doctrine. International law has also made considerable inroads into national legal systems in various ways, for instance by stipulations in treaties for states to take effective legislative, administrative or other measures to implement treaty provisions.[7] As already noted in the preceding chapter, the WTO treaty contains an entire range of obligations that has far-reaching systemic or constitutional repercussions for the Member's domestic legal systems (these are discussed in detail in the next chapter). There have also come into being ever more effective and "powerful" international adjudicative bodies with competence to review whether national legislative, administrative or judicial acts are in complete accord with international obligations. The European Community legal order, which in many respects partakes the characteristics of a domestic federal constitutional structure but yet remains an international treaty-based system, provides another instance where the traditional dividing lines between national and international law seem entirely inapt.[8]

Do these and other similar developments mean that the distinction between national and international law has became so vague that the contemporary international legal order is to be described as monist? The answer, of course, must be in the negative. Various reasons can be given

[7] See, for instance, the treaty provisions cited in Chapter 3, nn. 66–70.
[8] See, e.g., J. H. H. Weiler 1991; Bethlehem 1998; and Craig 2001.

for still treating the two legal orders as distinct: the methods of creation of rules of national and international law remain, as underscored in the traditional dualist doctrine, meaningfully different. And, it is still difficult to imagine that rules of international law can have effect within the national legal order without the sufferance of the latter.

However, if so inclined, one can take issue with these generalizations. For instance, the political organs of the European Community have authority to make laws that in some respect can be compared to the law-making power of national institutions.[9] Equally notable are the twin principles of direct effect and supremacy of EC law. According to the former, EC law – both treaty provisions and laws made by the European Community organs – become part of the national legal systems of member states without any intervention by national governments or legislatures to adopt or transform those provisions or laws as rules of national law.[10] And according to the latter, EC law takes precedence over both prior and subsequent national law.[11] But, again, with respect to the legislative power of the EC organs, it is of course the case that such power is delegated to those organs by the EC member states themselves under express treaty provisions. The principles of direct effect and supremacy can be somewhat more difficult to explain, because these were proactively developed by the European Court of Justice (ECJ) through a process of teleological interpretation of the EC Treaty, and in the absence of any explicit provision envisaging either of the two principles.[12] But, from a different perspective, it is difficult to overemphasize that the ECJ's enunciation of neither of these two principles could have any significance had they not been *accepted* at the national level. In other words, both principles became operative within the national legal systems of the member states only because they were allowed to become so operative, either by national legislative means or through accommodation by national courts.[13]

[9] See Weatherill & Beaumont 1999, chs. 2–5. [10] See ibid. ch. 11.

[11] See ibid. ch. 12; and Craig & de Búrca 1998, ch. 6.

[12] See Case 26/62, *Van Gend en Loos* v. *Nederlandse Administratie der Belastingen* [1963] ECR 1; and Case 6/64, *Costa* v. *ENEL* [1964] ECR 585 (these are the two seminal cases on direct effect and supremacy, respectively). The judgments of the ECJ in both of these cases, as well as other leading cases on the subject, are reproduced in Oppenheimer 1994. Cf. Spiermann 1999 (arguing that there is nothing innovative or proactive in the ECJ's judgments in these cases).

[13] Indeed, in this respect there exists a host of national court decisions that not only bear out an interesting discourse between those courts and the ECJ on issues of direct effect and supremacy but also demonstrate that in some instances the principles were

For present purposes it is also absolutely crucial to be mindful of the widely acknowledged *sui generis* nature of the EC legal system, which in the ECJ's own words is "a new legal order of international law."[14] Accordingly, attempts should not be made to theorize generally about the relationship between international and national law on the basis of features that are unique to the European Community legal order and are not to be found in other areas of contemporary international law.

At any rate, matters noted in the preceding paragraphs make it evident that, because of their "dichotomous" nature, the dualist and monist doctrines fail to reflect the diversity and the specificity of actual practice. A common difficulty of both doctrines is that they proceed from a-priori concepts of rather limited significance and then attempt to forge the practice into those concepts.[15] Thus, it is no wonder that in recent academic writings on the subject theories do not feature so prominently and there is a decisive preference for practice over theory.

As indicated in the last chapter, efforts are made throughout this work to understand the treatment of national law in WTO law in the light of the practice in international law in general. However, to set the scene, a few key aspects of the practice are briefly outlined below.

2 National law and international obligations

2.1 *National laws cannot be relied upon to avoid international obligations*

As a starting point, attention may be devoted to the question of fulfilment and/or implementation of international obligations in national laws. International regulation of this matter has a number of different dimensions: first, it is a well-established rule, supported by a range of

accepted somewhat grudgingly: see, for instance, the survey of cases in Craig & de Búrca 1998, 264–91.

14 *Van Gend en Loos*, n. 12 above, at 12.

15 It may be noted parenthetically that, as distinguished from the relationship between national and international law on the international plane, in respect of the relationship in a domestic context, the terminology of monism and dualism is sometimes used as a shorthand to categorize countries into two groups: (i) those that give direct domestic law effect to international rules (referred to as "monist" states); and (ii) those that do not give such direct effect but provide for the transformation of international rules into domestic law by statutory or other means (referred to as "dualist" states). Unlike the doctrinal controversy on the international plane surrounding the question of supremacy, this use of the terminology in a domestic context is less problematic. See, generally, Van Panhuys 1964, 14–15; Jackson 1992; and Higgins 2000.

judicial and arbitral decisions, that to justify violations of international obligations a state cannot refer to provisions in its constitution or its laws.[16] With respect to treaties, this rule is also provided for in Article 27 of the Vienna Convention on the Law of Treaties (VCLT), which lays down that provisions of national law may not be invoked as justification for failure to perform obligations imposed by a treaty.[17] Thus a state that has breached an international law obligation cannot plead that it acted lawfully under its domestic law or that its domestic law required the breach or that it was prevented from acting consistently with the international obligation because of the lack of or deficiencies in its own legislative provisions.[18] The rationale for this rule is self-evident: it prevents evasion of international obligations by means of domestic legislation and, as such, it is a sine qua non for the effectiveness of international law.[19]

However, the "negative" import of this rule is readily apparent. That is to say, it simply forbids something, i.e. opposing national law as a legal bar to the fulfilment of international obligations, and does not require a state to take any "positive" steps to implement international obligations in national laws. Unlike the issue of non-opposability of national laws, with respect to the issue of implementation there is no unequivocal international practice, and publicists also seem to hold divergent views. While many contemporary international treaties contain express provisions in this regard, the perplexing question is: what are the

[16] This principle was judicially endorsed as long ago as the *Alabama Claims* arbitration of 1872, where the Tribunal rejected the British argument that Britain had not violated its obligations as a neutral in the American Civil War because it did not have the legal means to prevent the private acts complained of: see J. B. Moore 1898, 653, 656. Both the PCIJ and the ICJ affirmed this principle on numerous occasions: see, e.g., *Wimbledon* case, PCIJ Ser. A No. 1 (1923) at 29–30; *Chorzow Factory* case, PCIJ Ser. A No. 17 (1928) at 33–34; *Greco-Bulgarian Communities* case, PCIJ Ser. B No. 17 (1930) at 32; *Free Zones* cases, PCIJ Ser. A No. 24 (1930) at 12, and PCIJ Ser. A/B No. 46 (1932) at 167; *Polish Nationals in Danzig* case, PCIJ Ser. A/B No. 44 (1932) at 24; *Reparation for Injuries* case, ICJ Rep. 174 (1949) at 180; *Fisheries* case, ICJ Rep. 116 (1951) at 132; *Nottebohm* case, ICJ Rep. 4 (1955) at 20–21; *Guardianship of Infants* case, ICJ Rep. 55 (1958) at 67; and *Headquarters Agreement* case, ICJ Rep. 12 (1988) at 34 (para. 57).

[17] See, further, Chapter 3, pp. 58–59. See also the ILC's Draft Declaration on Rights and Duties of States 1949, Article 13; and the ILC's Draft Articles on Responsibility of States for Internationally Wrongful Acts 2001, Articles 3 and 32, reproduced in: Crawford 2002, 86, 207.

[18] Another aspect of the same principle is that the unlawfulness of an act of a state under its domestic law does not entail that the act in question is unlawful in international law: see *Elettronica Sicula S.p.A. (ELSI)*, ICJ Rep. 15 (1989) at 51 (para. 73), 74 (para. 124).

[19] See Morgenstern 1950; and Fitzmaurice 1957, 85–86, and 1959, 185.

requirements for implementation in the absence of express provision and as a matter of general (customary) international law? As regards treaty obligations, Articles 26 and 27 of the VCLT can be seen as the codification of the general international law requirements. But, as discussed in the next chapter, these two Articles hardly speak of any positive implementation measures that states are obliged to take. Not surprisingly, in the WTO treaty the issue of implementation is dealt with expressly and with due emphasis. Article XVI:4 of the WTO Agreement, which requires Members to ensure the conformity of their laws, regulations and administrative procedures with the WTO obligations, is one of the more notable provisions on this subject. While a comparative discussion of this Article, Articles 26 and 27 of the VCLT and provisions on implementation contained in other international treaties is postponed for the next chapter, as a prelude to that discussion it may be in order to make some general remarks and to note the views of some of the publicists on issues relating to implementation.

2.2 *Is there a duty to ensure conformity of national laws with international obligations?*

The question of implementation of course has more than one component. As regards the *means* of implementation, it is clear that general international law gives each state complete freedom: that is to say, it does not regulate the manner in which a state may choose to put itself domestically in the position to meet its international obligations.[20] Thus, each state can determine in accordance with its own constitutional practice whether to give direct domestic law effect to international rules or whether to "transform," "adopt" or "incorporate" those rules into domestic law by statutes or by some other (e.g. judicial or administrative) means.[21] There is a related issue of whether a state must have laws that are compatible with international obligations or, conversely, must not have laws that are not so compatible; and with respect to this issue, the situation is far from clear. In the *Exchange of Greek and Turkish Populations* case, the Permanent Court of International Justice stated that: "a State which has contracted valid international obligations is bound to make in its legislation such modifications as may be necessary to

[20] See, e.g., Jennings & Watts 1992, 82–83; Malanczuk 1997, 64; Cassese 2001, 168; and Denza 2003, 415–16. See also *LaGrand* case, ICJ Rep. 466 (2001) at 514 (para. 125).

[21] See, generally, Jackson 1992; and the works cited in n. 20 above.

ensure the fulfilment of the obligations undertaken."[22] However, the above dictum has not settled the matter once and for all. First, although it is eighty years old, the dictum has hardly been judicially reiterated. Second, on this issue publicists seem to hold widely divergent views. Some have argued – apparently on the basis of the dictum of the PCIJ – that states have a general duty to bring national laws into conformity with international obligations.[23] Others take the view that it is uncertain whether under international law a state has an obligation to possess laws enabling it to comply with its international obligations, and not to have laws that do, or may, result in violations of those obligations.[24] And yet others deny, altogether, the existence of any general duty to ensure the conformity of national laws with international obligations.[25] Furthermore, commentators who contend that there exists such a general duty add that a state does not commit a direct breach of international law by merely failing in that duty, and a breach occurs only if the state concerned fails to carry out its obligations on a specific occasion.[26]

The view that there is no such general duty seems more plausible for a number of reasons. Firstly, as one commentator has rightly pointed out, had there been such a duty, each time a state failed to fulfil an international obligation because of the deficiencies in its laws, it would have breached both the obligation in question and the general duty. But a perusal of state practice reveals that when a state violates an international obligation owing to the lack or flaws in its laws, other states claim a mere cessation of the wrongful act and/or reparation for the specific breach. Thus the complaining states do not usually concern themselves with the factors that led to the violation or protest against the defects in the domestic laws or constitution; they are only interested in the final outcome, namely compliance or non-compliance with the obligation at issue.[27]

[22] PCIJ Ser. B No. 10 (1925) at 20.

[23] See, e.g., Fitzmaurice 1957, 89; and Brownlie 1998, 35.

[24] See, e.g., Jennings & Watts 1992, 85. [25] See, e.g., Cassese 2001, 167.

[26] See Fitzmaurice 1957, 89; and Brownlie 1998, 35. See also McNair 1961, 100.

[27] See Cassese 2001, 167. See further the *Arrest Warrant* case, ICJ Rep. 3 (2002), discussed below at p. 39. Cf. also the *Headquarters Agreement* case, ICJ Rep. 12 (1988), in which the United States adopted a statute providing for the closure of the office of the PLO Mission to the United Nations in New York in contravention of the US treaty obligations towards the United Nations under the Headquarters Agreement of 1947; but the UN Secretary-General took the view that the mere adoption of the legislation would not violate the Agreement if assurances were given that the PLO Mission would not be closed in pursuance of the statute.

Secondly, in each case the question really is whether the particular international obligation at issue requires the possession or non-possession of certain laws, or the performance or non-performance of certain acts, or some form of combination of both. Thus it is not possible to speak, in the abstract, of any general duty for states to ensure the conformity of their laws with each and every international obligation, and whether a state is required to bring its national laws into conformity with a particular international obligation depends on the content and interpretation of that obligation. While in some cases national laws may be a test of compliance or non-compliance with the international obligation at issue, in others they may not be.[28]

Thirdly, many international treaties explicitly require the contracting states to adopt legislative measures to implement specified treaty obligations.[29] The fact that, with respect to some obligations, the members of the international community take care to provide expressly for a duty to enact implementing legislation lends support to the point of view that a general duty to this effect may not exist.

In addition, there are persuasive grounds for arguing that the statement of the PCIJ quoted earlier also does not entail that there is a general duty. First, the statement was prompted with reference to Article 18 of the Treaty of Lausanne of 1923, which expressly required the contracting parties to introduce changes in their domestic laws for purposes of implementing the treaty.[30] Accordingly, it may not be accurate to cite that statement in support of the proposition that, even in the absence of an explicit provision and irrespective of the content of the obligation in question, there exists a general duty to ensure conformity. Second, the interpretation or application of Article 18 or of a general duty to bring national laws into conformity was not an issue before the Permanent Court. Thus, in jurisprudential terms, the PCIJ's statement is nothing more than an *obiter dictum*[31] – and hence it is not convincing to distill a principle of general international law by stretching the authority of that dictum.

2.3 *Can national legislation by itself violate international obligations?*

As alluded to in the last chapter, a large number of disputes before the WTO adjudicative bodies are about the WTO-compatibility of national

[28] See Jennings & Watts 1992, 85–86.
[29] See, for instance, the treaty provisions cited in Chapter 3, nn. 66–70.
[30] PCIJ Ser. B No. 10 (1925) at 20. [31] See ibid. 7, 20–21.

laws; and indeed in many cases national laws were found to be WTO/GATT-inconsistent by WTO (and before it GATT) panels and the Appellate Body.[32] This is sometimes put forward as a distinguishing feature of the WTO legal system. That is to say, it is suggested that in international law the mere enactment by a state of legislation incompatible with international obligations, does not, by itself, constitute a breach of those obligations and a breach could only occur if the legislation is actually implemented in a given case. Accordingly, the position in WTO law is regarded as distinctive because, under it, incompatible legislation by itself (i.e. even in the absence of any specific application of the legislation) constitutes a breach.[33]

However, the above view does not seem entirely accurate. For instance, in the *LaGrand* case the International Court of Justice stated that it

> can determine the existence of a violation of an international obligation. If necessary, it can also hold that a domestic law has been the cause of [the] violation.[34]

Thus, it is not only WTO obligations but apparently other international obligations can also be breached by the mere enactment of incompatible legislation. The question that immediately follows is when can a law in and of itself amount to a breach? In this respect there are some differences between WTO law and international law in general. In international law this question is not susceptible to a precise answer in the abstract. All that can be said is that, like the duty to bring national law into conformity with international obligations, whether a law by itself breaches a particular international obligation or whether the law has to be implemented for the breach to occur would depend on the content and interpretation of that obligation.[35] By contrast, in the WTO context, it is possible to answer the question in a more clear-cut manner. Firstly, all WTO obligations can possibly be violated by incompatible national laws.[36] Secondly, in the WTO there is a specific tool of

[32] As some of the more prominent examples, see WTO cases, *US – FSC*; *Canada – Pharmaceuticals*; *US – 1916 Act I & II*; *US – Copyright Act*; *US – Section 211*; *US – FSC 21.5 I & II*; *US – Offset Act*; *Japan – Apples*; *EC – Tariff Preferences*; *US – Gambling Services*; and *Mexico – Rice*; and GATT cases, *US – DISC*; *US – Manufacturing Clause*; and *US – Section 337*.

[33] See, e.g., Panel Report, *US – Section 301*, para. 7.80; and Naiki 2004, 25.

[34] *LaGrand* case, n. 20 above, at 513 (para. 125).

[35] This is also the view taken by the International Law Commission: see the ILC's Draft Articles on State Responsibility, Commentary to Article 12, para. 12, reproduced in: Crawford 2002, 130. Although the ILC did not mention it, it is possible to imagine that the answer may also depend on the content of the relevant national law.

[36] Cf. WTO Agreement, Article XVI:4. See, further, Chapter 3, pp. 55–62.

review that looks at the nature of the contested national legislation with a view to determining its WTO-compatibility. (This tool of review forms the subject-matter of Chapter 8 below.) Thus, in large measure, the WTO-compatibility of national legislation depends on the content of the legislation in question.

It may also be pertinent to note that instances can rarely be found in the jurisprudence of the PCIJ or the ICJ where national laws were held to be incompatible with international obligations. An obvious reason for the lack of such decisions is the general reluctance of states to pursue before the International Court claims against national laws. Recall in this context the point made earlier that complainant states usually concern themselves with the breach caused by the specific wrongful act rather than with the defects or flaws in domestic laws that led to the wrongful act.[37] The *Arrest Warrant* case before the ICJ provides a good example in this regard. A Belgian court issued an international arrest warrant against the incumbent foreign minister of the Congo. The warrant was issued under the explicit and clear authority of a Belgian law. Although initially the Congo claimed that both the law and the warrant were in breach of international law rules regarding diplomatic immunity, it later abandoned its claim against the Belgian law and made submissions only on the legality of the arrest warrant. Accordingly, while the warrant was found to be unlawful by the ICJ, no findings were made about the Belgian law.[38]

Indeed, despite the observation of the ICJ in the *LaGrand* case quoted above, it would be rather difficult, if not impossible, to succeed in a claim before the ICJ against national legislation per se (i.e. in respect of the legislation itself and not its application):[39] the reason being that it is very likely that the ICJ would apply much more stringent criteria than WTO panels and the AB in determining whether the claim fulfils the requirement of "ripeness." Ripeness is concerned with ensuring that cases presented to a court are not hypothetical or too speculative and that there exists a real controversy between the parties.[40] Thus, for instance, in the *Northern Cameroons* case the ICJ has observed that "it may pronounce judgment only in connection with concrete cases where there exists at the time of the adjudication an actual controversy

[37] See above, p. 36. [38] *Arrest Warrant* case, n. 27 above.

[39] Notably, the *LaGrand* case itself did not concern any challenge to a rule of domestic law per se, nor was in this case a domestic law rule found to be inconsistent with international obligations: n. 20 above, at 495, 497–98 (paras. 81, 90–91).

[40] Cf. Collier & Lowe 1999, 12–13, 156; and Davey 2001, 101–3.

involving a conflict of legal interests between the parties."[41] Consider now the following simple illustration. A treaty provision may make it unlawful to do something, which may be permitted or required under the national legislation of a state party. But if the state concerned has not applied the law and consequently there has not been an "injury," can it be held that the law by itself violated the treaty provision? Given that the International Court may pronounce judgment only in cases of actual controversy, should it not be possible to argue that in the absence of specific application of the law there is no "dispute"[42] that is "ripe" for judicial consideration?[43]

Unlike the PCIJ or the ICJ, courts that exercise supervisory jurisdiction in respect of a particular treaty regime have been called upon to review the compatibility of national laws with international obligations much more frequently; and such courts have also found national laws incompatible at regular intervals. (It is worth noting that there are important implications of this review for the effectiveness of the treaty regime concerned.) Thus, for instance, the European Court of Justice has made such findings in a very large number of cases.[44] Likewise, the

[41] ICJ Rep. 15 (1963) at 33–34.

[42] Cf. Article 38 of the Statute of the ICJ (providing that the function of the ICJ is to decide "such *disputes* as are submitted to it" – italics added).

[43] Cf., e.g., the *Headquarters Agreement* case. In this case the UN General Assembly sought an advisory opinion from the ICJ as to whether the United States was under an obligation to enter into arbitration for the alleged breaches of the Headquarters Agreement of 1947, caused by the adoption of a law prima facie inconsistent with that Agreement and of administrative decisions and measures to apply the law. To render its opinion the ICJ needed to determine whether there existed a "dispute" between the UN and the United States. The ICJ answered this question in the affirmative in the light of the entire factual circumstances of the case, including the fact that the US administration had decided to apply the law and resorted to US courts for enforcement. However, the Court did not address more specifically whether the dispute came into being because of the mere enactment of the law or whether it arose only after the administration had taken measures to apply the law: n. 27 above, at 30 (paras. 43–44).

The ripeness issue can be further illustrated by reference to the *Arrest Warrant* case. As noted before, in this case no claims or findings were made against the Belgian law under which the unlawful arrest warrant was issued. However, Judge Oda in his dissenting opinion criticized the Court's findings even in respect of the warrant, because in his view the warrant did not result in any "damage or injury" to the Congo. He also added a cautionary note that such lax exercise of jurisdiction by the ICJ "when no real injury has occurred" would lead to the withdrawal by states of their recognition of the Court's compulsory jurisdiction: n. 27 above, at 46–49, Dissenting Opinion of Judge Oda, paras. 3–7.

[44] See, e.g., Case 167–73, *Commission* v. *France* [1974] ECR 359; Case 104/86, *Commission* v. *Italy* [1988] ECR 1799; Case C-58/99, *Commission* v. *Italy* [2000] ECR I-3811; Case C-264/99,

European Court of Human Rights (ECHR) has found incompatibilities between domestic law and the law of the European Human Rights Convention (EHR Convention).[45] The ECHR's approach to this issue has some subtlety however. There is a settled case law of the ECHR to the effect that, in proceedings originating in an individual application, its task is not to rule *in abstracto* as to the compatibility of national law with the EHR Convention; rather, it should confine itself, as far as possible, to an examination of the concrete case before it.[46] But individuals may contend that a law violates their rights by itself, in the absence of a specific measure of implementation, if they run the risk of being directly affected by it.[47] Accordingly, in a number of cases the ECHR has held that domestic legislation violated the EHR Convention.[48] In addition, for purposes of rendering its judgment in the concrete case, the ECHR often implicitly addressed issues of compatibility of domestic laws and practices with the EHR standards.[49]

3 National laws as facts

It is a well-established principle of international law that national laws are facts before international courts and tribunals.[50] This principle has a number of different dimensions. Firstly, it means that judicial notice (pursuant to the principle *jura novit curia*) does not apply to matters of

Commission v. *Italy* [2000] ECR I-4417; Case C-160/99, *Commission* v. *France* [2000] ECR I-6137; Case C-162/99, *Commission* v. *Italy* [2001] ECR I-541; Case C-265/99, *Commission* v. *France* [2001] ECR I-2305; Case C-159/99, *Commission* v. *Italy* [2001] ECR I-4007; Case C-283/99, *Commission* v. *Italy* [2001] ECR I-4363; Case C-40/00, *Commission* v. *France* [2001] ECR I-4539; Case C-70/99, *Commission* v. *Portugal* [2001] ECR I-4845; and Case C-78/00, *Commission* v. *Italy* [2001] ECR I-8195.

45 Convention for the Protection of Human Rights and Fundamental Freedoms 1950.

46 See, e.g., *De Becker* v. *Belgium*, ECHR Ser. A No. 4 (1962), para. 14; *Axen* v. *Germany*, ECHR Ser. A No. 72 (1983), para. 24; *Bönisch* v. *Austria*, ECHR Ser. A No. 92 (1985), para. 27; and *Wingrove* v. *United Kingdom*, 1996-V ECHR Rep. 1937, para. 50.

47 See, e.g., *Klass* v. *Germany*, ECHR Ser. A No. 28 (1978), para. 33; *Johnston* v. *Ireland*, ECHR Ser. A No. 112 (1986), para. 42; and the cases cited in n. 48 below.

48 See, e.g., *Marckx* v. *Belgium*, ECHR Ser. A No. 31 (1979); *Dudgeon* v. *United Kingdom*, ECHR Ser. A No. 45 (1981); *Norris* v. *Ireland*, ECHR Ser. A No. 142 (1988); and *Modinos* v. *Cyprus*, ECHR Ser. A No. 259 (1993).

49 See, e.g., *Luedicke* v. *Germany*, ECHR Ser. A No. 29 (1978); *Abdulaziz* v. *United Kingdom*, ECHR Ser. A No. 94 (1985); *Ahmed* v. *United Kingdom*, 1998-VI ECHR Rep. 2356; *Rekvènyi* v. *Hungary*, 1999-III ECHR Rep. 867; *Hashman* v. *United Kingdom*, 1999-VIII ECHR Rep. 4; and *SBC* v. *United Kingdom*, 34 EHRR 619 (2002).

50 See, e.g., *German Interests in Polish Upper Silesia*, PCIJ Ser. A No. 7 (1926) at 19; and Brownlie 1998, 39.

national law, which must be proved by introducing necessary evidence, and different evidentiary rules including those on burden of proof for the establishment of facts are fully applicable in this regard.[51] Secondly, it also means that rules of national law constitute evidence of conduct by states that can be utilized by an international court in establishing the factual record so as to determine compliance or non-compliance with international obligations.[52]

In addition, sometimes it is suggested that because national laws are merely facts, an international tribunal does not interpret such laws.[53] This proposition, however, is difficult to substantiate.[54] It is problematic in that it fails to take into account that rules of national law do not lose their normative quality in relation to the rights, obligations and transactions that they seek to regulate, simply because their content or meaning is determined as a factual matter and on the basis of evidence.[55] And the normative import of a rule of law can hardly be ascertained without a certain amount of interpretation.

Chapter 7 of this book is devoted to an analysis of how, as facts, the content of national law is determined by the WTO panels and the AB. In that chapter evidentiary issues relating to proof of national law, the implausibility of the proposition that international courts do not interpret national laws and other pertinent issues concerning national laws as facts are taken up in fuller detail.

[51] See, e.g., *Brazilian Loans* case, PCIJ Ser. A No. 21 (1929) at 124.

[52] See, e.g., *German Interests in Polish Upper Silesia*, n. 50 above, at 19.

[53] See ibid.; and AB Report, *India – Patent I*, para. 66.

[54] Eminent authorities have questioned the "validity and wisdom" of this proposition: see, e.g., Jenks 1964, 548–603; Van Panhuys 1964, 23; and Brownlie 1998, 39–40 (the first of these works, after an extensive review of the relevant cases, concludes that both the PCIJ and the ICJ have interpreted national laws in a variety of circumstances).

[55] See Jenks 1964, 549.

3 Systemic WTO obligations regarding national law

1 Introduction

As already noted in Chapter 1, compared to many contemporary international treaties, the WTO agreements make it much more common for international and national legal norms to have endless points of contact between them. While the reasons for this have been discussed before,[1] it is worth emphasizing that, because the WTO treaty is a standard-setting regime (i.e. it sets out standards of treatment for goods, services and intellectual property rights and thus delineates the scope of lawful national conduct), most of the WTO obligations have implications for domestic laws of Members. While many other branches of international law are predominantly concerned with particular acts or conduct of states or non-state entities,[2] WTO law is concerned not only with specific acts or conduct,[3] but also – and even more – with Member countries' legislative or regulatory conduct.[4]

For purposes of discussing the implications of WTO obligations for national laws of Members, it may be useful to distinguish between substantive obligations and systemic obligations regarding national law. Substantive obligations are those that set out the standard of treatment to be accorded by one WTO Member to the goods, services or intellectual property rights originating in another WTO Member. Systemic obligations, by contrast, are those that perform a systemic function

[1] See above, Chapter 1, pp. 6–7.
[2] E.g. expropriation of property, unlawful occupation of embassy premises, aggression, war crimes, etc.
[3] E.g. unlawful import restriction, anti-dumping measures, etc.
[4] E.g. the WTO treaty contains requirements that laws and regulatory measures must not discriminate between domestic and foreign products, environmental or technical standards must not be more trade-restrictive than necessary, etc.

in respect of the relationship between WTO law and national law. As explained later, from the perspective of the relation between WTO law and national law, some of the obligations in both categories can also be seen as "constitutional" in character.[5]

It has been pointed out earlier that in the WTO treaty there are four categories of systemic obligations regarding national law:[6] first, obligations to implement WTO commitments in the domestic laws of Members (included in this category are obligations to ensure conformity of national laws with the WTO agreements); second, obligations relating to transparency, i.e. publication and notification of national laws; third, obligations concerning the administration of national laws; and fourth, obligations to make available under national laws procedures and remedies specified in various WTO agreements.

The first type of obligations, which are also most significant for present purposes, are both systemic and constitutional because they establish, inter alia, the hierarchy between WTO and national legal norms. It is widely acknowledged that norms that entrench some sets of rules over others and thus create primacy of rules are constitutional in character.[7] The remaining three categories perform systemic roles by providing guarantees of transparency, impartial administration of domestic laws and availability of remedies.

2 Substantive obligations and national law

While the main purpose of this chapter is to examine the systemic WTO obligations regarding national law, the implications of the substantive obligations for domestic laws of Members must also be duly underscored. At the core of the substantive WTO obligations, one finds the principles of most-favored nation and national treatment. In the context of trade in goods, the MFN principle requires each WTO Member to grant to every other Member the most favorable treatment that it grants to any country with respect to imports and exports of products;[8] and the national treatment principle calls for equal treatment of foreign and domestic goods, once the foreign goods have cleared customs and become part of the internal commerce.[9] The MFN and national treatment obligations also apply to trade in services and trade-related aspects of intellectual property rights under the GATS and the TRIPS Agreement,

[5] See pp. 49–52 below. [6] See above, Chapter 1, pp. 10–11.
[7] See, e.g., Petersmann 1997c, 428. [8] GATT 1994, Article I. [9] GATT 1994, Article III.

respectively.[10] Together, the MFN and the national treatment principles establish the WTO legal framework for non-discrimination. In essence, these non-discrimination rules prohibit WTO Members – in formulating and applying their domestic laws and regulatory measures – from discriminating between goods, services and IPRs originating in different nations or originating domestically and abroad. And, of course, the rules apply to the entire body of domestic laws or regulations, ranging from those on customs, tax and fiscal matters, dumping and subsidies, product standards, the environment, health and national security to those relating to just about anything and everything else that can affect and hamper movement of goods or services or the protection of IPRs.

For instance, the national treatment standard contained in Article III of the GATT 1994 requires every Member to accord to foreign products treatment no less favorable than that accorded to like domestic products in respect of *all laws, regulations, requirements*, etc. Thus, under this article Members are prohibited from maintaining in their laws provisions that discriminate between domestic and imported products.[11] Needless to say, this provision and the complex patchwork of rights, obligations and exceptions in which it operates incessantly shape the scope of national laws – be it at the stage of the formulation of those laws or afterwards as those laws are applied and interpreted by various domestic bodies.[12]

The anti-discrimination provisions apply to both explicit (commonly referred to as de jure) and implicit (commonly referred to as de facto) discrimination. A typical example of explicit or de jure discrimination is a domestic law that discriminates explicitly by providing different standards for goods, services or IPRs originating in different nations or originating domestically and abroad. Implicit or de facto discrimination typically involves a domestic law or measure that *on its face* appears to be non-discriminatory, but which has a discriminatory *impact* on goods, services or IPRs originating in different nations or originating domestically and abroad. It is not difficult to discipline national laws or measures that discriminate on their face between imported and domestic products or between products originating in different countries. This is so because such laws or measures are easy to detect and, given that they explicitly make the origin of products a criterion for their application, they do

[10] See GATS, Articles II and XVII; and TRIPS Agreement, Articles 3 and 4.

[11] See, generally, Verhoosel 2002; and Horn & Mavroidis 2004.

[12] WTO provisions have greater influence on the municipal laws of the major trading nations and the influence is also more apparent in respect of such nations, to an extent, because of their more frequent involvement in the dispute settlement process.

not purport to be something other than a trade policy measure (e.g. a health or environmental measure). By contrast, laws and measures that do not on their face discriminate between products of different origin but have a discriminatory effect are much more troublesome. First, such de facto discriminatory measures are quite often ingeniously designed by national authorities to serve – under the guise of a formally non-discriminatory measure – no legitimate purpose other than imposing a higher economic burden on foreign products or products of particular origin. Second, domestic policies adopted ostensibly for legitimate "non-trade" purposes (e.g. for the protection of health, the environment or culture) may sometimes affect the competitive conditions, or potential competitive conditions, between domestic and imported products or between products of different origin. Accordingly, ostensibly "non-trade" measures may need to be disciplined for being de facto discriminatory.

No doubt, without the prohibition of de facto discrimination, the GATT/WTO principles of non-discrimination would have been rather ineffective and their impact on national laws of Members would have lacked any depth or vigor. The application of the non-discrimination principles was extended to de facto discrimination through judicial interpretation. In 1987 a GATT dispute settlement panel for the first time decided that the national treatment obligation in Article III of the GATT applied to de facto as well as de jure discrimination.[13] This decision is remarkable both as a fundamental jurisprudential development for the effectiveness of GATT law and as a major building block of the GATT legal system.

WTO panels and the Appellate Body apply the non-discrimination principles scrupulously to both de jure and de facto discrimination.[14] They extend their investigation behind a state's claim of pure facial or formal equality of treatment and examine the actual outcomes, effects or results of a law or measure, as applied, with a view to determining whether any de facto discrimination exists. Indeed, the anti-discrimination principles have been significantly refined and augmented in WTO jurisprudence, to the extent that one commentator

[13] See *Japan – Alcohol I*. On the basis of his extensive study of GATT dispute settlement cases, Professor Robert Hudec has found that, of the first 207 legal complaints filed under GATT between 1948 and 1990, only a handful involved claims of de facto discrimination under Article III and the first affirmative ruling relating to a claim of de facto discrimination was made in *Japan – Alcohol I*: see Hudec 1998, 622 (citing Hudec 1993, 373–585).

[14] See, e.g., AB Reports, *EC – Bananas*, paras. 233–34; and *Canada – Autos*, para. 78.

has described them as reflecting a "sophisticated" and "constitutional" doctrine of "substantive non-discrimination."[15] *EC – Bananas 22.6* and *EC – Tariff Preferences* are two enlightening illustrations of the requirement of substantive non-discrimination.[16] In the former case, the Arbitrators have found that mere equalization of opportunities between service suppliers of different origin is inadequate to overcome past discrimination.[17] Thus, if past discrimination has a "carry on effect" on existing conditions of competition, something more than formally non-discriminatory treatment (perhaps some form of positive discrimination favoring those who have been previously discriminated against) may be required. The latter case concerned the question of whether different tariff preferences granted by the EC under the Enabling Clause[18] to different developing countries were discriminatory. While the Panel held that non-discrimination required identical treatment of all developing countries, the Appellate Body overturned that decision. The AB took the view that since different developing countries may have different development needs, it was possible, under the Enabling Clause, to treat *different sub-categories* of developing countries *differently*, as long as all *similarly situated* developing countries were treated *identically*.[19] Thus, what is required by WTO adjudicative bodies under the principles of non-discrimination is not mere formal equality of treatment but rather substantive equality.

From the preceding discussion it is not hard to understand that not only do the anti-discrimination principles have far-reaching implications for national laws of WTO Members, but also over the years they have become the backbone of the multilateral trading system through their guarantees of non-discrimination across frontiers. Yet, it is not uncommon to regard the principles of MFN and national treatment as negative integration rules – this is because these principles of non-discrimination are couched in negative terms, i.e. a WTO Member must *not* adopt or enforce a measure (including a law) that would disadvantage a foreigner vis-à-vis another foreigner or a national. Put differently, while these principles outlaw discrimination, they are not designed for positive integration of markets through harmonization of rules and policies.

[15] Cass 2005, 191–93. [16] Ibid. [17] See *EC – Bananas 22.6*, paras. 5.70, 5.78, 5.88.

[18] Decision on Differential and More Favourable Treatment, Reciprocity, and Fuller Participation of Developing Countries, GATT Document L/4903, November 28, 1979, BISD 26S/203 (generally referred to as the "Enabling Clause").

[19] See AB Report, *EC – Tariff Preferences*, paras. 153–54, 162, 165, 173, 180. For a comment on this case see Bartels 2005.

Rules of harmonization or positive integration can also be found in the WTO. Such rules are contained in the TRIPS Agreement and, to a lesser extent, in the SPS and TBT Agreements. The TRIPS Agreement establishes an international law of substantive minimum standards for national intellectual property laws, and thus seeks to achieve a certain harmonization on a worldwide basis. The SPS and the TBT Agreements incorporate obligations or admonitions to "harmonize" sanitary and phytosanitary measures[20] and technical regulations[21] (including domestic laws containing such measures and regulations) to international standards, where they exist, or require governments to justify why they have adopted laws and policies that deviate from international standards.[22]

There is a further set of provisions in the SPS and the TBT Agreements requiring WTO Members to ensure that SPS measures and technical regulations are not more trade-restrictive than necessary.[23] The requirement to apply only the least trade-restrictive SPS and TBT measures has its historical origin in Article XX of the GATT 1947. Clause (b) of Article XX of the GATT 1947 – or for that matter the GATT 1994 – permits states to adopt measures "necessary to protect human, animal or plant life or health" that are otherwise GATT-inconsistent. In dispute settlement cases concerning this provision, it was held by GATT panels that a respondent state could not justify a measure inconsistent with another GATT provision as "necessary," unless the measure was the least

[20] These are measures (including all relevant laws, decrees, regulations, requirements and procedures) adopted for protecting human, animal or plant life or health: see SPS Agreement, Annex A, para. 1.

[21] These are regulations (whether contained in a law or other document) concerning product characteristics or process and production methods of products, or terminology, symbols, packaging, marking or labelling requirements applicable to a product, process or production method: see TBT Agreement, Annex 1, para. 1.

[22] For instance, Article 3.1 of the SPS Agreement provides as follows: "To harmonize sanitary and phytosanitary measures on as wide a basis as possible, Members shall base their sanitary or phytosanitary measures on international standards, guidelines or recommendations, where they exist, except as otherwise provided for in this Agreement, and in particular in paragraph 3." Likewise, Article 2.4 of the TBT Agreement provides as follows:

> "Where technical regulations are required and relevant international standards exist or their completion is imminent, Members shall use them, or the relevant parts of them, as a basis for their technical regulations except when such international standards or relevant parts would be an ineffective or inappropriate means for the fulfilment of the legitimate objectives pursued, for instance because of fundamental climatic or geographical factors or fundamental technological problems."

[23] See SPS Agreement, Article 5.6, and TBT Agreement, Article 2.2 (the relevant parts of these two articles are quoted below in Chapter 6, p. 170.

trade-restrictive one from amongst reasonably available alternative measures.[24] This is now confirmed in the jurisprudence of the WTO Appellate Body.[25]

The above are but a few examples of how substantive WTO law impinges upon – and indeed restricts – national laws and regulations. It is also worth pointing out the constitutional ramifications of some of the substantive provisions, such as those prohibiting discrimination or outlawing health, environment, TBT or SPS measures that are more trade-restrictive than necessary.

Here the word "constitutional" is used in a rather modest sense. Recently, the questions of whether or not the WTO is – or is metamorphosing into – a constitutional entity as well as whether or not it can or should become such an entity have attained considerable prominence in international trade law circles.[26] In a recent book Deborah Cass puts forward a well-thought-out, yet tentative, thesis against constitutionalization of the WTO.[27] To begin with, she identifies six "core elements" of constitutionalization. These are: existence of rules or institutions that regulate and constrain social, economic or political behavior; emergence of a higher "new legal order"; presence of a constitutional community to authorize constitutionalization; having a process of deliberation according to which members of the community can contribute to the making of the rules of the legal order; rearrangement of the relationship between the constituting states and the central constitutional entity; and presence of social legitimacy in the sense of social acceptance of constitutionalization.[28] Cass rejects the idea that the WTO is a constitutional entity on the ground that either the above elements do not exist or, at best, only some of them exist partially, in the WTO. At the same time she also thinks that it is not possible to claim definitively that the WTO is not (or is) constitutionalizing.[29]

[24] See, e.g., *Thai – Cigarettes*, paras. 74–75.

[25] See, e.g., AB Reports, *Korea – Beef*, paras. 165–82; and *EC – Asbestos*, paras. 170–75.

[26] See generally on the WTO "constitution" and constitutionalism in international and WTO law, Petersmann 1997c, 1998a, 1999 and 2001; Jackson 1998 and 2001; Schloemann & Ohlhoff 1999; de Búrca & Scott 2001; Cass 2001 and 2005; Gathii 2001; Holmes 2001; Howse & Nicolaidis 2001 and 2003; Krajewski 2001; N. Walker 2001; Gerhart 2003; Cho 2004; Joerges *et al.* 2004; Dunoff 2006; and Trachtman 2006.

[27] Cass 2005. [28] Ibid. 28–57.

[29] Ibid. 18. As regards the question of whether the WTO should be constitutionalized, Cass, again, shows some ambivalence. On the one hand she seems to take the view that it should not be, because the resulting constitution is likely to be democratically deficient, harmful to state sovereignty and self-legitimizing in the face of persistent

It is, however, not surprising that in the international context constitutional discourse must be tentative rather than definitive. As one author has put it nicely, "constitutionalism and constitutionalization are conceived of not in black-and-white, all-or-nothing terms but as a question of nuance and gradation."[30] Ambivalence, therefore, is a key characteristic of WTO constitutionalization literature. For instance, in respect of Cass's six core elements, there are other authors who tend to argue that one or another of those elements is present in the WTO.[31] Yet others highlight different other dimensions of "constitutions" and argue that "the WTO 'constitution' has already grown along some of [those] dimensions."[32] Finally, there are those who take the view that constitutional features are entirely non-existent in the WTO.[33]

It has been mentioned in the last chapter that the EC legal system has been described by the ECJ itself as "a new legal order of international law."[34] In this new legal order a massive transfer of sovereignty by nation states in favor of the EC has taken place, which clearly deserves to be described, in Cass's terms, as a rearrangement of the relationship between the constituting states and the central constitutional entity. Although an international treaty-based system, in many respects the European Community legal order partakes the characteristic of a federal constitutional structure. No wonder the EC/EU has over the years provided a most fascinating field for both practical experimentation and scholarly analysis of constitutionalism in a non-state or *inter*-national context.

The WTO is not at all a constitutional entity in the way in which the EC is. There are also rather important reasons why it cannot – and also should not – become such an entity. From amongst such reasons, it is worth pointing out the existence of issues on which there is a deep-seated North–South divide. It is difficult to imagine a "constitution" without a full-blown integration of various subject-matters, policies and social values. In important ways the WTO does deal with a number of

doubts about the legitimacy of the WTO. On the other hand, she seems to endorse constitutionalization if there were a procedural transformation by a thorough-going democratization of the decision-making processes within the WTO and a reorientation of the WTO towards the goal of development: ibid. 238–46.

[30] N. Walker 2001, 33.

[31] Many such arguments are summarized in Cass 2005. Cass also acknowledges the existence of some of her core elements in the WTO. For instance, in respect of the element of "constitutional community" – an element whose existence is rather difficult to conceive in the WTO context – Cass notes that "a primitive form of distinguishable WTO community exists" and that this WTO community is "closer knit" than the diffused international community as a whole: ibid. 53–54.

[32] See Trachtman 2006, 623. [33] See, e.g., Dunoff 2006. [34] See Chapter 2, p. 33 above.

non-trade subjects, policies and values, such as protection of health and the environment, intellectual property, services, aspects of investment, etc. Yet, the WTO would have to become a much grander "linkage machine," if it were to metamorphose into a constitutional entity.[35] A growing list of ostensibly non-trade subjects (labor and competition policy crucial among them) receive easy espousal in developed countries, often backed by strong domestic (and, of course, northern) lobbies.[36] Developing countries, however, are skeptical about the imposition of "trade-unrelated" agendas on the WTO by the developed countries by simply adding the words "trade-related" before whatever the agendas are.[37] It is also difficult to imagine a "constitution" without an accompanying bill of human rights. And, again, the WTO is unlikely ever to have a bill of human rights due, not least, to the ominous North–South divide.[38]

Given the rather important shortcomings and imperfections of the "constitutional paraphernalia" of the WTO, references in this work to constitutional *ramifications* of principles, obligations and institutions of the WTO have a modest purpose.[39] They are not intended to suggest that the WTO is a constitutional entity. Instead, the intention is simply to underscore that some of the principles, obligations and mechanisms within the WTO promote, protect and guarantee values that are closely associated with constitutionalism.[40] The anti-discrimination principles, the requirements to apply the least trade-restrictive measure

[35] Cf. Alvarez 2002.

[36] See generally on the linkage between trade and non-trade issues, "Symposium: The Boundaries of the WTO," in 96 AJIL 1 (2002). In recent years the controversy over the so-called "Singapore issues" fatefully highlighted the North–South divide on issues of linkage. Four issues – namely, investment protection, competition policy, transparency in government procurement and trade facilitation – came to be known as Singapore issues because they were put on the agenda at the Singapore Ministerial Conference of the WTO in 1996. Developing countries were strongly against them, arguing that they centered on concerns of the developed countries, and the disagreements eventually led to a deadlock at the Cancún Ministerial Conference in 2003.

[37] Leading economists have also argued strongly against working "trade-unrelated" agendas into the WTO: see, e.g., Bhagwati 2002; and Stiglitz & Charlton 2005, 85–86.

[38] See generally on international trade and human rights, Alston 2002; Marceau 2002; Petersmann 2002a and 2002b; and Cottier *et al.* 2005. Unfortunately, however, none of these works adequately comes to terms with the important North–South divide that cuts across issues of interface between trade and human rights.

[39] The expression within quotation marks is taken from J. H. H. Weiler 2000b, 202. Joseph Weiler, a distinguished scholar of the constitution of Europe, remarks that "even at its strongest the WTO is still a far cry from the full constitutional paraphernalia of the EU" (ibid.) and that he finds "fanciful and even mischievous the advocacy of a constitutionalized GATT" (J. H. H. Weiler 2000a, 4).

[40] The existence of constitutional principles in the absence of a "constitution" has been recognized in other contexts as well: see, e.g., Orrego Vicuña 2004, 27.

or, on the systemic and institutional side, the obligations to ensure conformity of national laws with the WTO treaty and the WTO judicial review (a subject with which much of this work is concerned) are all tinged with constitutional values: they provide guarantees of non-discrimination, substantive equality, proportionality, non-arbitrariness, non-abuse of domestic trade and foreign policy power, supremacy of WTO law, judicial protection of treaty obligations and, above all, rule of law which are constitutional in character.[41] These constitutionally tinged principles, obligations and mechanisms are also fundamental building blocks of the WTO legal system.

Clearly, it is impossible to overemphasize the significance of the substantive provisions in respect of the interaction between WTO law and national law. However, the present study is not about the substantive coverage of the WTO agreements or about the substantive scope of the interaction between WTO and national legal norms.[42] Rather, it intends to examine the process of that interaction. Accordingly the next four sections of this chapter discuss the overarching systemic framework that the WTO treaty establishes concerning the relationship between WTO law and national law.

3 Obligations regarding implementation of WTO commitments

3.1 Background

As is well known, the WTO came into being through a "metamorphosis" of the predecessor GATT.[43] The WTO Agreement expressly states that the WTO is to be guided by "the decisions, procedures and customary practices" followed by the GATT.[44] So far as the implementation of the commitments was concerned, GATT had certain curious peculiarities, which Professor Jackson has even described as "birth defects."[45] The WTO has since overcome those defects. Nonetheless, a few brief remarks about the situation that existed under the GATT may be helpful both for a better understanding of the new WTO obligations regarding implementation

[41] Even ardent critics of the current state of trade liberalization under the WTO – for not having free or freer trade in agricultural products, for instance – recognize that "countries may benefit from having the 'rule of law' that the WTO provides for trade between nations": see Stiglitz & Charlton 2005, 75.

[42] There are many excellent works on substantive WTO law: see, e.g., Jackson 1997a; Lowenfeld 2002; Matsushita *et al.* 2003; and Van den Bossche 2005a.

[43] See Qureshi 1996, 3. For an account of how the WTO has evolved from the GATT, see Jackson 1998, 12–35.

[44] See WTO Agreement, Article XVI:1. [45] Jackson 1998, 15–18.

and for a proper insight into some of the GATT jurisprudence from which the WTO is expected to derive guidance.

The major peculiarity of the GATT 1947 was that, although during the period 1947–95 it operated as the principal treaty for trade relations, technically it never came into force as a treaty in accordance with its provisions on entry into force.[46] Instead, it was always applied "provisionally" through an ingenious device, namely the Protocol of Provisional Application (PPA).[47] Under the PPA the original GATT contracting parties agreed to apply by executive action and without legislative approval or ratification the substance of the GATT 1947 *provisionally*, i.e. temporarily until such time as the GATT 1947 itself came into effect. Ultimately, however, the GATT 1947 never came into effect as a treaty, and the PPA, which was intended to be a temporary device, became a permanent feature of the GATT.[48]

The main reason for resorting to the PPA was to facilitate the immediate acceptance of the GATT 1947 without any changes in domestic laws.[49] Accordingly, it implemented the GATT obligations in a rather curious fashion by providing as follows:

> The Governments . . . undertake . . . to apply provisionally on and after 1 January 1948:
>
> (a) Parts I and III of the General Agreement on Tariffs and Trade, and
> (b) Part II of the Agreement to the fullest extent not inconsistent with existing legislation.[50]

Thus, although Parts I and III were implemented fully, Part II, which, in Articles III through XXIII, contained most of the substantive provisions of the GATT and can be said to have had constituted its "code of conduct," was to be applied only to the extent that the obligations contained therein were not inconsistent with domestic legislation that pre-dated the PPA. This is commonly referred to as the "grandfather clause" for existing legislation. Countries that joined the GATT afterwards did so under accession protocols that incorporated the same grandfather exception.

[46] See GATT 1947, Article XXVI.

[47] The text of the PPA is reproduced in World Trade Organization 1995, 1071–72.

[48] See ibid. 923–24.

[49] For detailed accounts of the relevant history and generally on the PPA see: Jackson 1969, 108–17, and 1997a, 35–41; Roessler 1985; M. Hansen & Vermulst 1989; and World Trade Organization 1995, 1071–84.

[50] See PPA, para. 1.

In contrast to the pre-PPA or pre-accession national laws, post-PPA or post-accession national laws were effectively required to conform with the obligations under the GATT 1947. However, conformity was not required under any explicit treaty provision – rather, over the years, there developed specific dispute settlement practice to this effect. Thus, a contracting party could successfully challenge before GATT panels a national law of another contracting party on the ground that the law in and of itself amounted to a violation of GATT obligations. Such a challenge could be made even if the law was not yet applied against the complaining party or, more importantly, had not yet even entered into force, i.e. it had only been enacted and would enter into force, for example, after a certain period.[51]

For purposes of determining GATT-compatibility of national laws, a distinction used to be made between mandatory and discretionary legislation. In GATT/WTO parlance, the expression "mandatory legislation" refers to national legislation that *requires* the executive authority of a Member to act inconsistently with its GATT/WTO obligations, while the expression "discretionary legislation" refers to legislation that does not require but rather gives the executive a *discretion* to act in such a manner. According to this distinction, a mandatory law by itself violated GATT obligations, whereas a discretionary law did not by itself violate GATT obligations and a violation could only occur if that law was actually applied in a specific case and in a GATT-inconsistent manner.[52]

Turning now to the question of implementation of WTO obligations, unlike the GATT 1947, the WTO treaty has entered into effect "definitively," as a proper international treaty, and in accordance with its provisions concerning entry into force.[53] This means that all WTO Members have accepted and ratified the WTO texts in pursuance of their respective domestic procedures, including approval of the texts by national parliaments, enactment of implementing legislation, etc.[54] WTO agreements also do not contain any saving clause for national legislation pre-dating the WTO or even the GATT 1947.[55] And after the entry into force of the

[51] See, e.g., *US – Superfund*. [52] See, further, Chapter 8 below.

[53] See the Final Act embodying the results of the UR, paras. 2–3; and WTO Agreement, Article XIV.

[54] See, generally, Jackson & Sykes 1997. This publication comprises contributions that examine how the WTO agreements were implemented in eleven distinct jurisdictions, including the four largest and most powerful trading entities – the so-called "quad" group – the United States, the European Community, Japan and Canada.

[55] Cf. however, the preliminary notes to the GATT 1994, para. 3 (containing one rather lingering but very narrowly defined grandfather exception with respect to the operation of foreign vessels in national waters).

WTO Agreement, the provisional application of the GATT 1947 subject to the grandfather exception has come to an end.[56] Thus, the WTO has overcome all of the so-called GATT "birth defects."[57] In addition, it has introduced a new set of provisions that require Members to ensure the conformity of their laws with the WTO obligations – a requirement that is much more rigorous than the comparable obligations under public international law in general or under many contemporary international treaties.[58]

3.2 *Obligations to ensure conformity of national laws with the WTO agreements*

The principal provision requiring conformity of national laws is contained in Article XVI:4 of the WTO Agreement, which reads as follows: "Each Member shall ensure the conformity of its laws, regulations and administrative procedures with its obligations as provided in the annexed Agreements." Although the above requirement extends to all agreements and legal instruments in Annexes 1, 2 and 3 of the WTO Agreement, some of the annexed agreements also contain similar provisions. Specifically, such provisions are contained in the agreements on dumping, subsidies,[59] customs valuation,[60] preshipment inspection[61] and import licensing.[62]

Some differences in the language of these various provisions can be noticed. Unlike Article XVI:4, some of the other provisions make it

[56] See the Decision of the GATT Contracting Parties dated December 8, 1994, PC/12, L/7583, quoted in World Trade Organization 1995, 1084; and the preliminary notes to the GATT 1994, paras. 1(a) and (b). See generally on the transition from GATT to WTO: Marceau 1995; and P. M. Moore 1996.

[57] See Jackson 1997a, 49.

[58] Panel Report, *US – Section 301*, para. 7.80.

[59] See ADA, Article 18.4, and ASCM, Article 32.5, both of which employ the same language and provide as follows: "Each Member shall take all necessary steps, of a general or particular character, to ensure, not later than the date of entry into force of the WTO Agreement for it, the conformity of its laws, regulations and administrative procedures with the provisions of this Agreement as they may apply for [ASCM uses the word "to" instead of "for"] the Member in question."

[60] See Customs Valuation Agreement, Article 22.1. It reads as follows: "Each Member shall ensure, not later than the date of application of the provisions of this Agreement for it, the conformity of its laws, regulations and administrative procedures with the provisions of this Agreement."

[61] See PSI Agreement, Article 9.2. It provides as follows: "Members shall ensure that their laws and regulations shall not be contrary to the provisions of this Agreement."

[62] See Licensing Agreement, Article 8.2(a). It reads as follows: "Each Member shall ensure, not later than the date of entry into force of the WTO Agreement for it, the conformity of its laws, regulations and administrative procedures with the provisions of this Agreement."

explicit that conformity should be ensured from the date of entry into force of the WTO Agreement for the Member concerned. However, this difference is not significant because it is not in doubt that Article XVI:4 is also applicable from the date of entry into force of the WTO Agreement.[63] Another difference that can be of some consequence is that while Article XVI:4 requires conformity of national laws with the *obligations* as provided in the WTO agreements, the other articles require such conformity with the *provisions* of the agreement concerned. The latter requirement, it can be argued, is more onerous than the former. Under the latter requirement, national laws must conform not only with the WTO obligations but also with those treaty provisions that technically do not set out any obligations for Members, but deal with other incidental issues. Moreover, under Article XVI:4 it may be sufficient for national laws to be in conformity with the "substance" of the obligations, while under the other articles national laws may need to conform to the WTO *provisions themselves*. From this perspective, Article XVI:4 gives Members more latitude to choose the exact manner of ensuring conformity. By contrast, the threshold for the degree of correspondence or likeness between domestic laws and the relevant WTO provisions can be higher under the other articles. This is also supported by the drafting history of Article XVI:4. Some earlier versions of what became Article XVI:4 contained language that would have required conformity of national laws with the *provisions* of the WTO agreements, and for that reason were not acceptable to some countries. Apparently, to prevent a very expansive interpretation of Article XVI:4, it was accepted in its present form by clarifying that only *obligations* would be subject to it.[64]

In any event, the rest of the discussion focuses on Article XVI:4, not least because it is an umbrella provision that applies across the entire WTO treaty. The precise scope of this Article does not seem very clear.

[63] See AB Report, *India – Patent I*, paras. 78–84.

[64] See below, n. 76. It must be noted that no official *travaux preparatoires* were issued for the WTO agreements. There also do not exist many informal records of the negotiating history of Article XVI:4 apart from some earlier versions of the Article, two of which are reproduced in: T. P. Stewart 1993, vol. II, Annex 1. In *US – Section 301* the Panel requested the parties to provide any *travaux preparatoires* that might be relevant for the interpretation of Article XVI:4. In response to this request, the USA submitted to the Panel, as US Exhibit 23, various drafts of the WTO Agreement (including Article XVI:4) and informal records of the US negotiator. The descriptive part of the Panel Report (paras. 4.450–63) contains a description of these materials (from a US point of view) as well as some useful excerpts. For the lack of any other material, these materials are relied upon in discussing the drafting history of Article XVI:4.

Broadly, two questions may be asked about its scope. First, is Article XVI:4 obligation more rigorous than the comparable obligations under general public international law? Second, what exactly does Article XVI:4 require a Member to do? While it may not be difficult to answer the first question, the second does not have any quick answers.

3.2.1 Article XVI:4 vis-à-vis general public international law

It may be recalled from Chapter 2 that, although debatable, the better view seems to be that in public international law there is no general duty to bring national laws into conformity with international obligations. As already noted, in each case the question really is whether the particular international obligation concerned requires the possession or non-possession of certain laws or whether it simply requires the performance or non-performance of certain acts.[65] While in the former case it may be necessary to have conforming national laws, in the latter case it may not be. As examples of the former, reference may be made to provisions in various international treaties requiring states parties to adopt legislative measures to implement, if not the entire treaty, at least certain specified treaty obligations. Human rights treaties, for instance, require states parties to adopt laws or other measures that may be necessary to give effect to the rights recognized by them.[66] And treaties that create international crimes or offenses require contracting parties to make those offenses punishable by appropriate penalties.[67] Other examples include treaty provisions requiring states parties to adopt laws, regulations, etc.,

[65] See above, Chapter 2, p. 37.

[66] See, e.g., International Convention on the Elimination of all Forms of Racial Discrimination 1966, Article 2(1)(c) and (d); International Covenant on Civil and Political Rights 1966, Article 2(2); American Convention on Human Rights 1969, Article 2; African Charter on Human and Peoples' Rights 1981, Article 1; Convention Against Torture and Other Cruel, Inhuman or Degrading Treatment or Punishment 1984, Article 2(1); and United Nations Convention on the Rights of the Child 1989, Articles 3(2), 4, 19(1), 32(2) and 33.

[67] See, e.g., Convention on the Prevention and Punishment of the Crime of Genocide 1948, Article V; Geneva Conventions on the Victims of War 1949, Articles 49, 50, 129 and 146; Hague Convention for the Suppression of Unlawful Seizure of Aircraft 1970, Article 2; Montreal Convention for the Suppression of Unlawful Acts Against the Safety of Civil Aviation 1971, Article 3; International Convention on the Suppression and Punishment of the Crime of Apartheid 1973, Article IV; International Convention Against the Taking of Hostages 1979, Article 2; Convention Against Torture and Other Cruel, Inhuman or Degrading Treatment or Punishment 1984, Article 4; Convention for the Suppression of Unlawful Acts Against the Safety of Maritime Navigation 1988, Article 5; and Convention on the Safety of United Nations and Associated Personnel 1994, Article 9(2).

for the protection of the environment,[68] for facilitating cooperation with international judicial organs[69] and, less frequently, for making effective the treaty provisions in general.[70] However, none of these various treaty provisions entrench the "overall supremacy" of the relevant treaty in a manner that is comparable to Article XVI:4. Rather, these provisions are directed to domestic implementation of *specified* treaty obligations, and are couched in terms that give states much more latitude than what would be permissible under Article XVI:4.

Furthermore, in these instances the requirement to adopt legislative measures and thereby, to an extent, bring national law into conformity with international obligations applies as a kind of "*lex specialis*." In the absence of such explicit requirement, the rules of general (customary) international law regarding observance of treaties will be applicable; and under these rules it may not be necessary to adopt legislative measures. (At best, the law in this regard is far from clear.) Indeed, the relevant rules, as codified in the Vienna Convention on the Law of Treaties, do not make it explicit that states parties to a treaty must have conforming national laws. These rules are contained in Articles 26 and 27 of the VCLT. Article 26 (entitled "*Pacta sunt servanda*") reads as follows: "Every treaty in force is binding upon the parties to it and must be performed by them in good faith." And Article 27 (entitled "Internal law and observance of treaties") provides that: "A party may not invoke the provisions of its internal law as justification for its failure to perform a treaty." A textual comparison of the above two Articles and Article XVI:4 of the WTO Agreement does suggest that, with regard to national law, the latter puts in place more rigorous discipline. The VCLT provisions do not tell us anything about the necessity of having conforming national laws. Article 26 codifies the fundamental principle of *pacta sunt servanda*, and the emphasis, rightly, is on *good faith* performance.[71] It may not be argued plausibly that a party to a treaty has not acted in good faith simply because its laws are not in accord with the treaty obligations,

68 See, e.g., Geneva Convention on the High Seas 1958, Article 24; and United Nations Convention on the Law of the Sea 1982, Articles 207(1), 208(1), 209(2), 210(1), 211(2), 212(1), 213, 214, 217(1), 220(4) and 222.

69 See, e.g., Rome Statute of the International Criminal Court 1998, Article 88. See also Security Council resolution 827 (1993) on establishment and adoption of the Statute of the International Criminal Tribunal for the Former Yugoslavia, para. 4; and Security Council resolution 955 (1994) on establishment and adoption of the Statute of the International Criminal Tribunal for Rwanda, para. 2.

70 See, e.g., Convention on the Settlement of Investment Disputes between States and Nationals of Other States 1965, Article 69.

71 See, generally, Wehberg 1959; and McNair 1961, 493–505.

especially if another party is not injured thereby. Article 27 reproduces another well-established principle: namely, a state cannot oppose its national law as a legal bar to the fulfilment of its international obligations.[72] This, plainly, does not mean that national laws must be in accord with international obligations. Rather, this principle presupposes that there might be non-conforming laws and, accordingly, envisages that such laws cannot be relied upon to avoid international responsibility – if eventually the relevant obligations are not respected.[73]

In a recent work Anthony Aust expressed the following view about the implications of Articles 26 and 27 for the domestic law of a state party to a treaty:

> if a new law or modification of existing law, is needed in order to carry out the obligations which will be laid upon it by the treaty, a negotiating state should ensure that this is done at least by the time the treaty enters into force for it. If this is not done, not only will the state *risk* being in breach of its treaty obligations, but it will be liable in international law to another party *if as a result that party, or its nationals, is later damaged*.[74]

The above formulation is similar to the view expressed by certain other commentators to whom reference has already been made in the previous chapter. To recall, although these commentators argue that there exists a general duty to ensure the conformity of national laws with international obligations, they add that a state does not commit a direct breach of international law by merely failing in that duty, and a breach occurs only if the state concerned fails to carry out its obligations on a specific occasion.[75] This, in essence, means that while it is *desirable* to have conforming laws, strictly, a state is not "obliged" to ensure conformity (because a failure to do so does not result in a breach). By contrast, under Article XVI:4 of the WTO Agreement a Member *must* ensure the conformity of its national laws with the WTO obligations, and a failure to do so amounts – without more, i.e. without any resulting injury – to a breach.[76]

[72] Cf. Chapter 2, pp. 33–35 above.

[73] The principle codified in Article 27, although relevant for the law of treaties, can also be regarded as belonging to the topic of state responsibility: see Sinclair 1984, 84 (citing *Official Records, First Session*, 29th meeting [Sir Humphrey Waldock]). Cf. the ILC's Draft Articles on State Responsibility, Articles 3 and 32 and commentaries to those Articles, reproduced in Crawford 2002, 86–90, 207–8.

[74] Aust 2000, 144 (italics added).

[75] See above, Chapter 2, n. 26.

[76] In the drafting history of Article XVI:4 (although, as already noted, very little record is available: see above, n. 64), there is clear evidence that Members did not intend to create a *weaker* obligation than that under Articles 26 and 27 of the VCLT. In the Draft Final Act text, as well as in the second (dated March 25, 1992) and the third (dated

3.2.2 Article XVI:4 vis-à-vis national laws of Members

It must be evident from the above that Article XVI:4 obligation is more rigorous, *because*, unlike the VCLT, it *explicitly requires* Members to ensure conformity of their laws with the WTO obligations. However, it is not entirely clear *how* Members must ensure such conformity. In this context, a number of different constructions, each equally plausible, can be put on the Article. Shortly after the conclusion of the UR, two apparent extremes in the spectrum of possible interpretations were identified by Pieter-Jan Kuyper, who acted as the legal advisor to the EC negotiators during the UR and was also involved in the drafting of Article XVI:4. He made the following observation:

May 27, 1992) revised texts of the WTO Agreement, Article XVI:4 read as follows (see T. P. Stewart 1993, vol. II, Annex 1): "The Members shall endeavour to take all necessary steps, where changes to domestic laws will be required to implement the provisions of the agreements annexed hereto, to ensure the conformity of their laws with these agreements." It was believed that the term "endeavour" would call into question the obligatory nature of the provision. Hence, the following text omitting the endeavour language was subsequently proposed by the EC: "The Members shall take all necessary steps to ensure the conformity of their laws, regulations and administrative procedures with the provisions of the annexed agreements, in accordance with their individual constitutional or legal systems." Even the above formulation was rejected because it was also seen to weaken the generally applicable rules, as reflected in the VCLT. On November 12, 1993 the EC proposed another text, which read as follows: "The Members shall ensure the conformity of their laws, regulations and administrative procedures with the provisions of the annexed Agreements." The eventual text of Article XVI:4 largely reflects the above formulation (except that the phrase "obligations as provided in the annexed agreements" was added to clarify that only obligations would be subject to the provision). This formulation was acceptable because it did not create a weaker obligation than that under the VCLT.

There does not exist equally clear evidence as to whether the Members intended to create a *stronger* obligation than that under the VCLT. However, there are reasons to believe that they did so intend. It cannot be lightly assumed that none of the negotiating states were aware that, even without any explicit incorporation, the generally applicable rules concerning performance of treaty obligations, as reflected in the VCLT Articles 26 and 27, would be applicable to the WTO treaty (see, generally on this issue, Pauwelyn 2001). Moreover, there already existed at that time a considerable amount of GATT dispute settlement practice, which largely required the GATT-conformity of national laws; and the requirement under this GATT *acquis* was more rigorous than that under the VCLT (see above, p. 54). Thus, to conclude that the Members were not negotiating for a stronger obligation than that under the VCLT is to suggest that they knowingly involved themselves in a pointless exercise. Indeed, the EC, a major proponent of Article XVI:4, argued before the Panel on *US – Section 301* that several UR participants, including the EC, "worked for a strengthening of Article XVI:4 of the WTO Agreement beyond the 'natural obligation under international law' which finds its source in Articles 26 and 27 of the VCLT": see Panel Report, para. 4.486.

A provision that has been championed to a large extent by the Community, but which may have serious consequences for the Community itself, and for the Member States too, is Article XVI:4 of the WTO . . . This may turn out to be a very onerous obligation, requiring full conformity of all Community and national laws . . . with the precise provisions of the WTO's annexes. It may also have hardly any consequences at all, compared to the present situation, if it is interpreted in the light of standing panel case law which determines that a law or regulation is contrary to the GATT only if it is mandatory and as such contrary to GATT terms, but that such is not the case, if the text of the law or regulation permits a GATT conform application of the text. If conformity to WTO obligations is interpreted in this way – which would not be unreasonable in the light of the succession of the WTO to the "acquis gattien" – it should be clear that the added value of Article XVI:4 is rather limited.[77]

As noted earlier, under the GATT the principle that national laws per se – i.e. independently from their application in specific situations – could violate GATT obligations developed through dispute settlement practice and there was no textual basis for it. Needless to say, Article XVI:4 confirmed that principle[78] and, accordingly, what previously was a mere practice is now enshrined in lapidary treaty language. But the perplexing question is: what more does Article XVI:4 envisage? For obvious reasons, there does not exist any panel or Appellate Body jurisprudence that addresses this question in this abstract formulation. Given the difficulty of the matter, it is only natural that case law would develop gradually through an incremental process and not at a stroke. There is, however, a more specific question that attracted much attention (it also underlies Kuyper's observation quoted above): namely, does Article XVI:4 require WTO-conformity of discretionary laws in addition to mandatory laws? It seems that the answer to this must also await future litigation.[79]

How, then, has the Article been treated in dispute settlement cases so far? Panels and the Appellate Body have not made any unobvious use of Article XVI:4. They found violations of Article XVI:4 only if the domestic law at issue violated any other substantive provision of the annexed agreements.[80] Conversely, in the absence of a violation of a specific

[77] Kuyper 1995, 110 (footnotes omitted).

[78] Panel Report, *US – Section 301*, para. 7.41.

[79] Although in *US – Section 301*, the Panel in effect held that under certain circumstances discretionary laws can violate WTO obligations, its decision did not turn on Article XVI:4. See, further, Chapter 8 below.

[80] See, e.g., Panel and AB Reports, *US – 1916 Act I & II*; *US – Hot-Rolled Steel*; and *US – Offset Act*. Article XVI:4 was also invoked to confirm the conclusion that the WTO obligations are applicable to national laws that already existed at the date of entry into force of the WTO Agreement (no grandfather right): see, e.g., Panel Reports, *EC – Bananas*

substantive provision no violation of Article XVI:4 can occur.[81] From this perspective, Article XVI:4 can be seen as not imposing requirements regarding national law additional to the requirements that already arise under the substantive WTO obligations themselves. Its role is limited in making it clear that a cause of action can arise in respect of national laws per se. However, as already noted, even without Article XVI:4 the position was the same under the GATT in respect of post-PPA or post-accession national laws. Furthermore, it is difficult to imagine that the outcome in any of the WTO cases that concerned review of national law would have been different had Article XVI:4 not been there. Hence, one cannot resist wondering what would have been the difference in the WTO legal universe without Article XVI:4, *especially* when the WTO has succeeded to the GATT *acquis*?[82]

It is difficult to answer the above question, if attention were to be placed on the outcome of each individual case. By contrast, from a wider perspective, with Article XVI:4 it is now possible to speak of a constitutional principle enshrined in the WTO treaty that firmly establishes the supremacy of WTO norms in matters covered by the WTO agreements.[83] Article XVI:4 also provides a textual basis for the review of national laws by the dispute settlement panels and the Appellate Body.[84] There is no doubt that, in the absence of Article XVI:4 questions could have been raised more easily about the legitimacy of the WTO adjudicative process, so far as review of national law is concerned.[85]

3.3 *Implementation at sub-national levels*

An obvious consequence of the general international law rule (as reflected in Article 27 of the VCLT) that national laws cannot be opposed as a legal bar to the fulfilment of international obligations is that a

(Complaint by the United States), para. 7.308; and *EC – Hormones I*, para. 8.27; and AB Report, *EC – Hormones I & II*, para. 128.

[81] See, e.g., Panel Reports, *US – Section 129*; *US – Softwood Lumber III*; and *US – CRCS Sunset Review*; and AB Reports, *US – Carbon Steel*; *US – Countervailing Measures*; *US – CRCS Sunset Review*; and *US – Zeroing*.

[82] See above, p. 52. [83] See, e.g., Petersmann 1997c, 428.

[84] In addition, compared to the GATT *acquis*, it has broadened the scope of measures that can be reviewed per se. That is to say, while, under the GATT, "administrative procedures" were not subject to per se review (i.e. independently from their application), Article XVI:4 makes them so reviewable: Panel Report, *US – Section 301*, para. 7.41.

[85] See generally on the legitimacy of the WTO and its dispute settlement process: Howse 2000; Barfield 2001; Krajewski 2001; J. H. H. Weiler 2001; Esty 2002; and Beviglia Zampetti 2003.

federal state cannot rely upon its national constitutional distribution of competence between territorial and central governmental organs or entities to justify non-performance of international obligations.[86] This is also reflected in the rules of attribution of conduct to a state under international law of state responsibility. Under these rules, the conduct of a territorial unit of a state is regarded as an act of that state in the same manner as that of a central government entity.[87] It is possible, however, to derogate from both sets of rules under the terms of an express clause in a treaty. Such clauses are usually known as "federal clauses," and they take effect as *lex specialis* in respect of matters covered by the relevant treaty.[88]

Out of a total of twenty-two WTO agreements,[89] four – namely, the GATT 1994, the SPS Agreement, the TBT Agreement and the GATS – contain provisions that, at least apparently, look like federal clauses, that is to say, they purport to set limits regarding the implementation and observance of WTO commitments by territorial units of federal states.[90] The WTO Agreement itself – the provisions of which are applicable throughout the entire range of WTO agreements, and which also prevails in the event of any conflict between it and any other annex agreement[91] – does not contain any such clause. The applicability of the "federal limitation" of the four annex agreements is limited in respect of matters covered in those agreements. This means that the majority of the WTO agreements remain unqualified by any federal clause.

However, the existence of such clauses in four agreements creates imbalances between commitments under those agreements and other WTO agreements.[92] This can also give rise to interpretative difficulties where the same subject-matter is regulated by two or more agreements, of which one contains a federal clause. For instance, while the "federal limitation" of the GATT 1994 applies in respect of its provisions on dumping or subsidies, no such limitation exists in the ADA or the ASCM, which, respectively, deal with these two subjects. Although in respect of matters covered by them, the ADA and the ASCM take precedence

86 A more detailed account of the issues raised in this section has been published in the *Journal of World Trade*: see Bhuiyan 2004.

87 See, e.g., Brownlie 1998, 451; and Crawford 2002, 94–99.

88 See Crawford 2002, 98.

89 See above, Chapter 1, pp. 3–4.

90 See GATT 1994, Article XXIV:12; SPS Agreement, Article 13; TBT Agreement, Articles 3, 4 and 7; and GATS, Article I:3.

91 See WTO Agreement, Article XVI:3.

92 And, as hardly needs stating, these clauses also create imbalances between the rights and obligations of unitary and federal states.

over the GATT 1994,[93] the difficult question is whether they leave some aspects of the GATT 1994 provisions on dumping and subsidies unaffected, such that in respect of those aspects the federal limitation can be invoked.[94]

The federal clauses themselves present yet more difficult issues. And, as discussed below, it is possible to argue that, setting aside the TBT Agreement, the relevant provisions of the other three agreements are, in fact, devoid of any real meaning. For a proper insight into this issue it may be useful to note briefly the main features of the federal limitation as it existed under the predecessor GATT. Article XXIV:12 of the GATT 1947, which has since been carried into the successor agreement, the GATT 1994, required contracting parties having a federal constitutional system only to take "reasonable measures" to ensure the observance of the GATT by their political subdivisions. The Article read as follows: "Each contracting party shall take such reasonable measures as may be available to it to ensure observance of the provisions of this Agreement by the regional and local governments and authorities within its territories." In the early days of GATT some countries took the view that because of Article XXIV:12, local authorities were "not strictly bound" by the General Agreement.[95] GATT dispute settlement panels did not subscribe to that view, however; and they construed the provision more narrowly. Thus, it was held that Article XXIV:12 merely qualified the obligation to *implement* the General Agreement at local levels, but for that reason GATT obligations did not cease to be *applicable* to local governments.[96] This, in essence, meant that local measures – for instance, a provincial law – could still be found to be GATT-incompatible – and, indeed, in a number of cases they were so found[97] – but so far as bringing such measures into compliance with the GATT obligations was concerned, Article XXIV:12 could provide a defence. Furthermore, GATT panels had

[93] For purposes of federal limitation, the precedence may result either from the explicit conflict clause as contained in the General interpretative note to Annex 1A of the WTO Agreement, or because of the AB jurisprudence to the effect that the more onerous WTO obligation trumps the less onerous obligation: see AB Reports, *Guatemala – Cement I*, para. 65; *US – Hot-Rolled Steel*, para. 51; and Bhuiyan 2004, 130. Cf. also Montaguti & Lugard 2000; and Pauwelyn 2002b, 78–82.

[94] See, further, Bhuiyan 2004, 130–31.

[95] See Doc. EPCT/TAC/PV 19 at 33, quoted in World Trade Organization 1995, 830. See also Kuyper 1994, 244.

[96] *Canada – Alcohol II*, para. 5.36.

[97] See, e.g., *Canada – Alcohol I & II*; and *US – Malt Beverages*.

construed the term "reasonable measures"[98] very narrowly by holding that a federal government could be said to have taken reasonable measures only if it had made "serious, persistent and convincing efforts" to secure compliance by local authorities.[99] This proved to be a very high threshold, which respondent governments by and large failed to satisfy.[100] Thus GATT panels' interpretation tightly restricted the *lex specialis* effect of Article XXIV:12, and brought it much closer to the general international law rules on performance of treaties.[101]

As alluded to above, Article XXIV:12 of the GATT 1947 was carried forward to the GATT 1994. This was done subject, however, to an Understanding on the Interpretation of Article XXIV (the Understanding). The Understanding clarifies the meaning of Article XXIV:12 by adding a new clause to the effect that each Member is "*fully responsible*" for the observance of all provisions of the GATT 1994.[102] Like the Understanding, the federal clause of the SPS Agreement is also qualified by Members' "full responsibility."[103] Obviously, the introduction of this qualification means that the federal clauses of these agreements cannot be treated as having the same limiting effect as Article XXIV:12 of the GATT 1947 (note that GATT panels had already tightly restricted its effect), because otherwise the requirement of "full responsibility" would become meaningless.[104] In any case, the "real" significance of the GATT 1994, the SPS and the GATS[105] provisions is utterly diminished because, as discussed below, the standard WTO dispute settlement procedures are fully applicable to these three agreements.

In contrast to the provisions of the above-noted three agreements, the TBT Agreement does in fact establish a special regime for the implementation and observance of its obligations by local government

98 The GATT 1947 did not – and the GATT 1994 also does not – contain a general definition of this term. Cf., however, Interpretative Note *Ad* Article III, which provides some indication as to what could be regarded as reasonable measures for purposes of compliance with Article III.

99 *Canada – Alcohol II*, paras. 5.37–39.

100 See the cases cited in n. 97 above.

101 See Kuyper 1994, 244–45.

102 The Understanding, para. 13.

103 SPS Agreement, Article 13.

104 Cf. AB Reports, *US – Gasoline*, at 23; *Japan – Alcohol II*, at 12, 18; *Korea – Dairy*, paras. 80–82; and *Argentina – Footwear*, para. 88 (stressing that meaning must be given to all the terms of the treaty and a reading cannot be adopted that reduces an entire clause to redundancy or inutility). See also Lennard 2002, 58–61.

105 GATS, however, does not employ the language of "full responsibility" and simply provides that Members must take "reasonable measures" to ensure compliance by local authorities: see GATS, Article I:3.

bodies.[106] This Agreement, unlike any other agreement within the WTO framework, distinguishes between central and local governments at the level of providing for the relevant obligations. Thus it establishes different types of obligations for central[107] and local governments.[108] In addition, in respect of dispute settlement, the usual cause of action, i.e. nullification or impairment of benefits,[109] does not apply so far as local measures are concerned. Rather, the dispute settlement provisions may be invoked "where a Member considers that another Member has not achieved satisfactory results" and the "trade interests" of the former "are significantly affected."[110]

The WTO text on dispute settlement, namely, the DSU, explicitly confirms the GATT *acquis* that local measures are amenable to dispute settlement procedures. However, in case of a dispute settlement ruling that a local measure has violated a provision of any of the WTO agreements, "the responsible Member" is to "take such reasonable measures as may be available to it" to ensure compliance. But if those reasonable measures do not secure compliance, the DSU provisions concerning compensation and retaliation are to apply fully.[111] This means that a losing Member can choose not to bring a non-conforming local measure into conformity *only at the cost of* providing compensatory benefits to the successful party or of suffering likely retaliation by that party.

Generally – i.e. in respect of central government measures – the DSU establishes a clear preference for the performance of the dispute settlement rulings, and envisages compensation and retaliation as temporary remedies. But, strictly, even in respect of central government measures, a Member may choose to remain in violation and decide, instead, either to provide compensation or to suffer likely retaliation.[112] Thus, whatever special treatment there exists in respect of local government measures, in essence, its real content is very limited. To wit, it is limited in not prioritizing – of course, only after "reasonable measures" have already been taken – the type of remedy that otherwise would have

106 Cf. Villalpando 2002. 107 See TBT Agreement, Articles 2, 5 and 6.

108 See ibid. Articles 3 and 7.

109 Typically, a Member may invoke WTO dispute settlement procedures if "any benefit accruing to it" under the WTO agreements is "nullified or impaired" by another Member: see, further, Chapter 4, pp. 98–100.

110 TBT Agreement, Article 14.4.

111 See DSU, Article 22.9; and the Understanding, para. 14. For an analysis of why DSU Article 22.9 itself is not to be treated as a "federal clause," see Bhuiyan 2004, 133–35.

112 See, further, Chapter 4, pp. 109–12.

been given preference. And, as such, the WTO federal clauses are nothing but devices that are relevant only in respect of the "reputation" factor for inducing compliance. That is to say, compared to central government measures, a non-compliant Member would, possibly, lose its "reputation" less quickly in respect of local measures.

It may be noted that, notwithstanding the applicability of the DSU provisions on compensation and retaliation, the "federal limitation" of the TBT Agreement does not degenerate in a manner comparable to that of the other three agreements. This is because the substantive standard that is to be applied for finding an inconsistency is less exacting in respect of local TBT measures. That is to say, while under the GATT 1994, the SPS Agreement and the GATS local measures are to be judged by applying the same standard (i.e. nullification or impairment) as for central government measures, under the TBT Agreement they are to be judged, as already noted, on the basis of different standards. Therefore, local measures cannot, in the first place, be found to be inconsistent with the TBT Agreement as quickly as central governmental measures. This, in turn, secures some protection for local measures notwithstanding the applicability of the DSU provisions on compensation and retaliation.

Finally, it needs to be pointed out that the precise scope of the provisions on "federal limitation" vis-à-vis Article XVI:4 of the WTO Agreement is rather unclear. One view could be that these provisions, except the TBT Agreement provisions, are in conflict with Article XVI:4. Unlike the TBT obligations, the GATT 1994, the SPS and the GATS obligations are also applicable to local governments, because various provisions that set out those obligations refer in general terms to the "Member"[113] and, as such, they impose obligations on the Member as a whole, including its local governments.[114] Recall that Article XVI:4 requires Members to ensure the conformity of their laws, regulations, etc., with the WTO *obligations*, and does not, in this regard, make a distinction between central and local governments. Thus, if the relevant obligations are applicable to local governments, under Article XVI:4, conformity must also be ensured in respect of local government laws or regulations. By contrast, in pursuance of the GATT 1994, the SPS and the GATS provisions concerning

[113] Indeed, most of the provisions contained in various WTO agreements other than the TBT Agreement refer generally to "Members."

[114] It may be recalled that it was already decided under the GATT 1947 that the GATT obligations did not cease to be *applicable* to local governments because of the federal limitation: see above, text at n. 96.

territorial application, Members need not ensure such conformity, but need only to take "reasonable measures" for securing observance at sub-national levels. From this perspective the situation can be seen as one of "conflict." According to the WTO Agreement, it prevails in the event of a conflict between it and any other annex agreement.[115] As such, it can be argued that GATT 1994, SPS and GATS limitations on implementation at sub-national levels are, in fact, overridden by the WTO Agreement.[116]

The end result can be nearly as striking if the situation is not characterized as "conflict" – in that somehow it is possible to interpret the provisions "harmoniously"! To wit, while on the one hand, in Article XVI:4, the WTO treaty goes much further than the comparable rules under general public international law, it waters down those selfsame rules in respect of territorial application, on the other.

4 Obligations on transparency

In all fields of international law – trade, finance, investment, competition, human rights, labor, environment, arms control, etc. – much effort, quite rightly, is put into ensuring "transparency," i.e. publication and exchange of information. Under contemporary international treaties the information that a country may be required to publish, transmit or share can be of various kinds. It can relate to objective facts, e.g. facts concerning depletion of the ozone layer and data on a country's production of substances that cause such depletion;[117] or it can be about the domestic legal framework, e.g. the legal framework that exists for the protection of the ozone layer[118] or for the admission and protection of foreign investment; or it can also relate to measures – scientific, technical, socio-economic, legal or others – that a country has adopted for the implementation of the international agreement concerned.[119]

[115] See WTO Agreement, Article XVI:3.

[116] In the recent *EC – Customs Matters* case, the Panel took the view that Article XXIV:12 does not derogate from the other provisions of the GATT 1994. In support of this proposition the Panel referred to the Understanding and Article XVI:4 of the WTO Agreement: see Panel Report, paras. 7.136–45, footnote 287.

[117] See, e.g., Montreal Protocol on Substances that Deplete the Ozone Layer 1987 (revised several times), Articles 7 and 9.

[118] See, e.g., Vienna Convention for the Protection of the Ozone Layer 1985, Annex II, para. 6.

[119] See ibid. Article 5 and Annex II.

One common function that the publication and transmission of these various types of information perform is to secure implementation and increased observance of international obligations. However, apart from this general role, at different levels, transparency also serves some other very useful purposes; or, put differently, publication and transmission of *different types of information* lead to the same end result of increased observance of international obligations through *different means*. Thus, for instance, publication of information about depletion of the ozone layer and its severe adverse consequences, and data on the production of ozone-depleting substances, secures greater compliance with international commitments for the prevention of such depletion through, inter alia, increased public support for those commitments. Information about the national legal framework for the admission and protection of investment will have a somewhat different role so far as the public at large is concerned: it will help individuals and businesses to engage in the activity – in this case investment – that the international agreement concerned intends to promote; and by so helping it will further the objectives of the treaty. Needless to say, in both instances, if the relevant information brings into the open non-compliant behavior of a country, increased adherence may also result due to informal suasion by other countries to comply, as well as because of the inclination that the former may have for not losing its "reputation" by being labelled as a non-compliant. Thus, through publication, the same information serves different roles at different levels – even though, in one way or another, it is possible to reduce them all to that of securing increased adherence to international commitments.[120]

Two vital roles that the WTO obligations concerning transparency in respect of Members' trade laws and policies perform are: enabling individual traders and businesses to become acquainted with those laws and policies;[121] and contributing to improved adherence by Members to WTO rules and discipline.[122] The former is important because the realization

[120] As one commentator has put it nicely, "'transparency' is essentially an exercise in education – but with the implicit objective of inculcating a behavioral pattern": Qureshi 1996, 51.

[121] Indeed, the relevant WTO provisions not only require "transparency between Members" but "goes further and specifically references the importance of transparency to individual traders": Panel Report, *Argentina – Hides and Leather*, para. 11.76.

[122] On the role of transparency in implementing GATT/WTO norms, see generally: Blackhurst 1991; and Qureshi 1996. Sometimes the role of transparency in securing greater adherence to WTO commitments is not readily noticed, partly because of the

of the benefits of the WTO treaty by "expanding the production of and trade in goods and services"[123] depends, in large measure, on individual economic activity; and for this activity to flourish, it is essential that traders and businesses be acquainted with Members' trade laws and policies. In this respect, transparency is also important in providing guarantees of due process with regard to the adoption and/or modification of national trade laws or other measures.[124] The significance of the latter does not require explaining – it is difficult to think of any legal rules that are not framed with the intention of being observed.

For obvious reasons, presently the focus is on transparency in respect of national *laws*. But the WTO provisions concerning transparency are couched in more general terms and, in addition to Members' trade laws, they require transparency with respect to any other measures – e.g., administrative measures, international agreements entered into by Members, etc. – that may affect international trade. Two key ways in which WTO agreements seek to ensure transparency are: first, by requiring Members to *publish* their domestic laws *internally*, that is to say, publish the laws at the national level – in official journals, for instance; and second, by requiring Members to *notify* the laws to *the WTO Secretariat or various committees within the WTO*. Since 1989, another exercise in transparency has been put in place – this is known as the Trade Policy Review Mechanism (TPRM). The requirements of publication and notification are discussed together in the next section (because often it is the same provision that provides for both of these requirements). This discussion is followed by a consideration of the TPRM.

4.1 *Publication and notification of national laws*

Under the GATT 1947, Article X, which has since been carried into the GATT 1994, provided for requirements concerning publication of

existence of a very effective and efficient dispute settlement mechanism, which overshadows other means of implementation. Professor Weiss, for instance, has commented that in WTO agreements there has been little reliance on the transparency approach to ensure compliance: see E. B. Weiss 2000, 466. This suggestion, it may be noted, is not accurate. While it is true that in respect of various internal WTO meetings – for example, hearings before the dispute settlement panels – WTO does not ensure maximum transparency, in respect of Members' trade law and policy WTO does require complete transparency.

123 WTO Agreement, Preamble.

124 See observations of the Appellate Body in *US – Underwear* quoted at n. 217 below. Cf. Zoellner 2006, 603–4.

national laws. The obligation under Article X is applicable across the entire trade in goods sector; and its relevant part provides as follows:

> Laws, regulations, judicial decisions and administrative rulings of general application, made effective by any Member, pertaining to the classification or the valuation of products for customs purposes, or to rates of duty, taxes or other charges, or to requirements, restrictions or prohibitions on imports or exports or on the transfer of payments therefor, or affecting their sale, distribution, transportation, insurance, warehousing inspection, exhibition, processing, mixing or other use, shall be published promptly in such a manner as to enable *governments* and *traders* to become acquainted with them.[125]

In the following paragraph, Article X further provides that all legislative or other measures that result in increasing the burden on traders are to be made effective only after being officially published.[126]

The above requirements relate to "internal" publication of national laws. A number of other GATT articles – although they do not make explicit reference to national laws – require Members to notify other Members or the WTO Secretariat (formerly, GATT Secretariat) of their trade measures in general. Such notification is required, for instance, in respect of quotas,[127] subsidies,[128] state trading enterprises,[129] governmental assistance to economic development,[130] emergency action,[131] etc. To the extent that these various measures are contained in national laws, the notification requirement is applicable to such laws.

Furthermore, under the auspices of the GATT 1947, a considerable amount of practice had developed in respect of notification; and at various times GATT Contracting Parties as well as the Secretariat had adopted a number of recommendations, understandings or notes providing for, clarifying or summarizing notification obligations.[132] In a 1964 Recommendation on "Co-operation in the Field of Trade Information and Trade Promotion," the Contracting Parties recommended that "copies of the laws, regulations, decisions, [and] rulings" of the kind described in Article X should promptly be forwarded to the

[125] GATT 1994, Article X:1, first sentence (italics added). (The second sentence of Article X:1 requires publication of international agreements affecting trade; and the third sentence provides for a caveat in respect of confidential information, the disclosure of which would be contrary to public or legitimate commercial interests.) Cf. NAFTA, Article 1802(1) (containing a similarly worded provision).

[126] GATT 1994, Article X:2. However, prior publication does not validate a measure that is otherwise WTO-inconsistent: see AB Report, *US – Underwear*, at 21.

[127] GATT 1994, Article XIII:3(c). [128] Ibid. Article XVI:1.

[129] Ibid. Article XVII:4(a). [130] Ibid. Articles XVIII:7(a) and XVIII:14.

[131] Ibid. Article XIX:2. [132] For a list of these, see World Trade Organization 1995, 300.

Secretariat.[133] Thus, in addition to internal publication of national laws falling within the description of Article X, GATT contracting parties were also expected to furnish the Secretariat copies of those laws.

Under the WTO, GATT 1994 requirements for publication and notification have been supplemented by additional provisions. In the trade in goods sector, many of these provisions expressly require publication and notification of national laws and any changes in such laws,[134] while others require the same in respect of trade measures in general.[135] Thus, internal publication and/or notification to various WTO committees or the Secretariat is required in respect of Members' laws concerning balance-of-payment,[136] sanitary and phytosanitary measures,[137] trade-related investment measures,[138] dumping,[139] customs valuation,[140] pre-shipment inspection,[141] rules of origin,[142] subsidies,[143] safeguard measures,[144] etc.; or in respect of measures in general that concern safeguard action in the agriculture sector,[145] import restrictions in textiles,[146] technical regulations,[147] import licensing,[148] etc. In some instances Members are also obliged to notify about proposed legislative or other measures and to provide other Members copies of the draft laws, etc., reasonably in advance of their adoption, so that interested Members can make comments on them.[149] In relation to some of the agreements, Members are required to establish national enquiry points, with the responsibility to answer queries from Members or individuals and to provide relevant documents regarding specified trade laws, regulations or measures.[150]

[133] BISD 12S/49. See also Understanding Regarding Notification, Consultation, Dispute Settlement and Surveillance, adopted on November 28, 1979, BISD 26S/210, paras. 2–3.

[134] See below, nn. 136–44. [135] See below, nn. 145–48.

[136] See Understanding on the Balance-of-Payments Provisions of the GATT 1994, para. 9.

[137] See SPS Agreement, Article 7 and Annex B.

[138] See TRIMS Agreement, Articles 5.1 and 6.1. [139] See ADA, Article 18.5.

[140] See Customs Valuation Agreement, Article 12.

[141] See PSI Agreement, Articles 2.8, 3.2 and 5.

[142] See ARO, Articles 2(g), 3(e) and 5, and Annex II, paras. 3(c) and 4.

[143] See ASCM, Article 32.6. [144] See Safeguards Agreement, Article 12.6.

[145] See Agriculture Agreement, Article 5.7. [146] See ATC, Article 2.

[147] See TBT Agreement, Articles 2.9–11, 3.2, 5.6–8, 15.2.

[148] See Licensing Agreement, Articles 1.4(a) and 5.

[149] See, e.g., SPS Agreement, Annex B, para. 5; TBT Agreement, Articles 2.9 and 5.6; and ASCM, Article 8.3. Cf. NAFTA, Articles 718, 909, 1411(1) and 1802(2) (containing similar provisions on prior publication of proposed measures).

[150] See, e.g., SPS Agreement, Annex B, paras. 3–4; TBT Agreement, Article 10; and GATS, Article III:4. Cf. NAFTA, Articles 719, 910 and 1411(6) (containing similar provisions on enquiry points).

In addition to the goods sector, publication and notification requirements also extend to the new areas covered by the WTO. Thus, national laws pertaining to or affecting trade in services must be published as well as notified to the Council for Trade in Services.[151] Likewise, laws concerning the availability, scope, acquisition, enforcement and prevention of the abuse of intellectual property rights must be published and notified to the TRIPS Council.[152]

The UR single package also includes a Ministerial Decision on Notification Procedures. In this Decision, Members reaffirmed their commitment to publish and notify, to the maximum extent possible, their adoption and modification of trade measures. Notifications, however, are "without prejudice" to the question of the measures' consistency with or relevance to the WTO agreements.[153] A Central Registry of notifications is established under this Decision. The registry records information furnished by Members, which, on request, is made available to any Member. It also informs Members annually of their notification obligations for the following year; and draws individual Member's attention to notification requirements that remain unfulfilled.

4.2 *The Trade Policy Review Mechanism*

The Trade Policy Review Mechanism (TPRM) was first operationalized on a trial basis by the GATT Contracting Parties in 1989.[154] With the WTO, it has become a permanent institution – incorporated in the UR single package as Annex 3 to the WTO Agreement.[155]

The stated objectives of the TPRM are to contribute to improved adherence by Members to the WTO rules, disciplines and commitments, and to achieve greater transparency in, and understanding of, the trade policies and practices – including, of course, trade laws – of Members. As such, the review mechanism is directed to the "regular collective appreciation and evaluation of the *full range of* individual Members' trade policies and

[151] See GATS, Articles III and XXVIII:(a). [152] See TRIPS Agreement, Article 63.

[153] Thus, notifying a domestic law under a specific WTO agreement, e.g. the TBT Agreement, does not mean that that agreement is applicable to that law. The "without prejudice" language of the Decision also precludes the possibility of there being any "estoppel" against the notifying country regarding such applicability: see Panel Report, *EC – Asbestos*, para. 8.60.

[154] See World Trade Organization 1995, 305.

[155] See generally on TPRM: Qureshi 1990, 1992 and 1996, ch. 6; Mavroidis 1992; and Abbott 1993.

practices and their impact on the functioning of the multilateral trading system."[156]

Under the Mechanism all Members are subject to periodic trade policy review. The four Members with the largest share of the world trade are reviewed every two years, the next sixteen countries every four years, and other countries every six years.[157] To carry out the reviews a Trade Policy Review Body (TPRB) is established.[158] The process involves the submission of a so-called "full report" by the Member under review in relation to its trade policies and practices, including relevant domestic laws and regulations. In addition, the WTO Secretariat draws up a report on its own responsibility, based on information available to it or provided by Members. The Secretariat may also seek clarification from Members.[159] The criteria for the review is "to examine the *impact* of a Member's trade policies and practices *on the multilateral trading system*."[160] Apparently, this may involve legal as well as economic evaluation of the relevant information.[161] At the end of the process, the two reports, along with the minutes of the proceedings of the TPRB, are published as the trade policy review of the country concerned.[162]

The TPRM expressly states that it is not intended "to serve as a basis for the enforcement of specific obligations under the Agreements or for dispute settlement procedures, or to impose new policy commitments on Members."[163] While it may be true that the TPRM does not entail "enforcement" – albeit in a narrow sense – of *specific obligations*,[164] it nonetheless provides implementation incentives through transparency, evaluation, informal peer pressure, etc.[165] And, of course, information revealed in a review exercise is not "immune" from challenge before WTO dispute settlement bodies. Thus, even though the TPRM itself is not a dispute settlement process, it can, on occasion, *lead to* that process, by revealing WTO-inconsistent national laws or other trade measures.[166]

156 See TPRM, Section A. 157 Ibid. Section C.

158 Ibid. The TPRB is, in fact, the General Council of the WTO acting under a different name and organization: see WTO Agreement, Article IV:4.

159 TPRM, Sections C–D. 160 Ibid. Section A. 161 See Qureshi 1996, 117–22.

162 The reviews are available for purchase either in book format or on CD-ROM. A considerable amount of materials can also be obtained from the trade policy reviews gateway of the WTO website at www.wto.org/english/tratop_e/tpr_e/tpr_e.htm.

163 TPRM, Section A.

164 Thus, for instance, statements made in the TPRB or conclusions reached as a result of the reviews do not amount to "findings" with binding authority.

165 For analyses of various enforcement dimensions of the TPRM, see Qureshi 1990 and 1996, ch. 6.

166 See Qureshi 1996, 116.

5 Obligations regarding administration of national laws

Obligations to ensure the conformity of national laws with the WTO agreements and to publish and notify trade-related laws are supplemented by another group of systemic obligations regarding administration of those laws. In respect of laws relating to trade in goods, the relevant obligation is contained in Article X:3(a) of the GATT 1994, which reads as follows: "Each Member shall administer in a uniform, impartial and reasonable manner all its laws, regulations, decisions and rulings of the kind described in paragraph 1 of this Article."[167] Although the above is applicable throughout the entire trade in goods sector, some other goods agreements also contain analogous provisions. Specifically, such provisions are contained in the ARO[168] and the Licensing Agreement.[169] Administration of laws affecting trade in services is also subject to a similar obligation, in so far as and to the extent that the law relates to a service sector where the Member concerned has undertaken specific commitments.[170] However, no comparable provision exists in respect of administration of intellectual property laws. Then again, the TRIPS Agreement contains, as discussed in section 6 below, the most extensive provisions requiring Members to make available under their national law various enforcement procedures and remedies. Those provisions do not just counterbalance the lack of a provision regarding administration of national laws: at a practical level, their implications can be even greater.

Textually, there are some differences among the provisions regarding the administration of national laws. Thus, these provisions variously require "uniform," "impartial," "reasonable,"[171] "consistent,"[172] "neutral," "fair," "equitable"[173] and "objective"[174] administration of national laws. The Appellate Body apparently has said that the differences are not of much significance. In *EC – Bananas*, it made the following observation: "We attach no significance to the difference in the phrases 'neutral in application and administered in a fair and equitable manner' in

[167] (Paragraph 1 is quoted above at n. 125.) Cf. NAFTA, Article 1804. This somewhat differently framed provision requires NAFTA Parties to comply with certain procedural requirements "with a view to administering in a consistent, impartial and reasonable manner all measures of general application."

[168] See ARO, Articles 2(e) and 3(d). [169] See Licensing Agreement, Article 1.3.

[170] See GATS, Article VI:1; and Panel Report, *US – Gambling Services*, paras. 6.427–37.

[171] GATT 1994, Article X:3(a); ARO, Articles 2(e) and 3(d); and GATS, Article VI:1.

[172] ARO, Articles 2(e) and 3(d). [173] Licensing Agreement, Article 1.3.

[174] GATS, Article VI:1.

Article 1.3 of the Licensing Agreement and 'administer in a uniform, impartial and reasonable manner' in Article X:3(a) of the GATT 1994. In our view the two phrases are, for all practical purposes, interchangeable."[175] However, the above statement is correct only up to a point. In particular, it is correct in the context in which it was made in *EC – Bananas*. There the question before the Appellate Body was whether Article 1.3, Licensing Agreement, and Article X:3(a), GATT 1994, can have identical coverage in that they can apply to the administration of the same import licensing procedures. The Appellate Body concluded in the affirmative and made the above observation as an explanation for its conclusion.[176]

It is not in doubt that all of the provisions concerning administration of national laws target the particular manner of *administration* of national laws rather than the *substantive content* of those laws.[177] As such, notwithstanding textual differences, the provisions have "identical" coverage. Moreover, in paragraph 1 of Article X, a very wide range of national laws – virtually covering all conceivable types of laws concerning trade in goods – are enumerated. Accordingly, Article X:3(a) and analogous provisions in other goods agreements (e.g. the Licensing Agreement as in the *EC – Bananas* case) can be applicable with regard to the administration of the same national law. To this extent the Appellate Body's observation is accurate.

However, the textual differences can be important at a more specific level of *applying* the provision concerned to the administration of national laws. *Argentina – Hides and Leather* provides a good example. In this case, the Panel found, in respect of the administration of the same Argentine laws and on the basis of the same facts about their administration, that there was no violation of the standard of "uniform" application, while there were violations in respect of the other two Article X:3(a) standards, namely, "reasonable" and "impartial" administration.[178] Thus, clearly, the standards that must be satisfied under different criteria – "uniform," "impartial," "reasonable," "consistent," "neutral," "fair," "equitable" and "objective" – can vary to a considerable extent. The reason that the Appellate Body did not notice this aspect is that in *EC – Bananas*, it was not necessary to apply either of the above

175 AB Report, *EC – Bananas*, para. 203. 176 Ibid.

177 See ibid. para. 200; and AB Report, *EC – Poultry*, para. 115.

178 See Panel Report, *Argentina – Hides and Leather*, paras. 11.56–101. The Panel noted that the three Article X:3(a) standards are "legally independent" and, as such, the administration of laws must satisfy each of them (para. 11.86).

standards to the administration of the EC law. There the analysis ended at an earlier stage when the Appellate Body had found that the pertinent issue was one concerning the *substance* of the law at issue, rather than its *administration.*

Other critical interpretative issues also arise with regard to the group of provisions presently under consideration. The Appellate Body has noted more than once that these provisions relate to the *administration* of laws rather than to their *substance.*[179] Of course, in many instances laws will be administered through the discretionary acts of government officials. However, it is also possible for the manner *itself* of administration of a certain law to be provided for in another law or legislative instrument. In such circumstances the suggestion that the "substance" of a law cannot come within the scope of, e.g., Article X:3(a), may not seem accurate. Indeed, in *Argentina – Hides and Leather*, the Panel found a legislative instrument to be inconsistent with Article X:3(a), because the substance of that legislative instrument was administrative in nature.[180] This case was not appealed, so the AB's view on this particular issue is not yet known.[181]

Determining what is required under each of the various criteria – "uniform," "impartial," etc. – may not be straightforward either.[182] Two broad questions that arise in this context are: first, what is the relationship or difference between these criteria and other substantive WTO obligations? Second (and the most crucial part of the analysis), what kind of acts at the national level can constitute violation of each of these criteria?

[179] See, e.g., cases cited above at nn. 175, 177.

[180] Panel Report, *Argentina – Hides and Leather*, paras. 11.69–72. Cf. Panel Report, *US – Offset Act* (paras. 7.143–44), where the Panel found that the US law at issue was not administrative but substantive in nature and, accordingly, it fell outside the scope of Article X:3(a). Thus, applying Article X:3(a) or other analogous provisions to domestic laws gives rise to a threshold question of whether the law should be "characterized" as administrative or substantive in nature. On characterization, see, generally, Chapter 5 below.

[181] In the recent *EC – Customs Matters* case, the Panel adopted a stricter approach in determining that laws and regulations themselves cannot amount to "administration" within the meaning of Article X:3(a) of the GATT 1994: see Panel Report, paras. 7.94–119.

[182] Cf. AB Report, *US – OCTG Sunset Reviews*, para. 217, noting that allegations of biased and unreasonable administration of national laws and regulations should not be brought lightly and that a claim under Article X:3(a) of the GATT 1994 must be supported by solid evidence that reflects the gravity of the accusations inherent in claims under Article X:3(a).

As regards the first question, it has been suggested that these criteria should not be regarded as "duplicating" other substantive WTO obligations. For instance, the criteria of "uniform" application of laws should not be read as a broad anti-discrimination provision. To the extent that the administration of laws discriminates against the exports of one Member relative to another,[183] the relevant violation would be that of the most-favored nation treatment obligation as contained in Article I, GATT 1994, but not of Article X:3(a).[184] Thus, in determining "uniform" application, the focus should not be on how the products of *different Members* are treated or how *imported products* are treated compared to *domestic products*. Rather, "uniform" application pre-supposes that *individual traders* "should be able to expect treatment of the same kind, in the same manner both over time and in different places and with respect to other persons."[185] This formulation clarifies that the essential question is how individual traders are treated and not whether there has been MFN or national treatment violation. However, much of the abstract formulation still remains a matter to be applied on a case by case basis. Similar complex issues may arise with regard to the scope of the other criteria – not all of which have yet received judicial consideration – vis-à-vis substantive WTO obligations.

As regards the second question, panels have shown a general reluctance to test under Article X:3(a) the consistency of a Member's acts with its own domestic legislation.[186] As a consequence, departures from the established practice or policy under a domestic law were not regarded as non-uniform or unreasonable administration of the law.[187] This approach makes good sense. Firstly, as a matter of general public international law it is well established that the unlawfulness of an act of a state under its domestic law does not entail that the act in question is unlawful in international law.[188] Secondly, panels, of course, are not well suited to determine whether a Member has acted consistently with

[183] This is generally described as de facto discrimination, as opposed to de jure discrimination. That is to say, the discrimination exists not in the domestic law itself, but in how the law is applied as a matter of fact.

[184] See AB Report, *EC – Bananas*, para. 201; and Panel Report, *Argentina – Hides and Leather*, paras. 11.76, 11.83–84.

[185] Ibid. para. 11.83.

[186] See Panel Reports, *US – Stainless Steel*, paras. 6.50–51; and *US – Hot-Rolled Steel*, para. 7.267.

[187] See *US – Stainless Steel*; and *US – Hot-Rolled Steel*.

[188] See above, Chapter 2, n. 18, and the *ELSI* case cited there. See also Crawford 2002, 86–88.

its own laws. At the same time, it is possible to imagine circumstances where the violation by a Member of its own law could be such that a breach of Article X:3(a) may seem almost obvious.[189] In this context, it may also be noted that while international law does not concern itself with domestic legal conformity of acts of states, it is possible under an international law rule to make such conformity relevant for international law purposes.[190] In extreme cases, Article X:3(a) or other similar articles can be treated as partaking of the nature of such international law rules.

At any rate, under these provisions, panels and the Appellate Body may be presented with a host of arguments: ranging from arguments on treaty interpretation (e.g. interpreting the terms "uniform," "reasonable," etc.) to those on interpretation of municipal law and on evaluation of Members' acts against both international and municipal law benchmarks.[191]

6 Obligations to make available under national law specified procedures and remedies

There is a wide range of obligations in various WTO agreements requiring Members to make available under their national law specified procedures or remedies. Broadly, these obligations require the availability of two types of procedures: first, review procedures, i.e. procedures for the review and modification or reversal of administrative actions by independent authorities - for example by courts; and second, enforcement procedures, i.e. procedures for the enforcement of private rights by the right holders. The former is required in respect of matters concerning all three substantive areas - trade in goods, services and protection of

189 Cf. *Dominican Republic - Cigarettes*; and *EC - Customs Matters*. In the former case, the failure of the Dominican Republic to support certain decisions regarding tax administration by reference to provisions of its laws that were in force was found to be "unreasonable" administration of domestic laws, regulations, etc., within the meaning of Article X:3(a): see Panel Report, *Dominican Republic - Cigarettes*, paras. 7.365–94. In the latter case, the imposition by some member states of the EC of a requirement that was inconsistent with EC customs laws was held to be "non-uniform" administration of EC customs laws under Article X:3(a): see Panel Report, *EC - Customs Matters*, paras. 7.372–85.

190 Crawford 2002, 89.

191 See, e.g., *EC - Customs Matters* (this case and the eventual 357-page Panel Report almost entirely concerned questions of whether EC customs laws were administered in a "uniform" manner as required under Article X:3(a) of the GATT 1994).

intellectual property rights - covered by the WTO, while the latter is required only in respect of enforcement of IPRs. Needless to say, claims regarding non-fulfilment of these obligations can be raised in the WTO dispute settlement process. However, in that context, these obligations have not *yet* become highly contentious.[192]

6.1 *Review procedures*

The earliest provision requiring review procedures was contained in Article X:3(b) of the GATT 1947, which has since been carried into the GATT 1994. It requires Members to maintain or institute judicial, arbitral or administrative tribunals or procedures for the prompt review and correction of administrative actions relating to *customs matters*.[193] Such tribunals or procedures must be independent of the administrative agencies concerned. However, it is not necessary to substitute existing procedures which are not "formally independent" but which, nonetheless, ensure "an objective and impartial review."[194] An important question about the scope of Article X:3(b) is what meaning should be attributed to the expression "customs matters." Should it be understood in a "narrow" sense as including only those matters that are traditionally dealt with by the national customs authorities, for example determination of value or origin of goods, assessment of duties, etc.? Or, should it be given a "wider" meaning to include, for instance, matters concerning dumping, subsidies, product standards, etc.?

This difficulty is obviated, in part, by the UR texts: in addition to customs matters, independent review is now also required in respect of certain administrative actions concerning dumping and subsidies.[195]

[192] So far, only in one or two WTO cases have claims concerning violation of any of these obligations been seriously pursued: see *US - Section 211* (Panel Report, paras. 8.92–102, 8.160–62; and AB Report, paras. 203–32); and *EC - Customs Matters* (Panel Report, paras. 7.491–556) (the former case concerned Article 42 of the TRIPS Agreement, while the latter concerned Article X:3(b) of the GATT 1994).

[193] Cf. NAFTA, Article 1805 (providing for a similar obligation to establish independent procedures "for the purpose of the prompt review and, where warranted, correction of final administrative actions").

[194] GATT 1994, Article X:3(c).

[195] See ADA, Article 13 (entitled "Judicial Review"); and ASCM, Article 23 (also entitled "Judicial Review"). In addition, UR texts on customs valuation (see Customs Valuation Agreement, Article 11 and Annex I, Interpretative Note to Article 11) and rules of origin (see ARO, Articles 2[j], 3[h], and Annex II, paragraph 3[f]) contain similar requirements. However, the latter are matters that generally fall within the competence of national customs authorities.

There is, however, a host of other subjects covered in the UR texts on trade in goods, which cannot readily – or can hardly – be treated as "customs matters": for instance, internal taxation, sanitary and phytosanitary measures, technical regulations, investment measures, safeguards, etc. Thus, depending on how the expression "customs matters" is construed, with respect to some administrative actions concerning trade in goods, the requirement to institute or maintain review procedures will not be applicable.

In respect of administrative decisions affecting trade in services, Members are to maintain or establish either independent review procedures, or procedures that although not independent do "in fact provide for an objective and impartial review."[196] Then again, Members are not obliged to establish such procedures where that would be "inconsistent with its constitutional structure or the nature of its legal system."[197]

Finally, in the field of IPRs, obligations on judicial review procedures are closely related to those on enforcement procedures. Thus, parties to an enforcement proceeding against infringement of IPRs must be granted a right of judicial review in respect of administrative decisions, as well as of at least the legal aspects of initial judicial decisions.[198] In addition, judicial review procedures must also be made available in respect of administrative decisions concerning the acquisition, maintenance or revocation of intellectual property rights,[199] and decisions authorizing use of patents without the right holders' consent.[200]

6.2 *Enforcement procedures*

Obligations regarding enforcement procedures are unique to the TRIPS Agreement. Part III of that Agreement, comprising Articles 41 through 61 (in total ten pages of legal texts), sets out, in great detail, procedures and remedies that Members must put in place to ensure "effective action against any act of infringement of intellectual property rights."[201] The wide-ranging obligations cover subjects as diverse as civil procedures, remedies, interim relief, border measures, criminal liability, etc. However, these obligations do not create any requirement regarding "the distribution of resources as between enforcement of intellectual property rights and the enforcement of law in general."[202]

196 GATS, Article VI:2(a). 197 Ibid. Article VI:2(b). 198 TRIPS Agreement, Article 41.4.
199 Ibid. Articles 32 and 62.5. 200 Ibid. Article 31(i) and (j). 201 Ibid. Article 41.1.
202 Ibid. Article 41.5.

With respect to civil and administrative procedures for enforcement, it is required that they be fair and equitable (there are also specific requirements concerning written notice, representation by counsel, protection of confidential information, etc.[203]); that they are not unnecessarily complicated or costly; and that they do not entail unreasonable time-limits or unwarranted delays.[204] Decisions on merits are required "preferably" to be in writing and to contain reasons.[205] Judicial organs are to be given the authority to order production of evidence.[206] As regards remedies, the Agreement requires that judicial authorities be empowered to issue injunctions;[207] award damages and costs, including attorney's fees, to successful right holders;[208] and order the disposal of infringing goods "outside the channels of commerce," or their destruction.[209] In addition, such authorities are to be authorized to order – including, if need be, in *ex parte* proceedings – prompt and effective interim or provisional measures to prevent infringements or to preserve evidence.[210] Right holders are also to have access to appropriate border measures, whereby customs authorities can suspend "the release into free circulation" of counterfeit or pirated goods.[211] Lastly, Members are required to provide for criminal procedures and penalties "at least in cases of wilful trademark counterfeiting or copyright piracy on a commercial scale."[212]

Apparently, these obligations are highly intrusive in respect of Members' domestic legal systems. Commentators, for instance, have described them as constituting "a largely unprecedented degree of control by an international regime over domestic civil and administrative procedures."[213] However, at the same time, it must also be noted that the TRIPS Agreement contains an important qualification: if the *remedies*

[203] Ibid. Article 42. [204] Ibid. Article 41.2. [205] Ibid. Article 41.3.
[206] Ibid. Article 43. [207] Ibid. Article 44(1). [208] Ibid. Article 45. [209] Ibid. Article 46.
[210] Ibid. Article 50. [211] Ibid. Articles 51–60. [212] Ibid. Article 61.
[213] See Trebilcock & Howse 1999, 327. Cf. NAFTA Articles 1714–18, however. These provisions require NAFTA parties to make available procedures and remedies for the enforcement of IPRs that are fairly identical with those required under the TRIPS Agreement. In this regard both texts also employ largely identical language due, inter alia, to their contemporaneous negotiation. It is also notable that *generally* the EC/EU legal order is even more intrusive in respect of member states' domestic judicial systems. The principles of supremacy and direct effect of EC law ensure that individuals can have recourse to national courts to pursue and enforce claims based on EC law (see above, Chapter 2, p. 32, and the works and cases cited there). But, *specifically* in respect of the procedures and remedies to be made available to vindicate those claims, Community law has been less assertive. There is settled ECJ case law that the choice of procedures and remedies is a matter for the domestic legal system, subject to the requirements, first, that the applicable conditions are no less favorable than those applied to similar domestic matters (equivalence), and,

under the Agreement are inconsistent with domestic law, the latter is to prevail, *provided* that "declaratory judgments and adequate compensation" are always available.[214] Then again, this qualification, presumably, is applicable only in respect of provisions concerning "remedies" and not to those on, for instance, fair and equitable judicial and administrative procedures. These procedures, as the Appellate Body has noted, represent "an internationally-agreed minimum standard which Members are bound to implement in their domestic legislation."[215] Indeed, in *US – Section 211*, both the Panel and the AB did not consider themselves as precluded – because of the qualification regarding "inconsistent" domestic law – from examining whether the US law in question violated the obligations regarding civil judicial procedures as embodied in Article 42 of the TRIPS Agreement.[216] Certainly, it would be most interesting to see how in future cases this qualification is defined and interpreted vis-à-vis other provisions of Part III of the TRIPS Agreement.

7 Concluding remarks

It is worth concluding this chapter by pointing out the effectiveness and good governance dimensions of the WTO obligations discussed in the preceding pages. To start with, WTO obligations regarding

second, that the conditions do not make it impossible in practice to exercise the rights conferred by Community law (effectiveness): see, e.g., Case 33–76, *Rewe-Zentralfinanz* v. *Landwirtschaftskammer* [1976] ECR 1989, para. 5; Case 45–76, *Comet* v. *Produktschap* [1976] ECR 2043, para. 13; and Case C-224/01, *Gerhard Kobler* v. *Republik Osterreich* [2003] ECR I-10239, para. 46. Then again, the ECJ has shaped the second requirement in a fashion that resulted in significant incursions into national procedural and remedies law. For instance, in the well-known *Factortame* case, it ruled that to ensure full effectiveness of Community law a national court must set aside rules of national law that prevent it from granting interim relief in a case concerning Community law: Case C-213/89, *R* v. *Secretary of State for Transport*, ex parte *Factortame* [1990] ECR I-2433, para. 21. The *Francovich* case, in which the ECJ insisted that in appropriate circumstances national courts are obliged to award compensation to individuals suffering loss in consequence of violation of Community law, is another conspicuous example of incursions of Community law into national remedies law: Cases C-6/90, C-9/90, *Francovich* v. *Italy* [1991] ECR I-5357, paras. 28–37. On the enforcement of EC law through national legal systems, see, generally, Bridge 1984; Lewis 1996; and Vervaele *et al.* 1999.

214 TRIPS Agreement, Article 44(2).

215 AB Report, *US – Section 211*, para. 206.

216 See above, n. 192. In this case, the Panel made a finding of a violation of Article 42, which was reversed on appeal. However, the AB did so not because of the "saving clause" for inconsistent domestic law, but rather on the ground that the US legislation concerned did not fail to provide procedures that are required under Article 42.

implementation of WTO commitments are more rigorous in ensuring effectiveness of the WTO treaty than the comparable obligations under public international law in general or under many contemporary international treaties. In particular, the requirements to ensure conformity of national laws with the WTO obligations entrench the "supremacy" of the WTO treaty, and thereby ensure its effectiveness. The transparency obligations enhance effectiveness in two vital ways. First, they enable individual traders and businesses to become acquainted with Members' trade laws and policies and thereby help them to engage in the activity (i.e. international trade) that the WTO treaty intends to promote. Second, transparency obligations, including the Trade Policy Review Mechanism, act as useful implementation devices through identification and evaluation of WTO-inconsistent (and also consistent) domestic trade laws and policies, assessment of the impact of domestic laws and policies on the multilateral trading system, informal peer pressure to bring non-conforming laws and policies into conformity with the WTO treaty, etc. The obligations regarding administration of national laws and regulations provide guarantees of uniform, impartial, reasonable, consistent, neutral, fair, equitable and objective administration of domestic laws and regulations on matters covered by the WTO treaty. These obligations provide guarantees of fairness to individual traders and businesses on the one hand, and prevent evasion of WTO commitments by means of objectionable administration of domestic laws, and regulations on the other. The obligations to make available domestic review procedures, remedies and enforcement procedures provide guarantees of judicial protection to individual traders and businesses.

In some measure, individuals almost become the "surrogate" subjects of WTO law in respect of the WTO treaty provisions on transparency, fair administration of domestic laws, and domestic judicial procedures and remedies. In various ways all of these provisions seek to ensure a domestic legal environment in which individual traders and businesses can make optimum use of the multilateral trading system put in place under the WTO. It is true that, unlike the EU, the WTO treaty does not envisage direct effect of WTO law whereby individuals can rely on WTO norms before domestic courts even in the absence of adoption or transformation of those norms as rules of national law. Yet, the systemic obligations regarding national law go a long way towards ensuring effectiveness of the WTO treaty in the domestic legal systems of WTO Members through the international guarantees of "supremacy" of WTO law, as well as guarantees of transparency, fairness and judicial protection in favor of individuals.

The policy objective of good governance at domestic level is equally inherent in the WTO obligations examined in this chapter. It may be recalled that substantive obligations prohibiting discrimination or measures that are more trade-restrictive than necessary provide guarantees of non-discrimination, substantive equality, proportionality, non-arbitrariness, non-abuse of domestic trade and foreign policy power, and the like. These and other substantive WTO obligations secure some protection for the commercial interests of foreign states, who have little or no representation in the political life of a state enacting or implementing a trade or trade-related law or measure. Furthermore, they ensure that national trade policy is not unjustifiably biased in favor of one domestic constituency (e.g., exporters, producers) at the expense of another domestic constituency (e.g., importers, consumers). Thus, in various important ways, substantive obligations promote good governance.

Transparency obligations – including those requiring prior notification and publication of proposed legislative and other measures and draft laws, establishment of national enquiry points to answer queries and provide documents regarding trade laws and regulations – have crucial good governance and due process implications. The Appellate Body has aptly highlighted this aspect of transparency obligations: "transparency . . . obviously [has] due process dimensions. The essential implication is that Members and other persons affected, or likely to be affected, by governmental measures imposing restraints, requirements and other burdens, should have a reasonable opportunity to acquire authentic information about such measures and accordingly to protect and adjust their activities or alternatively to seek modification of such measures."[217] The obligations regarding consistent, fair and equitable administration of domestic laws and regulations are no less due process- and good governance-spirited. Finally, the requirements to establish and maintain in domestic legal systems judicial, arbitral or administrative tribunals or procedures for "the prompt review and correction of administrative actions" also promote good governance through judicial protection of individuals and by providing guarantees of checks and balances.

[217] AB Report, *US – Underwear*, at 21.

4 WTO dispute settlement procedures and national law

1 Introduction

The last chapter examined the systemic framework of interaction between WTO law and national law. The present chapter turns to the institutional framework of that interaction. On the institutional side, it is, as already noted in the introductory chapter, the WTO's unique dispute settlement mechanism that makes the interaction highly prominent as well as important from a policy point of view. Systemically, the supremacy of WTO norms (flowing, inter alia, from Article XVI:4 of the WTO Agreement), coupled, of course, with their extensive coverage, sets limits, more than any other contemporary international treaty, on the policy choices of national law-makers and other authorities. And, institutionally, it falls, in large measure, upon the WTO dispute settlement organs to oversee whether national constituencies (legislative, administrative or judicial) are respecting those limits.[1] The reasons for this have already been touched upon. To recall, because of characteristics such as compulsoriness, exclusivity and automaticity, the WTO dispute settlement system is used truly extensively. Thus, in case of disagreement between Members as to whether a national law or other measure has transgressed the limits set by the WTO treaty, it is often the dispute settlement organs which, as third party arbiters, have the last word.

On occasion, the application of WTO norms to national laws by these organs even evokes the idea of a national (constitutional) court applying constitutional norms to inferior laws. A good example of this is provided by the parallel cases before the US courts and the WTO regarding a law enacted by the US state of Massachusetts, namely the Act Regulating State Contracts with Companies Doing Business with or in

[1] For a related perspective, see Iwasawa 2002.

Burma (Myanmar). This law prohibited Massachusetts's public authorities from purchasing goods or services from companies engaged in business with Myanmar because of the human rights abuses by its military government. Against this Act, the EC and Japan invoked the WTO dispute settlement procedure claiming that it violated the WTO Agreement on Government Procurement (GPA),[2] while private businesses initiated proceedings in US courts on the ground that it infringed a number of provisions of the US Constitution.

Eventually, the United States Court of Appeals for the First Circuit declared the Act to be unconstitutional.[3] As a result of this ruling the EC and Japan abandoned the proceedings before the WTO.[4] But, clearly, the ultimate outcome could have been similar had there been no ruling on "constitutionality" by US courts and if there were a WTO decision in favor of the claimants. Even if one were to be mindful of the differences between the two sets of proceedings,[5] their likeness is also remarkable. To wit, in both cases a judicial organ was called upon to decide whether a legislative instrument violated some superior legal norms - constitutional in one case and international in another. From this perspective, WTO dispute settlement organs can be seen as possessing, with respect to national laws and measures of Members, the power of "judicial review"[6] in the classical *Marbury* v. *Madison*[7] sense, and WTO dispute settlement as a further layer of judicial review of such laws and measures.[8]

[2] See WTO documents: WT/DS/88 and WT/DS/95: www.wto.org.

[3] See *National Foreign Trade Council* v. *Natsios* 181 F.3d 38 (1st Cir. 1999). See also Murphy 1999, 898–99.

[4] See *United States – Measure Affecting Government Procurement*, WT/DS88/5, WT/DS95/5 (February 12, 1999).

[5] These relate to the claimants involved (sovereign states before the WTO and private individuals before the US courts) and the applicable law (the GPA before the WTO and the US Constitution before the US courts). Notably, the EC and its member states appeared before the US courts as *amici curiae*.

[6] Cf., however, Chapter 6, pp. 161–62 below (discussing different tools or techniques that WTO adjudicative bodies need to combine in reviewing national measures).

[7] 1 Cranch 137 (1803).

[8] Cf. Cass 2001, 54–57; and Krisch & Kingsbury 2006, 3 (putting forward similar theses). No wonder WTO law has been described as "functionally equivalent to supranational law" and its application through the dispute settlement mechanism as "a further layer of governance" just like the EU, which "arose as a second (and in federal systems a third) layer of governance in the EU member countries during the last decades": Krajewski 2001, 171. As such, the application of WTO norms by its dispute settlement organs can have an impact on national law that is comparable, to an extent, to that of the application of EU law by the European Court of Justice: ibid. 170. The point of departure between EU law and WTO law is that the latter lacks elements of "supranationality" in a domestic context. That is to say, unlike EU law, there is no direct effect or supremacy of WTO law as far as domestic courts are concerned.

While from a policy point of view, cases of review of national laws can be more important – or, put differently, in these cases the interface between WTO law and national law may seem more pronounced[9] – these are not the only cases where the WTO dispute settlement organs are required to examine domestic laws. Such examination is necessary even in cases where the WTO-consistency of not the law itself but its application is at issue. Thus, parties to a dispute settlement case may disagree as to the WTO-compatibility of the manner of implementation of a law of the respondent Member by its administrative branch, for instance. In order to determine the proper scope of the administrative measure in question, the WTO dispute settlement organs may need, in such cases as well, to look into the parent national legislation in pursuance of which the measure is taken.[10] In any case, it is impossible to overemphasize the significance of the institutional dimension of the interaction between WTO law and national law, which has at its core the WTO dispute settlement organs.

The principal objective of this chapter is to understand the institutional mandate, that is to say the jurisdiction and competence, of those organs under the WTO treaty. In addition, the key features of the dispute settlement process relevant for purposes of the present study are also discussed.[11] This analysis is undertaken in general terms, bearing in mind that some readers may not be familiar with the mechanics and the dynamics of the WTO dispute settlement system. Nonetheless, at

[9] And by now, in a large number of cases, such review has been undertaken. See, e.g., *Canada – Periodicals*; *EC – Hormones I & II*; *US – Shrimp*; *US – FSC*; *US – Section 301*; *Canada – Pharmaceuticals*; *US – 1916 Act I & II*; *US – Copyright Act*; *US – Hot-Rolled Steel*; *US – Exports Restraints*; *US – Section 211*; *US – FSC 21.5 I & II*; *US – Carbon Steel*; *US – Section 129*; *US – Countervailing Measures*; *US – Offset Act*; *US – Softwood Lumber III*; *US – Rules of Origin*; *Japan – Apples*; *EC – Tariff Preferences*; *US – Gambling Services*; *Dominican Republic – Cigarettes*; and *Mexico – Rice*.

[10] See, e.g., *US – Gasoline*; and *US – Shrimp 21.5*.

[11] As hardly needs stating, it is not possible here (nor is it necessary) to undertake a much broader analysis or to address the very many issues pertaining to WTO dispute settlement that have already been explored in the existing vibrant literature. (One commentator has noted, quite rightly, that amongst various areas of WTO law, dispute settlement has received the most extensive academic attention: see J. H. H. Weiler 2001, 191–92.) See generally on the WTO dispute settlement system: Davey & Morrison 1997; Petersmann 1997a and 1997b; Cameron & Campbell 1998; Weiss 2000b; Vermulst & Graafsma 2002; Waincymer 2002; Palmeter & Mavroidis 2004; Yerxa & Wilson 2005; Collier & Lowe 1999, ch. 6; Sands *et al.* 1999, ch. 5; Bronckers & Quick 2000, chs. 17–20; D. L. M. Kennedy & Southwick 2002, chs. 15–22; 1(2) JIEL (1998); 4(1) JIEL (2001); 5(2) JIEL (2002); and 6(1) JIEL (2003). A detailed bibliography can be found in Monroe 2003.

more specific levels, the chapter will also clarify the jurisdiction and competence of the dispute settlement organs vis-à-vis the national law of Members. From the perspective of the relationship between WTO law and national law, this analysis is important, as must be evident from what has already been said above, on its own. However, it will also provide a useful and necessary background for Part II of this book, where analyses of four specific issues of national law that arise in the dispute settlement context are undertaken in some detail.

2 General overview of the dispute settlement mechanism

2.1 The DSU, the dispute settlement organs and the key procedures

As has already cropped up once or twice in the earlier chapters, the Dispute Settlement Understanding (DSU) is the governing WTO text on dispute settlement.[12] It is set out in Annex 2 of the WTO Agreement, forms an "integral part" of that Agreement, is "binding on all Members" and is in principle applicable to all WTO disputes.[13] The mechanism established under the DSU comprises a Dispute Settlement Body (DSB), ad hoc panels and a standing Appellate Body (AB).

The DSB is a plenary (and also a political) organ comprising representatives from all WTO Members.[14] Although, strictly, the DSB does not have any "adjudicative" power, it is vested with the important overall authority of administering the entire dispute settlement process. As such, it supervises the process of consultations between disputing Members; establishes adjudicative panels on request of a party to a dispute; adopts panel or Appellate Body reports; maintains surveillance over the implementation of rulings and recommendations; and, if need be, authorizes retaliatory measures for non-compliance with adopted panel or Appellate Body rulings.[15]

The dispute settlement process is triggered by notification and consultation. In the event of a dispute between Members over their respective WTO obligations, a party may request the other to enter into consultations. Such requests must at the same time be notified to the

[12] Its more formal (and full) title is: "Understanding on Rules and Procedures Governing the Settlement of Disputes."

[13] WTO Agreement, Article II:2, and DSU, Articles 1 and 23. According to Article III of the WTO Agreement, one of the principal functions of the WTO is to administer the DSU.

[14] It is, in fact, the General Council of the WTO acting under a different name and organization: see WTO Agreement, Article IV:3.

[15] DSU, Article 2. On the role of the DSB, see Mueller-Holyst 2005.

DSB.[16] If consultations fail, parties may agree to avail good offices, conciliation or mediation.[17] Alternatively, the complainant[18] may request the DSB to establish an ad hoc panel, and the DSB is required to accede to this request, unless it decides by consensus not to establish a panel.[19] (Such consensus is a practical impossibility because it cannot be achieved unless the party requesting establishment of a panel agrees not to establish it.)

Panels are composed of three (unless the parties agree on a panel of five) "well qualified governmental and/or non-governmental individuals," who are to serve in their individual capacities.[20] Nominations of panel members are proposed by the WTO Secretariat, and the parties are not to oppose such nominations except for compelling reasons. If there is no agreement on the panelists within twenty days after the establishment of the panel, its composition is determined by the Director-General of the WTO in consultation with the chairman of the DSB and the chairman of the Council or Committee established under the WTO agreement in question.[21] Panels conduct hearings on the dispute referred to them, and issue a report on the merits of the case.[22] Technically, legal consequences attach to a panel report only after it is adopted by the DSB. Adoption, however, is automatic in that it can be prevented only through the unlikely procedure of "negative consensus," i.e. a consensus not to adopt the report.[23]

A panel report may be appealed before the standing Appellate Body established under the DSU. (And, in case of appeal, the DSB is not to consider the panel report for adoption until after the completion of the appeal.) The Appellate Body is composed of seven members who are "persons of recognized authority, with demonstrated expertise in law, international trade and the subject matter of the [WTO] agreements generally." Appeals are heard before a three-member division of the AB, which may uphold, modify or reverse the legal findings of the panel.[24] The Appellate Body report (along with the panel report as upheld or modified by the AB) is then adopted by the DSB and is to be "unconditionally accepted" by the parties to the dispute, unless, again, there is a

[16] DSU, Article 4. [17] Ibid. Article 5.

[18] The expression used in the DSU is "the complaining party."

[19] DSU, Article 6. Consensus on a decision means the absence of formal objection by any Member when the decision is taken: WTO Agreement, Article IX, footnote 1; and DSU, Article 2, footnote 1.

[20] Notably, a legal background is not essential for a panelist. [21] DSU, Article 8.

[22] Ibid. Article 12. [23] Ibid. Article 16. [24] Ibid. Article 17.

"negative consensus" – i.e. a consensus not to adopt the report – in the DSB.

The above, very briefly, is the standard procedure for the settlement of any dispute under the WTO agreements. In addition, the DSU provides for some further procedures regarding disputes that may arise in respect of implementation of recommendations and rulings issued in pursuance of the panel or appeal procedures, or, in respect of retaliatory measures taken for non-compliance with such recommendations and rulings. These procedures include arbitration, as well as recourse, once again, to the standard DSU procedures.[25] In respect of any "original" or "new" dispute, as distinguished from implementation disputes, the only alternative to the standard (and compulsory) panel and appeal process is "arbitration within the WTO" under Article 25 of the DSU. However, up till now, Article 25 arbitration has been used only once, and that too not in respect of an "original" dispute but in respect of an implementation dispute concerning the findings of the panel issued earlier regarding the same matter.[26] Thus, under the prevailing state of affairs, it is the panels and the AB which exercise most of the WTO adjudicative powers.

2.2 *Coverage of the mechanism*

While later sections of this chapter look more closely into the institutional mandate of the panels and the AB, as a prelude to that a few words need to be said about the coverage of the WTO dispute settlement process in general. According to its Article 1.1, the DSU is applicable to "disputes brought pursuant to the consultation and dispute settlement provisions of the agreements listed in Appendix 1 to [the DSU]." The agreements so listed are the WTO Agreement itself, and the agreements contained in Annexes 1, 2 and 4 of the WTO Agreement (i.e. all of the agreements on trade in goods (including the GATT 1994); the GATS; the TRIPS; the DSU itself; and the plurilateral agreements). Collectively these agreements are referred to as the "covered agreements,"[27] and only one of the WTO agreements, namely the TPRM, is not such a covered agreement.[28] Thus, put rather simply, the coverage of the DSU is

[25] See, further, section 5 below.

[26] See *US – Copyright Act 25*. Like the panel procedure, Article 25 arbitration can be resorted to in respect of both original and implementation disputes.

[27] DSU, Article 1.1 and Appendix 1.

[28] Also excluded from the scope of the DSU are the various ministerial decisions and declarations that form part of the UR Final Act.

coextensive, for the most part, with that of the WTO itself.[29] While positively this means that all WTO-related matters fall within the substantive jurisdiction (jurisdiction *ratione materiae*) of the WTO dispute settlement organs, negatively it means that non-WTO matters do not so fall.[30]

As regards national law, this gives rise to a threshold question of "characterization." That is to say, with a view to determining whether a domestic law falls within their sphere of competence, panels or the AB need to decide – of course, if the matter is contentious between the disputing parties – whether the law is "trade" or "non-trade" legislation. It may be noted, in passing, that this question can also be critical in determining the applicable rules of WTO law. For instance, it cannot be ascertained whether the GATT 1994 or the GATS is applicable to a domestic law, without first characterizing the law as either goods or services legislation. In a number of cases this question arose quite sharply; and it is taken up in greater detail in the next chapter.

2.3 *Applicable law*

While Article 1.1 of the DSU establishes with sufficient clarity that the substantive jurisdiction of the WTO dispute settlement organs is limited to claims under the covered agreements, neither the DSU nor any of the other covered agreements provides, with similar clarity, for the applicable law in WTO dispute settlement.[31] Nonetheless, it is not in doubt that the covered agreements form the preeminent part of the applicable law. A number of DSU provisions are relevant in this context; from amongst those it may be useful to quote Article 3.2 (not least because it is significant, as seen below, for other reasons as well):

[29] Cf. Article II:1 of the WTO Agreement, which defines the "scope of the WTO" as follows: "The WTO shall provide the common institutional framework for the conduct of trade relations among its Members in matters related to the agreements and associated legal instruments included in the Annexes to this Agreement." It may be noted, parenthetically, that the Appellate Body has ruled that the competence of the WTO dispute settlement organs under the covered agreements remains unaffected even where competence on the same matter is concurrently allocated under those agreements to the political organs of the WTO (such as the General Council or various other Councils or Committees established under the WTO agreements). See AB Reports, *India – Quantitative Restrictions*, paras. 80–109; and *Turkey – Textiles*, para. 60. For a critique, see Roessler 2000.

[30] See generally on jurisdiction: Waincymer 2002, ch. 3; and Palmeter & Mavroidis 2004, ch. 2.

[31] Cf., in this regard, Article 38 of the ICJ, Statute, which provides for the applicable law before the ICJ, or UNCLOS Article 293, which provides for the applicable law before the courts and tribunals having jurisdiction under that Convention. There is no Article 38 or Article 293 "equivalent" in the WTO agreements.

The dispute settlement system of the WTO is a central element in providing security and predictability to the multilateral trading system. The Members recognize that *it serves to preserve the rights and obligations of Members under the covered agreements*, and to clarify the existing provisions of those agreements in accordance with customary rules of interpretation of public international law. *Recommendations and rulings of the DSB cannot add to or diminish the rights and obligations provided in the covered agreements.*[32]

The mandate to the dispute settlement organs under the italicized language of the above provision, apparently, is to apply the covered agreements. Similarly, DSU Articles 7 (which provides for panels' terms of reference) and 11 (which deals with the function of panels) require panels to examine matters referred to them *in the light of the covered agreements.*[33]

The difficult question, however, is whether, in addition to the covered agreements, "non-WTO" rules of public international law are applicable in WTO disputes and, if so, to what extent. This issue has already generated a huge amount of doctrinal literature and debate.[34] And it seems that there is no easy solution to this problem. But for a better understanding of it a distinction should be made between the substantive or primary rules (e.g., WTO rules regarding treatment of products, UNCLOS rules on the protection of the environment, ILO labor standards, etc.) and the incidental or secondary rules (e.g. procedural rules of international adjudication, rules of treaty interpretation, rules of state responsibility, etc.) of international law. It can be stated with some certainty that WTO adjudicative bodies are not precluded from having recourse to secondary non-WTO rules of international law as may be relevant and which are not incompatible with the covered agreements. For instance, in the course of judicial settlement of disputes, many issues may arise on which express guidance can be lacking in the DSU or the covered agreements, which, accordingly, should be resolved by reference to the pertinent rules of

32 DSU, Article 3.2 (italics added).

33 Articles 7 and 11 are quoted below at nn. 68 and 77 respectively. See also DSU Articles 3.4 and 3.5, which provide that the recommendations or rulings of the dispute settlement organs must be consistent with the covered agreements.

34 See, e.g., Palmeter & Mavroidis 1998; Marceau 1999 and 2001; Trachtman 1999, 342–43; Bartels 2001; Cameron & Gray 2001; Pauwelyn 2001, 2003a and 2003b; Waincymer 2002, ch. 7; Hu 2004; Abi-Saab 2005; and Lindroos & Mehling 2005. See also AB Reports, *EC – Poultry* (where a covered agreement was held to prevail over a bilateral agreement between the disputing parties: paras. 79–81); and *Argentina – Textiles* (holding that a Member's commitments to the IMF cannot modify its obligations under the covered agreements: paras. 64–74); and cf. AB Report, *US – Gasoline* (noting that the WTO agreements are "not to be read in clinical isolation from public international law": at 16).

international law. Indeed, in various cases such references, quite rightly, have already been made by panels and the AB. An example relevant for the purposes of the present work is *India – Patent I*, where the AB, in the absence of any provision in the DSU as to how domestic laws should be assessed, referred to (and also applied) the pertinent principles of general public international law.[35]

The extent to which non-WTO substantive rules are to apply before WTO dispute settlement organs is much more difficult to reduce to a simple formula. Here both the applicability and the degree and manner of the application could depend on a range of factors including, for instance, whether the non-WTO rules are relied upon to found or enlarge a WTO claim or simply as a defence, whether they are relevant in clarifying meanings of WTO rules, whether the substantive WTO provisions concerned make reference to non-WTO rules, whether the non-WTO rules invoked are in conflict with the WTO treaty and, if so, whether they can prevail over the WTO treaty pursuant to the "relevant" conflict rules,[36] and so on.[37] Indeed, the variables that may affect the applicability and the manner of application of the non-WTO substantive rules are too numerous to be enumerated and examined here without going beyond the scope of this work.[38] Accordingly, no such attempt is

[35] See AB Report, *India – Patent I*, paras. 65–66 (referring to the international law principles that national laws are facts before international courts or tribunals and that such courts or tribunals are not to interpret national laws: see, further, Chapter 7 below). Various other examples are summarized in Pauwelyn 2001, 563. Notably, it is common for international courts and tribunals in general to refer to and apply secondary rules of international law in treaty relations, unless the treaty concerned expressly dispenses with their application: see e.g., *Legal Consequences for States of the Continued Presence of South Africa in Namibia (South West Africa) Notwithstanding Security Council Resolution 276 (1970)*, Advisory Opinion, ICJ Rep. 16 (1971) at 47 (para. 96); and *Elettronica Sicula S.p.A. (ELSI)*, ICJ Rep. 15 (1989) at 42 (para. 50).

[36] There are at least three different "sources" from which such conflict rules may be derived: namely, the WTO treaty, the non-WTO treaty concerned, and rules of general international law, for instance, the *lex posterior derogat priori* and the *lex specialis derogat generali* rules.

[37] Needless to say, this issue is not unique to the WTO and does arise before other international courts and tribunals as well. As a recent example, reference may be made to the *Mox Plant* case where the question of whether and to what extent an UNCLOS arbitral tribunal can apply non-UNCLOS rules arose quite sharply: see in particular the submissions of the United Kingdom on this point, Transcripts of Hearings, *Mox Plant* case, *Ireland* v. *United Kingdom*, Day 3, June 12, 2003, at 52–61 (Mr. Bethlehem), available at www.pca-cpa.org (containing a perceptive analysis to the effect that applicable law cannot be utilized to found or enlarge the jurisdiction of a tribunal).

[38] Elaborate analyses of many such variables can, of course, be found elsewhere: see, in particular, the works cited in n. 34 above.

made at present. Instead, just a few vital issues are noted below simply to illustrate the significance and complexity of the matter.

Although the question of the applicability of non-WTO substantive international law in WTO dispute settlement is not a central theme of this work, it certainly is one of the most crucial questions pertaining not only to the WTO or its dispute settlement mechanism, but also to the entire international legal architecture. As noted on several occasions, the WTO dispute settlement mechanism is by far the most effective and compulsory system of adjudication in international law – a system that enables each Member to bring unilaterally a claim against any trade-related policy of another Member. In many instances the contested trade measure can be contained in laws or regulations dealing predominantly with other concerns, such as health, environment, human rights, etc., or an apparent trade measure can have important non-trade implications. In such instances in particular, but also as a general matter, the respondent Members are likely to invoke any possible justifications for their measure that can be found in non-WTO international law to fence off the claim raised by the claimant "unilaterally." The way in which such non-WTO issues are dealt with by the WTO bodies is significant both for the WTO and for international law in general. It may even affect the negotiation and formulation of new rules of international law. That is to say, the availability of non-WTO defenses could be an incentive for the conclusion of treaties that can serve as justifications for trade measures.

Given that the WTO does not exist in an international legal vacuum, WTO adjudicative bodies do not – and should not – turn a blind eye to other rules of international law. Yet there are important reasons to be cautious. In many instances, it would be possible to interpret the WTO and non-WTO rules in a compatible manner, especially because the WTO agreements themselves have sufficient flexibility to accommodate different non-trade concerns such as health, environment, national security, etc.[39] However, the perplexing question is whether, in case of irreconcilable conflict, the non-WTO rules should be allowed to prevail over WTO rules in a manner that takes away the rights of a Member under the WTO treaty. Because the developed and the developing countries may have different priorities, their views on this question may also differ significantly. On the one hand, a developed country Member may find it unacceptable that a non-WTO defense cannot be pursued fully

[39] Cf., for instance, GATT 1994, Articles XX, XXI; GATS, Articles XIV, XIV *bis*; and TRIPS Agreement, Articles 8, 73.

before a WTO panel. On the other hand, it may be rather frustrating to a developing country Member if its market access rights are held to have become non-existent because of non-WTO norms.

As far as conflict is concerned, a few words need also to be said about the last sentence of DSU Article 3.2 and DSU Article 19.2, which prohibits WTO dispute settlement organs from "add[ing] to or diminish[ing] the rights and obligations provided in the covered agreements."[40] It does not require a considerable stretch of imagination to view this language as a conflict clause in favor of WTO law.[41] That is to say, the language can be viewed as precluding the possibility of applying non-WTO rules that are incompatible with the covered agreements, because to do so would amount to "adding to or diminishing the rights and obligations" provided in those agreements. While some commentators have already endorsed this view,[42] Joost Pauwelyn has mounted a serious challenge against it. In essence, he argues that, although the language precludes panels and the AB creating new rights and obligations, it does not preclude the WTO Members themselves creating new norms. And when Members themselves create new norms the WTO adjudicative bodies cannot deny giving them effect. Accordingly, he concludes that the "adding to or diminishing" language is not at all a conflict clause but rather it relates to how panels and the AB are to interpret the WTO treaty.[43]

While at first sight Pauwelyn's argument does seem quite plausible, it is not free from difficulties. True, Members themselves can create new norms. But this does not resolve the question of whether new norms created by WTO Members are to prevail over the WTO covered agreements irrespective of the *forum* where they are created. Members can create new norms under the auspices of the WTO system (e.g. by amendment of the WTO treaty, by revising a schedule of concessions, by granting a waiver to a Member or by negotiating new agreements) as well as in non-WTO forums (e.g. in a conference convened to combat terrorism). It can be the case that norms created *within* and *beyond* the WTO system would not prevail over the covered agreements in exactly the *same* manner. Thus, in order to argue that the WTO adjudicative bodies would

[40] (Article 3.2 is quoted at p. 93 above.) Article 19.2 provides as follows: "In accordance with paragraph 2 of Article 3, in their findings and recommendations, the panel and Appellate Body cannot add to or diminish the rights and obligations provided in the covered agreements."

[41] Another – and also more apparent – role of this language is to serve as an express caveat against judicial activism on the part of the panels and the AB.

[42] See, e.g., Bartels 2001; and Marceau 2001.

[43] See Pauwelyn 2003a, 352–55, and 2003b, 1002–3.

not add to or diminish the WTO treaty by giving precedence to norms created outside the WTO, grounds additional to the Member countries' ability to create new norms would be required.

Certainly, the question of whether non-WTO norms can prevail over WTO norms is much more complex than it may appear to be. And given this extreme complexity, the best way forward possibly is to avoid a generalized approach and to consider each individual case on its own merits and in the light of its particular facts and circumstances.

2.4 *Rules of treaty interpretation*

Another significant aspect of DSU Article 3.2 is that it provides for the rules of interpretation that WTO adjudicative bodies are to follow in interpreting the WTO treaty. Thus, panels and the AB are to "clarify the existing provisions of [the covered] agreements in accordance with *customary rules of interpretation of public international law*." These rules are regarded as contained, inter alia, in Articles 31 and 32 of the Vienna Convention on the Law of Treaties – and, indeed, the AB so concluded in the very first appeal that it considered.[44] As such, those two VCLT articles are relied upon by panels and the AB as the basic rules for interpreting the WTO agreements.[45]

An important respect in which the question of treaty interpretation is reverted to in a subsequent chapter concerns its relationship with standard of review. One of the WTO agreements contains language that apparently encourages panels and the AB to conclude, with a view to upholding the validity of national measures in borderline cases, that provisions of that agreement are susceptible to multiple meanings. This gave rise to a considerable amount of confusion as to whether the VCLT interpretative rules can be utilized in such a fashion, that is to say, whether or not VCLT rules can lead to multiple interpretations of treaty texts. This apparent tension between provisions on treaty interpretation and standard of review and possible solutions to this problem is one of the various issues explored in Chapter 6 on standard of review.

Not surprisingly, unlike for treaty interpretation, there is no express guidance in the WTO treaty as to how domestic legal texts are to be

[44] AB Report, *US – Gasoline*, at 16. See also AB Report, *Japan – Alcohol II*, at 9–11. It is notable that, although the VCLT interpretative rules apply in the WTO because of their express incorporation, even in the absence of such incorporation they would have applied as secondary rules of international law.

[45] An excellent account of treaty interpretation by WTO judicial organs is to be found in Lennard 2002. See also Skouteris 1999; and Waincymer 2002, ch. 7.

interpreted. And, in the absence of such guidance, panels and the AB have already developed their own "canons of statutory interpretation,"[46] which, interestingly, mirror (as seen in Chapter 7 below) much of their approach with regard to treaty interpretation under the VCLT rules.

3 Panels' jurisdiction and competence

Turning now more specifically to panels' jurisdiction and competence, a number of issues are vital in this context, including: substantive conditions for instituting proceedings before panels (i.e. causes of action); type of "measures" that can be challenged in such proceedings; terms of reference of panels; and adjudicative functions that panels are required to perform under the DSU. The following sections address these in turn.

3.1 *Causes of action*

The substantive conditions for initiation of panel proceedings can be found in Article XXIII of the GATT 1994, which has been carried forward without any change from the predecessor GATT 1947. Various other WTO agreements either expressly incorporate Article XXIII or contain a provision similar to its wording.[47] Under Article XXIII or the corresponding provisions of the other covered agreements, a claim may be presented by a WTO Member,[48] if:

(1) any *benefit* accruing to that Member under a covered agreement *is being nullified or impaired*; or
(2) the attainment of any *objective* of a covered agreement *is being impeded.*

In addition, it must be demonstrated that the above (i.e. the nullification or impairment of benefits or the impedance of objective) is a result of any of the following:

[46] This is a municipal law expression, which in that context refers to the detailed rules of statutory construction that one encounters in all well-developed municipal legal systems.

[47] DSU Article 3.1 also confirms the general applicability of the principles of GATT Article XXIII. A compilation of the provisions of the other covered agreements corresponding to Article XXIII is contained in World Trade Organization 2001, 33–58.

[48] It may be noted that the jurisdiction *ratione personae* of panels (or for that matter of WTO dispute settlement organs in general) encompasses all WTO Members and is also limited in respect of such Members (which are either sovereign states or separate customs territories possessing full autonomy in the conduct of their external commercial relations: see WTO Agreement, Article XII). Thus non-Members, including private entities or individuals, do not have a right of standing before panels.

(a) a failure by the respondent Member to comply with its obligations under the agreement concerned (i.e. a violation of the agreement); or
(b) the application by the respondent Member of any measure, whether it conflicts with the agreement concerned *or not* (commonly referred to as "non-violation"); or
(c) the existence of any other situation.

Thus, Article XXIII envisages six different types of complaints, that is to say, complaints for nullification or impairment of benefits resulting from any of the three different circumstances listed in (a) to (c) above, or for impedance of objectives resulting, similarly, from any of those three different circumstances.[49]

However, of the six types of complaints only two have been used in practice, namely, "violation complaints" for nullification or impairment of benefits; and "non-violation complaints" for nullification or impairment of benefits.[50] Again, the total number of GATT/WTO cases in which non-violation claims were raised is very few, and no such claim has yet been successful under the WTO.[51] Thus, as a matter of practice, violation nullification used to be the predominant cause of action under the GATT, and it has remained so under the WTO as well. Theoretically, under this cause of action a violation of the covered agreements by itself is not sufficient to entitle a complainant to relief, because to be so entitled the violation must result in nullification or impairment of benefits. However, in 1962, a GATT Panel ruled that a violation constitutes a prima facie case of nullification or impairment;[52] and this prima facie rule has ever since been applied as a presumption that is virtually irrefutable.[53] The net result is that, for all practical purposes, WTO litigation turns,

[49] See Petersmann 1997a, 72–74.

[50] Ibid. 73–74. Petersmann notes that, out of a total of more than 250 GATT disputes, only in 7 cases did the complainants refer to "impedance of objective" or the existence of "other situations" (ibid. 74). (See also Jackson *et al.* 1995, 348–64.) The position has not changed under the WTO. And, notably, no GATT/WTO panel has ever made a finding under the heads of impedance of objectives or the existence of situations. Cf. also DSU Article 26.2 which further restricts the use of situation complaints.

[51] Out of a total of 136 WTO cases in which panel reports have so far been issued, non-violation claims were put forward only in 4, but in none of those cases were such claims successful: see *Japan – Film*; *Korea – Procurement*; *EC – Asbestos*; and *US – Offset Act*. The AB has already noted that "non-violation" is an exceptional remedy which must be approached with caution: see AB Report, *EC – Asbestos*, para. 186. Cf. also DSU Article 26.1 containing special provisions on non-violation complaints. See, generally, Cottier & Schefer 1997; Cho 1998; and Williams 1999.

[52] *Uruguayan Recourse*, para. 15.

[53] *US – Superfund*, para. 5.1.7. The presumption is now codified in DSU Article 3.8.

like that in any other adjudicative system, on legality[54] – i.e., whether any provision of the covered agreements has been violated or not.[55]

3.2 *What can be challenged*

A WTO claim, then, is essentially a claim that the respondent Member has infringed obligations under the covered agreements (or, very exceptionally, that although it did not infringe such obligations it has nullified benefits accruing to the complainant under those agreements). But what can be the subject-matter of such a claim or, put differently, what can be challenged before WTO panels? The key word in this context is "measure" (or, in plural, "measures"), which is customarily used to refer to the "act" of the respondent Member that is challenged in panel proceedings.[56]

Although "measure/s" is one of the most frequently used words of the WTO treaty, no attempt has been made to define it either generally or for purposes of dispute settlement in particular. However, the WTO services agreement contains a definition of this term which usefully lists various heads that come under it. According to that definition: "'measure' means any measure by a Member, whether in the form of a *law*, regulation, rule, procedure, decision, administrative action, *or any other form*."[57]

As in the above definition, in WTO parlance in general, including its dispute settlement practice, the term "measure" has the widest possible connotation. Accordingly, a WTO Member can bring a dispute settlement claim against another Member in respect of any action (or omission[58]) attributable to the latter, regardless of the form that the action might take.[59] Furthermore, such a claim can be brought even

[54] Cf., for instance, EC Treaty, Articles 227, 230 and 232 (ex Articles 170, 173 and 175).

[55] Thus, while it is possible to be amazed at first sight by the departure of the WTO system, through its reliance on nullification of benefits rather than on infringement of rights or rules, from the traditional approach of formal adjudicative mechanisms (cf., for instance, Collier & Lowe 1999, 96–97), under the relevant practice, as it has evolved, the departure is not of much real significance. (It may be suggested in passing that the WTO treaty should be revised to reflect the actual position more accurately.)

[56] See, e.g., DSU Articles 3.7, 4.2, 6.2, 10.4, 12.10, 19.1, 21.2, 21.5, 21.8, 22.1, 22.2, 22.8, 22.9, 24.1 and 26.1; and Yanovich & Voon 2005.

[57] GATS, Article XXVIII:(a) (italics added).

[58] For instance, omission to take positive steps under Article XVI:4 of the WTO Agreement to ensure conformity of national laws with the WTO obligations. Cf. Panel Report, *Dominican Republic – Cigarettes*, para. 7.369.

[59] As regards attribution, WTO law does not depart in major respects from the general public international law principles concerning state responsibility. See, generally, the

against governmental measures that are technically not binding on private actors, but, nonetheless, are effective in bringing about certain specified behavior on the part of those actors.[60]

While the entire range of governmental measures – legislative, judicial or administrative – are amenable to WTO dispute settlement proceedings, in some of the subsequent chapters more attention is devoted, for obvious reasons, to cases concerning national laws, i.e. laws enacted by Members' legislatures. As already noted above, cases in which national law issues arise can be put into two broad groups: first, cases where the WTO-compatibility of the law itself is challenged (commonly referred to as challenge to national legislation per se); and second, cases where the WTO-compatibility of not the law itself but its application is challenged. The underlying factual circumstances of the second category of cases can be readily conceived: these are cases where a Member takes specific action, albeit in pursuance of a law, affecting particular trade or trading rights of another Member. But the first category of cases is also very common; and as hardly needs restating once again, the mere WTO-incompatibility of a piece of domestic legislation, even if it is not applied against any particular trade, renders it susceptible to dispute settlement claims.[61]

It is possible to imagine a number of circumstances in which panels may be called upon to decide WTO-conformity of legislation per se. A party may challenge a law prior to its entry into force.[62] A law which is not being enforced but which exists in the statute books of a Member may also be challenged.[63] A piece of legislation may be challenged because, although its application is consistent with GATT/WTO obligations,[64] or is claimed by the defendant government to be so consistent,[65] in the complaining party's view it contains GATT/WTO-incompatible

ILC's Draft Articles on State Responsibility, Articles 2 and 4ff. and commentaries to those Articles, reproduced in Crawford 2002, 81ff.; Garcia-Rubio 2001; and Villalpando 2002.

60 See, e.g., Panel Reports, *Japan – Agricultural Products I*, paras. 3.2.6, 3.4.32 and 5.4.1.4; *Japan – Semi-Conductors*, paras. 106–17; *Japan – Film*, paras. 10.42–56; and *Argentina – Hides and Leather*, paras. 11.15–21; and AB Report, *Korea – Beef*, para. 146.

61 This can be viewed as flowing from Article XVI:4 of the WTO Agreement. However, as may be recalled from the previous chapter, even before the coming into being of the WTO and the introduction of Article XVI:4, the dispute settlement practice of the predecessor GATT had already evolved to the same position.

62 See, e.g., Panel Reports, *US – Superfund*; and *Argentina – Textiles*, para. 6.45.

63 See, e.g., Panel Reports, *US – Malt Beverages*, para. 5.60; and *India – Patent I*, para. 7.35.

64 See, e.g., *Thai – Cigarettes* and *US – Tobacco*.

65 See, e.g., *India – Patent I & II*.

provisions.[66] Finally, in certain circumstances a party may want to challenge legislation per se in addition to challenging a measure taken under the legislation.[67]

3.3 *Terms of reference of panels*

DSU Article 7 provides for panels' standard terms of reference as follows:

> 1. Panels shall have the following terms of reference unless the parties to the dispute agree otherwise within 20 days from the establishment of the panel:
>
> > "To *examine, in the light of the relevant provisions in (name of the covered agreement[s]* cited by the parties to the dispute), the matter referred to the DSB by (name of party) in document . . . and to *make such findings as will assist the DSB in making the recommendations or in giving the rulings provided for in that/those agreement(s).*"
>
> 2. Panels shall address the relevant provisions in any covered agreement or agreements cited by the parties to the dispute.[68]

WTO panels generally act under the above terms of reference, because they apply automatically unless different terms are agreed upon by the disputing parties. This device entitles a complainant to define the subject-matter of litigation *unilaterally*; and, for this reason, it has been praised as "a decisive progress" over some other international adjudicative processes – arbitration for instance – where the terms of litigation are defined by agreement between the parties.[69] Setting aside the question of "praiseworthiness," it may be observed that, like many other characteristics of the WTO dispute settlement mechanism (recall its compulsory, automatic and exclusive nature), the ability to define unilaterally the terms of reference enables a complainant, if it so chooses, to commence proceedings even in respect of highly sensitive national legislation of a respondent Member.[70]

[66] See, e.g., *US – Section 301*.

[67] See, e.g., Panel Reports, *EEC – Parts and Components*; *US – Non-Rubber Footwear*, para. 6.12; and *Canada – Aircraft*, paras. 9.121, 9.204.

[68] Italics added. [69] Pescatore 1991 – loose-leaf, 24.

[70] Two cases that readily come to mind in this context are: *US – Section 301*; and *US – FSC*. The former concerned a US law that has been a subject of much criticism since the 1980s (see, e.g., Bhagwati & Patrick 1991; Puckett & Reynolds 1996; and Schaefer 1998), while the latter concerned another US law that was commonly perceived as GATT-inconsistent by other trading nations (see, e.g., Hudec 1993, 94–98, and 2003; Stehmann 2000; and Qureshi & Grynberg 2002). Although both pieces of legislation predated the WTO by many years, neither of them was challenged under the non-automatic and non-compulsory dispute settlement mechanism of the predecessor

A different facet of Article 7 concerns panels' substantive jurisdiction. To wit, the Article,[71] read in conjunction with DSU Article 1.1 and Article XXIII of the GATT 1994 and other similar provisions on causes of action, makes it abundantly clear that panels' jurisdiction comprises claims of violation of the *covered agreements* (or, rarely, non-violation nullification under *those agreements*). That it is a rather limited substantive jurisdiction hardly requires any mentioning.

A comparison of the jurisdiction of panels (or, for that matter, of the WTO dispute settlement organs in general) with that of the International Court of Justice (or its predecessor the PCIJ), which has, under Article 36(1) of its Statute, an unlimited substantive jurisdiction over "all cases which the parties refer to it,"[72] need not detain us here.[73] But it may be noted that the wider substantive jurisdiction – extending virtually to any case that the parties may wish to submit – makes it possible for the International Court to hear and adjudicate a particular type of disputes concerning domestic law that WTO panels are unlikely to confront.

Specifically, in certain cases decided by the PCIJ the essential issues were of pure national law, and the rules of international law, strictly speaking, were not at issue. In other words, in those cases, instead of international law, a particular municipal law was applied by the PCIJ as the applicable substantive law.[74] Because of their more limited jurisdiction (i.e. claims under the covered agreements), WTO panels are not likely to face such disputes.[75] Having said so, it needs to be pointed out that nonetheless a panel may find it necessary, albeit in a rather different context, to adjudicate an entirely factual dispute as to the meaning

GATT. By contrast, as soon as the WTO and its dispute settlement mechanism came into being, complaints were lodged against both of them.

71 Cf. the italicized language.

72 Statute of the International Court of Justice, Article 36(1).

73 For an interesting overview of the jurisdictional and other differences between the ICJ and the WTO adjudicative bodies, see Bethlehem 2000.

74 See *Serbian Loans* case, PCIJ Ser. A No. 20 (1929); and *Brazilian Loans* case, PCIJ Ser. A No. 21 (1929). Cf. *Norwegian Loans* case, ICJ Rep. 9 (1957) at 13, 31–32 (Separate Opinion of Judge Badawi).

75 However, the parties to a dispute may extend the jurisdiction of a panel beyond matters concerning the interpretation and application of the covered WTO agreements, either by agreeing to special terms of reference pursuant to Article 7.3 of the DSU or by referring the dispute to arbitration under Article 25 of the DSU. Thus, theoretically, it is possible for the parties to refer a dispute concerning solely the application of municipal laws to a panel, but as a practical matter it is difficult to imagine that such a possibility will be materialized.

of a domestic law. Thus, what can happen is that the disputing parties before a panel may hold opposite views as to the correct interpretation of a domestic law and the panel, though not required to *apply* that law, may be called upon to resolve the disagreement over its correct interpretation.

US – Section 129 provides a good example. In this case, Canada claimed that the US law at issue was inconsistent with a number of WTO provisions in that it required US authorities to take certain actions, which, if taken, would violate those WTO provisions. The Panel identified two distinct issues in this Canadian complaint: first, that the US law required the actions alleged by Canada; and second, that those actions would contravene the WTO provisions that had been invoked. The Panel thought that those two issues were capable of separate examination and that if Canada were to fail in establishing one of them an analysis of the other could be dispensed with. On this basis, the Panel first undertook an independent examination of the US law (i.e. an analysis of the law without any reference whatsoever to any of the WTO provisions invoked) and found that the law did not require the alleged actions. As a result, it was not necessary to examine or interpret the WTO provisions invoked, and the Panel was able to make its ruling *solely* on the basis of its findings regarding the meaning or scope of the US law.[76]

3.4 *Functions of panels*

So far, the sphere of competence of panels and the circumstances in which they may be seized of disputes concerning domestic laws have been discussed; the question that follows is: what are their functions when seized of a dispute? These are provided for in DSU Article 11, the pertinent part of which reads as follows:

> The function of panels is to assist the DSB in discharging its responsibilities under this Understanding and the covered agreements. Accordingly, *a panel should make an objective assessment of the matter* before it, *including an objective assessment of the facts of the case and the applicability of and conformity with the relevant covered agreements*, and make such other findings as will assist the DSB in making the recommendations or in giving the rulings provided for in the covered agreements.[77]

Thus, while generally a panel is required to make an objective assessment of the entire matter before it, more specifically it is required to make

[76] Panel Report, *US – Section 129*, paras. 6.23–25, 6.127–28. [77] Italics added.

such an assessment in relation to three different (but, of course, related) aspects of a case: (i) the facts; (ii) the applicability of the relevant rules; and (iii) the conformity of the facts with the relevant rules.

Part II of this book turns, in one way or another, on different aspects of these panel functions and accordingly details about them should not detain us here; but this seems an appropriate place to set out the organization and the basic features of the four chapters in Part II. Chapter 5, as already noted, concerns the threshold question of characterization – that is to say, typifying national laws for purposes of determining whether WTO rules are applicable and, if so, which particular rules are to apply. As such, this chapter relates in some respect to the function of determining the applicability of the relevant rules.

The problem of standard of review examined in Chapter 6 turns squarely on panels' functions regarding ascertainment of facts and determining the conformity of the facts with the relevant rules. There are different tools or techniques as well as standards and criteria that are applied both for purposes of ascertaining the relevant facts and for determining their conformity with the WTO agreements. Collectively, these form the subject-matter of Chapter 6.

The general analysis of the framework and the standards and criteria of review made in Chapter 6 is then carried forward in the next two chapters to look into two more specific aspects of WTO review of national measures. Thus, in the course of such review how the content or meaning of national law is determined as a factual matter is examined in Chapter 7. And Chapter 8 examines a particular tool, namely the distinction between mandatory and discretionary legislation, that is utilized in determining the WTO-compatibility of national laws.

4 Appellate jurisdiction

The mandate of the Appellate Body can be found in three rather short paragraphs of DSU Article 17, which provide as follows:

17.6 An appeal shall be *limited to issues of law* covered in the panel report *and legal interpretations* developed by the panel . . .
17.12 The Appellate Body shall address each of the issues raised in accordance with paragraph 6 during the appellate proceeding.
17.13 The Appellate Body may *uphold, modify or reverse the legal findings and conclusions* of the panel.[78]

[78] Italics added.

These provisions (cf. the italicized language) restrict appeals to questions of law and by implication exclude findings of fact from the scope of the appellate review.[79] It is not necessary for present purposes to go into the many intricacies of the appeal process;[80] instead, it will suffice to say how the appellate jurisdiction relates to the three panel functions noted in the preceding section.

The situation is fairly simple in respect of panel functions (ii) and (iii) which concern questions of law and accordingly are within the scope of appellate review. (Of course, one needs to be mindful that in any system of appeal limited only to legal questions, often – *as a practical matter and in specific instances* – the distinction between the facts and the law can be quite intractable.[81]) In respect of function (i) the position is not so straightforward, however. On the one hand, the AB is barred from deciding issues of fact; on the other hand, it can decide whether a panel has made an objective assessment of the facts as required by DSU Article 11, which, quite rightly, was held by the AB to be a legal question.[82] Again, as discussed in greater detail in Chapter 7, the AB has put the threshold for interfering with a panel's factual findings on the ground of a violation of Article 11 at too high a level, and thereby turned it into an almost impossible-to-use "escape hatch."[83] But, interestingly, that did not prevent the AB from reviewing in various cases, albeit on different grounds, panels' findings on national law. This is a notable development given that, under the DSU, "objective assessment" apparently is the only ground on which the AB can interfere with panels' factual findings. The AB's reasoning for its intervention in respect of questions of national law, as well as other related policy matters (e.g. whether such intervention is a welcome development or not), are discussed later in Chapter 7, after the issue of how panels, for their part, determine the content of national law is explored in the same chapter.

[79] AB Report, *EC – Hormones*, para. 132.

[80] See generally: Sacerdoti 1997; Lugard 1998; McRae 1998; Joergens 1999; Vermulst 1999; Bronckers & McNelis 2000; Kuyper 2000; Shoyer & Solovy 2000; Van den Bossche 2000 and 2005b; Bacchus 2002; Ehlermann 2002 and 2003; Steger 2002; Waincymer 2002, ch. 10; Smith 2003; Palmeter & Mavroidis 2004, ch. 6; V. Hughes 2005; and Voon & Yanovich 2006.

[81] Kuyper 2000, for instance, discusses a number of issues in the context of the WTO appeal process that lie "on the borderline between the facts and the law" and that concern panel functions (ii) and (iii).

[82] AB Report, *EC – Hormones I & II*, para. 132.

[83] Kuyper 2000, 318.

5 Dispute settlement recommendations and rulings and their implementation

5.1 *Background*

Preceding sections tried, inter alia, to understand two basic questions: what is the adjudicative competence of panels and the AB regarding national "measures" including laws? And what are the functions that they may need (or be called upon) to perform in adjudicating disputes concerning such measures or laws? The present section turns to two different, but by no means less pertinent, questions. First, what adverse rulings or recommendations can panels and the Appellate Body issue to a respondent Member at the end of the adjudicative process? And second, is a losing Member obliged, as a matter of WTO law,[84] to comply with those adverse recommendations and rulings? A clear-cut answer to the first question can be found in DSU Article 19.1; and it is in the following terms: "Where a panel or the Appellate Body concludes that a measure is inconsistent with a covered agreement, *it shall recommend that the Member concerned bring the measure into conformity with that agreement.* In addition to its recommendations, the panel or Appellate Body may suggest ways in which the Member concerned could implement the recommendations."[85]

Thus, clearly, in respect of a WTO-inconsistent national law, panels or the AB may – or indeed, should – recommend that the respondent Member bring the law into conformity with the relevant WTO obligations. But this does not tell us much about whether it is at all possible for the WTO dispute settlement process to compel a Member to secure legislative changes, either by introducing new laws or by repealing or amending existing ones. If Members are not obliged to bring non-conforming national laws into conformity in pursuance of panel or Appellate Body recommendations, and may, instead, provide "reparation" to the successful party in some other form, then the process is one which does not compel legislative changes by Members. Accordingly, unless and until the second question is answered, it is not possible to know how intrusive the WTO dispute settlement system really is – whether it can in fact be used to force internal legal reform or legislative changes.

[84] Thus the position that may exist under the national law of Members is not considered here: see, e.g., Zonnekeyn 1999; and Rosas 2001.

[85] Italics added; footnotes omitted.

However, unlike the first question, the second does not have any ready-made answer/s. And it is also not possible to come up with a general answer that either can explain the outcomes of the 136 cases in which panel reports have so far been issued or will be accurate in respect of the outcomes of all future cases. The relevant DSU provisions present an interesting paradox such that two diametrically opposite viewpoints have been put forward in the literature.[86] On the one hand, many prominent commentators argue that Members indeed are obliged to "specifically perform" dispute settlement recommendations by bringing non-conforming measures into conformity,[87] while on the other hand it is argued by other commentators with equal force that no such specific performance is required under the DSU, and a losing Member may, instead of specific performance, provide compensation or suffer retaliation by the successful party.[88] Clearly, to explore the answer/s to the second question one needs to understand the remedies available under the DSU.

If the above has not already generated enough curiosity about WTO remedies and the related enforcement mechanism, and demonstrated their significance for purposes of the present study, the following certainly will. Setting aside the issue of how leniently or strictly the DSU provisions concerned can be interpreted at a theoretical level, practically, some of the "judgments" issued by the WTO adjudicative bodies cannot but impress upon close observers the idea of a "regime" that has grave implications – implications far more profound than what can transpire from the DSU provisions – for Members' legislatures. For instance, those bodies not only directed Members to bring national laws into conformity but in a number of cases also issued "judgments" as to *how expeditiously national parliaments* – including parliaments as powerful as the US Congress – *must act* in introducing the necessary legislative measures for that purpose.[89] Even though many lawyers who do not specialize in WTO law, coming either from the public international law tradition or from municipal legal traditions, may be utterly surprised (some even shocked!) if they are told that such judgments were issued,

[86] In this regard the DSU does not contain clear or explicit language – language as clear and explicit as Article 94 of the United Nations Charter, for instance. Under that article every UN Member is "to comply with the decision of the International Court of Justice in any case to which it is a party."

[87] See, e.g., Jackson 1997b and 2004; Waincymer 2002, ch. 9; and, for a traditional public international law perspective, Gray 2000, 411–12.

[88] See, e.g., Bello 1996; Sykes 2000; Palmeter & Alexandrov 2002; and Schwartz & Sykes 2002.

[89] See the cases cited in n. 112 below.

given the WTO implementation mechanism the decisions concerned are not at all unusual.[90] And, as discussed below, compared to other formal international dispute settlement mechanisms, the WTO system is far more effective in ensuring compliance with dispute settlement rulings or "judgments."

Having said so, from a different perspective, it needs to be borne in mind that it is only international law and its processes that one is talking about. These are rules and procedures agreed upon by "sovereign" nations, which, unlike municipal law and its courts, are not backed by any monopoly of force that can secure compliance even where it is not forthcoming easily. As Judith Bello puts it:

> Like the GATT rules that preceded them, the WTO rules are simply not "binding" in the traditional sense. When a panel established under the WTO Dispute Settlement Understanding issues a ruling adverse to a member, there is no prospect of incarceration, injunctive relief, damages for harm inflicted or police enforcement. The WTO has no jailhouse, no bail bondsmen, no blue helmets, no truncheons or tear gas.
>
> Rather, the WTO – essentially a confederation of sovereign national governments – relies upon voluntary compliance. The genius of the GATT/WTO system is the flexibility with which it accommodates the national exercise of sovereignty, yet promotes compliance with its trade rules through incentives.[91]

5.2 *Remedies*

To turn now more specifically to WTO remedies, the DSU envisages three different types of remedies, which in traditional public international law terminology can be described as (i) *restitutio in integrum*; (ii) compensation; and (iii) countermeasures.[92] Despite this borrowing of terminology for purposes of putting the WTO remedies against the broader picture of public international law, it must be emphasized that under the DSU all three remedies have a WTO-specific meaning, which differs in some respects from that under international law in general.[93] For instance, unlike their international law counterparts, WTO remedies are prospective in nature and, as such, they do not aim to redress past injury but are concerned only with future conduct.[94]

[90] See, further, pp. 112–13 below. [91] Bello 1996, 416–17.

[92] See Kuyper 1997. Cf. Gray 1987, 11–21; and Crawford 2002, 211–30, 281–305.

[93] The "lex specialis" nature of WTO remedies and implementation mechanisms is well recognized in the literature: see, e.g., Crawford 2002, 307.

[94] Panel Report, *US – Certain Products*, para. 6.106. See also Kuyper 1997, 282–83; Grane 2001, 763–69; and Crawford 2002, footnote 863. Cf., however, Matsushita *et al.* 2003, 82–84; and *Australia – Leather 21.5*; for a critique of this case see: Goh & Ziegler 2003.

In international law *restitutio in integrum* is often divided into two categories: legal and material. The former essentially is an order for the repeal or modification of the offending measure of the respondent state's legislature, executive or judiciary, while the latter is an order for the return or restoration of territory, persons, property, etc.[95] There is no scope of material restitution under the DSU, not least because WTO remedies are prospective and not retrospective in nature. Thus, it is only legal restitution (in the WTO context, some authors also describe this remedy as "specific performance"[96]), which is available under the DSU. Legal restitution is also the most preferred WTO remedy and the only remedy that panels and the AB are expressly required to order at the end of the adjudicative process. (Recall that if it is found that a measure is WTO-inconsistent, under DSU Article 19.1, the panel or the AB is to recommend that the Member concerned bring the measure into conformity with the WTO obligations.)

The primacy of the remedy of legal restitution is also underlined in various other places within the DSU.[97] Article 3.7, for instance, provides that "the first objective of the dispute settlement mechanism is usually to secure the withdrawal of the measure concerned." The other two remedies are not available if the first remedy works; furthermore, even where the other remedies are resorted to, they are to be applied *only temporarily pending the withdrawal of the non-conforming measure.*[98]

Generally the DSU prefers "immediate" or "prompt" withdrawal of the non-conforming measure;[99] if, however, it is impracticable to comply immediately, the Member concerned must do so within a "reasonable period of time," which typically should not exceed fifteen months.[100] If the losing Member fails to withdraw the measure within a reasonable period of time, it must enter into negotiations with the complaining party with a view to developing "mutually acceptable compensation."[101] For WTO purposes, compensation is not monetary damages for past injury, but rather *trade advantages* to be granted in future. If agreement on satisfactory compensation is not possible, then, as the last resort, the DSU entitles the prevailing party to take countermeasures, subject

[95] Crawford 2002, 214–15; and Gray 1987, 13.
[96] See, e.g., Sykes 2000. For present purposes both expressions are used interchangeably.
[97] According to John Jackson, eleven DSU provisions are relevant in this context, which are Articles 3.4, 3.5, 3.7, 11, 19.1, 21.1, 21.6, 22.1, 22.2, 22.8 and 26.1(b): see Jackson 1997b, 63.
[98] DSU, Articles 3.7 and 22.1 [99] Ibid. Articles 3.7 and 21.1.
[100] Ibid. Article 22.3. [101] Ibid. Article 22.2.

to authorization by the DSB of such measures. The DSB, however, is to act under the negative consensus rule in this regard and accordingly, if requested, authorization is granted automatically.[102] For WTO purposes, countermeasures take the form of suspension of the application of trade concessions or other obligations under the covered agreements on a discriminatory basis vis-à-vis the losing Member.[103]

Commentators who argue that a losing Member need not specifically perform panel or AB recommendations rely mostly on the availability of compensation and countermeasures as alternative remedies. Thus, for instance, apart from her general sovereignty-based argument, Judith Bello argued, more specifically, that under the DSU bringing an offending measure into conformity is not the only option available to a losing Member. But rather, a losing Member may choose, if it so prefers, to remain in violation and decide either to compensate the successful party or to suffer likely retaliation (i.e. countermeasures) by that party. From this perspective the WTO system is viewed as one where all that matters is the maintenance of the balance of trade concessions or advantages agreed upon by Members. If a respondent Member upsets that balance by a non-conforming measure, it is possible to revert back to the delicately set equilibrium of concessions or advantages not only by the withdrawal of the offending measure, but also through the grant of compensatory concessions by the respondent Member or by suspension of concessions by the prevailing Member against the losing Member.[104]

Bello's arguments prompted an immediate response by John Jackson in support of the proposition that compliance with dispute settlement rulings is *obligatory*. For Professor Jackson, the mere availability of two alternative remedies, which in any case are expressly stated to be temporary, does not mean that a respondent Member is free to ignore panel or AB recommendations and provide compensation or suffer retaliation instead.[105] Subsequently, many other seasoned commentators joined in the debate highlighting many different threads and dimensions of both lines of arguments.[106]

While it may be the subject-matter of an ongoing debate whether Members are "obliged" to comply with panel or AB recommendations, and it may also be the case that as a matter of "realpolitik" occasionally Members may prefer the alternatives, one may not doubt that the DSU establishes a clear preference for the withdrawal of non-conforming

[102] Ibid. Article 22.6. [103] Ibid. Articles 3.7 and 22. [104] Bello 1996, 417–18.
[105] Jackson 1997b and 2004. [106] See, for instance, the works cited in nn. 87–88 above.

measures, and, for that matter, a clear preference for the remedy of legal restitution. This is a notable feature, because, although in pursuance of the well-known *Chorzow Factory* case,[107] *restitutio in integrum* is usually cited as the first remedy under traditional public international law, as a matter of practice, the actual award of restitution is not very common in international law.[108] And this is more so in respect of legal restitution, which is perceived as having important drawbacks in that it raises difficult issues of the relationship between international and municipal law. More specifically, it is viewed as problematic because it may require the repeal or amendment of laws duly adopted by parliaments whose constitutionality is not questioned by the highest courts of the country concerned.[109] By contrast, as hardly needs restating once again, each and every WTO panel or AB decision ends with an order for legal restitution.

5.3 *Enforcement mechanism*

In order to understand the degree to which the WTO can compel or induce the removal of non-conforming measures one needs to take into account – along with the prioritized system of WTO remedies – the mechanism for the enforcement of dispute settlement rulings and recommendations. In this regard three different tools available under the DSU are of particular interest.

First, if the disputing parties cannot agree as to the "reasonable period of time" within which to comply with the panel or AB recommendations, the matter is to be resolved through binding arbitration under DSU Article 21.3(c). An important feature of Article 21.3(c) arbitrations is that, because the jurisdiction is limited only to a determination of the reasonable period, disagreements as to the type of measures that may be needed to comply fall beyond the scope of such arbitrations. The parties often, however, have a common view as to the type of measure, e.g. legislative or administrative, that may be required for that purpose (although they may have disagreements about the details of the measure), and the submissions turn on how expeditiously that measure can be adopted by the respondent Member.

So far twenty-one Article 21.3(c) arbitration awards have been issued. (In every instance a current or former Appellate Body member served as the sole arbitrator.) Of these, fifteen concerned the question of how

[107] PCIJ Ser. A No. 17 (1928) at 48.

[108] Kuyper 1997, 282; and Gray 1987, 13–16. The two most commonly awarded remedies in international law are damages and declaratory judgments.

[109] Kuyper 1997, 282–83; and Gray 1987, 14–16.

expeditiously the necessary *legislative measures* could be taken by the respondent's parliament.[110] From the perspective of the relationship between WTO law and national law, these awards make very interesting reading. This is because parties' submissions in these cases covered the entire spectrum of issues and processes that the legislature concerned may need to address or follow for purposes of adopting the necessary legislative measures, including the following: the form (e.g. repeal or amendment of the non-conforming law), design, structure, complexity and so on of the proposed legislation; the existence and the length of any pre-legislative process (e.g. requirements for consultations between the administration and the parliament or parliamentary committees, between the government or the legislature and businesses and interest groups, etc.); the normal legislative procedures of the parliament including the dispatch with which it usually acts or has acted on previous occasions; the anticipated nature of parliamentary debate; the agenda or schedule of the legislature and its workload; the availability and the nature of any extraordinary or urgency procedures; the extent to which the administration has control over the legislature (i.e. whether the ruling party has majority in the parliament); whether a new administration or parliament has or is due to come into being following a national election; and so on.

In the face of such wide-ranging arguments – many of which were quickly dismissed by the arbitrators concerned – the arbitrator had to decide what in his view was "the shortest period possible within the legal system of the Member" for the implementation of the recommendations.[111] For one reason or another, the arbitrator's view almost never coincided with that of the respondent Member whose legislature would have to adopt the necessary measures. Thus Article 21.3(c) awards are good examples of the implications of the WTO dispute settlement mechanism for Members' legislatures, including those of the most powerful trading nations.[112]

[110] The rest concerned the adoption of administrative measures.

[111] Reasonable period was interpreted as meaning such shortest period: see *EC – Hormones 21.3(c)*, para. 26; and *Korea – Alcohol 21.3(c)*, para. 42.

[112] For instance, five Article 21.3(c) arbitrations concerned the issue of how expeditiously the US Congress can act: see *US – Copyright Act 21.3(c)*; *US – 1916 Act 21.3(c)*; *US – Hot-Rolled Steel 21.3(c)*; *US – Offset Act 21.3(c)*; and *US – Gambling Services 21.3(c)*. Other cases concerned Canada (see *Canada – Patent Term 21.3[c]*); Chile (see *Chile – Alcohol 21.3[c]*, and *Chile – Agricultural Products 21.3[c]*); the European Communities (see *EC – Bananas 21.3[c]*; *EC – Hormones 21.3[c]*; *EC – Tariff Preferences 21.3[c]*; *EC – Export Subsidies on Sugar 21.3[c]*; and *EC – Chicken Cuts 21.3[c]*); Japan (see *Japan – Alcohol II 21.3[c]*); and Korea (see *Korea – Alcohol 21.3[c]*). See, generally, Monnier 2001; and Zdouc 2005.

Second, under DSU Article 21.5 disagreements as to the WTO-compatibility of measure/s adopted to implement panel or AB recommendations are to be resolved through recourse, once again, to the DSU procedures, including, if possible, resort to the original panel. The ingenuity of this provision, which makes objective determination of compliance with the panel and AB "judgments" possible, is apparent. It invests WTO adjudicative bodies with competence that can be described as "comprehensive," enabling them to pronounce on the WTO-compatibility of national measures or laws not only in an original instance but also where they are adopted to replace measures that were previously found to be WTO-inconsistent.[113]

Third, at a political level the DSB continuously monitors the issue of implementation. This issue is placed on the DSB agenda within a specified period after the adoption of the panel or AB recommendations (which through adoption technically become DSB recommendations) and remains on the agenda until it is completely resolved. Once the matter is placed on the agenda, a written status report about the progress of implementation is required from the respondent Member prior to each DSB meeting.[114] This surveillance continues even where compensation is agreed upon or countermeasures are taken – i.e. until the non-conforming measure is withdrawn.[115]

It may be noted in passing that, although not designed to induce "specific performance" of panel or AB recommendations, there is yet another implementation device provided for in the DSU: disputes concerning the level of countermeasures are to be referred to arbitration by the original panel, if members are available, or, if not, by a different tribunal.[116] Last but not least, the two alternative DSU remedies of compensation and countermeasures themselves are useful implementation devices, in that a losing Member can choose not to comply with the DSB recommendations *only at the cost of* providing compensatory benefits to the successful party or of suffering likely retaliation by that party.[117]

[113] The *US – FSC* and *US – FSC 21.5 I & II* cases are obvious examples. In the former case a piece of US tax legislation was found to be WTO-inconsistent. With a view to complying with the Panel and AB recommendations the USA replaced that legislation by new laws. But the WTO-compatibility of the new laws was challenged in the latter cases under Article 21.5 procedures, which again went up to the Appellate Body and resulted in fresh findings on incompatibility. See, generally on Article 21.5 procedures, Kearns & Charnovitz 2002.

[114] DSU, Article 21.6. [115] Ibid. Article 22.8. [116] Ibid. Article 22.6.

[117] Notably, in DSU Article 22.6 arbitration awards concerning the determination of the level of countermeasures it has been recognized that the purpose of such measures is

In the light of the above, it is not surprising that the WTO enforcement mechanism has been described as "one of the most developed enforcement regimes in international law" and also as "a distinctive and important advance within the international arena."[118] In addition to effectiveness, important as it is, the clear and strong bias of the mechanism in favor of specific performance of panel and AB recommendations is of particular note.

While the elaborate rules and procedures, no doubt, go a long way to securing compliance, for a proper understanding of the matter it must also be borne in mind that compulsion is not always the only reason (according to some accounts its role is even negligible) for the observance of international obligations.[119] Informative in this regard is the compliance record of the GATT panel decisions. Under the GATT, the respondent virtually had a "veto" at every stage of the dispute settlement process, including the establishment of the panel, the adoption of its report or the authorization of countermeasures. Furthermore, the GATT system entirely lacked an enforcement mechanism, not to mention the ingenious devices put in place under the DSU. Yet, not only were most of the GATT panel reports adopted, but, more strikingly, most adopted reports were in fact complied with.[120] Indeed, apart from legal costs, reputational and other similar costs for the non-performance of a dispute settlement ruling can be considerable. Some of these were highlighted by John Jackson with reference to US non-compliance with a GATT panel decision in which a piece of US tax legislation was found to have violated GATT 1947 provisions on subsidies:

to "induce compliance" with the original panel and AB recommendations: see *EC – Bananas 22.6*, para. 6.3; *EC – Hormones I 22.6*, para. 40; *EC – Hormones II 22.6*, para. 39; *EC – Bananas (Ecuador) 22.6*, para. 76; *Brazil – Aircraft 22.6*, para. 3.44; *US – FSC 22.6*, paras. 5.59–60; *Canada – Regional Aircraft 22.6*, paras. 3.47–48; and *US – 1916 Act I 22.6*, paras. 5.5–7. This is also in accord with the relevant general public international law principles: see the ILC's Draft Articles on State Responsibility, Article 49, reproduced in Crawford 2002, 284. See generally Hudec 2000a, 386–93; Pauwelyn 2000; Valles & McGivern 2000; Charnovitz 2001; Anderson 2002; Palmeter & Alexandrov 2002; Jürgensen 2005; McGivern 2005; Renouf 2005; Fukunaga 2006; and Spamann 2006.

118 Pauwelyn 2000, 339. Indeed, in marked contrast to the DSU, the constitutive instruments of other international courts or tribunals provide very little on enforcement: see Gray 2000, 401–2.

119 See, generally, Chayes & Chayes 1995; and Koh 1997. The common tendency of states not to disregard their international obligations independently of any compulsion was underscored by Louis Henkin in a rather interesting formulation: "It is probably the case that almost all nations observe almost all principles of international law and almost all of their obligations almost all of the time" (Henkin 1979, 47).

120 See Hudec *et al.* 1993.

The United States, for example, found in the 1970s, when it refused to follow the results of the GATT *DISC* (Domestic International Sales Corp.) case relating to the subsidy rules, that it was having trouble capturing meaningful attention from other major trading entities with regard to their own subsidy rules, which the United States felt were quite inadequate. Other trading entities would simply note that the United States was not complying with its obligations, so why should they take US complaints against them seriously?[121]

The net result, to sum up, is that once an adverse ruling is issued against a domestic law it is truly difficult for the Member concerned to persist in not introducing any changes in (or, if need be, repealing) the law. Although occasionally it takes time (especially in cases where the domestic constituencies concerned are extremely powerful or some long-standing and entrenched national interests are involved[122]), panel and AB recommendations usually result in changes in domestic measures including laws. And this is true in respect of both developed and developing country Members.[123]

6 Concluding remarks

It must be evident from the preceding discussions that WTO dispute settlement can be effectively pursued by one WTO Member to force internal legal reform or legislative changes in another Member. Effectiveness, indeed, is a major hallmark of the WTO dispute settlement and it has two dimensions. Firstly, effectiveness is an attribute of the dispute settlement process itself. Recall in this context various features of the WTO dispute settlement mechanism noted above that ensure effective resolution of disputes between disputing parties, such as: compulsoriness, exclusivity and automaticity (including automatic establishment of panels, adoption of panel and AB reports, authorization of retaliatory measures for enforcement, etc.); ability of the complainant to define unilaterally the terms of reference of the panel; award of the remedy of legal restitution in each and every case, as well as primacy of this remedy over compensation or retaliation; existence of a highly developed regime in international law for the enforcement of judgments; and so on. Secondly, through its contribution to resolution of disputes between parties, the dispute settlement system contributes significantly

[121] Jackson 1997b, 61. [122] *EC – Bananas* and *EC – Hormones* are two glaring examples.
[123] An update of the implementation status of adopted panel and AB reports can be found in WTO, *Update of WTO Dispute Settlement Cases*, WT/DS/OV/30 (April 25, 2007). Cf. Carmody 2002; Horlick 2002; McRae 2004, 5; and Magnus 2005.

to the promotion of free trade in the international community and to the attainment of the WTO's objectives. The DSU expressly provides that prompt settlement of disputes "is essential to the effective functioning of the WTO and the maintenance of a proper balance between the rights and obligations of Members."[124] The dispute settlement mechanism, no doubt, is a vital element for the effectiveness of the WTO legal system as a whole.

Like effectiveness, good governance also has more than one dimension in WTO dispute settlement. First, the WTO dispute settlement system has been commended for its highly developed judicial character, reflected in its formal procedures, guarantees of procedural fairness or due process, rendering of rational and clear decisions or judgments at the end of the process, etc.[125] Accordingly, it has been suggested that the dispute settlement mechanism has provided the trade organization "with a reputation for fairness and rigor in upholding due process, and thus greater procedural legitimacy" and thereby has put "the WTO in a leadership position in terms of supranational good governance."[126] Second, as emphasized in this work on several previous occasions, WTO dispute settlement often operates as a further layer of judicial review of national laws and administrative measures. Genuine access to fair and impartial judicial review is widely considered to be an important element in ensuring good governance, because it acts as a check on legislative and administrative bodies and ensures rule of law. WTO dispute settlement also acts as a check on national legislators and executives and provides guarantees of rule of law.

In addition to the above-noted constitutive aspects of effectiveness and good governance, both of these policy objectives have important evaluative functions in WTO dispute settlement. As pointed out in the introductory chapter, effectiveness represents a standard or level of review against which the WTO-compatibility of national measures and laws is evaluated or tested by WTO adjudicative organs and good governance represents a significant criterion of such review. These evaluative aspects of effectiveness and good governance are discussed later in Chapter 6.

124 DSU, Article 3.3.

125 On the role of due process in WTO dispute settlement, see Mitchell 2005.

126 Esty 2006, 1546–47.

Part II

5 The problem of characterization

1 Introduction

As may have been noticed from the remarks made in this regard in the last chapter, different dimensions of WTO adjudicative organs' review of national measures/laws are the core and the recurring themes of this second part of the present work. However, before embarking on those issues, this chapter attempts to deal briefly with the problem of characterization that often arises in the context of WTO dispute settlement. Although it has not attracted much conscious attention, this problem also exists in other areas of public international law. In contrast to public international law, in the context of private international law, "characterization," as discussed below, is a very well-known term of art used to describe a particular process in the selection of the applicable law.

Because the present exercise involves the borrowing of a term of art and its introduction in a new setting it may be useful as a starting point to discuss the meaning of the term more generally and likewise to make general references to the judicial faculties that may be described by the term. When it comes to meanings of words, dictionaries can of course be of some assistance. According to the *Shorter Oxford English Dictionary* "characterization" means "the action or result of characterizing; *esp.* (a) portrayal in words etc., description," while the word "characterize" is defined inter alia as "describe the character or peculiar qualities of; describe *as*," "represent, portray," etc.[1] In these senses it may not be an overstatement to say that the whole function of adjudication concerns characterization, i.e. characterization of facts (or rules of law) with reference to given legal concepts. For instance, when a domestic court decides whether the defendant was negligent or whether

[1] Trumble & Stevenson 2002, 381.

the plaintiff contributed to that negligence the court in essence characterizes certain facts in terms of juridical concepts of municipal law, i.e. "negligence" and "contributory negligence."

The same is true for international courts and tribunals, although there is some added complexity given that an international court may need to characterize facts (or rules of law) in terms of familiar international legal concepts as well as concepts of municipal law to which the international court comes somewhat as a stranger. Thus, when an international court decides whether a claimant state has committed an armed attack so that the action of the respondent state can be justified as self defense, it, in essence, characterizes certain facts with reference to international legal concepts, i.e. "armed attack" and "self defense."[2] In contrast, when an international tribunal adjudicating upon a dispute concerning expropriation decides whether the rights that had allegedly been interfered with were proprietary in nature or whether those rights originated from a contract or administrative contract, it, in effect, characterizes certain facts with reference to juridical concepts of municipal law,[3] i.e. "property,"[4] "contract"[5] and "administrative contract."[6] There can be even more complex situations in which an international court may need to characterize a set of facts in terms of both municipal and international legal concepts at the same time. Disputes concerning exhaustion of local remedies are obvious examples.

Although, if viewed from a broad perspective as noted above, the whole process of adjudication can be described under the "rubric" of characterization of facts,[7] in the following pages the word is used in a more limited sense and as such this chapter does not address the

[2] See, e.g., *Nicaragua* case, Merits, ICJ Rep. 14 (1986). International political bodies such as the UN Security Council or General Assembly may also be required to characterize facts with reference to juridical concepts. Thus, for instance, in the context of the conflict in Bosnia and Herzegovina during the early 1990s, UN political bodies were faced with the question of whether the conflict should be characterized as civil war or inter-state conflict: see Gray 1996.

[3] Even though in these instances the characterization is made for purposes of international law, it cannot be denied that the same is made by reference to a particular system of municipal law or at least in the light of the general principles of law and the teachings of comparative law. Cf. Staker 1987, 169–74.

[4] See, e.g., *LIAMCO* v. *Libya*, 62 ILR 140 (1977) at 189.

[5] See, e.g., *Saudi Arabia* v. *Aramco*, 27 ILR 117 (1958) at 204; and *Texaco* v. *Libya*, 53 ILR 389 (1977) at 438–41.

[6] See, e.g., *Texaco* v. *Libya*, 463–68.

[7] Cf., for instance, AB Report, *EC – Hormones I & II*, para. 132 (noting that the determination of the consistency or inconsistency of a given fact or set of facts with the obligations under the WTO treaty is an issue of "legal characterization" of facts).

problem of characterization of *all* facts. Its aims are more modest; and it focuses only on characterization by a court of rules of an "external" legal system, which come before the court as *facts*. Nonetheless, it needs to be noted that the characterization of the facts *qua* facts may involve a parallel exercise in characterization of the rule of law by reference to which the facts are characterized. However, since every court is presumed to know the law that it applies, the characterization of the rules of law of the forum does not ordinarily surface in the decisions of the municipal and international courts alike. In contrast, when rules of one legal system come as facts before a court of another legal system, the issue of characterization of rules of law (of both systems) becomes more apparent. This is because, although rules of an external legal system are treated by both national and international courts as facts, they are facts, so to speak, of a very special nature; and they interact with the rules of law of the forum differently from other types of facts. Thus when a court decides a case that concerns rules of another system of law, it is likely for that court to find it necessary to determine the respective spheres of application of the relevant rules of the external and its own systems of law, and in so doing the court characterizes, explicitly or implicitly, rules of both legal systems.

It hardly needs stating that in a domestic context rules of a foreign legal system may come as "facts" before a court in private international law (conflict of laws) cases, while before an international court or tribunal rules of various national systems of law may come as "facts" in disputes concerning the existence, enactment or application of national laws. Thus the problem of characterization of rules of another system of law is common to both private and public international law. However, while in the context of private international law the problem has been subjected, beginning from as early as the end of the nineteenth century, to extensive judicial and academic examination,[8] in the context of public international law it hardly generated any critical analysis. One reason for the absence of such study could be the lack of a sufficient body of case law generated by international courts and tribunals that concerned national laws. The paucity of relevant case law did not create an interest in the problem and also did not call for a study of it.

Given that an increasing number of WTO disputes concern national legislation or other regulatory measures, a study of the problem in the WTO context may not be a futile exercise. But apart from arithmetic,

[8] See Collins 2000, 33.

there are other important policy reasons for which such studies should be undertaken in the contexts of both WTO law and public international law in general. Foremost among them is the fact that the way in which an international forum characterizes rules of national law may have important consequences for the appropriate relationship between national legislative or other authorities and the international regime concerned. WTO adjudicative organs' competence does not extend, for instance, to matters concerning labor standards, competition or double taxation.[9] Hence a mischaracterization of national laws and regulations dealing with these subjects as trade measures and thereby exercising jurisdiction over them would amount to a grave encroachment on the legislative freedom of Members. On the contrary, in appropriate cases WTO panels and the Appellate Body (as well as other international tribunals) may defer to the national regulatory competence by characterizing the laws and regulations at stake as falling outside the sphere of international norms over which they have jurisdiction.

The implications of characterization for national regulatory competence are not limited only to the situations noted above, namely characterizing laws as falling either within or beyond the scope of the international regime concerned. Rather, characterization may have important implications even when it is done at an intra-regime level. To take again the WTO as an example, in reviewing the compatibility of a national legislative or other measure, as a threshold issue it may be necessary to determine whether the measure is a technical regulation falling within the scope of the TBT Agreement or a sanitary measure falling within the scope of the SPS Agreement.[10] It hardly needs stating that the choice of the legal base from which to start is never "neutral,"[11] because the applicable standard may vary considerably in respect not only of two different agreements but even of different provisions within the same agreement. Thus even at the intra-regime level accurate characterization is vital in ensuring that the WTO adjudicative bodies do not unduly interfere with Members' legislative freedom.

In addition to the proper allocation of competence between national legislative or other authorities and international tribunals, characterization can also be critical in ensuring that disputes that appropriately belong to one international forum are not forced into another. It is now quite well known that the increase in the number and activity of

[9] Cf. Chapter 4, pp. 91–92 above. [10] See, e.g., Marceau & Trachtman 2002.
[11] See Pescatore 1991 – loose-leaf, 54.

international courts and tribunals in recent years has created not just a theoretical but indeed the practical possibility for states to engage in forum and norm shopping.[12] While a certain amount of forum shopping may not be harmful,[13] every international judicial organ should, nonetheless, be cautious to make sure that it is not adjudicating upon disputes that fall beyond its field of expertise. In this context characterization can be of immense help. Thus, for instance, WTO panels, by characterizing disputed national laws and regulations as non-trade measures, may ensure that they are not adjudicating disputes for which they are not well suited; this in some cases may also leave the parties to the dispute with the choice to go to another and possibly more appropriate forum.

There are, then, important reasons for undertaking a study of the problem in the WTO context. However, before proceeding to do that, in the following two sections the wider private and public international law dimensions of the problem are discussed with a view to exploring afterwards whether there is any potential for cross-fertilization. Besides, some attention to the problem as it exists in private international law is necessary for the simple reason that, as a term of art, "characterization" has its root in that field.

2 Characterization in private international law

In both civil and common law systems of private international law, the choice of law process necessarily involves the problem of characterization. For this purpose two stages of characterization are generally distinguished, namely characterization of the cause of action (this is also described as the characterization of the facts or of the legal issue raised by the facts) and characterization of the relevant rule of law.[14]

Characterization of the cause of action refers to the process by which the issue raised by the factual situation is assigned to its appropriate juridical category. In other words, it means determining whether the matter before the court concerns breach of contract, the commission of a tort, succession to movables or immovables, matrimonial rights, and so on. The subject-matter of this characterization is essentially a set of *facts*.[15] Once the correct juridical nature of the issue is determined and

[12] See generally Guruswamy 1998; Ohlhoff & Schloemann 1998; Helfer 1999; Kingsbury 1999; Schwebel 2000; Romano 2001; and Shany 2003.

[13] See, e.g., Guruswamy 1998, 296–97.

[14] See North & Fawcett 1999, 35–45.

[15] See, e.g., *Macmillan Inc.* v. *Bishopsgate Investment Trust Plc. (No. 3)* [1996] 1 WLR 387.

thereby the relevant choice of law rule is revealed, it becomes necessary to characterize rules of law with a view to determining whether a rule falls within a legal category with regard to which the law chosen by the relevant choice of law rule is paramount. Thus, for instance, in an action for breach of contract brought in Utopia, if the law of Arcadia governs matters of substantive validity of the contract and Utopian law governs questions of procedure, it may be necessary to determine whether a rule of Arcadian law relates to matters of substance or procedure with a view to ascertaining whether the rule is to be applied. If the rule is characterized as procedural in nature it will not be applicable, and if it is characterized as relating to substantive validity of contracts it will be applicable. By contrast, a rule of Utopian law will not be applicable if it relates to matters of substance but will be applicable if it is procedural in character. Evidently, the subject-matter of this characterization is rules of law – either domestic or foreign.

Characterization of rules of national law by an international judicial organ can be seen as characterization of rules of an external (or "foreign," in the sense of being "unfamiliar") legal system. Accordingly, for present purposes it is appropriate to confine the discussion regarding private international law to characterization of rules of foreign legal systems only. There are many examples of such characterization in most jurisdictions. An English case is considered below to illustrate concretely the nature of the problem and the methods used by the courts in characterizing rules of an external legal system.

The case of *Maldonado*[16] concerned a person domiciled in Spain who died intestate leaving no next-of-kin. She left movables in England. In Spanish law the movables passed to the Spanish state as a successor, while in English law the Crown was entitled to them as ownerless property. According to the relevant conflict rules, the law of the deceased's domicile governed succession to movables and the law of the place where the property was situated governed confiscation of ownerless property. Consequently, the court had to determine whether the Spanish state took the property as a successor or confiscated it as a sovereign. If the rule under which the Spanish state claimed the property was characterized as a rule of succession, then it would be applicable and the property would pass to Spain. Conversely, if it was characterized as a rule of confiscation it would not be applicable, because the property was in England;

[16] *Re Maldonado's Estate* [1954] P 223.

and, as such, the English rule would apply and the Crown would take the property.

The court characterized the Spanish rule as a rule of succession. In so characterizing the rule, the court looked at similar rules in a number of jurisdictions and found that, although it was almost a universal rule that in the absence of next-of-kin movables of a deceased who died intestate passed to the state, yet the capacity in which the state took the movables was not uniform throughout the world. In some countries, such as Germany, Italy and Switzerland, the state took by way of succession as an ultimate heir, while in others, such as England, Austria and Turkey, the state as a sovereign confiscated the property as being ownerless goods. As a result, even though the English rule under which the movables were to pass to the Crown was confiscatory in nature, the court did not impose the same characterization on the Spanish rule. Rather, the court was of the view that the meaning and scope of the term "succession" and the capacity in which the Spanish state claimed the property must be decided in accordance with Spanish law. In private international law terminology, this is often referred to as characterization in accordance with the *lex causae*, as opposed to *lex fori*. Put more simply, this means characterizing a foreign rule in the way in which it would be characterized under the relevant foreign law, rather than forcing on a foreign rule a characterization of a similar rule of the law of the forum. *Re Maldonado* also highlights the importance of the methods of comparative law in characterizing rules of an external legal system.

Although the above provides an example of characterization on the basis of the *lex causae*, it needs to be noted that English courts have not adopted any consistent theory of characterization in accordance with the *lex causae* or the *lex fori*. Indeed, there are many cases where characterization of a foreign rule was effected on the basis of the *lex fori*.[17] The opinion of academic writers, both English and continental, is also equally divided as to whether characterization should be made on the basis of the *lex causae* or the *lex fori*.[18] Some of the arguments put forward in support of each of these two approaches and whether those arguments have any relevance in the WTO context, are discussed later in section 5 below, while the following section turns to the problem as it exists in public international law in general.

[17] See, for instance, *Ogden* v. *Ogden* [1908] P 46; and *Adams* v. *National Bank of Greece* [1961] AC 255.

[18] See, for instance, Clarkson & Hill 1997, 486–91; North & Fawcett 1999, 40–45; Collins 2000, 35–36; and Morris & McClean 2000, 494–95.

3 Characterization in public international law

An early instance in which the International Court of Justice faced the problem of characterization is the *Guardianship of Infants* case.[19] This case concerned the Hague Convention of 1902 on guardianship of infants, which provided for the application of the national law of an infant for the institution and operation of guardianship. Stated simply, the facts were as follows. Swedish courts placed a Dutch infant under the regime of protective upbringing in accordance with the Swedish law on that subject. As a result of this measure the infant could not be handed over to the guardian appointed under Dutch law. The Netherlands claimed that the measure violated the 1902 Convention, because it prevented the infant from being put under the custody of the guardian appointed under the Convention.

Sweden did not dispute the fact that protective upbringing impeded the exercise of custody by the guardian. Its key submission was that the Swedish law on protective upbringing and the jurisdiction conferred by that law upon Swedish authorities were beyond the scope of the 1902 Convention. This was so because the Convention governed conflicts of law regarding guardianship, while the Swedish law was concerned with *ordre public* and not guardianship.[20] On the contrary, it was submitted on behalf of the Netherlands that the measure was one "virtually amounting to guardianship," and that it constituted a "rival guardianship" such that the Dutch guardianship was completely "absorbed, whittled away, overruled and frustrated."[21] Thus, the essential question before the ICJ was one of characterization – namely, whether the Swedish law should be characterized as a law on guardianship or as a law concerning a "different subject-matter."[22]

The Court concluded that the Swedish law was not a law on guardianship.[23] It found that the purpose of the Convention was to eliminate divergence of views as to whether guardianship should be governed by the national law of the infant, the law of his place of residence, or some other law,[24] while the aim of the Swedish law was to contribute to the protection of children and, more importantly, to protect society against dangers of improper upbringing, inadequate hygiene, or moral corruption of young people.[25] Thus a comparison between the purpose of the Convention and that of the Swedish law showed that the purpose of the latter placed it "outside the field of application of the Convention."[26]

[19] ICJ Rep. 55 (1958). [20] Ibid. 64–65. [21] Ibid. 65.
[22] Ibid. 68. [23] Ibid. [24] Ibid. 67. [25] Ibid. 69. [26] Ibid.

This conclusion was reached in spite of the fact that the Court found that there were points of contact between the law and the Convention and that, indeed, protective upbringing created obstacles for the exercise of the right of custody provided for under the Convention. In the judgment those obstacles were even referred to as "encroachments revealed in practice."[27]

In this case the Swedish measures whose consistency with the 1902 Convention was directly at issue before the ICJ were various judicial and administrative decisions taken in pursuance of the Swedish law on protective upbringing. Accordingly, the ICJ was not concerned with the conformity of the Swedish law, as such, with Swedish international obligations. Nevertheless, it is apparent that a mischaracterization of the law as a law on guardianship could have deprived it of real meaning, and, as a result, would have abridged the competence of Sweden to regulate matters concerning protection of children. Evidently, the ICJ's purposive interpretation of both the Convention and the Swedish law resulted in a high degree of deference to national legislative, judicial and administrative competence. This case provides a clear example of the importance of characterization in determining the applicability of international norms to national legislative and other measures, as well as in ensuring proper deference by international judicial organs to national authorities.

Possibly the most remarkable body of public international law jurisprudence on characterization can be found in the case law of the European Court of Human Rights (ECHR). This statement needs to be understood in perspective, because the case law to which references are about to be made pertains to a specific ECHR doctrine, namely the doctrine of "autonomous concepts," and, as such, is not commonly labeled as being on characterization. The doctrine of autonomous concepts, however, was developed by the ECHR as it confronted the question of characterization of rules of national law or national legal institutions by reference to certain legal terms used in the European Human Rights Convention (EHR Convention) that apparently refer back to the national law of the state concerned.

A convenient way to explain both the doctrine and the underlying problem of characterization that it addresses is to consider a concrete example. Article 6 of the EHR Convention grants every individual certain rights in respect of the determination of any "criminal charge"

27 Ibid. 71, 66.

against him, such as fair and public hearing by an independent tribunal; presumption of innocence; legal and, if need be, interpreter's assistance; etc. In *Engel*[28] five conscript soldiers serving in the Netherlands armed forces claimed that there were violations of Article 6 in the imposition of penalties on them by military courts for military offenses. In response, the government of the Netherlands took the view that there was no violation of Article 6, because the proceedings against the applicants did not involve the determination of a "criminal charge" as the article requires. It argued that under Netherlands law, the military penalties imposed constituted strictly *disciplinary*, and not *criminal*, offenses and that therefore Article 6 of the Convention was not at all applicable.

The ECHR accepted the distinction between disciplinary and criminal proceedings and offenses, which it found to be a long-standing distinction made in domestic legislation of contracting states. This could have meant that Article 6 was not applicable in respect of the applicants. However, the Court did not end its analysis at that point, but rather it formulated the real issue to be as follows: "Does Article 6 cease to be applicable just because the competent organs of a contracting state classify as disciplinary an act or omission and the proceedings it takes against the author, or does it, on the contrary, apply in certain cases notwithstanding this classification?"[29] The ECHR was concerned that if the contracting states were able at their discretion to classify offenses and proceedings as disciplinary instead of criminal, the operation of Article 6 "would be subordinated to their sovereign will."[30] To prevent this manner of circumvention of the Convention rights, the Court resorted to the idea of autonomous concepts. Thus the concept of "criminal charge" cannot be understood by mere reference to domestic law, but must be given an *autonomous* Convention meaning. The characterization in national law can have only a relative value and provide no more than a starting point; and the Court must look behind the appearances and investigate the realities of the rules and procedures in question in the light of the common denominator of the respective legislation of the various contracting states.[31] On this basis the ECHR characterized the rules and procedures of Netherlands military law as "criminal" rather than "disciplinary"; and, as a result, the applicants

[28] *Engel* v. *Netherlands*, ECHR Ser. A No. 22 (1976).

[29] Ibid. para. 80. [30] Ibid. para. 81.

[31] Ibid. para. 82. See also *Deweer* v. *Belgium*, ECHR Ser. A No. 35 (1980), para. 44; and *Chassagnou* v. *France*, 1999-III ECHR Rep. 858, para. 100.

could claim violations of Article 6 in respect of those rules and procedures. This theory of autonomous concepts is consistently applied by the ECHR in characterizing rules and institutions of domestic law, be it with reference to the expression "criminal charge" in Article 6 or other similar Convention terms that apparently refer back to domestic law, such as "association," "civil rights and obligations," "possessions," "tribunal," etc.[32]

4 Characterization in WTO law

Turning now to the problem of characterization in WTO law, for analytical purposes it is possible to distinguish between three different circumstances in which WTO panels and the Appellate Body may need to characterize rules of national law with reference to given legal concepts. Two of them were mentioned before: first, to determine whether the disputed measure falls within or beyond the scope of the WTO agreements (this can be described as extra/intra-regime characterization); and second, to determine which of the two or more prima facie applicable WTO norms or sets of norms are applicable to the national law at issue (i.e. intra-regime characterization). The third circumstance concerns cases, which, unlike the first two, do not involve more than one legal category (such as labor standards *versus* trade measure, sanitary measure *versus* technical regulation, etc.), but, nonetheless, characterization is necessary simply to determine whether a specific WTO norm or a specific set of WTO norms is applicable (for convenience this may be referred to as provision-specific characterization).

4.1 *Extra/intra-regime characterization*

The problem of extra/intra-regime characterization arose most strikingly in *US – 1916 Act I & II*.[33] In these cases the complainants, the EC and Japan, claimed that Title VIII of the United States Revenue Act of 1916 violated WTO provisions regarding anti-dumping measures as contained in the GATT 1994 and the ADA. In defense of the Act, the central US argument was that those provisions were not applicable to the Act, because it was an antitrust and not an anti-dumping legislation. As a result, both the

32 See, generally, Harris *et al.* 1995, 16–17; Clayton & Tomlinson 2000, 267; and Letsas 2004.

33 The Panels in these two cases were composed of the same three persons; accordingly, it is convenient to refer to these Panels as "the Panel." A detailed comment on these cases can be found in Keyser 2001.

Panel and the Appellate Body had to address the question of whether the law should be characterized as an anti-dumping or antitrust legislation. They arrived at the same conclusion, namely that the Act was an anti-dumping legislation. While it is difficult to imagine (and almost certainly is also not the case) that the Panel or the AB was influenced by the ECHR jurisprudence on autonomous concepts, an analysis of their approach to the problem reveals some interesting parallels.

Put simply, there are three key aspects of the WTO provisions regarding anti-dumping measures. First, they set out a definition of dumping which is to be understood as the introduction of products of one country into the commerce of another country at less than the normal value of the products, i.e. price discrimination between two markets, one located in the country of importation and the other in the country of production or a third country of exportation.[34] Second, the provisions authorize Members to take measures against dumping only if the dumping causes or threatens to cause certain detrimental effects in the importing country, such as material injury to an established industry.[35] Third, the provisions set out three specific types of remedies or measures that Members are allowed to take against dumping, namely: provisional measures, price undertakings, and imposition of anti-dumping duties.[36]

The US legislation in question, i.e. the 1916 Act, corresponded with the WTO provisions in respect of the first aspect, but differed significantly in respect of the second and the third aspects. That is to say, like the WTO provisions, the Act addressed transnational price discrimination. However, unlike the WTO provisions, the Act targeted price discrimination that was undertaken with a specific predatory *intent* to destroy or injure an industry or restrain or monopolize any part of trade and commerce in the United States, and not simply a price discrimination that caused or threatened the detrimental effects envisaged in the GATT 1994 and the ADA. Finally, the remedies provided in the 1916 Act were not the ones set out in the GATT 1994 and the ADA, but rather they were the same as, or similar to, those under various US antitrust statutes.

The reason for which both the Panel and the AB characterized the 1916 Act as anti-dumping legislation was that it addressed the same

[34] See GATT 1994, Article VI:1; and ADA, Article 2.
[35] See GATT 1994, Article VI:1; and ADA, Articles 3–4.
[36] See GATT 1994, Article VI:2; and ADA, Articles 7–9.

type of price discrimination as the GATT 1994 and the ADA. In other words, since the pricing practices targeted by the Act fell within the WTO definition of dumping, the fact that the Act targeted such pricing practices when undertaken with a particular intent having antitrust ramifications, or that the remedies provided for were those of antitrust legislation in general, was of no relevance. Thus the second and the third aspects of the WTO provisions on dumping relating, respectively, to effects of dumping and remedies against dumping were completely ignored in characterizing the Act.[37] In terms of effectiveness of international rules and supervision, this makes good sense because treating the effects and remedies aspects as having a bearing on the characterization would have subordinated the application of the WTO provisions on dumping, to borrow the expression used by the ECHR, to the sovereign will of the Members. To wit, if these were regarded as relevant, a Member would have been able to insulate entirely its laws and measures dealing with the same type of commercial activity and pricing practices as dumping from international regulation and supervision, by simply adding some additional requirements regarding intent or by providing for remedies that differed from the ones set out in the GATT 1994 and the ADA.

Thus, apparently, in both the ECHR and the WTO contexts, the approach to the problem of characterization is tuned by the same underlying concern of ensuring effectiveness of international rules and supervision. But what about autonomous concepts? In the *1916 Act* cases it was not necessary for the Panel or the AB to resort to an autonomous concept of "dumping," which is a clearly and elaborately defined WTO concept. But did they tend to develop an autonomous notion of antitrust (or competition) legislation, which for WTO purposes is a domestic legal concept? It is not possible to find an answer to this question in the reports of the Panel and the Appellate Body. While at a conceptual level it is not difficult to imagine that in many circumstances complete acceptance of domestic characterization could fly in the face of effectiveness of international rules and supervision, neither the Panel nor the AB dealt with the matter as explicitly as the ECHR.

Remarks about the analytical or methodological framework for characterizing rules of national law can be found only in one short paragraph of the Panel reports, which reads as follows:

[37] See Panel Reports, *US – 1916 Act I*, paras. 6.93–165; and *US – 1916 Act II*, paras. 6.108–84; and AB Report, *US – 1916 Act I & II*, paras. 103–33.

Panels need not accept at face value the characterization that the respondent attaches to its law. A panel may analyse the operation of the domestic legislation and determine whether the description of the functioning of the law, as made by the respondent, is consistent with the legal structure of that Member. This way, it will be able to determine whether or not the law as applied is in conformity with the obligations of the Member concerned under the WTO Agreement.[38]

The above formulation, no doubt, reflects a more cautious approach than the doctrine of autonomous concepts. Thus, while the characterization put forward by the respondent is not to be accepted at face value, characterization is not to be done independently of national law either. Rather, a panel must seek to establish a characterization that reflects the operation and function of the domestic legislation in question and is consistent with the legal structure of the Member concerned. This methodology, however, will work only up to a point. That is to say, where the national law characterization is wholly irreconcilable with the Member's international obligations, greater resourcefulness on the part of the panels and the AB would be required.

4.2 Intra-regime characterization

The problem of intra-regime characterization can be conveniently illustrated by discussing the *Canada – Periodicals* case. This case concerned Part V.1 of the Canadian Excise Tax Act, which imposed on every split-run edition[39] of a periodical an excise tax of an amount equivalent to 80 percent of the value of all advertisements contained in the edition. The United States claimed that the law was inconsistent with the national treatment obligation contained in Article III:2 of the GATT 1994, because the tax discriminated against imported split-run periodicals vis-à-vis domestic non-split-run periodicals.

The Canadian defense was that Part V.1 was not a measure affecting trade in goods and, as such, was not subject to the GATT 1994; rather it was a measure pertaining to advertising services and, therefore, was within the scope of the GATS. According to Canada, magazines are both

38 Panel Reports, *US – 1916 Act I*, para. 6.51; and *US – 1916 Act II*, para. 6.50. Cf. AB Report, *US – Softwood Lumber IV*, para. 56 (quoted below at n. 59).

39 The term 'split-run' is used to refer to an edition that is published by splitting, i.e. by dividing, the editorial content (e.g. articles, photographs, artworks, etc.) and the advertising content of a single issue of a magazine, whereby two or more separate regional editions of the same issue are published. Each edition shares some or all of the editorial content, but the advertisements differ. Because each edition is distributed in a different geographical market, the advertisements are directed at the specific market in which each edition is distributed.

consumer goods and a means of providing advertising services, having two distinct revenue sources, namely revenue from the sale of a product (i.e. the magazines themselves) and from the sale of a service (i.e. advertisement spaces to advertisers). Since the excise tax was imposed on the advertising revenues, it was a tax in respect of advertising services. Referring to the fact that Canada did not undertake any commitments in respect of advertising services in its Schedule of Specific Commitments under the GATS, Canada argued that it was not required to grant national treatment to foreign publishers providing such services. And the US challenge of the Act on the basis of the GATT 1994 was an indirect attempt to gain access to a service sector to which the US was not entitled under WTO law.

Accordingly, the applicability of the GATT 1994 to the Excise Tax Act was a central issue before the Panel; and to resolve this issue it was necessary to decide whether the Canadian law could be characterized as a measure affecting trade in goods. But, apparently, the Panel failed to capture the nuances of the parties' arguments; and it concluded that the GATT 1994 was applicable by simply pointing out that both the GATS and the GATT 1994 may apply concurrently to the same measure.[40] The reasoning of the Panel is deficient in that, from the proposition that both the GATT 1994 and the GATS may apply to the same measure (this is self-evident anyway), it does not follow that the GATT 1994 was applicable to the Excise Tax Act. Indeed, both GATT and GATS obligations may apply to the same measure, but unless a measure is characterized as being one pertaining to trade in goods, how is it possible to say that the GATT 1994 applies to that measure?[41] The failure to address this matter while considering the applicability of the GATT 1994 was compensated, somewhat imperfectly, in the course of the Panel's examination of the issue of violation of Article III of the GATT 1994. At that stage, the Panel concluded that the tax was imposed on periodicals themselves (i.e. on *goods*) within the meaning of Article III, given that it was applied to each split-run edition on a "per issue" basis.[42]

[40] See Panel Report, *Canada – Periodicals*, paras. 5.13–19 (at one place the Panel, however, noted that it was not fully convinced by Canada's characterization of the Act as a measure regarding advertising services).

[41] Cf., for instance, AB Report, *Canada – Autos*, para. 152. In this case the Appellate Body ruled that the Panel erred in its interpretative approach by not considering "as a threshold question" whether the contested measure concerned trade in services, and, instead, proceeding directly to examine the consistency of the measure with the GATS.

[42] See Panel Report, *Canada – Periodicals*, para. 5.29.

In upholding the Panel's conclusion that the GATT 1994 was applicable, the Appellate Body dealt more precisely with the question of characterization. It thought that a number of factors indicated that the Canadian law was a measure concerning goods: the title of the legislation was "tax on split-run periodicals" and not "tax on advertising"; the tax, even though calculated in terms of the value of the advertisements, was applied on a "per issue" basis; it was not the advertiser but the publisher (or, in the absence of a publisher resident in Canada, the distributor, printer or wholesaler) who was liable to pay the tax; etc.[43]

While the *Canada – Periodicals* case illustrates the goods/services dimension of intra-regime characterization,[44] the problem arises, and does so quite frequently, in numerous other contexts and circumstances. To mention just a few of them, in order to determine which is/are the relevant or most pertinent WTO norm/s, it is often necessary to ascertain whether the contested national measure is a technical regulation coming under the TBT Agreement or a sanitary/phytosanitary measure falling within the scope of the SPS Agreement;[45] a general ban on import covered by the GATT 1994 or a technical regulation covered by the TBT Agreement;[46] an investment measure falling within the purview of the TRIMS Agreement or a more simple discriminatory measure covered by GATT 1994 Article III;[47] an internal regulation coming within the scope of GATT 1994 Article III or a quantitative restriction covered by Article XI;[48] a measure concerning customs duties falling under GATT 1994 Article II or internal taxation covered by Article III,[49] etc.

Because intra-regime characterization is done by reference to concepts of WTO law, unlike extra/intra-regime characterization, the issue of attributing meaning ("autonomously" or otherwise) to a purely domestic legal concept does not arise. But, of course, it is more likely than not

43 See AB Report, *Canada – Periodicals*, at 16–20.

44 Other cases in which this issue arose include *EC – Bananas*; and *Canada – Autos*.

45 See, e.g., Panel Reports, *EC – Hormones I*, para. 8.29; and *EC – Hormones II*, para. 8.32.

46 See, e.g., Panel Report, *EC – Asbestos*, paras. 8.15–73; and AB Reports, *EC – Asbestos*, paras. 59–76; and *EC – Sardines*, paras. 175–76.

47 See, e.g., Panel Report, *Indonesia – Autos*, paras. 14.60–62.

48 See, e.g., Panel Reports, *US – Tuna I*, paras. 5.8–14; *US – Tuna II*, paras. 5.6–10; *US – Shrimp*, paras. 7.11–17; and *EC – Asbestos*, para. 8.85. See also Hudec 2000b (containing an interesting analysis of how the problem of internal regulation / quantitative restriction characterization has shaped the doctrine of "production or processing methods" (PPM) that was introduced by GATT panels in addressing the question of whether regulatory burdens can be imposed on goods based on their production or processing methods, for purposes of protecting the environment, health and the like).

49 See, e.g., Panel Report, *EEC – Parts and Components*, paras. 5.4–10.

that the relevant WTO law concept will have a domestic law counterpart. Thus, for instance, concepts such as customs duties or internal taxation may have a WTO meaning, but they equally belong to domestic law and can be understood in a particular way by the respondent Member. As such, the issue of accepting or departing from domestic law characterization arises in the intra-regime context as well. With reference to GATT 1994 Articles II and III, this issue was highlighted by the Panel in the *EEC – Parts and Components* case. The Panel noted that if the characterization of a measure under domestic law is regarded as providing the "required connection" for the applicability of one or the other article, contracting parties would be able to "determine themselves" which of the two provisions would apply to their measures: a solution which the Panel thought would undermine the basic objectives – and hence effectiveness – of Articles II and III.[50]

4.3 Provision-specific characterization

Given that unless a national law or measure falls within the scope of a WTO agreement or provision, the WTO adjudicative bodies cannot properly exercise jurisdiction over it, the issue of provision-specific characterization is omnipresent – in either explicit or implicit manner. While in the predominantly larger number of cases the matter may remain unnoticed, in some cases this form of characterization may also become contentious and raise difficult issues regarding the proper balance of authority between national governments in regulating domestic affairs and the WTO dispute settlement process in "policing domestic regulatory measures."[51]

The *US – FSC* case provides a good example in this regard. This case concerned sections 921–27 of the US Internal Revenue Code (IRC) establishing special tax treatment for Foreign Sales Corporations (FSCs). The EC alleged that the law constituted subsidies prohibited under the WTO agreements on subsidies (the ASCM) and agriculture. From the various issues that the Panel and Appellate Body had to address with a view to deciding whether the ASCM and the Agriculture Agreement were applicable to the FSC tax legislation, it is possible to discern at least four different questions of characterization. These were: should the legislation be characterized as a subsidy? Should it be characterized as an *export* subsidy? Should it be characterized as a subsidy to reduce the

[50] Ibid. para. 5.7.

[51] The words within quotation marks are taken from Hudec 1999, 359.

cost of marketing exports of agricultural products? And should it be characterized as a subsidy not listed in Article 9.1 of the Agriculture Agreement that was applied in a manner resulting in or threatening to lead to circumvention of export subsidy commitments under that Agreement?

Under WTO law, tax legislation may be characterized as a subsidy, because the definition of subsidy contained in the ASCM provides for that possibility.[52] According to ASCM Article 1, a subsidy exists if there is a "financial contribution by a government or any public body"[53] and a "benefit is thereby conferred";[54] and a financial contribution may occur where, inter alia, "government revenue that is otherwise due is foregone or not collected."[55] Thus it is not extraordinary that in *US – FSC* a tax legislation was characterized as a subsidy; rather, it is the type of arguments put forward by the USA that makes the case worth discussing.

The key US argument was that the FSC tax exemptions did not constitute a subsidy because those exemptions were not granted with regard to taxes that were "otherwise due" within the meaning of Article 1. It argued that the exemptions were granted in respect of the *foreign-source income* of FSCs and there is no WTO rule requiring countries to tax such income and therefore the exempted taxes were not "otherwise due." The USA pointed out that there are two principal systems of taxation: first, the system of taxing the *worldwide* income of persons resident within the jurisdiction of the country; and second, the system of taxing only the income earned within the *territory* of the country. The US tax laws generally operate on a worldwide basis and thus all income earned "worldwide" by US citizens and residents is subject to taxation. In contrast, many European countries impose taxes on a territorial basis and, as such, provide more favorable tax treatment to exporters than the USA. To obviate this imbalance in the tax burden on the exporters, the USA, in the exercise of its "*tax sovereignty*," had incorporated through the FSC legislation features of a territorial system into its

[52] Indeed, in various other cases, under both the GATT and the WTO, such characterization has been made: see, e.g., *US – DISC*; *Belgium – Tax Legislation*; *France – Tax Legislation*; *Netherlands – Tax Legislation*; *Indonesia – Autos*; and *US – FSC 21.5 I*. But it needs to be noted that generally taxation is one of the gray areas of WTO jurisdiction. On the one hand, there is no direct jurisdiction over taxation matters; on the other hand, in a number of WTO provisions taxation issues are dealt with directly or indirectly in a rather important manner: see Waincymer 2002, 146.

[53] ASCM, Article 1.1(a)(1). [54] Ibid. Article 1.1(b). [55] Ibid. Article 1.1(a)(1)(ii).

otherwise worldwide system, with a view to granting exemptions to certain categories of foreign-source income. The USA argued that, because European countries exempt *all* foreign-source income from taxation, if the FSC legislation was a subsidy, so too were the tax systems of many European countries.

Both the Panel and the AB accepted and underscored the proposition that the WTO agreements do not impose any obligation to levy taxes and Members in principle are absolutely free to decide which particular categories of revenue are to be taxed, and likewise to decide not to levy any taxes at all. However, they disagreed with the USA that a Member which opts for a particular method of taxation does not forgo revenue "otherwise due" if it exempts in a selective manner certain limited categories of income from taxation. Since in the absence of the FSC legislation income insulated from taxation by that legislation would have been subject to taxation, the legislation, it was held by both the Panel and the AB, amounted to a subsidy.[56] This ruling in essence means that, while a Member in the exercise of its "tax sovereignty" (as put by the USA) is free to choose whatever method/s of taxation that it deems appropriate, be it worldwide, territorial or something else, a Member cannot tailor – by combining different methods or otherwise – its tax regime in a manner that results in the evasion of WTO discipline on subsidies.[57] Again, it is evident that the issue of the effectiveness of international rules and

[56] See *US – FSC*, Panel Report, paras. 7.35–130 (in particular, paras. 7.92, 7.119), and AB Report, paras. 77–121 (in particular, paras. 90, 99).

[57] It may be noted parenthetically that the tension between the United States and the GATT/WTO in the area of tax exemption / export subsidies is quite long-standing. The FSC legislation was in fact adopted by the USA to replace the earlier and almost identical DISC (Domestic International Sales Corporations) legislation. The latter was found to be GATT-inconsistent in the 1970s by a GATT panel and resulted in protracted diplomatic means of settlement between the USA and the EC, which eventually led to the adoption of the FSC legislation by the US Congress. When the FSC legislation was again found to be WTO-inconsistent, the USA adopted a third similar legislation, namely the Extraterritorial Income Exclusion Act (ETI). This legislation once again was found to be WTO-inconsistent in the *US – FSC 21.5 I* case. In response to this ruling the USA enacted the American Jobs Creation Act, which again was found to be WTO-inconsistent in the *US – FSC 21.5 II* case. Thus, even after more than three decades of judicial and diplomatic means of settlement, the matter still remains unresolved. The tension is also well documented in the extensive academic literature dealing with the dispute settlement efforts regarding DISC, FSC and ETI legislation: see, e.g., Jackson 1978; Hudec 1993, 59–100 and 2003; Stehmann 2000; and Qureshi & Grynberg 2002.

discipline lies at the heart of the problem of how national laws are to be typified by WTO adjudicative bodies.

The interesting parallel between characterization by WTO bodies and ECHR jurisprudence on autonomous concepts has already been pointed out; the *US – Softwood Lumber IV* case perhaps is the most conspicuous example of it. This case also involved the question of whether national measures fell within the definitions of subsidy and financial contribution contained in Article 1 of the ASCM. The definition of financial contribution in that article covers situations where a government provides *goods*. Canada claimed that it did not provide goods to timber harvesters by making available to them standing timber attached to the land, i.e. trees. It argued that trees did not fall within the definition of goods, because the term "goods" must be understood by reference to the concept of "personal property" and trees were not such property.[58] These contentions were rejected by the Appellate Body in the following terms:

> the arguments put forward by Canada relating to the nature of "personal property," raise issues concerning the relevance, for WTO dispute settlement, of the way in which the municipal law of a WTO Member classifies or regulates things or transactions . . . However, municipal laws – in particular those relating to property – vary amongst WTO Members. Clearly, it would be inappropriate to characterize, for purposes of applying any provisions of the WTO covered agreements, the same thing or transaction differently, depending on its legal categorization within the jurisdictions of different Members. Accordingly, we emphasize that municipal law classifications are not determinative of the issues raised in this appeal.[59]

These observations illustrate that it is difficult for an international system of dispute settlement to work properly and effectively without some autonomy from concepts that are creatures of municipal law.

5 Concluding remarks: is there any scope for cross-fertilization?

From the preceding discussion it must be evident that there are obvious differences between the contexts in which the problem of characterization arises and the reasons that necessitate characterization in private and public international law. In private international law, rules of foreign law are characterized to determine their applicability; and if a rule is characterized as falling within the scope of a choice of law rule it is applied as the applicable law. On the contrary, in public international

[58] See AB Report, *US – Softwood Lumber IV*, paras. 48, 54, 65. [59] Ibid. para. 56.

law, rules of national law are characterized to ascertain whether they come within the purview of the international legal norms over which the international court concerned has competence. Here characterization is not made with a view to applying the national law rules as applicable law, but rather those rules form the very subject-matter of the dispute. These differences mean that the methods of characterization may not always converge in the two contexts. For instance, one of the basic concerns of public international law in acceding to the national law characterization of a rule is whether thereby the international rules would become ineffective. This concern does not exist so profoundly in the private international law context. That is to say, characterization in accordance with the *lex causae* rather than *lex fori* would hardly, if ever, render the law of the forum ineffective.

While it would be unfortunate to play down the differences that are rather important, it is also notable that at a technical level the problem has much in common in the two contexts. This can be demonstrated by pointing out some of the basic arguments that are put forward in support of the contending methods of characterization, e.g. approaches based on the *lex causae*, the *lex fori* or comparative law.

The main argument in favor of the *lex causae* approach of private international law is that, as one commentator has put it, "every legal rule takes its characterization from the legal system *to which it belongs*."[60] In cases where foreign law governs, not applying its characterization could be tantamount to not applying it at all. Against this argument, consider the following remarks made by Judge Matscher of the ECHR regarding the EHR doctrine of autonomous concepts:

> Even if it is necessary, for purposes of autonomous qualification of a concept in an international convention, to depart from the formal qualification given to an institution in the legislation of a given state and to analyse its real nature, this process must never go too far – otherwise there is a danger of arriving at an abstract qualification which may be philosophically valid, but which has no basis in law. In point of fact, the "real nature" of a legal institution is conditioned above all by the legal effects to which it gives rise under the legislation concerned.[61]

Clearly, the point raised by Judge Matscher is quite similar to the *raison d'être* of the *lex causae* approach of private international law. This highlights that, even in the public international law context, the

[60] Wolff 1950, 154 (italics in original).
[61] *Ozturk* v. *Germany*, ECHR Ser. A No. 73 (1984) (Dissenting Opinion of Judge Matscher).

characterization accorded by a state to its own laws should not be rejected very quickly and without a thorough analysis of the reasons and the necessity for doing so.

Turning now to the *lex fori* approach, here the principal argument in private international law is that if the foreign law were allowed to determine the characterization and, consequently, whether that law must be applied, the forum would lose all control over the application of its own private international law rules and "would no longer be master in its own house."[62] This emphasis on retaining control over the dispute can be compared to the general concern that exists in public international law regarding the effectiveness of international rules and supervision.

In the private international law context it has not been possible to argue in absolute terms that one approach is better than the other. This is also reflected in the attitude of the courts, which usually show much flexibility in characterizing rules of foreign law, turning to either the *lex causae* or the *lex fori* as the circumstances may require.[63] In addition, it is often suggested that the process of characterization should not be constrained by particular notions of the *lex fori* or the *lex causae* and that, given the international dimension of the matter, the process should be "internationalist" and be based on the principles of analytical jurisprudence and comparative law.[64] This suggestion has much significance for public international (including WTO) law courts and tribunals as well. It is no wonder that, in formulating the doctrine of autonomous concepts, the ECHR has underscored the importance of comparative legal analysis. Thus, as may be recalled from earlier discussions, to attribute an autonomous characterization to domestic law rules and institutions, they must be examined "in the light of the common denominator" in the laws of the states parties to the EHR Convention.[65]

Finally, quite apart from methodological similarities or dissimilarities, an important reason why references to private international law seem relevant is that, in that field, the problem has always been a subject of extensive judicial and scholarly analysis. By contrast, in the public international law sphere, the problem has not only failed to generate adequate judicial or academic attention, but, more strikingly, sometimes

62 Morris & McClean 2000, 495. 63 See above, p. 127.

64 See, e.g., Beckett 1934, 58–60; Rabel 1945, 54–56; and Morris & McClean 2000, 496. See also the *Maldonado* case discussed at pp. 126–27 above; and *Macmillan Inc.* v. *Bishopsgate Investment Trust Plc. (No. 3)* [1996] 1 WLR 387, at 407 (per Auld LJ).

65 See above, p. 130.

it even remains unnoticed. (Recall, for instance, that the Panel in the *Canada – Periodicals* case did not properly understand parties' arguments on characterization.) It can hardly be doubted that there is a need on the part of the courts, as well as professionals and scholars of public international law, to impress themselves – as their private counterparts have – with the idea that the problem is not a trifling one, and, as such, requires not just incidental but focused and thorough analysis and discussion.

6 Standard of review

1 Introduction

This chapter explores one of the thorniest issues of WTO dispute settlement, namely that of the standard – or, in plural, standards – of review.[1] Put simply, this involves the manner in which panels and the Appellate Body should *review* Members' measures for their conformity with the WTO obligations: the crucial issue is the *degree* of intensity, rigor, thoroughness or severity – or, alternatively, the *lack* of these – with which such measures are to be reviewed. Given the extent of coverage of the WTO obligations, their varying impact on the legislative, judicial and administrative competence of Members,[2] the finesse and intricacy of questions of both fact and law that are put before panels and the AB (this list no doubt can be prolonged considerably), it is only natural that one particular standard will not be apposite in reviewing every national measure. Nor will the same standard be appropriate in resolving every issue in the course of such review. Thus, while the expression "standard of review" in its singular form is not an inaccurate description of the underlying problem, it should also be borne in mind that the benchmark of intensity, rigor, thoroughness or severity of review ought to vary for a number of reasons and so should the standard of review. To

[1] It is not only the WTO jurisprudence and the emerging academic discourse that are perplexed with this concept – increasingly it is generating much political discussion and debate in the major trading nations. A previous member and chairman of the WTO Appellate Body has noted that, over the recent period, the question of standard of review has become "one of the most controversial aspects" of the WTO dispute settlement jurisprudence: see Ehlermann 2002, 621. The political sensitivities surrounding this concept are discussed below in section 6.

[2] Recall, for instance, the discussion in Chapter 3 regarding the obligations to implement WTO commitments in national laws and to put in place specified civil, judicial and administrative procedures and other similar issues.

be sure, it is not a particular standard that WTO adjudicative bodies apply, but increasingly it is possible to identify a range of standards of review that are applied in practice – either explicitly or implicitly (more on these issues in section 5, below). From this perspective, the plural form of the expression is not inapt either.

1.1 *Scope of the chapter*

It may be recalled from Chapter 4 that the term "measure/s" has the widest possible connotation covering all governmental "acts" and, as such, panels and the AB may be called upon to review the WTO-compatibility of the entire range of administrative, judicial or legislative measures. Thus the question of standard of review does arise in respect of WTO dispute settlement organs' review of Members' administrative acts or decisions, and decisions of their domestic courts, as well as their national laws.[3] However, the question of standard of review has, so far, acquired greatest prominence and received comparable attention – be it in academic discourse, political debate or in the real world of WTO dispute settlement – in the context of review of administrative measures.

There are a number of reasons for this. First (as discussed below in more detail), the WTO treaty does not contain any general provision on standard of review that is applicable across the entire range of WTO disputes; nor does each of the individual WTO agreements contain such provisions applicable to disputes under each of them. The only exception is the Anti-Dumping Agreement (ADA), which expressly provides for a particular standard of review in respect of certain anti-dumping measures.[4] In most Members, these measures, by and large, are imposed by the administrative branch.[5] In these instances of administrative measures, the specific requirement on standard of review necessitates a more explicit and detailed consideration of the problem by panels and the AB. Likewise, in academic and political discourse the question of whether panels and the AB have kept within the bounds of the required standard of review attracts considerable attention. There also exist strong domestic economic interests that are deeply concerned that the WTO adjudicative bodies should keep within the specified parameters in reviewing anti-dumping measures.[6] And, indeed, it is this overwhelming concern

[3] See Trebilcock & Howse 1999, 69; and Waincymer 2002, 353, 525.

[4] See ADA, Article 17.6 (quoted below at p. 154).

[5] See, e.g., *Mexico – HFCS; Thailand – H-Beams; Guatemala – Cement II; US – Stainless Steel; US – Hot-Rolled Steel; Mexico – HFCS 21.5; US – Steel Plate; Egypt – Rebar*; and *Argentina – Poultry*.

[6] Croley & Jackson 1996.

of certain domestic interests (mostly in the United States) that was the major driving force for the insertion, in the first place, of a standard of review provision in the ADA.[7] Second, disputes concerning administrative measures are often highly fact-intensive. That is to say, at issue before the panels are administrative decisions arrived at on the basis of voluminous factual record – be it economic data, scientific evidence or something else. And, hence, in these disputes it is absolutely crucial to adopt and apply a well-articulated standard in reviewing the decisions against their factual backdrop. There is also a further reason pertaining to arithmetic: because disputes concerning the WTO-compatibility of administrative measures outnumber those regarding national legislation or court decisions, they naturally attract more scrutiny and analysis.

Having said the above, it must also be recognized that the legal systems of the Members vary considerably; and while in some Members certain types of trade measures may be administrative in nature, in others those same types of measures may be taken by a judicial or quasi-judicial body or may even partake of the nature of legislation. Anti-dumping measures taken by the European Community as a WTO Member are good examples. These are usually contained in "regulations" of the Council or the Commission of the EC[8] and, as such, are nothing less than Community legislation.[9] Furthermore, while the Commission can be described as something of a hybrid of a legislature and an executive,[10] the Council, indeed, is the principal legislative organ of the EC.[11] In addition, clear distinction between measures as legislative, judicial, administrative, etc., may be blurred because, for instance, an administrative (or legislative) agency may act on the basis of findings or recommendations made by other administrative,[12] judicial or quasi-judicial bodies.[13] It is also possible for an administrative measure to come before the WTO after certain domestic judicial review or appeal procedures have been pursued against it.[14]

At any rate, the question of standard of review is not unique to administrative measures – be it in the context of the specific standard of review clause of the Anti-Dumping Agreement or in general. And, of course, the question arises equally where a stand-alone measure – whether legislative, judicial or administrative – is challenged or where the situation is

[7] Ibid. 194, 199–200. [8] See, e.g., *EC – Bed Linen; EC – Bed Linen 21.5*; and *EC – Pipe Fittings*.
[9] See Weatherill & Beaumont 1999, 150. [10] Ibid. 72. [11] Ibid. 73.
[12] See, e.g., *Thailand – H-Beams*; and *Argentina – Poultry*.
[13] See, e.g., *US – Stainless Steel; US – Hot-Rolled Steel*; and *US – Steel Plate*.
[14] See, e.g., *US – Steel Plate*.

more complicated and two or more different measures (e.g., a domestic law and an administrative decision taken under it or an administrative act and a judicial decision upholding the same) are challenged at the same time.

While the subject-matter of this book is the relation between WTO law and national *law*, the analysis in this chapter is not confined to standard of review of legislation only. A broader analysis is undertaken for a number of reasons. First, it is difficult to understand the problem of standard of review of national laws, unless it is put against the backdrop of issues that arise in other contexts. Second, it may be the case that in respect of particular types of trade measures – emergency safeguard measures,[15] for instance – the existing jurisprudence predominantly concerns "acts" of, say, quasi-judicial bodies of Members. This, however, does not mean that the same types of measures cannot be contained in legislation;[16] and, in that context, the jurisprudence pertaining to quasi-judicial measures may be germane to a review of legislation. Third, and more importantly, certain benchmarks for the review of the acts or decisions of the administrative, judicial or quasi-judicial authorities of Members can have important implications for national legal institutions and procedures – or, more broadly, national legal systems. To give a simple example, in a number of cases panels and the AB have concluded, as part of their review of the decisions of different domestic authorities, that in order for the decisions concerned to be treated as WTO-compatible, they must be adequately reasoned.[17] An obvious consequence of applying such a criterion of review is that the relevant domestic procedures (whether administrative, judicial, quasi-judicial or legislative), which, as a matter of course, have their source in Members' *domestic laws*, must be such as to ensure the outcome of adequately reasoned decisions.

1.2 *Effectiveness and good governance*

The policy objectives of effectiveness and good governance have a certain evaluative function in WTO dispute settlement in general, and in respect of standard of review in particular. The role of effectiveness can be best explained by reference to Article 3 of the DSU, which sets forth

[15] These are measures taken to protect domestic producers against an unforeseen surge in imports.
[16] EC measures that are challenged before the WTO, for instance, are most often contained in EC legislation.
[17] See the cases cited in nn. 179, 182, 184, below.

the objectives of the WTO dispute settlement system. It states that the system "is a central element in providing security and predictability to the multilateral trading system" and "serves to preserve the rights and obligations of Members under the covered agreements."[18] The article further provides that prompt settlement of disputes "is essential to the effective functioning of the WTO and the maintenance of a proper balance between the rights and obligations of Members."[19] These provisions illustrate the importance attached by WTO Membership to a cohesive, stable and effective trading regime where WTO rules are applied in a similar, consistent, and predictable manner from Member to Member. Panels and the Appellate Body play a critical part in achieving these goals by providing for a uniform interpretation and application of WTO law.[20] As explained later in section 3, formulating and applying the appropriate standard of review concerns issues of whether and to what extent panels and the AB are to *defer* to matters of fact as well as law put forward by the respondent party to a dispute. Undue deference to questionable interpretation and application of WTO law by individual WTO Members would defeat the uniform interpretation and application - and hence effectiveness - of WTO law. In such circumstances, the rights and obligations of WTO Members would differ from Member to Member, undermining the core objectives of security, predictability and effectiveness. Accordingly, the level of deference to be accorded by panels and the AB to contested national laws or measures is - indeed, should be - conditioned by the objective of ensuring effectiveness of WTO rules and discipline. Put differently, the standards or benchmarks for the assessment and evaluation of the WTO-compatibility of national laws and measures must correspond to the policy objective of effectiveness of the multilateral trading system.

Standard of review is an important mechanism that guarantees separation of powers within and between legal systems. It involves the nature and intensity of a court's or judicial organ's review of the legal validity of legislative, administrative or other decisions. In a domestic context and within domestic legal systems, it concerns the degree of deference that a national judge should accord to national legislators and regulators. In an international, including WTO, context and between international and domestic legal systems, it concerns the degree of deference that an international judge should accord to national legislators and regulators. Thus, standard of review defines the parameters within which judges

[18] DSU, Article 3.2. [19] Ibid. Article 3.3. [20] See Ehlermann & Lockhart 2004, 498.

and, correspondingly, legislators and regulators should work. Ehlermann and Lockhart have put it nicely in the following terms: "[Standard of review] establishes 'no go' areas for judges, requiring them to respect the choices made by legislators or regulators. Within these 'no go' areas, the first decision-maker has discretion to make choices that the judge cannot reconsider. Beyond the 'no go' areas, the judge has the authority to verify the legal – but not political – validity of the decision."[21] Clearly, standard of review is a crucial part of the system of checks and balances in governance, both domestic and international, helping to ensure the accountability of decision-makers. It functions to allocate decision-making authority and resources in an efficient fashion among different branches and levels of governance.[22] Thus, in essence, standard of review is concerned with good governance.

Apart from the above-noted general relationship between standard of review and good governance, at a more particular level, good governance serves as an explicit tool or standard of review of national laws and measures. As will be seen, in certain circumstances panels and the AB apply a two-pronged standard of review: they examine whether the contested measure is adopted after evaluating *all relevant facts or factors* and whether a *reasoned and adequate explanation* is provided by the national authority as to how those facts/factors support the contested measure. A national measure that does not duly take into account the interests of all relevant stakeholders – both foreign and domestic – may well fall short of the first criterion of this standard of review. A deliberative decision- or rule-making process that gives stakeholders the opportunity to be heard is more likely to take into account "all relevant facts or factors" than a secretive, non-participatory process. Accordingly, the first criterion may in effect lead to greater deference to measures based on adequate *public deliberation*. The second criterion directly promotes rational and transparent decision- and rule-making as it tests whether a contested measure is explicitly supported by sufficiently reasoned analysis. It also has implications for deliberative decision-making, because the competing interests of various stakeholders must presumably be addressed – and resolved – as part of the reasoned and adequate explanation for adopting a measure. Thus, these criteria of review in effect test the legality of national measures on the basis of essential ingredients of good governance, namely deliberative, rational and transparent decision- and rule-making.

[21] Ibid. 493. [22] Ibid.

Furthermore, as explained below in section 5, there are a number of variables that have bearings on the standard of review. One such variable is the WTO provision/s concerned, i.e. provision/s under which the legality of the contested national measure is assessed. It may be recalled from Chapter 3 that there are various "good governance-tinged" substantive and systemic WTO obligations, such as those concerning non-discrimination, proportionality, non-arbitrariness, transparency, procedural fairness and due process, judicial remedy and the like. Whenever the legality of a national measure is determined under such a provision, "good governance" becomes an essential tool of review. Thus, in various important ways good governance already functions as an evaluative tool in the context of the standard of review analysis in WTO dispute settlement. There is, however, greater scope to use good governance-spirited standards of review in WTO dispute settlement. The question of the relevance of effectiveness and good governance in the potential evolution of standard of review in WTO dispute settlement is addressed later in section 6, after both the conceptual and the practical dimensions of the problem of standard of review are adequately explored in the forthcoming sections.

1.3 *The wider international legal context*

Before proceeding to the substantive analysis, it may be useful to underscore, as a further introductory matter, the wider international legal significance of the topic of standard of review. Although in recent years this topic has become particularly important in the WTO context, the problem of standard of review is not at all unique to the WTO. Rather, it arises whenever an international court or tribunal is called upon to *review* the conformity of national measures with international obligations.[23] Thus, for instance, standard of review is not simply a subject dealt with explicitly and elaborately in the NAFTA (or its predecessor the US–Canada FTA[24]) treaty, but it is also a most crucial issue that the NAFTA dispute settlement bodies confront on a regular basis.[25] Similarly, in the EC/EU context, the ECJ reviews the conformity of national measures with

[23] However, it is not suggested that the question always becomes contentious or that in all cases it is adequately argued or given the required amount of judicial consideration.

[24] Free Trade Agreement between Canada and the United States, January 2, 1988. On dispute settlement under the FTA (including issues of standard of review), see Lowenfeld 1991; and Mercury 1995.

[25] It may be noted in passing that NAFTA provides for a number of distinct procedures for dispute settlement. Two principal sets of provisions are contained in its Chapters 19 and 20. Chapter 19 establishes a mechanism for the review of anti-dumping and

EC law, and for this purpose applies criteria such as "proportionality," "subsidiarity," etc.[26] When these criteria are applied for determining the compatibility of national measures with international obligations, they assume the character of specific tools of review; and, accordingly, they can – and should – be understood in the light of the general problem of standard of review.

The problem is not confined to the area of international trade or economic affairs either. In the field of human rights, the ECHR has for many years dealt with this issue under its well-known doctrine of "margin of appreciation." In addition, it is also apparent that the problem

countervailing duty measures. The central feature of this mechanism is the replacement of domestic judicial review of administrative acts or decisions with international review by ad hoc bi-national panels (Article 1904[1]). In accordance with NAFTA Article 1904(2)-(3) and Annex 1911, these bi-national panels apply both the law of the country whose measure is being reviewed and that country's standard of review. As a result, the standard of review varies significantly in respect of the three NAFTA member states. The standard for the review of the US measures is whether the administrative agency's decision is based on substantial evidence on the record and is otherwise in accordance with the US law. The relevant Canadian law provides for more detailed grounds of review including whether the agency has acted beyond jurisdiction, committed any legal or perverse or capricious factual error, violated principles of natural justice, procedural fairness, etc. The grounds of review under Mexican law include whether the administrative agency lacked jurisdiction, whether it failed to observe formal legal requirements or furnish a reasoned decision, whether there have been defects of procedure, factual error or violations of the applicable law, etc. The bi-national panel system of Chapter 19 is most unique in international law because, while these panels are established under a treaty and as such are international law organs, in every other respect they partake the character of domestic administrative courts. On Chapter 19 procedure (including issues of standard of review), see Moyer 1993; T. J. Weiler 1995; Winham 1998; Pan 1999; and Pippin 1999.

Chapter 20 provides for the general dispute settlement mechanism of NAFTA; and this chapter applies to all NAFTA disputes other than those for which provisions are made elsewhere in the NAFTA treaty (e.g. in Chapter 19) (Article 2004). The adjudicative bodies envisaged in Chapter 20 are ad hoc five-person arbitral panels (Articles 2008, 2011). Unlike Chapter 19 panels, Chapter 20 panels are purely international legal organs and they are to review the conformity of national measures with the relevant NAFTA provisions (Articles 2004, 2012[3]). However (and again unlike Chapter 19), Chapter 20 does not contain any express provision on standard of review. But this does not mean that the question of standard of review is not relevant in respect of Chapter 20. So far three cases have been decided under this chapter. The question of standard of review was raised in one of those cases. The Panel in that case, although it avoided dealing with the matter elaborately, applied the criterion of whether the relevant domestic agency provided adequate and reasoned explanation for its decision: see *US Safeguard Action Taken on Broom Corn Brooms from Mexico*, Final Panel Report, January 30, 1998 (NAFTA), paras. 39–42, 57, 65–78, available at www.nafta-sec-alena.org. On Chapter 20 procedure, see, generally, Gantz 2000; and Sher 2003.

26 These are discussed in section 3 below.

will become increasingly important in respect of international dispute settlement in general. That is to say, it will be raised, more and more, before international forums other than the ones that have traditionally confronted it (such as those noted above, namely, the GATT/WTO, the US–Canada FTA/NAFTA, the ECJ or the ECHR). In a recent article, Yuval Shany has proposed that a doctrine akin to the ECHR's doctrine of margin of appreciation should be developed and introduced into general international law and that the International Court of Justice should make use of such a doctrine in reviewing decisions of national authorities.[27] "The *Ospar* case between Ireland and the United Kingdom before the Permanent Court of Arbitration provides a practical example of the

[27] See Shany 2005. Shany criticizes the ICJ for what he calls explicit or implicit rejection of the margin of appreciation doctrine in the *Oil Platforms* case, ICJ Rep. 161 (2003), and the *Wall in the Occupied Palestinian Territory* case, ICJ Rep. 136 (2004). In the former case the United States claimed that it was entitled to "a measure of discretion" in protecting its essential security interests under its treaty with Iran on amity, economic relations and consular rights. The ICJ, however, did not address the matter, because it took the view that, irrespective of the treaty, the relevant rules of general international law on self-defense left "no room for any measure of discretion": ICJ Rep. 161 (2003) at 196, para. 73. Shany considers the latter case as a rejection of the margin of appreciation doctrine because in that case the ICJ held that Israel was obliged to wipe out all the consequences of the breaches of international obligations due to the construction of a wall in the occupied Palestinian territory, and thus did not accord any discretion to Israel in remedying the breaches: ICJ Rep. 136 (2004) at 197–98, paras. 149–53. He contrasts these two cases with the following: first, cases where the ICJ apparently allowed some discretion to the responsible state in remedying breaches of consular obligations (*LaGrand* case, ICJ Rep. 466 [2001] at 514, 516, paras. 125, 128(7); and *Avena* case, ICJ Rep. 12 [2004] at 60, 62, 73, paras. 122, 131, 153[11]); and second, cases where the Court's ruling apparently did not foreclose the possibility of some discretion for a state in determining whether certain measures were necessary to protect its essential security interests (*Nicaragua* case, ICJ Rep. 14 [1986] at 116, 141–42, paras. 222, 282) or in invoking the plea of a "state of necessity" for breaches of international obligations (*Gabcikovo-Nagymaros Project* case, ICJ Rep. 7 [1997] at 39–46, paras. 49–57). For none of the aforementioned cases does Shany's interpretation seem to be entirely sound. The discretion allowed in the *LaGrand* and the *Avena* cases did not concern *whether or not* the consequences of the illegal act were to be wiped out, but rather *how* they were to be wiped out. From this perspective, these two cases are quite distinct from the *Wall in the Occupied Palestinian Territory* case. The differences between the Court's opinion in the *Oil Platforms* case and that in the *Nicaragua* and *Gabcikovo-Nagymaros Project* cases can be attributed to the differences in the content of the substantive rules that were at issue. (These cases, accordingly, highlight that the level of deference to national authorities – and hence the standard of review – may well vary depending on the applicable substantive rules. Section 5 of this chapter discusses this matter in fuller detail.) Nonetheless, the very fact that the question of discretion or deference to be accorded to national authorities in reviewing the legal validity of national measures has arisen before the ICJ shows that the full potential of the concept of standard of review is yet to be realized in that context.

relevance of standard of review in international dispute settlement in general. In this case the question of standard of review arose quite sharply and was extensively argued by the parties, drawing on the jurisprudence of both the WTO and the ECHR.[28] Similar attempts can, of course, be made in other cases and before other international courts and tribunals. Thus, as the international adjudicative process grows and develops, the relevance and importance of the topic of standard of review will become even greater.

While the main purpose of this chapter is to explore the problem in WTO dispute settlement, it is also cognisant of the wider significance of the topic. Accordingly, it endeavors to discuss the problem in WTO law along with some of the analogous or related concepts in other areas of international law to which reference has already been made, i.e. margin of appreciation, proportionality and subsidiarity. This is done with a view to developing a more comprehensive understanding of this aspect of international dispute settlement in general.

2 Textual framework

To put the relevant texts of the WTO treaty on or concerning standards of review in their proper perspective it may be useful to note briefly how some of the texts – or, specifically, the standard of review clause of the ADA (which, of course, is the only provision that addresses the matter expressly and directly) – came into being. GATT 1947, the rather modest predecessor of the WTO treaty, did not contain any provision regarding standard of review. Not surprisingly however, the issue, although not always explicitly labeled as such by the dispute settlement panels concerned, arose quite sharply in a number of GATT cases.[29] Thus, as the Uruguay Round negotiations,[30] which resulted in the signing of the WTO treaty, were going on, some of the most powerful trading nations as well

[28] See Transcripts of Hearings, *Dispute Concerning Access to Information under Article 9 of the OSPAR Convention, Ireland* v. *United Kingdom*, Day 2, October 22, 2002, at 105–8, and Day 3, October 23, 2002, at 4–16, available at www.pca-cpa.org.

[29] See, e.g., *US – Fur Hats*, para. 48; *Swedish Anti-Dumping Duties*, paras. 15, 23; *New Zealand – Transformers*, paras. 4.3–4; *Canada – Grain Corn*; *Korea – Polyacetal Resins*, paras. 209–13; *US – Softwood Lumber II*, paras. 334–35; *US – Norwegian Salmon I*, paras. 491–94; *US – Norwegian Salmon II*, paras. 257–60; and *Brazil – Milk Powder*, paras. 282–96. See also Akakwam 1996, 295–304; and Gomula 1999, 585–89.

[30] The brief remarks made here about the negotiating history are intended simply to put matters in perspective by pointing out the reasons for the absence of a general standard of review clause in the WTO treaty. More detailed accounts of the relevant negotiating history can be found in: Croley & Jackson 1996; Horlick & Clarke 1997;

as their domestic constituencies were already cognisant of the centrality of the problem in respect of third-party trade dispute settlement.[31] Deepest concern existed in the United States; and during the later stages of the negotiations a number of efforts were made by the USA to narrow significantly – either generally or at least in respect of anti-dumping measures – the scope of review by dispute settlement panels of questions of both fact and law.[32] Most other trading nations, however, were opposed to a generally applicable restrictive standard of review and feared that such a provision might unnecessarily constrain panels' supervisory role in respect of national trade measures and compromise the effectiveness of the WTO dispute settlement system.

As a result, the USA abandoned its proposals for a generally applicable standard of review clause and focused, instead, on the Anti-Dumping Agreement.[33] Eventually it succeeded in securing the agreement of the other negotiating countries on what is now Article 17.6 of the ADA.[34] This provision reads as follows:

> 17.6 In examining the matter referred to in paragraph 5:[35]
> (i) in its assessment of the facts of the matter, the panel shall determine whether the [domestic] authorities' establishment of the facts was proper and whether their evaluation of those facts was unbiased and objective. If the establishment of the facts was proper and the evaluation was unbiased and objective, even though the panel might have reached a different conclusion, the evaluation shall not be overturned;
> (ii) the panel shall interpret the relevant provisions of the Agreement [i.e. the ADA] in accordance with customary rules of interpretation of public international law. Where the panel finds that a relevant provision of the Agreement admits of more than one permissible interpretation, the panel shall find the [domestic] authorities' measure to be in conformity with the Agreement if it rests upon one of those permissible interpretations.

Needless to say, the carefully crafted language of Article 17.6 gives rise to some interesting interpretative issues. These, however, are dealt with

and Oesch 2003b, 72–80. It must be borne in mind, however, that under the customary rules of interpretation of treaties as contained in the VCLT, recourse may be had to the negotiating history or *travaux préparatoires* only as supplementary means of interpretation.

31 See Croley & Jackson 1996, 194.

32 For details of some of the US proposals, see Horlick & Clarke 1997, 317–18.

33 Ibid. 318–19.

34 The final language of Article 17.6, however, is a much watered-down version of the text that the USA originally intended to push through: see Croley & Jackson 1996, 199–201.

35 (Footnote inserted.) Paragraph 5 provides for the establishment of panels by the DSB to examine disputes regarding the imposition of anti-dumping measures.

in the later sections of this chapter; and, presently, attention is devoted to other pertinent aspects of the textual framework or the lack of it. It has now been stated more than once that the WTO treaty *does not* contain any express provision on standard of review (other than ADA Article 17.6 applicable *only* to anti-dumping measures).[36] The absence of a standard of review clause should not, however, be a matter of great surprise or shock. While it may not be unreasonable to think, or expect, that some guidance should exist somewhere in the treaty,[37] it is also true that treaty provisions on a subject such as this are most likely to be formulated at a level of considerable abstraction. In other words, even if there were a standard of review clause, in all likelihood it would have addressed the matter in broad general terms by reference to abstract notions such as "objective," "reasonable," "permissible" or the like.[38] The factual and other circumstances can be so diverse in real cases that treaty provisions, quite understandably, can neither anticipate nor seek to address specifically all the precise standard of review questions that may arise in practice. Thus, whether or not there exists any express

[36] It may be noted parenthetically that the Uruguay Round Final Act contains a Ministerial Decision (entitled "Decision on Review of Article 17.6 of the Agreement on Implementation of Article VI of the General Agreement on Tariffs and Trade 1994": this is the formal title of the ADA) which, in an attempt to give countenance to the original US intentions to have a generally applicable restrictive standard of review, states that the standard of review in ADA Article 17.6 "shall be reviewed after a period of three years with a view to considering the question of whether it is capable of general application." Although the stipulated three years have elapsed long since, as yet no action has been taken under this Decision; and it is also most unlikely that Article 17.6 will ever be declared to be generally applicable: see, further, Oesch 2003a, 646.

Also part of the UR Final Act is a Ministerial Declaration (entitled "Declaration on Dispute Settlement Pursuant to the Agreement on Implementation of Article VI of the General Agreement on Tariffs and Trade 1994 or Part V of the Agreement on Subsidies and Countervailing Measures"), in which the Ministers recognized "the need for the consistent resolution of disputes arising from anti-dumping and countervailing duty measures." In *US – Lead and Bismuth*, the United States sought to argue that, as a result of this Declaration, the standard of review clause as contained in ADA Article 17.6 was applicable to the ASCM. This argument was rejected by both the Panel and the Appellate Body (see Panel Report, paras. 6.8–18; and AB Report, paras. 44–51).

[37] See, e.g., Oesch 2003a, 645.

[38] This should not be taken as a suggestion that abstract notions are not important. Indeed, they are vital for any system of judicial dispute settlement and sometimes, quite rightly, are viewed as having constitutional attributes: see, e.g., Cass 2001. They are also not ignored in the present study, but are discussed with due emphasis in section 3 below. By contrast, the intention here is to highlight the equally important question of applying, as a practical matter, appropriately nuanced standard/s of review to the details of a particular case.

provision on standard/s of review, judicial organs (here panels and the AB) cannot but be left to their "reasoned judgments in confronting the endless and ever-changing ebb and flow of real facts in real cases in the real world"[39] (more on these and other related issues in subsequent sections).

In this context it may also be mentioned that some of the most celebrated doctrines on or concerning standard of review, in both international and domestic law, have developed not on the basis of express treaty or legislative provisions, but through judicial interpretation. The foremost example in international law is the doctrine of margin of appreciation as developed by the ECHR.[40] Although this doctrine has become an integral part of European human rights jurisprudence, the European Human Rights Convention under which the ECHR exercises jurisdiction does not contain any reference to it.[41]

At any rate, the earliest WTO panels which faced the question of standard of review thought that it would be more prudent to base their analysis on some text, rather than giving the impression that they were addressing the matter "out of the ether."[42] And the provision that was resorted to for this purpose was Article 11 of the DSU. Thus, in *US – Underwear* and *US – Shirts and Blouses*, both of which concerned the textiles agreement (ATC), the Panels, while noting that neither the ATC nor the DSU contains any provision on or reference to standard of review, considered DSU Article 11 to be "relevant."[43] (The Panel reports in these two cases were issued in late 1996 and early 1997 respectively; and these were also the first WTO cases to address the question of standard of review.) Subsequently, in *EC – Hormones* the Appellate Body confirmed the relevance of DSU Article 11 and made the following

39 These words in quotation marks are taken from the AB Report, *Japan – Alcohol II*, at 32 (the AB was not categorically addressing the question of standard of review, however).

40 In addition to the ECHR, the now-extinct European Commission of Human Rights also contributed to the development of this doctrine.

41 This doctrine is discussed in greater detail in the following section. Examples in domestic law include the English public law doctrine of *Wednesbury* unreasonableness (see *Associated Provincial Picture Houses, Limited* v. *Wednesbury Corporation* [1948] 1 KB 223) and the *Chevron* doctrine in US administrative law (see *Chevron USA, Inc.* v. *Natural Resources Defense Council, Inc.* [1984] 467 US 837). Under both of these doctrines courts can exercise the power of judicial review over administrative acts or decisions on very limited grounds only, and cannot reconsider the matter *de novo* as a court of appeal.

42 This expression is taken from the submissions of the United Kingdom on standard of review in the *Ospar* case before the Permanent Court of Arbitration: see Transcripts of Hearings, Day 3, October 23, 2002, n. 28 above, at 7 (Mr. Bethlehem).

43 See Panel Reports, *US – Underwear*, paras. 7.8–9; and *US – Shirts and Blouses*, para. 7.16.

observation:[44] "In our view, Article 11 of the DSU bears directly on this matter and, in effect, articulates with great succinctness but with sufficient clarity the appropriate standard of review for panels in respect of both the ascertainment of facts and the legal characterization of such facts under the relevant agreements."[45] From then on, it became a standard practice to refer to DSU Article 11 as the legal basis for the appropriate standard/s of review under each of the WTO covered agreements other than the ADA.[46] Although Article 11 has been quoted before,[47] it may be reproduced once again for ease of reference. The relevant part reads as follows:

> The function of panels is to assist the DSB in discharging its responsibilities under this Understanding and the covered agreements. Accordingly, a panel should make an objective assessment of the matter before it, including an objective assessment of the facts of the case and the applicability of and conformity with the relevant covered agreements, and make such other findings as will assist the DSB in making the recommendations or in giving the rulings provided for in the covered agreements.

3 Definitional, terminological and thematical issues

Of course, issues of interpretation as well as the practical implications of both of the textual benchmarks for the review of Members' measures are recurring subjects of this chapter. But, for a moment, it may be useful, as a further background analysis, to devote some attention to the thematical aspects of the problem of standard of review. Accordingly, this section explores in some detail the true nature and character of the

[44] Although both *US – Underwear* and *US – Shirts and Blouses* were appealed, the question of standard of review was not at issue before the AB.

[45] AB Report, *EC – Hormones I & II*, para. 116. However, like the earlier Panels, the AB also recognized the absence of any standard of review clause in the covered agreements other than the ADA: see ibid. para. 114.

[46] This is a notable development in that DSU Article 11 was hardly conceived earlier as a standard of review clause. The text of Article 11 is not something that has been introduced for the first time in the DSU through the Uruguay Round negotiations, rather, it was carried forward almost verbatim from a 1979 instrument adopted under the auspices of the GATT: see Understanding on Notification, Consultation, Dispute Settlement and Surveillance, adopted November 28, 1979, BISD 26S/210 (para. 16). Thus, although this provision was there for more than a decade, Professor Jackson, a leading scholar in the field, in a 1996 article (co-authored with Steven Croley) did not consider it to be relevant for purposes of standard of review, but rather thought that a different provision (namely, DSU Article 3.2) could be relevant: see Croley & Jackson 1996, 199–200.

[47] See above, Chapter 4, p. 104.

problem that is conveniently labeled as "standard of review" and seeks to identify the vital policy issues that lie beneath this shorthand label.

3.1 *Standard of review, deference and margin of appreciation*

Rather than attempting to describe the nature of the problem of standard of review in the abstract, it may be more apt to do so by reference to a concrete example; and for this purpose the well-known *EC – Hormones* case may be considered. This case concerned certain EC legislation prohibiting imports of meat products derived from cattle to which hormones had been administered for growth-promotion purposes, because such meat products were considered "unsafe" for human consumption. These types of measures are known as SPS (sanitary and phytosanitary) measures.[48] Article 5.1 of the WTO SPS Agreement requires that SPS measures be "based on an assessment, as appropriate to the circumstances, of the risks to human, animal or plant life or health." This is commonly referred to as "risk assessment." The complainants claimed that the EC measure (i.e. the legislation at issue) violated Article 5.1, while the EC, of course, took the view that its measure satisfied the risk assessment requirement.

The Panel could have adopted a number of different alternative approaches in reviewing the WTO-compatibility of the EC measure, including the EC's determination of the relevant risks. Two such alternatives were highlighted by the EC in its submission on appeal: namely, "*de novo* review" and "deference." The former, according to the EC, was a standard that would allow a panel "complete freedom to come to a different view" than that of the competent authority of the Member whose act or determination was being reviewed. Under this standard a panel could verify whether the determination by the national authority was "correct both factually and procedurally." By contrast, under the deference standard, a panel could not "seek to redo the investigation conducted by the national authority" but instead could only examine whether the procedure required by the relevant WTO rules had been followed.[49]

In addition to these, it is possible to conceive of other alternatives as well. Thus, more concretely, one could ask: should the *EC – Hormones* Panel have conducted a *de novo review of the entire matter*, e.g. investigating for itself whether there really existed the relevant risks?[50] Or should it have confined its review to an evaluation of the issues and evidence

[48] See SPS Agreement, Annex A, para. 1. [49] See AB Report, *EC – Hormones I & II*, para. 111.
[50] Cf. the GATT case, *Swedish Anti-Dumping Duties*, paras. 15, 23.

expressly noted in some EC public document or, alternatively, those *actually* considered or relied upon by the EC?[51] Should it have conducted a *de novo review of the evidence or issues* considered by the EC (that is to say should it have reviewed those issues or evidence afresh, rather than confining itself to an assessment of the conclusions drawn by the EC on those issues or on the basis of that evidence)?[52] Or should it have just reviewed whether the *EC itself* had properly determined the existence of the relevant risks?[53] What should have been the standard or criterion for determining the "propriety" of the EC's risk assessment, or for determining the WTO-compatibility of the EC's SPS measure? Should the criterion have been whether the EC's determination of risks and its interpretation of the WTO SPS Agreement were reasonable?[54] Or should it have been whether a reasonable person could have reached that interpretation or determination?[55] Or, in respect of the risk assessment for instance, should the criterion have been simply whether the EC had failed to take duly into account matters that it ought to have taken into account, or, conversely, whether it had taken into account matters that it ought not to have taken into account?[56]

Indeed, not much resourcefulness is needed to think of yet other alternatives; but this is not an endeavor to list all possible options that, rightly or wrongly, the Panel on *EC – Hormones* could have adopted. The purpose of noting some of the alternatives was to illustrate the nature of the problem that is described as "standard of review"; and, against those alternatives, the following definition given by two seasoned commentators can be put quite perceptively:

> It would seem clear that the international agreement does not permit a national government's determination *always* to prevail (otherwise the international rules could be easily evaded or rendered ineffective). But should the international body approach the issues involved (including factual determinations) *de novo*, without any deference to the national government? Certainly, . . . panels should respect national government determinations, up to some point. That "point" is the crucial issue that has sometimes been labeled the "standard of review."[57]

[51] Cf. the GATT cases, *Korea – Polyacetal Resins*, paras. 209–11; and *Brazil – Milk Powder*, paras. 282–95.

[52] Cf. the GATT case, *Canada – Grain Corn*.

[53] Cf. the GATT cases, *US – Norwegian Salmon I*, paras. 491–94; and *US – Norwegian Salmon II*, paras. 257–60.

[54] Cf. the US administrative law case of *Chevron*, n. 41 above, at 844, 865–66.

[55] Cf. the GATT case, *US – Softwood Lumber II*, para. 335.

[56] Cf. the English public law case of *Wednesbury*, n. 41 above, at 233–34. See also the GATT case, *US – Fur Hats*, para. 48.

[57] Croley & Jackson 1996, 194.

While the above definition assimilates the notion of "standard of review" with that of the "appropriate standard of review," the assimilation is not amiss. It hardly needs stating that any discussion about standard of review must as a matter of course focus on the "appropriateness" and/or "inappropriateness" of the relevant "standards," because otherwise it will be an entirely pointless exercise.

In this context (to wit, in the context of formulating and applying the appropriate standard/s of review), reference is often made to the need on the part of the panels to accord *due* (i.e. some) *deference* to matters of fact as well as law put forward by the respondent party to a dispute.[58] Similarly, sometimes it is argued (on appeal, by the complainant) that a panel showed *undue* (i.e. too much) *deference* to the respondent.[59] Thus the word "deference" (often preceded by a qualifier, such as, due, undue, appropriate, inappropriate, reasonable, unreasonable, considerable, substantial, total, etc.) has become a part of the vocabulary of standard of review in WTO dispute settlement.[60]

Returning once again to the *EC – Hormones* case, there the AB articulated the appropriate standard and noted the relevance of deference to it, in the following manner:

> So far as fact-finding by panels is concerned, their activities are always constrained by the mandate of Article 11 of the DSU: the applicable standard is neither *de novo* review as such, nor "total deference," but rather the "objective assessment of the facts." Many panels have in the past refused to undertake *de novo* review, wisely, since under current practice and systems, they are in any case poorly suited to engage in such a review. On the other hand, "total deference to the findings of the national authorities," it has been well said, "could not ensure an 'objective assessment' as foreseen by Article 11 of the DSU."
>
> In so far as legal questions are concerned – that is, consistency or inconsistency of a Member's measure with the provisions of the applicable agreement . . . it is appropriate to stress that here again Article 11 of the DSU is directly on point.[61]

58 See, e.g., Panel Report, *US – Section 301*, para. 7.19.

59 See, e.g., AB Reports, *US – Lamb*, paras. 42–43, 119; *US – Wheat Gluten*, para. 24; and *US – Softwood Lumber VI 21.5*, para. 100.

60 Many of the recently published works on this subject, for instance, include the word "deference" as part of their title: see Stuart 1992; Croley & Jackson 1996; Davey 2001; Bloche 2002; Trebilcock & Soloway 2002; and Durling 2003. References in the dispute settlement reports are also abundant. See, e.g., AB Reports, *EC – Bed Linen*, paras. 22, 65; *Australia – Salmon*, paras. 12, 262, 267; *Korea – Alcohol*, paras. 39, 68; *US – Wheat Gluten*, para. 147; *US – Lamb*, para. 101; *US – Cotton Yarn*, para. 69; and *Japan – Apples*, paras. 150, 165. The word has also been used in both the EHR and NAFTA contexts: see, e.g., O'Donnell 1982, 495; and T. J. Weiler 1995.

61 AB Report, *EC – Hormones I & II*, paras. 117–18 (footnotes omitted).

Thus the AB has explicitly excluded *de novo* review and total deference from the spectrum of acceptable standards or deference – albeit in so far as *fact-finding* by panels is concerned. (The varying dimensions of standard of review in respect of questions of fact and questions of law are considered below.) However, apart from this, the AB's formulation does not identify – to borrow an expression used by Croley and Jackson[62] – the "point" or "points" in that spectrum that in different circumstances can be the appropriate benchmark/s of review or deference.

The AB, of course, underscored the "objective assessment" criterion of DSU Article 11, which in its view sets out the appropriate standard with "sufficient clarity"![63] Quite contrarily, this provision says almost nothing about standard of review. Panels, no doubt, should make an "objective assessment" of the matter, because WTO Members did not set up the elaborate formal dispute resolution mechanism for panels to render "skewed" judgments. But it is not possible to distill from the criterion of objectivity any guidance on the level of intensity or thoroughness with which national measures are to be reviewed.[64] (Consider, for instance, the function of a first instance domestic trial court which hears and decides a case *de novo* and that of another domestic court which can review the legality of the acts of administrative agencies on certain limited grounds only: neither of these two courts acts less objectively than the other.)

Having said the above, the difficulty of articulating with great precision the appropriate level of scrutiny (or "point" of deference) needs also to be recognized. The function of adjudication is barely an exact science;[65] and for an international adjudicative body the situation is all the more complicated for a number of reasons.

Firstly, while in a domestic context it is possible to put cases in clearly defined categories such as "new," "appeal" or "judicial review," in an international context such categorization is much more difficult. *EC – Hormones*, again, is a good example. There the Panel's factual finding with respect to risk assessment came quite close to *de novo* review;[66] and the AB, although expressly excluding the possibility of *de novo* review, did not

[62] N. 57 above. [63] N. 45 above.
[64] Desmedt 1998, 697. [65] See, e.g., Bedjaoui 2000, 2.
[66] See Panel Reports, *EC – Hormones I*, paras. 8.98–159; and *EC – Hormones II*, paras. 8.101–62. The Panel not only reviewed *de novo* the evidence submitted by the EC, but also relied heavily on the views of the scientific experts appointed by it. See Waincymer 2002, 350; Wirth 1998, 758; L. Hughes 1998, 926; and T. P. Stewart & Johanson 1999, 244–45.

overturn that finding.[67] Yet it is difficult to criticize the Panel or the AB for failing to apply an appropriately deferential standard of review. This is because Article 5.1 of the SPS Agreement requires that SPS measures be "*based on*" risk assessment. Accordingly, in reviewing conformity with this provision, a panel, to a certain extent, needs to satisfy itself whether the alleged risks really exist – even if it means engaging in a *de novo* review of the matter; otherwise a respondent government could very well render the WTO obligation (and the complainant's rights) ineffective by simply asserting that it found, on whatever basis, those risks to exist.[68] Clearly, a very restricted criterion of review – as may be the case, for instance, in respect of "judicial review" in a domestic context – will not be apposite here. Rather, a panel needs to be much more resourceful in combining various techniques, some of which may be similar to tools or standards of "judicial review" in a purely domestic context, while others may pertain to fact-finding in a "new" matter, and yet others may be reminiscent of an "appeal."[69]

Secondly, the authority of international adjudicative organs rests on the relatively fragile foundations of the consent of "sovereign" nations. This greatly changes the entire scene; and these organs must incessantly be concerned to strike an appropriate balance between national sovereignty and international obligations.[70] In some circumstances

[67] AB Report, *EC – Hormones I & II*, paras. 196–208.

[68] See, generally, Quick & Blüthner 1999, 617; Pauwelyn 1999, 648–49; and Hurst 1998.

[69] Any strict domestic analogy breaks down not least because international adjudicative organs have an entirely different relationship to domestic authorities whose acts or decisions they may review from that between domestic courts and other domestic authorities, over whom such courts may exercise the power of judicial review. The likelihood of conflict between the interests pursued by the reviewing and the reviewed authorities is greater in the former context, while in the latter context it is not only smaller but, in fact, the interests may even coincide. Consequently, an international court or tribunal needs to be more open to "second-guess" national measures (be it with regard to factual or policy determinations) than may be the case in respect of judicial review of administrative measures in a domestic context, for instance.

Croley and Jackson have argued at great length and quite convincingly as to why some of the common justifications for a restrictive standard of judicial review in a domestic context are completely out of place in an international context: see Croley & Jackson 1996, 208–11. Another commentator has gone as far as to argue that the actually applied standard of review cannot be found in formulations such as "objective assessment" or the like, but rather "in the relationship of the 'judge' to the 'judged'": see McNelis 2001, 189.

[70] See, generally, Jackson 1997c, 175–83 and 2003; Barfield 2001; Raustiala 2003; and Sarooshi 2005, 95–97.

applying an intrusive standard of review might entail a damaging confrontation between a panel and the respondent WTO Member over their respective spheres of authority, while in others applying a lax standard might empty the rights of the complainant, which again is a WTO Member, of real meaning and effectiveness. The task no doubt is a very delicate one; and this, by itself, calls for a certain amount of flexibility.[71]

While in *EC – Hormones* the substantive provision at issue tipped the standard more towards *de novo* review of a factual matter, in other cases, different obligations – or, indeed, other factors and issues[72] – may cause the appropriate balance to move in the opposite direction. The real outcome in any particular case can be so much dependent on the relevant context and circumstances that it is hard to formulate a-priori principles.

It is not only in the context of trade dispute settlement under the WTO that the appropriate level of review or deference defies precise definition – such difficulty exists in other areas of international adjudication as well. In the European human rights law context for instance, the concept of margin of appreciation – a much older and also more well-known and closely scrutinized tool of international review of national measures – has been widely critiqued as being incapable of precise formulation.[73]

This may be an appropriate place to note briefly the nature and character of the doctrine of margin of appreciation. Apart from pointing out the difficulties of precise formulation that exist in that context, there are other, and perhaps more compelling, reasons to do so. Some of the academic analyses of standard of review in WTO law refer to "margin of appreciation" in a footnote without further clarifying what, if any, are the similarities or dissimilarities between these two concepts;[74] nor have attempts been made to develop a more comprehensive understanding of this aspect of international dispute settlement in general, by discussing these two rather important concepts together. Accordingly, some discussion of these issues is overdue and has a certain analytical appeal.

[71] Cf. de Búrca & Scott 2000 (this volume contains a set of interesting articles on the role of flexibility in the EU legal order).

[72] Some of these are considered in section 5 below.

[73] See, e.g., Morrisson 1973, 284; O'Donnell 1982, 475, 495; Macdonald 1993, 85; and Lavender 1997, 380.

[74] See, e.g., Croley & Jackson 1996, 194 (footnote 11); and Oesch 2003a, 638 (footnote 7). Although a short discussion of the margin of appreciation doctrine can be found in Oesch 2003b, unlike the present work, the view taken there is that standard of review and margin of appreciation are entirely distinct concepts: see Oesch 2003b, 51–54.

Put simply, the margin of appreciation refers to the latitude allowed to the states parties to the EHR Convention in their observance of the Convention obligations.[75] The margin, or the width of the margin, is said to vary from case to case.[76] The wider the margin is, the less exacting is the scrutiny to which the impugned act or decision of the defendant state is subjected and, as a result, the less likely is a finding of a violation of the Convention. Conversely, the narrower the margin is, the less lax (or more rigorous) is the scrutiny and the greater is the possibility for the ECHR to find the defendant state to be in breach.[77] Clearly, the underlying problem that this doctrine seeks to address is analogous to the problem of standard of review. Consider, for instance, the following observations by a former judge of the Human Rights Court, which usefully highlight the affinity between the two concepts as well as their common difficulty of precise formulation:

> Being concerned with the appropriate scope of review, the margin is not susceptible of definition in the abstract, as it is, by its very nature, context-dependent. To search for its "ambit" or "scope" in the abstract again misunderstands its nature and leads only to tautology, for it is the equivalent of attempting to define the scope of review. *The margin of appreciation is really just the other side of the scope of review coin.*[78]

At least apparently, the expression "margin of appreciation" tends to be evocative of one particular dimension of standard of review, namely, that of deference. Specifically, if the margin is wide, more deference is given to the defendant state, and if narrow, less deference is given.[79] While this aspect should not be de-emphasized, there is in fact much more to the doctrine of margin of appreciation. For instance, on various occasions the ECHR has attempted to devise *the appropriate structure/s of review* to be conducted by it of the acts or decisions of national (legislative, judicial or administrative) authorities so that the "margin of appreciation" of such authorities is duly respected.[80]

In this context two extreme alternatives have been espoused at different times. The first alternative would have the ECHR ignore the decision of the national authorities and seek to apply the provisions of

[75] See, e.g., O'Donnell 1982, 475; and Macdonald 1993, 85.

[76] See, e.g., *Rasmussen* v. *Denmark*, ECHR Ser. A No. 87 (1984), para. 40; and Macdonald 1993, 84.

[77] O'Donnell 1982, 475.

[78] Macdonald 1993, 85 (italics added).

[79] The margin of appreciation doctrine has indeed been described as "a doctrine of deference in the exercise of judicial review": O'Donnell 1982, 495.

[80] Lavender 1997, 390.

the Convention directly to the facts of each case,[81] while the second alternative would have it confine itself to checking only whether the national authorities had acted reasonably, carefully and in good faith.[82] (Notably, these alternatives are quite similar to *de novo* review and total – or nearly so – deference that are generally put forward as extreme alternatives in the WTO context.) The ECHR, however, has rejected both of these alternatives.[83]

As regards the first, in *Handyside* the ECHR has noted categorically that its task is not "to take the place" of national authorities but rather to review their acts or decisions under the Convention.[84] This case concerned the Convention provision regarding interference with the right to freedom of expression for the protection of morals;[85]and the ECHR has identified two factors that would form part of its "review" of the acts or decisions of national authorities in cases concerning that provision. These are: (i) the interference must be *proportionate* to the legitimate aim pursued; and (ii) the *reasons given* by the national authorities to justify the interference *must be relevant and sufficient.*[86]

The second extreme alternative noted above was also rejected by the ECHR, notably, in the *Sunday Times* case, where the majority took the view that the Court's supervision was not limited to ascertaining whether a respondent state had exercised its discretion reasonably, carefully and in good faith.[87] Subsequently, in the *Observer and Guardian* case, the judgment of the majority (of fourteen out of twenty four) has summarized the Court's function as follows:

The Court's task, in exercising its supervisory jurisdiction, is not to take the place of the competent national authorities but rather to review under Article 10 the decisions they delivered pursuant to their power of appreciation. This does not mean that the supervision is limited to ascertaining whether the respondent

[81] This view was taken, for instance, by the minority of the European Commission of Human Rights in the *Handyside* case (see *Handyside* v. *United Kingdom*, ECHR Ser. A No. 24 [1976], para. 47).

[82] This view was taken, for instance, by the majority of the European Commission of Human Rights in the *Handyside* case (see ibid.) and by the minority of the ECHR in the *Sunday Times* case (see *Sunday Times* v. *United Kingdom*, ECHR Ser. A No. 30 [1979], Joint Dissenting Opinion of Judges Wiarda *et al.*, para. 8).

[83] Lavender 1997, 382.

[84] *Handyside*, n. 81 above, para. 50. Indeed, the ECHR has throughout been very scrupulous in expressing its unwillingness to take the place of national authorities, whether a court, the administration or the legislature: see, e.g., the survey of cases in Macdonald 1993.

[85] EHR Convention, Article 10(2).

[86] *Handyside*, n. 81 above, paras. 49–50.

[87] *Sunday Times*, n. 82 above, para. 59.

State exercised its discretion reasonably, carefully and in good faith; what the Court has to do is to look at the interference complained of in the light of the case as a whole and determine whether it was "proportionate to the legitimate aim pursued" and whether the reasons adduced by the national authorities to justify it are "relevant and sufficient."[88]

While the above formulation draws on the particular language of Article 10(2) of the EHR Convention, one nonetheless encounters criteria that are capable of some, even if limited, general application, e.g. proportionality or the sufficient reasons test. Then again, the difficulty of the actual application of these rather indeterminate concepts in real cases persists no less significantly. It is no wonder that the "margin" allowed to states parties in fulfilling their obligations varies considerably even in respect of a single Convention provision. Thus, for instance, in real cases the margin varied depending on whether an interference with the right to freedom of expression was for the protection of morals, or for the protection of the reputation and rights of others, or for the protection of confidential information, and so on.[89] And it is needless to say anything about the changes in the "context-dependent spectrum" of the margin that occur across the Convention and in respect of different rights.[90]

In the case law there is also equally clear evidence of the ECHR's constant struggle in getting to grips with the appropriate structure, scope or standard of review (so as to respect the margin of appreciation of the national authorities). Thus, for instance, while in some cases the ECHR took the view that it should not substitute its own evaluation for that of the national authorities, where such authorities had acted on reasonable grounds,[91] in others such an approach proved to be inadequate and too restrictive of the ECHR's supervisory function and the effectiveness of the Convention.[92] These difficulties on the one hand highlight the point that questions of standard of review do not belong to the realm of pure

88 *Observer and Guardian* v. *United Kingdom*, ECHR Ser. A No. 216 (1991), para. 59(d).

89 See the survey of cases in Macdonald 1993; and Arai-Takahashi 2002, 101–37.

90 The words in quotation marks are taken from Macdonald 1993, 84. See, generally, ibid. and Arai-Takahashi 2002.

91 See, e.g., *Markt Intern* v. *Germany*, ECHR Ser. A No. 165 (1989), para. 37; and *Demuth* v. *Switzerland*, 38 EHRR 423 (2004), para. 48.

92 See, e.g., *Observer and Guardian*, n. 88 above, para. 3. Cf. *Margareta and Roger Andersson* v. *Sweden*, ECHR Ser. A No. 226 (1992), Partly Dissenting Opinion of Judge Lagergren; and *Hertel* v. *Switzerland*, 1998-VI ECHR Rep. 2301, Dissenting Opinion of Judge Bernhardt: both of these opinions criticize the majority of the Court for substituting their own evaluation for that of the national authorities.

mathematics, and on the other hand demonstrate their indispensability in any large-scale international dispute settlement.

To summarize, and looking beyond the problem of precise formulation, the role that the doctrine of margin of appreciation plays in the European human rights context is this: states are allowed some choice when delimiting human rights; and in a given case the ECHR does not seek to answer the question of whether the measure taken by the respondent state is the best one or the most adequate one, because several measures may be equally consistent with the Convention. (In this respect, the ECHR, it has been suggested, is not a court of cassation, but compares better with a national constitutional court, which also often leaves to the legislator a certain margin of appreciation to legislate under the state constitution, for instance.[93])

A final point that needs to be stressed in this part of the analysis of the present chapter is that, because of the "elusive"[94] nature of the problem of standard of review, it is of utmost importance that all relevant actors – the litigants, but, more importantly, the adjudicating bodies – are constantly aware of the underlying policy issues that are at stake. In the EHR context these had long since been understood as pertaining to the proper allocation of power between a supranational (or centralized) institution and national (or local) authorities[95] – and they are no less so in the WTO context.[96] Certainly, in today's complex, interconnected and interdependent world, centralized institutions have vital roles to play. This, however, does not lessen the importance of decision-making closer to the constituencies affected, not only for reasons of democratic accountability and legitimacy but also as a check and balance against centralized power.[97] Thus, in each case, questions of standard of review must, of necessity, be probed by trying to understand who is better placed to make a particular decision: is it the international judge or the national authority? Only a constant awareness and vigilance in this regard can ensure that appropriately nuanced standard/s of review are applied in practice – standards that, on the one hand, do not sacrifice

[93] Bernhardt 1993, 33. [94] O'Donnell 1982, 495.

[95] See, e.g., *Handyside*, n. 81 above, para. 48; *James* v. *United Kingdom*, ECHR Ser. A No. 98 (1986), para. 46; Ryssdall 1996, 24–25; and Singh *et al.* 1999, 17.

[96] See, e.g., Croley & Jackson 1996, 194, 211–13.

[97] Indeed, issues concerning the appropriate allocation of power lie at the heart of any system of layered governance and the related adjudicative process, be it at a federal, regional or global level: see, e.g., O'Connor 2001. And, it hardly needs stating that the WTO is a key institution in global economic governance: see, generally, Kelly 2001; and Sampson 2001.

the effectiveness of international dispute settlement and, on the other hand, do not usurp legitimate national authority.

In the light of the above, the following observations of the WTO Appellate Body, which countenance the concerns regarding the proper allocation of power, are of particular note:

> The standard of review appropriately applicable in proceedings under the SPS Agreement, of course, must reflect the balance established in that Agreement between the jurisdictional competences conceded by the Members to the WTO and the jurisdictional competences retained by the Members for themselves. To adopt a standard of review not clearly rooted in the text of the SPS Agreement itself, may well amount to changing that finely drawn balance; and neither a panel nor the Appellate Body is authorized to do that.[98]

3.2 *Proportionality?*

As may have been noticed during the preceding discussion, in the EHR context the principle of proportionality is used as a specific tool within the margin of appreciation / standard of review analysis.[99] While proportionality as a legal principle has a much wider significance, and differing but comparable versions of this principle can be equally found in international law[100] and regional[101] and domestic law,[102] this is not the place for an extensive or comparative study of the principle. (Such studies, of course, can be found elsewhere.[103]) But a few remarks about the nature of the principle when it is applied as a tool of international review of national measures, as well as some attention to the question of what, if any, the relevance of the principle may be in WTO dispute settlement, are obviously not beside the point.

"Proportionality" again is a rather indeterminate concept and there is no universally settled meaning for it. It may be applied and interpreted

[98] AB Report, *EC – Hormones I & II*, para. 115 (footnote omitted).

[99] See text at nn. 86, 88 above.

[100] In traditional public international law the most notable examples of the principle of proportionality can be found in the law of countermeasures and in the law of armed conflict: see, e.g., Crawford 2002, 294–96; Cannizzaro 2001; and Gardam 1993. Beyond that, the ICJ has referred to "proportionality" in cases concerning maritime delimitation: see, e.g., *North Sea Continental Shelf*, ICJ Rep. 3 (1969) at 52, 54 (paras. 98, 101D[3]); *Continental Shelf (Tunisia/Libya)*, ICJ Rep. 18 (1982) at 75–78, 91–93 (paras. 103–4, 108, 130–31, 133B[5]); *Continental Shelf (Libya/Malta)*, ICJ Rep. 13 (1985) at 45–46, 53–55 (paras. 58, 74–75); and Brownlie 1998, 225–26. However, in these instances, "proportionality" is not applied as a tool of *review* of national measures, as is the case in the *lex specialis* international legal fields of European human rights law or EC/EU law: see, e.g., the works cited in n. 101 below.

[101] See, e.g., Emiliou 1996; and Ellis 1999.

[102] See, e.g., Emiliou 1996; and Thomas 2000.

[103] See, e.g., the works cited in nn. 101–2 above.

differently depending not only on the legal area at stake (e.g., international law, EC/EU law, human rights law, domestic administrative law, etc.) but also on the questions or issues at stake within one legal area. Nonetheless, some generalization for present purposes may be attempted and is also necessary. Put simply, as a tool of international review of national measures (and in the EC/EU context, also as a tool of review by the European Court of Justice of the acts of other European Community organs), the application of the criterion of proportionality involves a balancing of different rights, interests, values, etc.

There is more than one way in which the balancing itself is done. The ECHR, for instance, applies two types of balancing (or, indeed, proportionality) tests in cases involving interference with the individual rights guaranteed under the Convention. Firstly, an analysis of the "fair balance" between the individual rights and the general public interests of the society as whole (e.g. between the individual right to freedom of expression and the public interests of protection of morals by preventing publication of obscene materials) forms a part of the ECHR's review of national measures. Secondly, the ECHR applies a balancing test between the means employed by the respondent state and the public ends pursued by those means, that is to say it enquires whether there exists a rational means–ends relationship.[104] In this latter context, the review may also involve a determination of whether the means chosen is the *least restrictive* one, i.e. whether from amongst available alternative means the one that is least restrictive of the individual rights is chosen.[105]

Proportionality in EC/EU law, where this concept has definitely found the most fertile ground,[106] involves similar balancing techniques. Here the exact content of proportionality may vary depending on whether a national measure or an EC act is being reviewed by the ECJ. As regards national measures, proportionality involves – at a very general level – a due balance between the interests in free "intra-European Community" trade and the interests in, for instance, national health or environmental protection. One of the ways in which the balancing is done, again, is through an analysis of whether the means chosen by the defendant state is the *least restrictive* one, i.e. whether it is least restrictive of free

[104] Arai-Takahashi 2002, 193; and Eissen 1993. [105] Arai-Takahashi 2002, 194.

[106] Proportionality is not only a general principle of EC/EU law that has, since the Maastricht Treaty of 1991, been explicitly incorporated into the EC Treaty, but in "*inter*national" (as distinguished from domestic) law the most impressive and nuanced jurisprudential development of this principle can also be found in EC/EU law: see Emiliou 1996, 134–42.

intra-Community trade.[107] This least restrictive means test is also applied in respect of judicial review of EC acts by the ECJ. Other balancing techniques applied in this respect include a suitability test, which focuses on whether the means chosen is suitable for the purpose of achieving the desired objective, that is to say, on the means–ends (suitable/rational) relationship.[108]

Thus, as a minimum, proportionality concerns the following. First, at a general level, it is concerned with having the proper equilibrium between different rights, interests or values, for instance between individual rights and protection of morals or between free trade and health or environmental protection.[109] Second, at a more specific level, a number of techniques are employed in establishing that equilibrium, for instance means–ends rationality test, least restrictive means test, or the like. In these senses, the concept of proportionality is not only present in a number of provisions of the WTO treaty, but also a commonly used tool of review of national measures under those provisions.[110]

Consider, for instance, the following two provisions contained in the SPS Agreement and the TBT Agreement, respectively:

- Members shall ensure that [sanitary or phytosanitary] measures are not more trade-restrictive than required to achieve their appropriate level of sanitary or phytosanitary protection, taking into account technical and economic feasibility.[111]
- [T]echnical regulations shall not be more trade-restrictive than necessary to fulfil a legitimate objective, taking account of the risks non-fulfilment would create.[112]

It is almost immediately apparent that, in reviewing the compatibility of national measures with the above provisions, panels and the AB are to apply a least trade-restrictive means test,[113] which, needless to state once again, is a specific form of proportionality analysis.

[107] Weatherill & Beaumont 1999, 527, 541. [108] Emiliou 1996, 191–94.

[109] Although sometimes these are projected as "competing" interests or values, it is equally true that often none of these are preeminent by themselves. It has, for instance, quite sensibly been noted that "environmental protection policy as well as trade policy are both appropriately aimed at promoting, in different ways, human welfare, broadly understood": R. B. Stewart 1992, 1332. See also Trachtman 1998, 33; and Dunoff 1992, 1450.

[110] One author has even suggested that "proportionality is one of the more basic principles" underlying the WTO legal system: see Hilf 2001, 120.

[111] SPS Agreement, Article 5.6. [112] TBT Agreement, Article 2.2.

[113] See, e.g., Panel Reports, *Australia – Salmon*, paras. 8.161–83; *Japan – Agricultural Products II*, paras. 8.64–104; and *Australia – Salmon 21.5*, paras. 7.115–53; and AB Reports, *Australia – Salmon*, paras. 179–213; and *Japan – Agricultural Products II*, paras. 95–101. A detailed account of these cases in the light of the proportionality principle can be found in Desmedt 2001, 453–62.

Notably, the least trade-restrictive means test, as contained in the SPS and the TBT Agreements, was derived from earlier GATT panel decisions on the interpretation of the word "necessary," as it existed in clauses (b) and (d) of Article XX of the GATT 1947. This Article, of course, has been carried into the successor agreement, the GATT 1994. It bears the title "General Exceptions" and contains a number of provisions permitting WTO Members to adopt measures that are otherwise GATT-inconsistent. The following are permitted under clauses (b) and (d), respectively:

- [measures] necessary to protect human, animal or plant life or health.
- [measures] necessary to secure compliance with laws or regulations which are not inconsistent with the provisions of this Agreement.

In cases concerning both of the above provisions, it was held by GATT panels that a respondent state could not justify a measure inconsistent with another GATT provision as "necessary," unless the measure was the least trade-restrictive one from amongst reasonably available alternative measures.[114] This is now confirmed in the jurisprudence of the WTO Appellate Body.[115]

Another prominent WTO provision that requires proportionality analysis (in this instance a means–ends rationality test) is Article XX(g) of the GATT 1994. This provision entitles Members to adopt measures "relating to the conservation of exhaustible natural resources" that are otherwise GATT-inconsistent. The AB has already held that a measure can be treated as "*relating to*" conservation, if there exists a "substantial" or a "close and genuine" relationship "of ends and means."[116] That is to say, the means chosen is to be "reasonably related to the ends" and is not to be "disproportionately wide in its scope and reach in relation to the policy objective of protection and conservation" of resources.[117]

In *Japan – Apples*, the proportionality test has been applied in the context of the requirement under Article 2.2 of the SPS Agreement that sanitary or phytosanitary measures must not be maintained "without sufficient scientific evidence." This case concerned a Japanese phytosanitary measure restricting importation of apples in connection with fire blight (a disease of fruits and plants).[118] The Panel found that the measure was not supported by sufficient scientific evidence within the

[114] See, e.g., *US – Section 337*, para. 5.26; *Thai – Cigarettes*, paras. 74–75; and *US – Malt Beverages*, para. 5.43.
[115] See, e.g., AB Reports, *Korea – Beef*, paras. 165–82; and *EC – Asbestos*, paras. 170–75.
[116] AB Report, *US – Shrimp*, para. 136. [117] Ibid. para. 141.
[118] For a comment on this dispute, see Goh 2006.

meaning of Article 2.2, because it was "clearly disproportionate" to the risk of fire blight identified on the basis of the available scientific evidence. Such clear disproportionality resulted from the lack of "a rational or objective relationship" between the measure and the relevant scientific evidence.[119] On appeal, these findings were upheld by the Appellate Body.[120] (It is worth noting that, although under both GATT 1994 Article XX[g] and SPS Agreement Article 2.2 the proportionality test concerns "rational relationship," the test is not exactly the same. In the former context it involves a "means–ends" relationship, while in the latter context it concerns a "measure–evidence" relationship.)[121]

Requirements pertaining to the more general proportionality analysis of balancing different rights, interests or values can also be found in the WTO treaty. These exist, for instance, in the introductory provision (commonly referred to as the chapeau) of Article XX of the GATT 1994. This provision imposes certain requirements regarding non-discrimination, non-arbitrariness and the like in respect of invoking any of the various "general exceptions" of Article XX (including clauses [b], [d] and [g] noted above). The Appellate Body has described the task of applying this provision as follows:

> The task of interpreting and applying the chapeau is . . . one of locating and marking out a line of equilibrium between the right of a Member to invoke an exception under Article XX and the rights of the other Members under varying substantive provisions . . . of the GATT 1994, so that neither of the competing rights will cancel out the other and thereby distort and nullify or impair the balance of rights and obligations constructed by the Members themselves in that Agreement.[122]

Thus, under the WTO, proportionality is not an uncommon tool of review of national measures. However, having said that, two particular points need to be stressed.

First, although in various forms proportionality analysis is undertaken by panels and the AB, often they do not explicitly put that label on it.

119 See, Panel Report, *Japan – Apples*, paras. 8.101–3, 8.180–81, 8.191, 8.197–98.

120 See, AB Report, *Japan – Apples*, paras. 147, 162–63.

121 In addition to the examples noted above, reference to "proportionality" has been made in reviewing national measures under Article 6.4 of the ATC concerning attribution of serious damage caused by imports (see AB Report, *US – Cotton Yarn*, paras. 119–20) and Article 5.1 of the Safeguards Agreement providing that safeguard measures can be applied only to the extent "necessary" to prevent or remedy serious injury to a domestic industry (see AB Report, *US – Line Pipe*, paras. 253–60).

122 AB Report, *US – Shrimp*, para. 159. See also Appleton 1999, 492.

It is also understandable why they prefer not to do so. Unlike the ECJ or the ECHR, WTO panels and the AB exercise jurisdiction on a global basis. Accordingly, it is natural for them to show less readiness to refer to legal concepts (indeed, concepts that may be well known in some of the Member countries but may not be quite so in others) that are not expressly mentioned in the WTO treaty.[123] Then again, not adding the label does not change the nature of the underlying proportionality enquiry or convert it into something else.

Second, in WTO law, as yet, there is no "unwritten" and "autonomous" proportionality principle. In other words, unlike European human rights law or EC/EU law, under WTO law proportionality has not yet been developed into a generally applicable standard of review. Rather, in each case, its application is dependant on the substantive provision concerned, and it is applied only if that provision incorporates tests or criteria pertaining to the concept of proportionality.

3.3 *Subsidiarity?*

Subsidiarity is another legal principle that can be found in both EC/EU law[124] and European human rights law.[125] Although it is variously defined depending on the context, in rather general terms it can be described as the principle that calls for decisions – legislative, executive or judicial – to be taken as closely as possible to the most concerned constituencies. This principle is better known not as a tool of "judicial review," but as a check on the exercise of executive and legislative powers. In the EC context, for instance, there exists explicit treaty language that legislative or administrative actions are to be taken at the EC level only if the objectives of the proposed actions cannot be achieved by actions taken by the EC member states.[126] Presently, however, attention is devoted, for obvious reasons, not to the role of "subsidiarity" in

[123] Cf. Abi-Saab 2005, 11 (noting that in one case reference by the Appellate Body to the principle of proportionality as a general principle gave rise to a lot of criticism). Also recall in this context DSU Articles 3.2 and 19.2 (discussed in Chapter 4), which forbid panels and the AB from engaging in "judicial activism" by requiring them not to add to or diminish the rights and obligations provided in the WTO agreements. In addition, right from the beginning, the AB was extremely cautious to avoid referring to terms and expressions not contained in the WTO agreements and was equally (and sometimes even unnecessarily) critical of panels, which made such references: see, e.g., AB Reports, *US – Gasoline*, at 18; and *US – FSC*, para. 91.

[124] See, e.g., Toth 1994; Gonzalez 1995; Swaine 2000; and Estella 2002.

[125] See, e.g., Petzold 1993; Mahoney 1997; Lord Lester 1998; and Carozza 2003.

[126] See, EC Treaty, Article 5.

international governance and rule-making,[127] but rather to its significance in respect of international (judicial) review of national measures.

Because the principle of subsidiarity is expressly incorporated in the EC Treaty, it is an obvious criterion against which not only EC acts but also national measures may be tested by the ECJ.[128] In the latter context, the ECJ may review whether a member state has violated this principle by introducing legislation or taking some other action that falls exclusively within the competence of the EC.[129] In the WTO, subsidiarity, of course, is not such a criterion of review. Firstly, the WTO treaty does not incorporate this principle. And, secondly, unlike the EC, the WTO itself as an international organization does not have much competence (even by consensus) for rule-making or taking substantive actions.[130] As a result, the question of encroachment of the WTO's competence by a Member does not arise.

However, quite apart from the above-noted aspect, there is a much more generalized dimension of the subsidiarity principle, which does bear out the vital policy issues that underlie the question of standard of review in any large-scale international dispute settlement. These policy issues concern, as already noted, the proper allocation of power between international adjudicative bodies and national authorities;[131] and, generally speaking, power allocation is exactly what subsidiarity aims to address.[132] From this perspective, the margin of appreciation doctrine of European human rights law has been described as stemming from the principle of subsidiarity.[133] That is to say, the respondent state is allowed "a margin" so as to ensure decision-making closer to the affected constituencies.[134] Likewise, in the EC context, instances have been given where, on the basis of the subsidiarity principle, the responsibility for decision-making as between the ECJ and national courts is allocated according to their comparative institutional expertise.[135] Considerations such as these, it may be noted, are no less significant in the WTO context. (Indeed, it is not an extremely uncommon criticism of the WTO panel and AB decisions that they affect not only the economic but also

[127] Analyses of these issues in the WTO context can be found in Bourgeois 2000b; Sauvé & Zampetti 2000; and Jackson 2002.

[128] Toth 1994, 273–85. [129] Ibid. 276–78.

[130] Rule-making in the WTO must, of necessity, take the form of new agreements entered into by the WTO Members in accordance with the international law rules regarding conclusion of treaties.

[131] See above, pp. 167–68. [132] See, e.g., Trachtman 1998.

[133] Ryssdall 1996, 25; and Mahoney 1997, 369.

[134] Ryssdall 1996, 27; and Mahoney 1997, 364. [135] See, e.g., Pager 2003, 68.

the social policies of nations in a manner that does not ensure effective participation by the affected societies.[136])

Finally, in the context of public international law in general, the exhaustion of local remedies rule ensures subsidiarity by rendering inadmissible claims for which redress was not sought, in the first place, at the national level. As noted before, in the WTO there is no requirement to exhaust local remedies and the non-applicability of this rule in WTO dispute settlement contributes to the effectiveness of the WTO legal system in general and its dispute settlement in particular.[137] Yet, given the absence of this rather common and inherent safeguard which exists in other areas of international law, WTO panels and the AB need to be especially attentive to the values of subsidiarity.

4 Standard of review and treaty interpretation

For a proper understanding of the questions of standard of review, it is necessary to be mindful of the rather fine and subtle distinction between those questions and questions of treaty interpretation. This distinction requires emphasizing all the more because some of the academic analyses of the WTO standards of review confuse these two quite discrete matters.[138] Given that academic discourse in this area is relatively new, it is not surprising to detect one or two instances of the lack of clarity and precision that are otherwise called for. However, the analysis needs to be put right not only for the sake of clarity, precision and an accurate exposition of the emerging WTO jurisprudence on standards of review, but also to avoid any damaging effect that an incorrect premise may have on that jurisprudence.

Some of the confusions in this respect are due to the particular language of the standard of review clause of the ADA. To recall, while the first sentence of ADA Article 17.6(ii) directs panels to interpret the ADA in accordance with the customary rules of treaty interpretation, the second sentence stipulates that if a provision admits of more than one permissible interpretation, the national measure concerned is to be found consistent with the ADA, if it rests upon one of those permissible

[136] See, e.g., Kelly 2002, 372–73. [137] See above, Chapter 1, pp. 20–23.

[138] The recent works of Matthias Oesch, which attempt to discuss the standard of review of WTO law, as distinguished from national law or national measures, are obvious examples: see Oesch 2003a, 656–58, and 2003b, 173–87. That this is a non sequitur is readily apparent, because panels and the AB do not "*review*" WTO law, but rather they "*apply*" WTO law in reviewing national laws or measures.

interpretations. Accordingly, it is thought that, in interpreting the ADA, panels and the AB ought in certain circumstance (i.e. in circumstances envisaged in Article 17.6[ii], second sentence) to *defer* to the interpretation put forward by the respondent Member. And, because Article 17.6(ii), second sentence, is seen as a requirement for *deference* to a Member's interpretation of the ADA, questions of interpretation are mistakenly assimilated with questions of standard of review.

On a closer look, however, it is evident that Article 17.6(ii) does make a distinction between those two types of questions. Questions of interpretation are to be resolved by applying the customary rules of treaty interpretation, which, as noted before, can be found, inter alia, in the VCLT.[139] By the application of these rules, panels or the AB may or may not come to the conclusion that the relevant ADA provision admits of more than one permissible interpretation. But, in any event, this is purely an exercise in treaty interpretation in accordance with the VCLT rules and can be distinguished from the further and the discrete part of the analysis pertaining to the *review* of the Member's interpretation in the light of the interpretation that the panel or the AB has settled on. This, however, is not to suggest that the process of interpretation, as distinguished from the process of review, is, or is to be, performed in the abstract. Of course, questions of interpretation, like any other questions that come before panels or the AB, are addressed in relation to the particular circumstances of the case and in the light of the arguments put forward by the parties. Furthermore, a panel's or the AB's interpretation may entirely coincide with that of the respondent, as it may with that of the complainant, or it may not coincide with that of any of the parties. But because the parameters of the questions of interpretation, like other questions, are most often determined by the parties' arguments, one need not confuse the interpretative and the review functions of panels and the AB.[140]

Unlike some of the academic analyses, panels and the AB, however, have not confused treaty interpretation with standard of review. The following observations of the Panel in *US – Stainless Steel*, for instance, bear out the distinction quite clearly:

> in considering those aspects of the United States' [anti-dumping] determinations which stand or fall depending on the interpretation of the ADA itself rather than or in addition to the analysis of facts, *we first interpret the provisions of the ADA*. As the Appellate Body has repeatedly stated, panels are to consider the

[139] See above, Chapter 4, p. 97.

[140] See, Panel Reports, *US – DRAMS*, footnote 499; and *US – Section 301*, para. 7.16.

interpretation of the WTO agreements, including the ADA, *in accordance with the principles set out in the Vienna Convention on the Law of Treaties*. Thus, we look to the ordinary meaning of the provision in question, in its context, and in light of its object and purpose [as required under Article 31 of the VCLT]. Finally, we may consider the preparatory work (the negotiating history) of the provision, should this be necessary or appropriate in light of the conclusions we reach based on the text of the provision [as envisaged in Article 32 of the VCLT]. *We then evaluate whether the United States' interpretation is one that is "permissible"* in light of the customary rules of interpretation of international law.[141]

The above approach has also been endorsed by the Appellate Body on a number of occasions.[142]

While it is not difficult to discern the distinction between the interpretative and the review functions in respect of ADA Article 17.6(ii), more problematic is the *inter*-relation between those two functions. This provision, as must be evident by now, requires panels or the AB to defer to the respondent Member if a particular ADA provision "admits of *more than one permissible interpretation*," when interpreted under the VCLT rules. Recall that panels and the AB are also directed to interpret all of the other WTO agreements in accordance with the VCLT rules.[143] But, in respect of those other agreements, there is no provision that envisages multiple permissible interpretations. Does this mean that the application of the VCLT rules should result in different outcomes in respect of the ADA and the other WTO agreements? Specifically, should it result in multiple interpretations in respect of the former and a single or uniform interpretation in respect of the latter? If so, one cannot but wonder how it could be that the same rules of interpretation are to bring about such divergent outcomes. If not, one is equally compelled to wonder how then panels and the AB could ever be able to show deference to a Member's interpretation of the ADA as being one of the various permissible interpretations.

This is a difficulty that almost entirely defies analysis, and although some attempts have been made to rationalize this aspect of Article 17.6(ii), none is satisfactory. A few remarks about an argument that at least has some apparent plausibility may be in order. It has been suggested that, in very rare cases, a full VCLT interpretative analysis may indeed leave open the possibility of at least two permissible

[141] Panel Report, *US – Stainless Steel*, para. 6.4 (italics added).
[142] See e.g., AB Reports, *EC – Bed Linen*, paras. 63–65; *Thailand – H-Beams*, paras. 122–27; and *US – Hot-Rolled Steel*, paras. 57–60.
[143] See above, Chapter 4, p. 97.

interpretations, and that the second sentence of Article 17.6(ii) addresses that situation by requiring deference to the respondent's interpretation.[144] This view is presented as one that gives meaning to both the first (providing for the application of the customary rules) and the second (envisaging more than one permissible interpretation) sentences of Article 17.6(ii). Thus, it is premised, inter alia, on the principle of effectiveness in treaty interpretation, which requires a treaty interpreter to give meaning to all the terms of the treaty and not to adopt a reading that reduces an entire clause to redundancy or inutility.[145]

Notably, the AB, with a view to remaining faithful to the language of Article 17.6(ii), has not foreclosed the possibility of at least two interpretations of some ADA provisions. In *US – Hot-Rolled Steel* it observed as follows:

> This second sentence of Article 17.6(ii) *presupposes* that application of the rules of treaty interpretation in Articles 31 and 32 of the Vienna Convention could give rise to, at least, two interpretations of some provisions of the ADA, which, under that Convention, would both be "*permissible* interpretations." In that event, a measure is deemed to be in conformity with the ADA "if it rests upon one of those permissible interpretations."[146]

However, the above view is not entirely unassailable. First, the proposition that the application of the customary rules of interpretation may lead to multiple readings is not that strong. Although it is possible to detect some doubts expressed in academic writings as to whether the VCLT rules can solve all interpretative issues, it has equally been argued that they probably would.[147] Indeed, the purpose of interpretation is not to create ambiguity by establishing multiple meanings, but rather it is to resolve them by attributing a coherent meaning to the terms. Thus it is not surprising that, although in some instances the panels or the AB have agreed with the respondent's interpretation (as being permissible), they are yet to so agree on the basis of Article 17.6(ii) and on the ground that the relevant ADA provision is susceptible to *multiple*

[144] See, e.g., Lennard 2002, 80–85.

[145] The AB in a long line of decisions has rightly treated this principle as forming part of the customary rules of interpretation of public international law: see, for instance, the cases cited above in Chapter 3, n. 104.

[146] AB Report, *US – Hot-Rolled Steel*, para. 59 (italics in original). In the next paragraph the AB emphasized that a permissible interpretation is one that is found to be appropriate only *after* the application of the VCLT rules.

[147] See, generally, Sinclair 1984, 114–58; Jennings & Watts 1992, 1266–82; Croley & Jackson 1996, 200–1; and Brownlie 1998, 631–38.

interpretations.[148] Furthermore, even if the application of the VCLT rules presents a treaty interpreter with two or more meanings of a particular provision, some of the many other interpretative principles and maxims that are not explicitly referred to in the VCLT but also form part of the customary rules of interpretation may be applicable.[149] These may operate to provide the interpreter with a clear choice between the two (or more) apparent alternatives. One such principle, namely the principle of *in dubio mitius*, is highly relevant for present purposes; and, as discussed below, considered in the light of this principle, the second sentence of Article 17.6(ii) seems rather superfluous.

Second, if the application of the VCLT rules can indeed lead to multiple interpretations, then that possibility must be open not only in respect of the ADA but also in respect of all of the other WTO agreements. For all such cases, a solution that is similar to Article 17.6(ii) can be found by the application of the *in dubio mitius* principle. However, this solution may be chosen (in respect of any WTO agreement, including the ADA) not because of Article 17.6(ii), but because of the general requirement to apply the customary rules of interpretation. The Appellate Body has already endorsed the applicability of this principle in WTO disputes and has also given a description of it:

> The interpretative principle of *in dubio mitius*, widely recognized in international law as a "supplementary means of interpretation," has been expressed in the following terms:
>
> "The principle of *in dubio mitius* applies in interpreting treaties, in deference to the sovereignty of states. If the meaning of a term is ambiguous, that meaning is to be preferred which is less onerous to the party assuming an obligation, or which interferes less with the territorial and personal supremacy of a party, or involves less general restrictions upon the parties."[150]

[148] See, e.g., AB Reports, *EC – Bed Linen*, paras. 63–65; *Thailand – H-Beams*, paras. 122–28; *EC – Bed Linen 21.5*, para. 118; *US – Softwood Lumber V*, paras. 113–16; *Mexico – Rice*, paras. 170–71; *US – Zeroing*, para. 134; and *US – Softwood Lumber V 21.5*, para. 123. See also Tarullo 2002 and 2003; Cunningham & Cribb 2003, 163; Durling 2003; Oesch 2003a, 657; and Spamann 2004, 511, 517.

[149] It may be noted that Articles 31 and 32 of the VCLT do not provide a comprehensive catalog of all principles and maxims that, from time to time, are used as aids to interpretation, and for this reason the Articles have been described as an "economical code of principles": Brownlie 1998, 633. See also Sinclair 1984, 153; and Jennings & Watts 1992, 1276–82.

[150] AB Report, *EC – Hormones I & II*, footnote 154 (quoting Jennings & Watts 1992, 1278, and citing, inter alia, *Nuclear Tests* case, ICJ Rep. 253 [1974] at 267; *Access of Polish War Vessels to the Port of Danzig*, PCIJ Ser. A/B No. 43 [1931] at 142; *Air Transport Services Agreement Arbitration*, 38 ILR 182 [1963] at 243; and *De Pascale Claim*, 40 ILR 250 [1961]).

It can easily be imagined that, from among multiple permissible interpretations of an ambiguous provision, the one put forward by the respondent Member would be least burdensome to it. Accordingly, in pursuance of the *in dubio mitius* principle deference must be given to that interpretation, whether or not the provision concerned is one of the ADA or another WTO agreement. Thus, again, it is difficult to conceive how ADA Article 17.6(ii) can lead to a solution that is different from other WTO agreements.

The difficulty with Article 17.6(ii), second sentence (including its superfluity) results, it may be noted, from the fact that it represents a wholesale transplantation of a US administrative law doctrine, namely the *Chevron* doctrine,[151] made without giving any serious thought as to whether and how that might fit in an international adjudicative process. The fallacies that lie behind the assumption that something akin to the *Chevron* doctrine may be fully applied in an international context have been discussed elsewhere in great length and with convincing sharpness.[152] So, without repeating that analysis, it may simply be noted here that, unlike international courts, US courts have a long tradition of accepting the susceptibility to multiple readings of a statute (especially when they review the acts of an administrative agency entrusted with the implementation of that statute). Moreover, US courts apply, as hardly needs stating, the rules of statutory construction of US domestic law and not the "customary rules of interpretation of public international law." Because of these and other systemic and structural differences,[153] more caution is needed before suggesting that the WTO panels and the AB should follow the footsteps of the US courts.[154]

In an international context, the necessity of attributing multiple readings to a treaty provision for purposes of applying a deferential standard of review may also be questioned. Rather than attributing multiple interpretations to a provision, it is equally possible to uphold national measures even in some extreme cases by remaining true to a single and coherent interpretation of that provision. This can be achieved if the single interpretation is wide and flexible enough for accommodating different national measures taken by different Members in different circumstances. The doctrine of margin of appreciation offers a good illustration. Thus, for instance, different national measures interfering

[151] See above, n. 41. [152] See, Croley & Jackson 1996; and Vázquez 2004.

[153] See above, n. 69.

[154] See, Croley & Jackson 1996, 205–11; Petersmann 1997a, 227–28; and Gomula 1999, 599.

with the right to freedom of expression are upheld under Article 10 of the EHR Convention, not because that Article has different meanings but because it is given a single and yet a flexible interpretation that allows different "margins" of appreciation in different circumstances.[155] Although this distinction between multiple interpretations and a single flexible interpretation is rather subtle (and unless looked at closely may even appear as "artificial"), it is nevertheless an important distinction. And, between multiple interpretations and a single flexible interpretation, the latter is clearly preferable because it does not affect the integrity of the "customary rules of interpretation of public international law."

Apart from the interpretative policy (and paradox) discussed above, a variety of other policy arguments can be put forward in support of the proposition that interpretation of the WTO agreements ought to be a province of the WTO judiciary and not of individual Members. Recall, for instance, the point made in the introduction to this chapter about the importance of uniform interpretation of WTO norms by panels and the Appellate Body for the effectiveness of the WTO legal system. If panels or the AB were to defer to the interpretation of individual Members, they would be deferring to 150 potentially different interpretations of the same legal provision or instrument. Such multiplicity of interpretations would undermine the core objectives of "security and predictability" of the multilateral trading system, which the dispute settlement mechanism must ensure in accordance with Article 3.2 of the DSU.[156] Deference to individual Members' interpretation of WTO law would result in normative ambiguity and subjective and relativist application of WTO law, detracting thereby from the conduct-regulating quality of the law. The dilution of objective legal certainty resulting from multiplicity of interpretations would encourage evasion of WTO obligations, whether for reasons of domestic political convenience or otherwise. This would undermine the authority and perceived fairness (for instance, the expectation that like cases will be treated alike) of the

155 See above, n. 89 and corresponding text.

156 It is perhaps worth noting that, while the possibility of multiple interpretations envisaged in ADA Article 17.6(ii) has its origin in the *Chevron* doctrine of US administrative law, *Chevron* deference does not result in multiple interpretations. This is so because, under that doctrine, multiple US courts defer to the interpretation of a single US administrative agency entrusted with the enforcement of a given law. Thus, rather than leading to multiple interpretations, *Chevron* deference in fact prevents multiplicity and ensures uniformity of interpretation: see Croley & Jackson 1996, 210; and Vázquez 2004, 603.

legal norms and seriously jeopardize the legitimacy and effectiveness of the WTO legal system.

National authorities of individual Members also do not enjoy any comparative institutional advantage over WTO panels and the Appellate Body in respect of treaty interpretation. It is not unlikely for individual Members to have incentives to resort to self-serving interpretations that are advantageous to them individually but detrimental to other Members and the multilateral trading system as a whole. Being interested parties in disputes, domestic interests (including domestic political and "rent-seeking" interests) of an individual Member may not always ensure the required fidelity to the terms of an international agreement.[157] By contrast, there do not exist any similar interests for WTO panels and the Appellate Body to engage in self-serving interpretations. They are better placed to interpret the WTO treaty in the light of the international coordination efforts that underpin the treaty. Thus, meaningful normative guidance can come from interpretations by the WTO judiciary (and not individual Members) that are both uniform and faithful to the terms of the WTO agreements.

Accountability of a decision-maker is often treated as an important policy reason for deference to that decision-maker. For instance, judicial deference to decisions of administrative agencies under the US *Chevron* doctrine is justified on the ground that such agencies, and not the courts, are accountable to both the executive and the legislative representatives of the citizenry.[158] An individual WTO Member, however, does not represent, nor is accountable to, the WTO membership as a whole. Instead, it is the WTO panels and the Appellate Body that are the membership's delegates and are accountable as such. Accordingly, interpretation of the WTO norms by panels and the AB will not displace the interpretation of any entity that is accountable to the WTO Members as a whole.[159]

It may be recalled from Chapters 1 and 3 that an important way in which the WTO legal system promotes good governance is by guaranteeing some protection for the commercial interests of foreign states, who have little or no representation in the political life of a state enacting

[157] Again, it is worth pointing out that the *Chevron* deference under US administrative law does not result in self-serving interpretations of statutes by interested parties. Under that doctrine, courts do not defer to the interpretations of those sought to be "regulated" by a given statute but rather to the interpretation of the "regulator" administrative agency charged with the administration of the statute: see Vázquez 2004, 604.

[158] See Croley & Jackson 1996, 207.

[159] Ibid. 209; and Vázquez 2004, 603–4.

or implementing a trade or trade-related law or measure.[160] Self-serving interpretations of the WTO norms by national authorities of individual Members, who are not accountable to the WTO membership, will erode the WTO agreements and wipe out the guarantees that the agreements provide in favor of foreign states and individual traders and businesses. Thus, the policy objectives of both effectiveness and good governance suggest that the ultimate authority to interpret the WTO treaty must rest with the WTO judiciary and not individual Members.

In contrast to questions of interpretation, questions of fact and legal characterization (i.e. applying the law to the facts and determining the conformity of the facts with the law) properly belong to the realm of standard of review. The type of review and the level of deference applicable in respect of these latter issues are addressed in the next section.

5 Emerging standards

This section discusses some of the standards that have so far been applied in WTO dispute settlement cases and that also represent an emerging body of principles in this regard. But first recall the comments made earlier about the difficulty of discussing standards of review in the abstract. (It is notable that, because of this difficulty, all studies of the European human rights law doctrine of margin of appreciation focus, in one way or another, not on the margin itself, but on the variables that affect the margin.) The present analysis is of course mindful of this difficulty. Accordingly, while at the outset a few general issues are treated, in due course specific attention is devoted to the premise that there is not a single standard of review in the WTO, rather the standard does and could vary for a variety of reasons.

5.1 In general

Discussions of the review standards must of necessity begin by underscoring the distinction between questions of fact and of law.[161] This is because, although the problem of standard of review does arise with respect to both types of questions, it arises rather differently. For absolute clarity it must be mentioned that the point that is now being made about the relevance of standard of review with regard to questions of law does not detract from the earlier observation that standard of review and

[160] See Chapter 1, p. 17, and Chapter 3, p. 85, above.

[161] Some questions may of course defy precise categorization; and there may be mixed questions of fact and law or questions that lie on the borderline between the fact and the law: see above, Chapter 4, n. 81; and Stuart 1992, 762–63.

treaty interpretation are quite distinct matters. Interpretative questions, no doubt, are questions of law, but so are questions of qualification or characterization of facts in the light of the law. And, while the former cannot be addressed by the tools of standard of review, such tools can certainly be applied in respect of the latter.

The discreteness of the three types of question noted above (namely, questions of treaty interpretation, legal qualification and facts) is also recognized in the AB jurisprudence. Thus while discussing the scope of appellate review (which, as noted earlier, is confined to issues of law[162]), the AB referred to "legal interpretations" and "legal characterizations," and distinguished these from "findings of facts."[163] The AB also aptly described the nature of the legal characterization and factual questions, which may be usefully quoted to illustrate the type of questions that are amenable to a standard of review analysis:

> [1] The determination of whether or not a certain event did occur in time and space is typically a question of fact . . . Determination of the credibility and weight properly to be ascribed to (that is, the appreciation of) a given piece of evidence is part and parcel of the fact finding process . . . [2] The consistency or inconsistency of a given fact or set of facts with the requirements of a given treaty provision is, however, a legal characterization issue. It is a legal question.[164]

Recall now that, while noting that DSU Article 11 sets out the appropriate standard of review, the AB made reference to the "ascertainment of facts" and the "legal characterization of such facts," but not to treaty interpretation.[165] Thus, clearly, the AB did not think that treaty interpretation is something that is to be addressed by the tools of standard of review. Of course, treaty interpretation is undertaken with a view to legal qualification or characterization of facts, but, still, it is possible to distinguish between them. A good example is *US – Gasoline*, where the AB, although it agreed with the Panel about the interpretation of a WTO provision concerned, disagreed about the qualification of the facts in the light of that provision.[166] This clearly bears out the distinction between treaty interpretation and legal qualification. And, while there is not much scope for "deference" to a Member in respect of treaty interpretation, there certainly is in respect of legal qualification. For instance, in the *US – Gasoline* case itself, although both the Panel and the AB had the same interpretation of a provision, the AB was more deferential

[162] See above, Chapter 4, p. 106. [163] AB Report, *EC – Hormones I & II*, para. 132. [164] Ibid.
[165] See text at n. 45 above. [166] This example is taken from Kuyper 2000, 311.

to the respondent in respect of legal qualification of facts under that provision.[167]

In the panel and AB jurisprudence, numerous statements can be found that deal at a more or less general level with the issue of standard of review of questions of fact; and compared to that, not many observations concerning questions of legal qualification can be found. An obvious reason is that the latter, being greatly dependent on the substantive obligation concerned, more readily defies abstract analysis. However, there are certain quite important general matters concerning legal qualification (especially concerning the determination of the WTO-compatibility of national laws), which are discussed later. Presently, the issue of standard of review of questions of fact is taken up.

With regard to these questions, the guidance that can be obtained from DSU Article 11 is simply that panels are to make "an objective assessment of the facts." By contrast, ADA Article 17.6(i) sets out the criteria of review in more detail. To recall, it provides that a panel is to determine, first, whether the domestic authorities' "establishment of the facts was proper" and, second, whether the authorities' "evaluation of those facts was unbiased and objective." If these criteria are satisfied, the domestic authorities' factual determinations are not to be overturned "even though the panel might have reached a different conclusion."[168] However, as the AB has made abundantly clear, there is no conflict between DSU Article 11 and ADA Article 17.6(i):

> Article 17.6(i) requires panels to make an "*assessment* of the *facts*." The language of this phrase reflects closely the obligation imposed on panels under Article 11 of the DSU to make an "*objective assessment* of the *facts*." Thus the text of both provisions requires panels to "assess" the facts and this, in our view, clearly necessitates an active review or examination of the pertinent facts. Article 17.6(i) of the ADA does not expressly state that panels are obliged to make an assessment of the facts which is "*objective*." However, it is inconceivable that Article 17.6(i) should require anything other than that panels make an *objective* "assessment of the facts of the matter." In this respect, we see no "conflict" between Article 17.6(i) of the ADA and Article 11 of the DSU.[169]

[167] See AB Report, *US – Gasoline*, at 18–19; and Kuyper 2000, 311–12.

[168] See, e.g., Panel Reports, *Mexico – HFCS*, para. 7.95; *Thailand – H-Beams*, para. 7.51; *Guatemala – Cement II*, para. 8.19; *EC – Bed Linen*, para. 6.45; *US – Stainless Steel*, para. 6.3; *US – Hot-Rolled Steel*, para. 7.26; *Argentina – Ceramic Tiles*, paras. 6.1–3, 6.27; *Egypt – Rebar*, paras. 7.8–14; *EC – Bed Linen 21.5*, para. 6.6; *EC – Pipe Fittings*, para. 7.6; and *Argentina – Poultry*, paras. 7.43–45, 7.48–49.

[169] AB Report, *US – Hot-Rolled Steel*, para. 55 (italics in original).

The above is to be understood subject to the caveat that the ADA Article 17.6 contemplates a particular type of national measures, namely anti-dumping measures. These measures can be adopted by a Member only after an investigation has been conducted by that Member which has led to certain determinations regarding dumping of products by another Member, injury to domestic goods and the like.[170] The determinations are usually contained in documents issued by a domestic administrative, quasi-judicial or judicial body that has conducted the investigation. (In the case of the EC, the determinations are, however, contained in EC legislation.) Thus, in cases concerning anti-dumping measures, at issue before panels is the WTO-compatibility of certain determinations made in pursuance of a domestic fact-finding and/or "adjudicative" process. This sets the scene for the review at the WTO level rather uniquely, as can be seen from the following observations made by the AB:

> In considering Article 17.6(i) of the ADA, it is important to bear in mind the different roles of panels and [domestic] investigating authorities. Investigating authorities are charged, under the ADA, with making factual determinations relevant to their overall determination of dumping and injury. Under Article 17.6(i), the task of panels is simply to review the investigating authorities' "establishment" and "evaluation" of the facts.[171]

Thus, clearly, in respect of review of anti-dumping measures under the Article 17.6(i) standard, panels need not, nor are expected to, engage in any new fact-finding. This, however, may not always be the case with regard to the DSU Article 11 standard, when the review concerns other national measures and other WTO agreements. To give just one example, in a number of cases panels, for a variety of reasons, engaged in a process of fact-finding not simply by recourse to the evidence requested from or submitted by the parties but also by seeking information or evidence from independent experts.[172] Indeed, DSU Article 13 expressly

[170] See ADA, Articles 1–3.

[171] AB Report, *US – Hot-Rolled Steel*, para. 55. It is no wonder that the review of anti-dumping measures under the WTO along with that under the NAFTA has been described as "a rudimentary form of international administrative law": see Winham 1998, 78, 83.

[172] See the cases discussed in Pauwelyn 2002a. It is pertinent to note that, in certain respects, standard of review concerns evidentiary matters, including admissibility of evidence and panels' role in collecting evidence, as well as appreciation of evidence by panels: see, e.g., Cameron & Orava 2000, 226–42.

authorizes a panel to appoint experts or seek information or advice from any individual or body which the panel deems appropriate.[173] It may also be mentioned that the standard applied with respect to the process of *fact-finding* (albeit, undertaken if and when the circumstances so required) has been variously described as "thorough," "comprehensive," "searching," "intrusive," "inquisitorial" (as opposed to "adversarial"),[174] or even as "*de novo* review."[175] Compared to *fact-finding* by panels, the scope of review under ADA Article 17.6(i) is much more limited, not least because here panels are called upon to determine the WTO-compatibility of determinations that have been issued through a prior domestic investigative and fact-finding process.[176]

Notably, it is not only the anti-dumping measures that are adopted in pursuance of a domestic investigative and fact-finding process, but rather the WTO treaty imposes obligations to conduct investigations and/or make specific (factual) determinations with respect to other measures as well. Two obvious examples are countervailing and safeguard measures. The former can be adopted by a Member only after determinations have been made by that Member regarding subsidization of products by another Member, injury to domestic goods and the like,[177] while the latter can be adopted upon determinations of surges in imports, injury to the domestic industry and the like.[178] (These measures, along with anti-dumping measures, are collectively referred to as "trade remedy measures.") Not surprisingly, with regard to countervailing and safeguard measures as well, a limited standard of review is applied, although in these instances DSU Article 11 rather than ADA Article 17.6(i) provides the relevant textual framework.

In *US – Cotton Yarn*, the AB, after referring to a number of earlier panel and AB reports, spelled out two "key elements of panels' standard of review under Article 11 of the DSU" insofar as review of *determinations* made by national authorities is concerned:

[173] The right granted to panels in DSU Article 13 has even been described as an "almost unfettered right to seek information" from any individual or body deemed appropriate: see Pauwelyn 2002a, 329.

[174] Oesch 2003a, 650–51. [175] Ehlermann & Lockhart 2004, 518.

[176] Differences in the applicable standard of review when a panel acts as "the initial fact-finder" and when it reviews factual determinations have also been expressly recognized in the jurisprudence: see, e.g., Panel Report, *US – Steel Safeguards*, paras. 10.25–27.

[177] See ASCM, Articles 10–23. [178] See Safeguards Agreement, Articles 2–4.

> [First,] panels must examine whether the competent [national] authority has evaluated all relevant factors; they must assess whether the competent authority has examined *all the pertinent facts*, and [second, they must] assess whether an *adequate explanation* has been provided [by the national authority] as to how those facts support the determination.[179]

In *US - Lamb*, the AB described the first element (i.e. review of whether the national authority has evaluated all relevant factors/facts) as the "formal aspect," and the second element (i.e. review of whether a reasoned and adequate explanation has been provided by the national authority) as the "substantive aspect" of the standard of review.[180] (As regards the second element, it may be interesting to recall that in reviewing decisions of national authorities, the ECHR also applies a similar criterion of "relevant and sufficient reasons."[181])

The two-pronged test, as noted in the preceding paragraph, has been applied in a long line of safeguard cases,[182] and it is also possible to find references to both criteria of the test in the Safeguards Agreement itself.[183] But still, the general relevance of the test cannot be excluded. Indeed, the test was articulated in the first place not in respect of the Safeguards Agreement but in respect of another WTO agreement, namely the Agreement on Textiles and Clothing (ATC), which does not

179 AB Report, *US - Cotton Yarn*, para. 74 (italics added).

180 AB Report, *US - Lamb*, para. 103. There are certain consequences that flow from both elements of this two-pronged standard of review. Thus, in reviewing determinations, panels cannot consider evidence that was not in existence when the determination was made by the national authority: see AB Report, *US - Cotton Yarn*, paras. 77–80. However, insofar as arguments (as opposed to evidence) are concerned, panels are not confined by those made in the course of the domestic procedures. This is because arguments at the domestic level are unlikely to focus on WTO law: see AB Report, *US - Lamb*, paras. 110–15. An obvious corollary of the second element is that if a reasoned and adequate explanation of the determination is not provided in the course of the domestic procedures, that deficiency cannot be cured by providing explanations before the panel: see AB Report, *US - Wheat Gluten*, paras. 156–63.

181 See text at nn. 86, 88, above. See also the NAFTA case of *Broom Corn Brooms*, n. 25 above.

182 See, e.g., AB Reports, *Argentina - Footwear*, paras. 116–21; *US - Lamb*, paras. 97–114; and *US - Steel Safeguards*, paras. 273–80; and Panel Reports, *Korea - Dairy*, para. 7.30; *US - Wheat Gluten*, para. 8.5–6; *US - Line Pipe*, para. 7.194; and *Argentina - Peaches*, para. 7.93.

183 Specifically, Article 3.1 of the Safeguards Agreement requires Members to publish, following investigations undertaken to apply safeguard measures, a report setting forth "findings and reasoned conclusions" on all pertinent issues of fact and law; and Article 4.2(a) requires the investigating authorities of Members to "evaluate all relevant factors" in making determinations concerning injury to the domestic industry.

contain any reference to either of the two criteria.[184] This is indicative that the test is not tied to the specific language of the Safeguards Agreement and that it may be applied in reviewing national determinations under any WTO agreement.

Furthermore, the *raisons d'être* of the test can be equally pertinent in respect of review of many national decisions or determinations under various WTO agreements. In this context, the wider significance of the criterion of "reasoned and adequate explanation" can be usefully illustrated by reference to the *US – Steel Safeguards* case. In this case the USA contended before the AB that the Panel erred in extending that criterion to Article XIX of the GATT 1994, which, unlike the Safeguards Agreement, does not contain any requirement for national authorities to issue reasoned findings and conclusions. In rejecting this contention, the AB made certain observations that highlight the general relevance of the criterion. According to the AB, the US contention that national authorities need not provide a reasoned and adequate explanation "cannot be reconciled" with DSU Article 11 requiring panels to make an "objective assessment" of matters before them.[185] The AB further elaborated the point as follows:

> We do not see how a panel could examine objectively the consistency of a determination with Article XIX of the GATT 1994 if the competent authority had not set out an explanation supporting its conclusions . . . Indeed, *to enable a panel to determine whether there was compliance* with the prerequisites [of Article XIX] . . . *the competent authority must provide a "reasoned and adequate explanation"* of how the facts support its determination for those prerequisites.[186]

More recently, in the *US – CVD Investigation on DRAMS* case,[187] the Appellate Body observed that the standard of review articulated by it in the context of review of decisions or determinations of domestic agencies

[184] The first WTO case in which the two-pronged standard of review of national determinations was articulated is *US – Underwear*. In this case the standard was set out with respect to the ATC, and for this purpose the Panel relied not on any specific language of the ATC or other WTO agreements, but rather on a number of GATT panel reports: see Panel Report, paras. 7.12–13. (Later in the *US – Cotton Yarn* case the AB confirmed the applicability of the two-pronged test in respect of the ATC: see AB Report, paras. 70–76.) Notably, prior to WTO panels and the AB, GATT panels applied this test in reviewing anti-dumping and countervailing measures: see, e.g., *US – Norwegian Salmon I*, para. 492; and *US – Norwegian Salmon II*, para. 258.

[185] AB Report, *US – Steel Safeguards*, para. 278.

[186] Ibid. para. 279 (italics added). Exactly the same proposition was put forward by the NAFTA Panel in the *Broom Corn Brooms* case, n. 25 above, para. 71.

[187] For a comment see Becroft 2006.

under the Safeguards Agreement "is instructive for cases under the ASCM that also involve agency determinations."[188] However, the AB rightly pointed out that the "objective assessment" under Article 11 of the DSU "must be understood in the light of the obligations of the particular covered agreements at issue in order to derive the more specific contours of the appropriate standard of review."[189] (The issue of variations in the standard of review on the basis of substantive provisions is discussed below.) In the light of the provisions of the ASCM that were at issue in the *DRAMS CVD* case, the AB spelled out the following standard of review for subsidy determinations: "the 'objective assessment' to be made by a panel reviewing [a domestic] investigating authority's subsidy determination will be informed by an examination of whether the agency provided a *reasoned and adequate explanation* as to: (i) how the evidence on the record supported its factual findings; and (ii) how those factual findings supported the overall subsidy determination."[190] The above formulation seems to be an elaboration – albeit in the context of the relevant ASCM provisions – of the second element (i.e. review of reasoned and adequate explanation) of the two-pronged standard of review articulated in the long line of safeguard cases.[191] Other than the general remark noted earlier that the standard of review under the Safeguards Agreement is instructive for cases under the ASCM, in the *DRAMS CVD* case the AB did not make any explicit reference to the first element (i.e. review of whether the national authority has evaluated all relevant factors/facts) of the two-pronged standard. Yet, the relevance of the first element does not seem any less than the second element. A subsidy determination by a domestic authority that does not take into account all relevant facts and factors and provide an adequate explanation of those, can hardly be regarded as a determination supported by "a reasoned and adequate explanation." Indeed, in a later subsidy case the AB observed that an assessment of whether a domestic determination is "reasoned and adequate" would require a panel to consider whether the domestic authority has evaluated "all of the relevant evidence."[192] In that case the AB also repeatedly emphasized the duty of a panel to examine whether a domestic determination was based on, supported by, and explained in terms of "positive evidence."[193]

It may have been noticed that, like the standard of review of national determinations under DSU Article 11, the standard of review under ADA

[188] AB Report, *US – CVD Investigation on DRAMS*, para. 184. [189] Ibid.
[190] Ibid. para. 186 (italics added). [191] See above, n. 182.
[192] AB Report, *US – Softwood Lumber VI 21.5*, para. 97.
[193] Ibid. paras. 93, 96, 99, 103, 109, 113, 132, 135, 147.

Article 17.6(i) is also two-pronged. Yet they are not exactly the same. The two criteria in the former context, to restate once again, are whether the national authority has considered all relevant facts/factors and whether it has provided a reasoned and adequate explanation, while in the latter context these are whether the national authority's establishment of the facts has been proper and whether its evaluation of those facts has been unbiased and objective. While these differences in the criteria may lead to similar differences in panels' analysis, it is also possible that, because of the similarity of the relevant substantive obligations, the same standard of review will apply in respect of national anti-dumping, subsidy or safeguard determinations. The recent *US – Softwood Lumber VI 21.5* case provides a good example. In this case Canada challenged a single US determination of threat of material injury to the US domestic softwood lumber industry under both the ADA and the ASCM. Theoretically, it was necessary to scrutinize the US determination under two separate standards of review, namely, ADA Article 17.6 and DSU Article 11. Yet, neither the Panel nor the AB made any separate assessment of the US determination. Rather, they applied a single standard of review derived from DSU Article 11 and the relevant (identical) provisions of the ADA and the ASCM.[194]

Having noted the similarities and dissimilarities between the standard of review of trade remedy determinations under the ADA, ASCM and the Safeguards Agreement, it is worth emphasizing that in these instances the standard of review is decisively limited and also results in a comparable amount of deference to Members. This is so not least because trade remedy determinations are made pursuant to a domestic investigative and fact-finding process required by the WTO agreements themselves. Accordingly, in these instances, panels are neither to reinvestigate the matter nor to substitute their own conclusions for those of the national authorities.[195] Thus, the exclusion of *de novo* review has its full significance in respect of these measures.[196] However, in many situations where national measures are not preceded by any investigative or fact-finding process, panels themselves, as noted a few pages ago, may need to engage in a rigorous fact-finding exercise.[197]

5.2 *Factors that have bearings on the standard of review*

References have already been made in preceding discussions to some of the factors that affect the applicable standard of review. Thus it has been

[194] Ibid. paras. 91–92. [195] See for instance, the cases cited in nn. 168, 182, 184 above.
[196] See Ehlermann & Lockhart 2004, 503–13. [197] See above, pp. 186–87.

seen that the standard can vary in respect of matters of fact and of law. In respect of factual matters, the standard varies again as between fact-finding and review of factual determinations. And, with regard to factual determinations, the analysis may vary further depending on whether the review is under ADA Article 17.6 or DSU Article 11. Certain other factors that can and do have a bearing on the standard of review are discussed below. The intention is not to provide an exhaustive catalog of all conceivable and inconceivable factors that may have such a bearing, but simply to underscore some of the more pertinent issues that adequately illustrate the context-dependent multidimensional character of the problem of standard of review.

5.2.1 Type of the measure

An important factor that affects the standard of review is the type of the measure that is being reviewed. As seen above, in reviewing the WTO-compatibility of (trade remedy) determinations or decisions issued by domestic judicial, quasi-judicial or administrative authorities, criteria such as whether those authorities took into account all relevant facts/factors or whether those authorities had established and evaluated the facts properly, objectively and without bias are applied. It hardly needs stating that these criteria will be quite inapposite when, instead of administrative or judicial decisions, the review concerns the WTO-compatibility of *national laws* (except, possibly, certain EC legislation that may be specifically directed against particular products or imports and accordingly can be more akin to administrative measures). To give a simple example, in reviewing whether a particular piece of domestic legislation of a Member is consistent with the WTO TRIPS Agreement – that is to say, whether or not the legislation falls short in securing protection for the intellectual property rights recognized under that Agreement[198] – the criteria mentioned above can hardly have any relevance.[199] Rather, in such cases, the panel's analysis must of necessity turn on what meaning or interpretation is to be attributed to the

[198] See, e.g., *India – Patent I & II*; *Canada – Pharmaceuticals*; *Canada – Patent Term*; *US – Copyright Act*; and *US – Section 211*.

[199] As another example it may be mentioned that the special standard of review of ADA Article 17.6 applies only in respect of review of anti-dumping measures taken against specific imports by, say, national administrative authorities, and does not have any relevance when the review concerns the ADA-compatibility of Members' (anti-dumping) laws that are applicable in general: see, e.g., *US – 1916 Act I & II*; *US – Section 129*; and *US – Offset Act*.

legislation and how it is to be assessed against the standards of the TRIPS Agreement.

Because national laws are facts before international courts and tribunals,[200] the determination of the content or meaning of a national law involves purely factual issues. While this aspect of the review of national laws forms the subject-matter of the next chapter, presently a few brief remarks may be made simply to underscore the differences in the methodology and the criteria of review between national *laws* and administrative, quasi-judicial or judicial *decisions*.

In establishing the content or meaning of a national law, it is of utmost importance that panels should not attribute to the law an interpretation that is at odds with how the law is actually interpreted and applied by the relevant Member. This is a challenging task. Firstly, it is almost inconceivable that a Member will not have its own methods of statutory interpretation. Secondly, often the text of a domestic law will carry with it interpretations from various other sources, for example legislative history, administrative guidelines, judicial decisions, etc. Thus the proper establishment of the content of a domestic law as facts demands on the part of a panel not only sufficient ad hoc expertise in the canons of statutory interpretation of the relevant Member, but also an effort to address and deal with a wide range of arguments and materials concerning the interpretation of the law.[201] This is an exercise that is entirely different from the task of ordinary fact-finding or assessment of factual determinations, which is commonly undertaken in the context of the review of administrative, quasi-judicial or judicial decisions.

Postponing further consideration of the factual aspect of the standard of review of national laws for the next chapter, attention may now be devoted to the legal qualification (i.e. the determination of the WTO-compatibility) aspect. Members, of course, are obliged to ensure the conformity of their laws with the WTO obligations by, inter alia, Article XVI:4 of the WTO Agreement. Certain interpretative issues surrounding this Article and how the Article is treated in dispute settlement cases have been discussed in Chapter 3. An issue raised there concerned the threshold for the degree of correspondence or likeness between domestic laws and the relevant WTO provisions/obligations. In this context, it has also been pointed out that the precise scope of the Article is far from clear.[202]

200 See above, Chapter 2, p. 41. 201 See further, Chapter 7, pp. 221–38.
202 See above, Chapter 3, pp. 60–62.

According to certain remarks made by the AB (although not by reference to Article XVI:4) in the *India – Patent* case, it seems that the standard is that of providing a "sound legal basis" to ensure compliance with the WTO obligations and not of removing every "reasonable doubt" regarding conformity of domestic laws with those obligations.[203] A different facet of the "latitude" that must be allowed to Members was highlighted by the Panel in the *US – Section 301* case:

> When evaluating the conformity of national law with WTO obligations in accordance with Article XVI:4 of the WTO Agreement account must be taken of the wide-ranging diversity in the legal systems of the Members. Conformity can be ensured in different ways in different legal systems. It is the end result that counts, not the manner in which it is achieved. Only by understanding and respecting the specificities of each Member's legal system, can a correct evaluation of conformity be established.[204]

It is possible to identify certain tools that are – or, can be – applied in determining the WTO-compatibility of national laws. A prominent one is the distinction between mandatory and discretionary legislation, which has already been touched on briefly in an earlier chapter[205] and which also forms the subject-matter of Chapter 8 below. According to this distinction, as may be recalled, national legislation mandating a violation of WTO obligations can be WTO-incompatible, whereas legislation that merely gives the executive branch of the government a discretion to violate those obligations cannot, by itself, be WTO-incompatible. While the matter is considered in detail in Chapter 8, presently it is worth emphasizing that the distinction is nothing but a specific tool of review of WTO-compatibility of national laws.

Transparency in the application and administration of national laws can also be a relevant criterion for determining their WTO-compatibility.[206] For instance, in the *India – Patent* cases the lack of transparency was one of the main reasons that led to findings of violations. In those cases the Panels rejected India's interpretation of its own law adopted in certain "instructions" issued by the Indian administration, inter alia, on the ground that the instructions concerned were

203 AB Report, *India – Patent I*, paras. 57–58. See also Panel Reports, *US – 1916 Act I*, para. 6.50; and *US – 1916 Act II*, para. 6.49.

204 Panel Report, *US – Section 301*, para. 7.24 (footnote omitted).

205 See above, Chapter 3, p. 54.

206 See, e.g., Cottier & Schefer 1998, 86–87; P. I. Hansen 1999, 1057–67; and Zleptnig 2002, 453–56.

"unwritten and unpublished."[207] The concept of "proportionality" discussed above can be mentioned as another example of a tool relevant for "legal qualification" of national measures including laws.[208] There are other tools as well, and many are inextricably related to the substantive provisions concerned. However, to discuss all such provisions with a view to identifying the precise standards of review applicable under each of them would go beyond the scope of this study and accordingly needs to be postponed for another occasion.

5.2.2 Substantive provisions

While presently an examination of various substantive provisions cannot be undertaken, the point that the standard of review does vary depending on the provision/s concerned must be duly punctuated. In the recent *US – CVD Investigation on DRAMS* and the *US – Softwood Lumber VI 21.5* cases, the Appellate Body also recognized that the proper standard of review needs to be understood "in the light of the specific obligations of the relevant agreements that are at issue in the case."[209] The concept of proportionality can again be taken as an example. As seen above, so far this has been found to be relevant in respect of certain provisions of the SPS and the TBT Agreements, Article XX of the GATT 1994, Article 6.4 of the ATC, Article 5.1 of the Safeguards Agreement, etc.[210] It may also be relevant in respect of certain other WTO provisions,[211] but in respect of many others its significance may not be readily apparent. Recall also that the two-pronged test of whether the national authority concerned has evaluated all relevant facts/factors and provided a reasoned explanation has a particular relationship with the Safeguards Agreement.[212] While this test (as elaborated above) is capable of some general application, panels and the AB cannot be blamed if they do not apply it with the same rigorousness in respect of safeguard and other measures. It is crucial to be mindful of the link between standard of review and

[207] See Panel Reports, *India – Patent I*, para. 7.42; and *India – Patent II*, para. 7.56; and Chapter 7 below, pp. 233–34. See also AB Report, *US – Shrimp*, paras. 181–83. It may be noted that transparency as a criterion of review (and as applied in the *India – Patent* cases) is distinguishable from the specific and express WTO obligations regarding transparency that were discussed in Chapter 3 above.

[208] It may be mentioned parenthetically that, while the mandatory/discretionary distinction is relevant *only* in respect of national *laws*, both transparency and proportionality are relevant in respect of all types of national measures.

[209] See AB Reports, *US – CVD Investigation on DRAMS*, para. 184, and *US – Softwood Lumber VI 21.5*, para. 92.

[210] See above, pp. 170–73 and n. 121. [211] E.g. GATS Article XIV. [212] See n. 183 above.

substantive obligations, because in many instances extrapolating specific criteria of review from their particular substantive context may give an entirely inaccurate picture of their relevance and significance.

5.2.3 The area in which the contested measure falls

Another factor that affects the standard of review is the area in which the contested national measure falls. This can be exemplified by a comparison between safeguard measures and health protection measures. Safeguard measures are taken to grant domestic industries a temporary respite from increases in *fairly* traded imports.[213] By their very nature these measures are "protectionist" in respect of domestic products and industries and discriminatory against imports. In contrast, health measures are adopted not for any protectionist purpose but rather with the aim of preserving human life and health, an objective that is "both vital and important in the highest degree."[214] These differences can of course lead to different standards of review and levels of deference in respect of safeguard and health measures. It has, for instance, been argued rather forcefully that "in sharp contrast" with anti-dumping, countervailing and safeguard measures, panels and the AB have been "highly deferential" to Members' measures falling in the area of health protection.[215] This argument – whether or not one entirely agrees with it – is suggestive that the standard of review does vary depending on the area in which the contested measure falls.

As another conspicuous example, take the case of security exceptions provided for in GATT 1994 Article XXI, GATS Article XIV *bis* and TRIPS Article 73. These provisions authorize a Member, inter alia, to take "any action which it considers necessary for the protection of its essential security interests taken in time of war or other emergency in international relations." It hardly needs stating that a security measure, as envisaged in these provisions, would raise issues and concerns that are quite unique. Accordingly, the standards that are applied in economic disputes relating, for instance, to subsidies, dumping, taxation or fiscal regulation may not be apposite in the area of national security.[216]

Some of the differences in the standard of review across different subject areas result from differences in the wording and nature of the

213 See, generally, Jackson 1997a, 177–78. 214 AB Report, *EC – Asbestos*, para. 172.

215 Bloche 2002, 831–35. See also Trebilcock & Soloway 2002.

216 An analysis of certain tentative standards of review in respect of national security measures can be found in Schloemann & Ohlhoff 1999, 447–49. See also Kuilwijk 1997.

substantive provisions and obligations concerned. But the standard can vary even beyond that: for instance, depending on the subject matter, the standard can vary in respect of the *same* substantive provision. Recall in this context GATT 1994 Article XX(d) discussed above, which entitles Members to adopt measures "necessary" to secure compliance with WTO-consistent laws and regulations. That the standard entailed by the word "necessary" as contained in Article XX(d) could vary due to the relative importance of the interests or values pursued (e.g. prevention of deceptive or anti-competitive practices, protection of the environment or health, etc.) by the relevant national laws or regulations has been recognized by the AB in the following manner:

> It seems to us that a treaty interpreter assessing a measure claimed to be necessary to secure compliance of a WTO-consistent law or regulation may, in appropriate cases, take into account the relative importance of the common interests or values that the law or regulation to be enforced is intended to protect. *The more vital or important those common interests or values are, the easier it would be to accept as "necessary" a measure designed as an enforcement instrument.*[217]

Other WTO provisions can similarly entail different standards of review and/or levels of scrutiny and deference in different subject areas; and, in fact, the AB itself has underscored the point on several other occasions.[218]

5.2.4 Underlying facts and the nature of the evidence

The standard of review can also vary because of the nature of the facts and evidence on the basis of which a contested measure is adopted. For instance, whether a national authority has acted on the basis of scientific evidence involving *scientific uncertainty*,[219] or on the basis of economic evidence or data that are more definite in nature, will have important consequences in respect of the rigorousness with which panels may "second guess" that national authority. A comparison between the facts and evidence underlying a safeguard measure and a health measure can usefully highlight the difference. A safeguard measure may be adopted when imports cause or threaten serious injury to the domestic industry. This is determined on the basis of economic evidence or data bearing on the state of the industry. By contrast, a health

[217] AB Report, *Korea – Beef*, para. 162 (italics added).

[218] See, e.g., AB Reports, *US – Shrimp*, paras. 120, 159; and *EC – Asbestos*, para. 172; and McRae 2000, 225, 229.

[219] See, generally, Christoforou 2000; and V. R. Walker 1998.

measure may be adopted in respect of products that pose risks to human health, a matter that is to be determined by reference to scientific evidence. Against this background consider the following two standards set out by the AB in respect of economic data and scientific evidence, respectively.

- [A] panel can assess whether the competent authorities' explanation for its determination [of serious injury to the domestic industry] is reasoned and adequate *only if* the panel *critically examines* that explanation, *in depth*, and in the light of the facts before the panel. Panels must, therefore, review whether the competent authorities' explanation fully addresses the nature, and, especially, the complexities, of the data, and responds to other plausible interpretations of that data. *A panel must find*, in particular, *that an explanation is not reasoned, or is not adequate, if some alternative explanation of the facts is plausible*, and if the competent authorities' explanation does not seem adequate in the light of that alternative explanation.[220]
- [A] Member may rely, in good faith, on scientific sources which, at [a given] time, may represent a divergent, but qualified and respected, opinion. A Member is not obliged, in setting health policy, automatically to follow what, at a given time, may constitute a majority scientific opinion. Therefore, *a panel need not, necessarily, reach a decision . . . on the basis of the "preponderant" weight of the [scientific] evidence.*[221]

It is apparent from the above that, between measures taken on the basis of economic data and of (uncertain) scientific evidence, the latitude allowed to Members may be wider in respect of the latter.

6 Future perspective

The foregoing analysis by no means exhausts the range of standards or criteria of review that may be relevant under different provisions in different circumstances, nor those that have been applied in dispute settlement cases. It has had more modest aims: to understand the nature of the problem that is commonly labeled as standard of review and the vital policy issues that lie beneath this shorthand label; and to explore on

220 AB Report, *US – Lamb*, para. 106 (italics added). See also AB Report, *US – Cotton Yarn*, para. 72; and Panel Reports, *US – Line Pipe*, para. 7.216; and *US – Steel Safeguards*, para. 10.23.

221 AB Report, *EC – Asbestos*, para. 178 (italics added). See also AB Report, *EC – Hormones I & II*, para. 194.

the basis of the dispute settlement jurisprudence some of the more prominent benchmarks or criteria of review. The analysis has probed into the context-dependent nature of the problem of standard of review. Because a range of variables would have bearings on the proper standard of review applicable in a given case, it is not possible to articulate, in the abstract, the appropriate level of scrutiny (or "point" of deference) in reviewing national measures.[222] Therefore, presently no attempt will be made to set out an abstract prescriptive position as to what specific standard of review the WTO should adopt. It is, however, possible to hypothesize about the path that the standard of review should follow. The appropriate standard of review may well change over time. For the WTO, such change or evolution could be influenced by the tension that exists between its judiciary and domestic civil, political or other bodies within Member countries that represent affected domestic constituencies or are keen to preserve national regulatory competence. The viability of the WTO dispute settlement mechanism rests on the political support for its decisions by WTO Members. Accordingly, before embarking on any thought-experiment as to the future path of the WTO standard of review, a few remarks about the evolution and politicization of standard of review seem relevant.

6.1 *Evolution and politicization of standard of review*

The ECHR jurisprudence clearly illustrates that standard of review evolves over time. The ECHR has a practice of adjusting the margin of appreciation allowed to the states parties to the EHR Convention in their observance of the Convention obligations in the light of the contemporaneous circumstances.[223] This means that the standard of review could change over time in view of developments such as new value choices that place a higher premium on legal certainty, changes in comparative institutional capacities of international courts and national authorities, and the like.[224]

Since the WTO dispute settlement system is still relatively new, standard of review in WTO dispute settlement will evolve over time.[225] As

[222] Cf. Ehlermann & Lockhart 2004, 493 (noting that there is "no single or 'right' standard of review").

[223] See, e.g., *Tyrer* v. *United Kingdom*, ECHR Ser. A No. 26 (1978), para. 31; and *Rees* v. *United Kingdom*, ECHR Ser. A No. 106 (1986), para. 47.

[224] Shany 2005, 939.

[225] A previous member and chairman of the WTO Appellate Body, in an article written with Nicolas Lockhart, has also recognized this possibility: see Ehlermann & Lockhart 2004, 493, 521.

pointed out earlier, standard of review functions to allocate decision-making authority among different levels of governance. The tensions regarding decision-making authority that exist between the WTO judiciary and domestic policy makers, adjudicators and administrators play out in the standard of review. Consequently, the standard of review adopted by WTO panels and the AB can generate heated domestic political debate and can also be influenced by such debate.

In this context, recall that ADA Article 17.6, the only express WTO treaty provision on standard of review, was inserted at the instance of certain US economic interests and was also modeled on a US (the *Chevron*) doctrine. It is, therefore, not surprising that within the United States the subject of standard of review has much political sensitivity. These political sensitivities are well demonstrated by attempts made in the US Congress to establish a commission of jurists with the responsibility to examine, inter alia, whether WTO panels and the Appellate Body have applied the appropriate standard of review in cases where rulings adverse to the USA are issued.[226] In the end such a commission was not established, but nonetheless there have been other attempts made by the US Congress to assess standards of review applied in WTO cases. For example, it requested the General Accounting Office (GAO)[227] to undertake a study of the standards of review that the WTO applies when ruling on trade remedy disputes. The report issued by the GAO did not accuse the WTO of any grave error, yet concerns have been expressed that the WTO has not always properly applied the correct standards and has imposed obligations on Members that are not found in the WTO agreements.[228] In any event, the heated US domestic political debate over standard of review is unlikely to abate in the near future.

It seems that the US outcry against what the US calls "judicial activism" in trade remedy cases has already impacted WTO standard of review jurisprudence. The recent *US – CVD Investigation on DRAMS* case is a notable example. In this case the Appellate Body overturned the

226 See, for instance, the proposed World Trade Organization Dispute Settlement Review Commission Act, S 676 (March 20, 2003), available at http://thomas.loc.gov.

227 The GAO is an agency of the US Congress. Information on its activities can be found at www.gao.gov.

228 GAO 2003. Similar concerns have been expressed by the United States in Doha negotiations, as it has called upon Members to consider whether ADA Article 17.6 should be addressed to ensure that panels and the AB properly apply the article. It has also called upon Members to consider whether a provision similar to ADA Article 17.6 should be included in the ASCM: see WTO Document, TN/RL/W/130 (June 20, 2003), available at http://docsonline.wto.org.

findings of the Panel that the United States had acted inconsistently with the ASCM, on the ground that the Panel had failed to apply the correct standard of review. Three different aspects of the Panel's treatment of the evidence were found to be incorrect: first, the Panel's examination of individual pieces of evidence in isolation and failure to examine the evidence in its totality; second, its refusal to admit certain evidence; and third, its conclusion that the relevant US agency should have made certain factual inference from the evidence.[229] Note that, by and large, these errors relate to the Panel's appreciation of the evidence.[230] The AB concluded that, because of these errors, the Panel "went beyond its role as the reviewer of the [domestic] investigating authority's decision" and, instead, conducted its own *de novo* assessment, relying on its own judgment, of much of the evidence before the US agency.[231] In a long line of earlier cases, including a number of trade remedy cases, the AB has held that panels enjoy "a margin of discretion" in respect of "appreciation of the evidence."[232] In view of those cases, the conclusion of the AB in the *DRAMS CVD* case seems particularly odd.

The signal that the Appellate Body has sent by overturning the Panel in the *DRAMS CVD* case has subsequently resulted in the application of rather superficial standards of review in the *US – Softwood Lumber VI 21.5* case. This case concerned determinations of threat of material injury to the US softwood lumber industry by a US agency. The Panel upheld the determinations on the basis that they were "not unreasonable" or that the complaining party had not demonstrated that an objective and unbiased authority "could not" have reached those determinations.[233] On appeal, the Appellate Body, however, found both of these standards of review to be "inadequate."[234] Thus, the serious restrictions on the review powers of panels that have been imposed in the *DRAMS CVD* case have been relaxed in some measure by the Appellate Body itself in

229 AB Report, *US – CVD Investigation on DRAMS*, paras. 141–79. 230 Cf. Becroft 2006, 215.

231 AB Report, *US – CVD Investigation on DRAMS*, paras. 188–90.

232 See, e.g., AB Reports, *EC – Hormones I & II*, paras. 132–33, 135–36; *Australia – Salmon*, para. 267; *Korea – Alcohol*, para. 164; *Japan – Agricultural Products II*, para. 141; *US – Wheat Gluten*, para. 151; *EC – Asbestos*, para. 161; *EC – Sardines*, para. 299; *US – Carbon Steel*, para. 142; *EC – Bed Linen 21.5*, paras. 177, 181; *Japan – Apples*, paras. 221–22; *US – OCTG Sunset Reviews*, para. 313; *US – Upland Cotton*, para. 399; *US – Gambling Services*, para. 363; and *Dominican Republic – Cigarettes*, paras. 84, 112.

233 Panel Report, *US – Softwood Lumber VI 21.5*, paras. 7.27, 7.39, 7.57, 7.63. It is notable that, while the WTO Panel accepted the US determinations of threat of material injury, a NAFTA committee concluded that the evidence did not support a finding of threat of material injury: see Pauwelyn 2006.

234 AB Report, *US – Softwood Lumber VI 21.5*, paras. 99, 112–13, 118, 130, 138–39.

the *Lumber* case. Yet, it is apparent that political heat cannot fail to have some impact on the evolution of the standard of review.[235]

6.2 *Looking forwards*

As noted above, political support for its rulings from WTO Members is needed for the viability of the WTO dispute settlement system. Accordingly, it is unreasonable to suggest that panels and the AB should not pay any heed to domestic political debates. However, giving way to sheer political pressure without any principled basis would undermine the credibility of the system and, paradoxically, political support for it. In the light of these considerations a few final remarks can be made about the path that the standard of review should follow.

Recall that standard of review is concerned with good governance because it functions to allocate decision-making authority and resources in an efficient fashion. Section 4 of this chapter has discussed various important policy arguments that suggest that the ultimate authority to interpret the WTO treaty must rest with the WTO judiciary and not individual Members. Such arguments include those stemming from the policy objectives of effectiveness and good governance. For instance, uniform interpretation of WTO norms by panels and the Appellate Body is crucial in securing fairness, legitimacy and effectiveness of the WTO legal system. Interpretative authority of the WTO panels and the AB can be supported on the basis of good governance, because these bodies are accountable to the WTO membership as a whole and also have comparative institutional advantages over individual Members in interpreting the WTO treaty. It has been argued that, in the exercise of their interpretative authority, panels and the AB should remain true to a single and coherent interpretation of treaty provisions. But there can be flexibility within a single and coherent interpretation for accommodating different national measures taken by different Members in different circumstances.

In contrast to questions of interpretation, questions of fact and legal characterization (i.e. applying the law to the facts and determining the conformity of the facts with the law) properly belong to the realm of standard of review. Determination of these questions, unlike questions of interpretation, is not an exclusive province of an international judiciary. National authorities enjoy comparative institutional advantages

[235] Cf. Davey 2006, 15 (noting that the AB "realizes that it cannot deviate too far from the views of the Members").

over international courts in respect of fact-finding or fact-assessment exercises. In respect of legal characterization, which involves interactions between facts and the law, the institutional advantages of international courts and national authorities are relatively equipoised. Consequently, an international court should accord considerable deference to national authorities on matters of fact, while also according some deference on matters of legal characterization.

Some of the arguments that suggest that the ultimate authority on interpretative questions should rest with the international judiciary can be relevant for legal characterization as well. Thus, for instance, it may be argued that to ensure fair, predictable and effective application of WTO law to the facts, panels and the AB should intensively review legal characterization issues. Furthermore, compared to certain other international treaties, the scope of deference and normative flexibility under the WTO treaty can be more limited. In this context the European Human Rights Convention can be taken as an example. This Convention regulates the internal or domestic conditions of states. Societies should be entitled to particular discretion in adopting internal social arrangements, which reflect the wishes, values and perceived interests of the population. The application of the EHR Convention by domestic authorities of a state remains accountable to the citizens of that state, whose rights the Convention intends to protect.[236] The WTO treaty, however, regulates international trade and foreign policy powers of states. Domestic authorities of a WTO Member would not have a similar accountability to foreign nationals or countries whose trading interests the WTO treaty intends to protect. Besides, human rights norms may admit of considerable flexibility in their application, appropriately suited to local circumstances and needs. By contrast, since the WTO treaty regulates market conditions, ensuring security and predictability in the market place may demand consistent application of WTO norms. Thus, the policy objectives of both good governance and effectiveness may suggest that, compared to the ECHR, the WTO judiciary should retain greater control over legal characterization issues.

Considerable deference can be accorded to national authorities on factual matters. In some instances panels themselves may need to engage in fact-finding, while in others (mostly in trade remedy cases) their role

[236] Cf. Shany 2005, 920–21 (noting that international norms that regulate domestic conditions are more amenable to the application of a margin of appreciation-type doctrine).

is limited to a "second tier" review of the factual determinations made by national authorities. In the latter instances, WTO review is strictly limited and falls far short of a review of whether the national authority's determination is "right" or "wrong." Thus, in respect of trade remedy determinations under the ASCM or the Safeguards Agreement, the review is limited to a consideration of whether the national authority has evaluated all relevant factors/facts and provided reasoned and adequate explanations for its determination. These standards of review focus on the governance processes that underpin the adoption of domestic measures and promote good governance by making deliberative, transparent and rational decision- and rule-making relevant for the review of their legality.

Although good governance-spirited standards of review have so far been used mostly – but not exclusively – in trade remedy cases, there is a lot of scope for much wider application of such standards of review in WTO dispute settlement. For example, in respect of factual (scientific or technical) determinations made for the adoption of SPS or TBT measures, criteria such as whether the determinations have taken into account all relevant evidence and factors, afforded interested parties an opportunity to be heard, and have been adopted through transparent and rational processes can be applied.

It needs to be acknowledged that there are some differences in the structure of the trade remedy agreements and the SPS and TBT agreements. As discussed earlier, trade remedy agreements themselves require national authorities to conduct investigations for making factual determinations. They also incorporate elaborate procedural guarantees for those investigations. No similar requirements prescribing a formal process for the adoption of SPS or TBT measures are contained in the SPS and TBT Agreements. Accordingly, doubts may be expressed as to whether it would be appropriate for panels to apply to these measures, even in cases where they are adopted in pursuance of a formal process, a "second tier" review that is identical to the review of the trade remedy measures.[237] Such doubts certainly have some merit; nevertheless, between two national determinations, one of which *is*, and the other *is not*, adopted through a transparent, rational and deliberative process, the former seems to be a better candidate for greater judicial deference. Another difference between the trade remedy agreements and the SPS and TBT Agreements is that under the former the determinations must

[237] Cf. Ehlermann & Lockhart 2004, 514.

be made by the Member adopting the trade remedy measure, while under the latter a Member can rely on determinations made by another Member or by international standards-setting organizations. In a perceptive article, Joanne Scott has argued that deference to international standards by the WTO judiciary should depend on the legitimacy and transparency of the decision-making and governance processes leading to the adoption of the relevant standards.[238] Thus, as a tool of review, good governance can be relevant even where a Member relies on factual determinations made by another Member or an international body.

Good governance is relevant in respect of not only factual determinations but also legal characterization. Recall that there are various "good governance-tinged" substantive and systemic WTO obligations, such as those concerning non-discrimination, proportionality, non-arbitrariness, transparency, fair and equitable administration of laws, judicial remedy and the like. Whenever the legality of a national measure is determined under such a provision, "good governance" becomes an essential tool of review. The Appellate Body ruling in the *US – Shrimp* case well illustrates the potential that good governance has as a criterion of review. In this case the AB extrapolated far-reaching good governance-spirited standards of review from the chapeau of Article XX of the GATT, such as: transparency; procedural fairness and due process; opportunity to be heard; providing formal, written and reasoned decisions; availability of review or appeal procedures, etc.[239] The AB, quite innovatively, went much further than the text of Article XX in promoting deliberative decision- and rule-making by condemning the contested US measure for its "unilateralism":

> the United States [has failed] to pursue negotiations for establishing consensual means of protection and conservation of the living marine resources here involved . . . The principal consequence of this failure may be seen in the resulting unilateralism evident in the application of Section 609 . . . The [US] system and processes of certification are established and administered by the United States agencies alone. The decision-making involved in the grant, denial or withdrawal of certification to the exporting Members, is, accordingly, also unilateral. The unilateral character of the application of Section 609 heightens the disruptive and discriminatory influence of the import prohibition and underscores its unjustifiability.[240]

Similar good governance-spirited standards of review can be applied in respect of other WTO provisions as well.

[238] Scott 2004. [239] See AB Report, *US – Shrimp*, paras. 180–83. [240] Ibid. para. 172.

The principle of proportionality has obvious good governance dimensions. It prevents arbitrariness and abuse of power by ensuring the proper equilibrium between different rights, interests or values and a rational relationship between the means and the ends or the measure and the underlying evidence. The full potential of this principle as a standard of review in WTO dispute settlement is yet to be realized. It has been discussed that, in a number of contexts and in various forms, proportionality analysis is undertaken by panels and the AB. Although reference to proportionality gave rise to criticism by WTO Members, Appellate Body Member Georges Abi-Saab has posed the following sensible question: "Can there be any system of law that can work without a reasonable concept of proportionality?"[241] In the light of the experience of other international and regional courts (i.e. the ECHR and the ECJ) it can be suggested that the WTO dispute settlement will benefit from a greater use of proportionality review of national measures.

Review of national measures on the basis of the decision-making and governance processes leading to their adoption can be recommended for reasons of subsidiarity as well. Testing the legality of a measure by examining whether it was adopted in pursuance of a transparent process that took into account all relevant factors and facts, provided interested parties opportunities to be heard and resulted in reasoned decisions would encourage national authorities to engage in a rational and fair balancing of the interests of various stakeholders before adopting any measure.[242] Consequently, affected constituencies would be able to raise their concerns and obtain redress in domestic forums, and not all conflicts of interest would need to be resolved by the WTO judiciary. As pointed out earlier, due to the non-applicability of the exhaustion of local remedies rule, a common and inherent safeguard in favor of subsidiarity that exists in other areas of international law is absent in the WTO. This gap can be filled by reviewing national measures on the basis of the decision-making and governance processes leading to their adoption.

So, to conclude, it is worth emphasizing that, as standard of review evolves in future, panels and the Appellate Body would be well advised to bear in mind the relevance and significance of the policy objectives of effectiveness of WTO rules and supervision, and good governance at domestic level, for that evolution.

[241] Abi-Saab 2005, 11.

[242] Cf. P. I. Hansen 1999, 1061–68; and Zleptnig 2002, 452–57.

7 National law as a question of fact

1 Introduction

This chapter deals with two particular aspects of WTO adjudicative organs' review of national laws, namely, *proof* of national law and *interpretation* of national law. Both of these are related to the basic international law principle that national laws are *facts* before international courts and tribunals. The connection between proof of national law and the principle that national laws are facts is rather obvious. That is to say, because national laws are facts, judicial notice (pursuant to the maxim *jura novit curia*) does not apply to matters of national law. Instead, national law needs to be proved and an international tribunal will consider evidence of such law furnished by the parties, or, if necessary, may undertake its own researches.[1] This dimension of the national law as facts principle is easily understandable and is genuinely reflected in the practice of international courts and tribunals – be it the PCIJ/ICJ, the ECHR, the WTO bodies or other international tribunals.

The issue of interpretation of national law by international courts and tribunals is less straightforward, or, to be exact, this issue has unnecessarily been shrouded in confusion. It is, of course, clearly and plainly the case that in a variety of circumstances international courts and tribunals need to interpret national laws.[2] But despite this reality, it is sometimes suggested – as a corollary to the principle that national laws are merely facts – that an international tribunal "does not interpret

[1] See, e.g., *Mavrommatis* case, PCIJ Ser. A No. 5 (1925) at 29–30; *Brazilian Loans* case, PCIJ Ser. A No. 21 (1929) at 124; and Brownlie 1998, 40.

[2] See, e.g., Jenks 1964, 548–603; and Brownlie 1998, 40–41.

national law as such."[3] While earlier reference to this proposition (i.e. national laws are not interpreted) was quite sporadic and confined to a very limited number of dicta or individual (separate or dissenting) opinions of the judges of the PCIJ/ICJ,[4] WTO panels and the AB have made it almost a fashion to refer to this proposition whenever they confront issues of national law. They do so again and again like a *mantra* and without giving any serious thought to what it really means or whether it actually reflects what they or international courts and tribunals in general do with municipal law. The fallacies of the proposition are canvassed in due course and in necessary detail in section 3 below, while presently it is appropriate to redirect attention to other introductory matters.

Three points require mentioning specifically. First, although proof of national law and interpretation of national law can be seen as functionally discrete, they have the common aim of establishing the content of national law. Proof is the process whereby the necessary evidence – such as text of legislation, evidence on pertinent legislative history, judicial decisions, administrative guidelines, etc. – on the relevant national law issue is gathered. Interpretation is the process of construing the evidential materials to determine what is it that the national law provides on the particular issue/s that are at stake. The process of gathering evidential materials is important, because without such materials the content of national law cannot be established, and, if the gathering of evidence is defective, the interpretation and consequently the establishment of the content of national law is also likely to be defective. The process of interpretation is no less important either, because the simple gathering of even the most comprehensive and the most voluminous evidential record on a particular national law point would barely shed light on that point unless the evidential materials are construed in some manner, usually in accordance with the canons of interpretation of the Member concerned. Thus, it is through a combination of the processes of proof and of interpretation that the content of national law is established.

The second point that requires mentioning is that the general theme of this chapter, i.e. establishment of the content of national law, bears

[3] See, e.g., *German Interests in Polish Upper Silesia*, PCIJ Ser. A No. 7 (1926) at 19; Dissenting Opinion of Judge Read, *Nottebohm* case, ICJ Rep. 4 (1955) at 36; and Separate Opinion of Judge Lauterpacht, *Guardianship of Infants* case, ICJ Rep. 55 (1958) at 91.

[4] See n. 3 above.

directly on the issue of *standard of review of national laws*. While the relationship may not be readily apparent in respect of proof, it nonetheless exists, because a question can be posed as to what should be the level of rigorousness in accumulating evidential materials on national law. In respect of interpretation, the standard of review issue arises much more conspicuously because a crucial methodological question is: how far should panels accept (i.e. *defer* to) the interpretation or meaning attributed by a Member to its own laws, either internally by various governmental organs (e.g. courts and administrative bodies) or in the context of submissions before the panels?[5] These are particular dimensions of standard of review of national laws as *facts* and must be understood in conjunction with issues of standard of review of facts and legal characterization discussed in the last chapter. For instance, if a national law embodies factual determinations concerning health or environmental risks, injury to domestic industry, necessity of technical or sanitary regulations, etc., the analysis contained in the last chapter relating to review of factual determinations will be relevant in respect of review of that national law. But, in addition, it will be necessary for the reviewing panel to determine the content of the national law, which is addressed in this chapter. Similarly, everything that has been discussed in the last chapter regarding legal characterization (i.e. applying the WTO law to the facts / domestic law and determining the conformity of the facts / domestic law with the WTO law) is relevant in reviewing national law.

The third point is an obvious one. Yet duly highlighting it may be useful for a proper appreciation of the significance of various matters discussed in this chapter. The content of a national law is established for determining its WTO-compatibility.[6] Hence, the outcome of a case can depend on what materials are relied upon and how they are interpreted in establishing the content of a law. Take, for instance, the question of the mandatory/discretionary nature of national legislation, to which references have been made on a few earlier occasions and which also forms the subject-matter of the next chapter. Because a mandatory law by itself violates WTO obligations and a discretionary law does not, the outcome of a case can, of course, turn entirely on whether the contested domestic law is held to be – i.e. on the basis of the *evidential materials* is *interpreted* to be – mandatory or discretionary.

[5] See, further, pp. 218–19 below.

[6] Or sometimes the compatibility of a specific measure taken under the law: cf. Chapter 4, pp. 100–2 above.

2 Proof of national law

Turning now to proof of national law, this can be dealt with rather briefly, not least because there does not exist much controversy in this regard. The issue of proof is of course inextricably related to burden of proof.[7] And the basic WTO law rule on burden of proof can be stated quite simply: "the party who asserts a fact, whether the claimant or the respondent, is responsible for providing proof thereof."[8] In respect of national law the Appellate Body has further clarified this rule as follows:

> The party asserting that another party's municipal law, as such, is inconsistent with relevant treaty obligations bears the burden of introducing evidence as to the scope and meaning of such law to substantiate that assertion. Such evidence will typically be produced in the form of the text of the relevant legislation or legal instruments, which may be supported, as appropriate, by evidence of the consistent application of such laws, the pronouncements of domestic courts on the meaning of such laws, the opinions of legal experts and the writings of recognized scholars. The nature and extent of the evidence required to satisfy the burden of proof will vary from case to case.[9]

While the above observations focus on assertions made by a party regarding the law of the opposite party, they apply, *mutatis mutandis*, in respect of assertions made by a party regarding its own law. For instance, if a complainant claims that the law of the respondent provides for certain things and, in response to that claim, the respondent asserts that its law does not provide for those things or that its law provides something entirely different, the respondent is to furnish the necessary evidence regarding its own law to substantiate its assertions. This, however, is not a suggestion that the respondent has, *ab initio*, an evidentiary burden to show that its law is WTO-consistent. In other words, the respondent can certainly sit back and watch until the claimant has adduced sufficient evidence to raise a presumption that its claims regarding the

[7] See, generally, Kazazi 1996; and Pauwelyn 1998.

[8] AB Report, *US – Shirts and Blouses*, at 14. This is also the basic rule on burden of proof in respect of international dispute settlement in general: see Kazazi 1996, 117, 378; and Rosenne 1997, 1083. See also Bethlehem 2000 (containing a comparative analysis of pleading of facts before the ICJ and the WTO organs).

[9] AB Report, *US – Carbon Steel*, para. 157 (footnote omitted). See also AB Report, *Dominican Republic – Cigarettes*, paras. 111–12 (noting that different types of evidence may be relevant in ascertaining the meaning and scope of an impugned domestic law and that a panel enjoys a margin of discretion in weighing such evidence, commensurate with its role as trier of fact).

WTO-incompatibility of the respondent's law are valid.[10] Once the claimant has been able to raise such a presumption, the respondent has the evidentiary burden to rebut that presumption and, for that purpose, to adduce the necessary evidence to substantiate any affirmative assertions that it makes regarding its own law.[11]

Thus, succinctly, a party that affirmatively puts forward a national law point - be it in respect of its own law or the law of the opposite party - has the burden and the responsibility to furnish the necessary evidence on that point. In addition, and if the circumstances so require, the panel itself may engage in fact-finding by seeking information from any source or expert that it deems appropriate or by appointing expert/s to advise it on national law issues. This can be done in pursuance of the general authority given to a panel under DSU Article 13 to seek information and technical advice from any individual or body which the panel deems appropriate or to appoint experts to advise it on technical factual issues.[12] However, except in one case[13] where questions of translation were involved, panels have not found it necessary to consult experts for purposes of determining national law issues. The usual practice has been for the parties to furnish the relevant domestic legal texts and documents as exhibits to their written submissions.[14] And panels have been able to determine national law issues on the basis of such party-led documentary evidence and the written and oral submissions/arguments - turning largely on the interpretation of the documentary evidence - of the parties before the panels.[15]

However, the situation can be somewhat less straightforward where, as has just been hinted at, the relevant legal texts and documents are not available in the working language of the panel. An example of the translation problem is the *Japan - Film* case. In this case the Panel had to consider various documents, including legislation and other statutory instruments, which were in the Japanese language. Although provisions are made, as already noted, in DSU Article 13 for consultation with and appointment of experts, there is no express guidance in the DSU

[10] See AB Report, *US - Shirts and Blouses*, at 14.

[11] Ibid. See further, Waincymer 2002, 549–58.

[12] See above, Chapter 6, n. 173. [13] I.e. *Japan - Film*.

[14] See, e.g., Panel Reports, *US - Copyright Act*, footnotes 6, 8; and *US - Countervailing Measures*, footnotes 89, 294.

[15] Thus the position is diametrically different from that of the proof of foreign law as facts before national courts, which involves not simply the submission of written expert evidence but more standardly, and more often, the examination of expert witnesses in open court: see, generally, Fentiman 1998, 173–202.

regarding either translation of documents or resolving any disagreement between the parties about the correct translation. Due to the absence of such guidance, the Panel, in consultation with the parties, drew up a procedure to address both of these matters, i.e. translation and resolution of disagreements about translation.

Under that procedure the party relying on a Japanese-language document was required to provide copies of the entire document and English translation of the relevant parts at the time it first referred to the document in the Panel proceedings. If an additional part was relied on subsequently, translation of that part was required when reference to that part was made for the first time. A party that disagreed with a translation provided by the other was required to submit an alternative translation along with supporting written arguments, if necessary. The procedure further provided that the Panel would attempt to resolve any translation issue submitted to it either by recourse to independent experts appointed by it or by such other means as it deemed appropriate. Eventually the Panel appointed two law professors as translation experts, and their responses on various translation issues raised by the parties were annexed to the Panel report.[16]

It is possible to imagine that the above procedure may put constraints on panels' limited time and resources and, on occasion, may put panels in a difficult situation of choosing between widely divergent opinions of experts. Relying on official translations, or, in their absence, accepting translations on the basis of official authentication by an appropriate organ of the country whose law is in question is a simpler way to resolve translation issues.[17] In the WTO, reliance may also be placed on the official WTO translations of notifications of laws and regulations that Members are required to make under different transparency provisions of the WTO agreements.[18] However, there could be circumstances where the disputing parties may have disagreements about the accuracy of a translation, despite its official nature or authentication. In such cases, reliance by a panel on a disputed translation would not

[16] See Panel Report, *Japan – Film*, paras. 1.8–11.

[17] Cf. the *Lighthouses* case, where in respect of a Turkish law the PCIJ relied on an official translation produced to the Court by the Greek government, while in respect of another it referred to a translation from a Turkish official source, submitted by the Greek Agent, which did not encounter any objection from the French Agent: PCIJ Ser. A/B No. 62 (1934) at 20–23. See also Jenks 1938, 90–91, and 1964, 588.

[18] For instance, in *Mexico – Rice* the Panel relied on the official WTO translations of the notifications of Mexican laws made by Mexico to the WTO Anti-Dumping Committee: see Panel Report, para. 7.252; and AB Report, para. 330.

be compatible with the panel's obligation to make an "objective assessment" of the matter. Thus, some cases may indeed require the assistance of translation experts.

3 Interpretation of national law

3.1 *In general*

Before turning to interpretation of national law by WTO panels, it may be useful to note briefly the wider international legal context of the issue and, in particular, comment on the unnecessary confusions that have apparently been created. The origin of the confusions lay in the following oft-quoted 1926 dictum of the PCIJ:

> From the standpoint of International Law and of the Court which is its organ, municipal laws are merely facts which express the will and constitute the activities of States, in the same manner as do legal decisions or administrative measures. *The Court is certainly not called upon to interpret the Polish law as such*; but there is nothing to prevent the Court's giving judgment on the question whether or not, in applying that law, Poland is acting in conformity with its obligations towards Germany under the Geneva Convention.[19]

The italicized language of the above quote is commonly seen and put forward as the authoritative pronouncement that an international tribunal does not interpret national law.[20] But not much ingenuity is needed to see that the language is far from clear and that it raises more questions than it answers. Thus, for instance, the PCIJ did not simply state that an international tribunal does not interpret national law, but rather it made a qualified statement that national law is not interpreted *as such*. What the PCIJ meant by the qualifier "as such" will possibly always remain a mystery. A sensible way to understand the language would have

[19] *German Interests in Polish Upper Silesia*, PCIJ Ser. A No. 7 (1926) at 19 (italics added).

[20] In addition, reference is sometimes made to a few separate or dissenting opinions of individual judges of the PCIJ/ICJ. However, it is difficult to treat such individual opinions as significant, given that it is readily possible to find other individual opinions which suggest the contrary – namely, that in certain circumstances an international tribunal may need to interpret national laws. Thus, for instance, Judge Anzilotti in his individual opinion in the *Danzig Legislative Decrees* case referred to the possibility that an international court may be required "to *interpret* a municipal law . . . simply as a law which governs certain facts": PCIJ Ser. A/B No. 65 (1935) at 63 (italics added); and Judge Basdevant in his dissenting opinion in the *Norwegian Loans* case suggested that the questions of fact that might arise in the case would include "questions of the *interpretation of such Norwegian laws* as may call for consideration": ICJ Rep. 9 (1957) at 78 (italics added). For other references, see Jenks 1964, 551.

been to view it as an indication that an international tribunal does not *authoritatively* interpret national law, which can only be done by domestic courts. That is to say, the interpretation of national law by an international court is not authoritative within the internal legal system of the country whose law is interpreted. This, of course, does not mean that an international tribunal need not interpret – i.e. determine the content or meaning – of national law for purposes of international adjudication. But this is not how WTO panels and the AB have understood the dictum. They refer to the dictum in a rather mechanistic way to make flat assertions – assertions that demonstrate a total failure to appreciate the finer dimensions of the problem – that they are not engaged in interpretation of national law.

Given the ambiguous and unconvincing nature of the PCIJ dictum, it is no wonder that the dictum has not remained unchallenged.[21] The most perceptive and well-researched challenge has been mounted by Wilfred Jenks, who notes that the proposition that international courts and tribunals take cognizance of municipal laws only as facts and do not interpret municipal law as such "falls well short of being established law. It is, at most, a debatable proposition the validity and wisdom of which are subject to, and call for, further discussion and review."[22] He then engages in an extensive review of the relevant cases decided by both the PCIJ and the ICJ and concludes that it is "neither necessary nor desirable to describe municipal law . . . as a fact,"[23] and suggests that there should be "a franker and fuller recognition than there has been that in a variety of cases the functions of the Court necessarily include the *interpretation* and application of municipal law."[24]

Other authorities have observed that the dictum in the *Upper Silesia* case "is not unequivocal" in its remark with regard to the interpretation of municipal law.[25] Rather, it is simply an indication of the manner in which national law can be treated in certain types of cases, which does not foreclose the possibility that in other types of cases it may be necessary to treat national law quite differently.[26]

[21] See, for instance, the works cited above in Chapter 2, n. 54.

[22] Jenks 1964, 552. The statement is approvingly quoted in Brownlie 1998, 39–40.

[23] Jenks 1964, 603. [24] Ibid. 600 (italics added).

[25] See Brownlie 1998, 40, footnote 52 (and the authorities cited there).

[26] See, e.g., Jenks 1964, 548. Jenks also argues for a restrictive interpretation of the dictum on the ground that it was made at a very early stage when the varied elements of the problem of interpretation and application of national laws by international tribunals had not been brought into proper focus: ibid.

A further trend of argument focuses on cases decided by the International Court where, instead of international law, a particular municipal law was applied as the applicable substantive law.[27] Commentators have referred to these types of cases as disputes involving solely the *interpretation* of municipal law;[28] and the Court itself, in the course of elucidating how it should proceed in such a case, has used language that reflects that the Court hardly considered interpretation of national law as something beyond the realm of its functions.[29] Thus, with regard to these types of cases, the proposition that international courts do not interpret national law breaks down overtly and shockingly.[30]

While the most compelling argument that international tribunals do interpret national law can be made on the basis of the cases concerning the application of such law, it needs to be noted, however, that this argument has an important flaw. To a certain extent, it may imply that in other types of cases, for example cases concerning the determination of international legal conformity of national legislation, an international tribunal does not interpret national law. The inaccuracy of such an implication, if there is one, should be duly underscored. Indeed, the entire proposition that international courts do not interpret national law is deficient in that it fails to take into account that, although before an international tribunal national laws are facts, they are facts, so to speak, of a special nature. Even in cases where an international tribunal examines a municipal law or determines its content so as to apply the

[27] See, e.g., *Serbian Loans* case, PCIJ Ser. A No. 20 (1929); and *Brazilian Loans* case, PCIJ Ser. A No. 21 (1929). Cf. *Norwegian Loans* case, ICJ Rep. 9 (1957) at 13, 31–32 (Separate Opinion of Judge Badawi). See also Chapter 4, p. 103, above.

[28] See, e.g., Shaw 1997, 104; and Harris 1998, 72.

[29] For instance, in the *Serbian Loans* case the PCIJ described itself as having "to decide as to the *meaning* and scope of a municipal law": PCIJ Ser. A No. 20 (1929) at 46 (italics added); and in the *Brazilian Loans* case the PCIJ considered itself "bound to apply municipal law when circumstances so require": PCIJ Ser. A No. 21 (1929) at 124. In the latter case, the Court also referred to its authority to select, from among uncertain or divided interpretations of national law by domestic courts, the interpretation that it (the PCIJ) "considers most in conformity with the law": ibid. 125. Certainly, this task of selecting the most appropriate interpretation from amongst the diverging interpretations by domestic courts cannot be performed without interpreting, to a certain degree, the relevant national law. See also Harris 1998, 72, who describes certain passages of the judgment of the PCIJ in *Brazilian Loans* as relating to the Court's view as to "how it [the PCIJ] should go about interpreting municipal law when called upon to do so."

[30] Cf. also the *US – Section 129* case discussed in Chapter 4, p. 104, above. In this case, as may be recalled, a WTO panel was able to make its ruling solely on the basis of its findings regarding the meaning or interpretation of the contested domestic law.

relevant international law rules, simply for that reason the municipal law in question does not lose its normative quality in relation to the rights, obligations and transactions that it seeks to regulate.[31] It is this normative quality which makes national law different from other types of facts. Unlike ordinary facts relating to events that take place in a certain time and space, establishing the content or meaning of a national law as a fact entails the determination of its normative significance. And the normative import of a law – be it national or international – cannot be ascertained without a certain amount of interpretation.

Various international courts and tribunals, however, have faced from time to time cases where the meaning of the domestic law at issue was either straightforward or else the parties did not dispute it.[32] In these cases the content of the domestic law was established rather simply; and it is not apparent from the relatively brief discussion of the matter in the judgments that the tribunals concerned were interpreting national law. By contrast, the law reports contain numerous other examples in which the matter was far from simple, and it was necessary to determine the meaning of complex national laws in the face of differing interpretations put forward by the parties. Even on a cursory review of international tribunals' elaborate examination of national law in this latter type of case, it becomes evident that the suggestion that international tribunals do not interpret national law (as such?) is without merit.[33]

Although both the clarity and the accuracy of the PCIJ dictum in the *Upper Silesia* case are thus open to question, the WTO Appellate Body, quite regrettably, has seized the very first opportunity to affirm it. In *India – Patent I*, India argued that the Panel erred in its treatment of Indian municipal law because it did not assess the law as a fact to be established, but rather as a law to be interpreted by the Panel. The Appellate Body, after quoting the dictum, continued as follows:

> It is clear that an examination of the relevant aspects of Indian municipal law . . . is essential to determining whether India has complied with its obligations under Article 70.8(a) [of the TRIPS Agreement]. There was simply no way for the Panel to make this determination without engaging in an examination of Indian law. But, *as in the case cited above before the Permanent Court of International Justice, in this case, the Panel was not interpreting Indian law "as such."*[34]

[31] See Jenks 1964, 549. [32] See, for instance, the cases cited in n. 44 below.

[33] See, e.g., *Fisheries* case, ICJ Rep. 116 (1951); *Nottebohm* case, ICJ Rep. 4 (1955); and *Guardianship of Infants* case, ICJ Rep. 55 (1958). In these cases the ICJ has examined at great length national laws relating, respectively, to fisheries zones, nationality, and guardianship and welfare of infants.

[34] AB Report, *India – Patent I*, para. 66 (italics added).

To the above, a gloss in the following terms was added by the Panel in the *US – Section 301* case: "we do not, as noted by the Appellate Body in *India – Patent I*, interpret US law 'as such', *the way we would, say, interpret provisions of the covered agreements* [i.e., the WTO agreements]. We are, instead, called upon to establish the meaning of [the US law] as factual elements."[35] Since then it became a standard practice to utter this *mantra* before commencing an examination of national law. It is, however, not difficult to understand why panels and the AB find the *mantra* so attractive. Any hints by panels or the AB of the existence and invocation of even minimalist powers to interpret national law would generate a huge outcry by the Members of the WTO. For panels and the AB the *mantra* also serves as a useful and convenient refuge when they confront arguments by Members that they cannot and should not interpret national laws.

Given the Members' perspective on the matter, it will not be possible for panels and the AB to overcome the confusions that have already been created unless Members also realize that it is not possible for panels and the AB to perform their adjudicative and supervisory functions in respect of national law without interpreting such law. But why is it essential to acknowledge the necessity to interpret national law? To mention just an obvious reason, because national laws are interpreted anyway, an acknowledgment of it would enable both the parties to canvass the relevant issues adequately and the panels to deal with them in a more befitting manner. Likewise, critical evaluations would be able to assess more constructively the extent and manner of interpretation of national law as well as the degree to which such interpretation is desirable and appropriate, rather than being confined to the sterile question of whether or not national laws are interpreted.

3.2 *Methodological issues*

While it is not to be doubted that international tribunals do interpret national law, it is equally true that, compared to the interpretation by a domestic court of its own law, the interpretation by an international tribunal is limited in both purpose and scope. International tribunals interpret national law, as already alluded to, for purposes of international adjudication only; and their interpretation is not authoritative as a matter of domestic law. The interpretation is limited in scope because it is not the task of an international tribunal to interpret a national law autonomously or independently of how the law is actually interpreted

[35] Panel Report, *US – Section 301*, para. 7.18 (italics added).

or is likely to be interpreted by national organs including courts. Thus, for instance, an international tribunal cannot come up with its own preferred interpretation in disregard of the interpretation by domestic courts.[36] Some even suggest that interpretation by national courts is binding on an international tribunal.[37]

In this respect there is some grey area, however. To pose a simple example, suppose that an issue arises before a domestic court as to whether a domestic legislation is compatible with certain WTO norms, and the domestic court after a thorough examination of the matter decides that the legislation is not incompatible with the WTO rules. Now, if the WTO-compatibility of the same legislation comes before a WTO panel, what should be the weight to be attached to the decision of the domestic court? The panel should certainly pay the utmost regard to that decision, but should the interpretation by the domestic court be binding on the panel? The answer can hardly be in the positive. It is equally possible to conceive of other circumstances where interpretation by domestic courts may command near-binding authority. Thus a panel is unlikely to depart from the interpretation by a domestic court of a national law that does not bear directly on WTO law – a statute of limitation, for instance.

At any rate, it is apparent that in interpreting national law a crucial methodological issue is: how far should panels accept the interpretation or meaning attributed by a Member to its own law? And this question arises in respect both of the interpretation attributed internally by various national governmental organs (e.g. courts and administrative bodies) and of the interpretation put forward by a Member by way of submissions before a panel.[38] The DSU does not contain any explicit provision as to how domestic laws should be assessed. In the absence of such a provision guidance can be sought only from DSU Article 11, which, as may be recalled from the last chapter, requires panels to make "an objective

36 See *Serbian Loans* case, PCIJ Ser. A No. 20 (1929) at 46; *Brazilian Loans* case, PCIJ Ser. A No. 21 (1929) at 124; *Deweer* v. *Belgium*, ECHR Ser. A No. 35 (1980), para. 52; *Van Droogenbroeck* v. *Belgium*, ECHR Ser. A No. 50 (1982), para. 54; *Malone* v. *United Kingdom*, ECHR Ser. A No. 82 (1984), para. 79; and *Eriksson* v. *Sweden*, ECHR Ser. A No. 156 (1989), para. 65.

37 See, e.g., Brownlie 1998, 40; and Bernhardt 1993, 31.

38 This distinction between the meaning attributed internally and that presented in the course of submissions before panels is important, because, in the former case more caution needs to be exercised before rejecting a Member's interpretation than in the latter.

assessment of the facts of the case."[39] However, given the general and abstract nature of this provision, it is not particularly helpful in this regard, except to the limited extent of making it clear that mere acceptance of a Member's description *before the panels* of its own law may not meet the required standard.[40] This is self-evident anyway, and it does not resolve the crucial methodological issue as to the "point" up to which a Member's description of its own law should be accepted by panels.[41] In one case it has been suggested that considerable deference should be given to Members' interpretation of their own laws.[42] This, again, begs the question: how much deference is considerable deference? Thus, in this regard, panels cannot but be left, as in respect of many other standard of review questions, to make "reasoned judgments" on a case by case basis.[43]

A second methodological issue regarding interpretation of national law concerns the manner in which various elements of a law are to be treated. There were cases under both the GATT and the WTO in which the meaning of the domestic law at issue was apparent simply from a textual reading of the law.[44] In contrast, in numerous cases the meaning of the law in question was more diffused, in the sense that a statutory text carried with it interpretations from various other sources, for example legislative history, administrative guidelines, judicial decisions, etc.[45] In these latter types of cases, it is important to formulate a methodological approach that is nuanced enough to establish a meaning of the law as actually applied by the Member concerned. Thus, as has rightly been noted, in evaluating many modern, complex, economic and regulatory

[39] See Panel Reports, *US – 1916 Act I*, para. 6.40; and *US – 1916 Act II*, para. 6.36.

[40] See above, Chapter 6, p. 161. See also Panel Reports, *US – Section 301*, para. 7.19 (quoted in n. 42 below); *US – 1916 Act I*, para. 6.51; and *US – 1916 Act II*, para. 6.50.

[41] See above, Chapter 6, pp. 159–62.

[42] In *US – Section 301* the Panel made the following observation: "in making factual findings concerning the meaning of . . . [the US law] we are not bound to accept the interpretation presented by the US. That said, any Member can reasonably expect that *considerable deference* be given to its views on the meaning of its own law" (para. 7.19) (italics added). Cf. Panel Reports, *EEC – Parts and Components*, para. 5.7; *US – 1916 Act I*, paras. 6.50–51; and *US – 1916 Act II*, paras. 6.49–50.

[43] Cf. Chapter 6, p. 156 above.

[44] See, e.g., Panel Reports, *Canada – FIRA*; *EEC – Parts and Components*; *US – Non-Rubber Footwear*; *Argentina – Textiles*; and *EC – Asbestos*. There are also some instances in which the parties were more or less in agreement as to the meaning of the law: see, e.g., Panel Reports, *US – Section 337*, paras. 5.4, 5.8; and *Argentina – Textiles*, para. 6.45.

[45] See, e.g., Panel Reports, *US – Malt Beverages*; *India – Patent I & II*; *US – Section 301*; *US – 1916 Act I & II*; *US – Exports Restraints*; *US – Section 211*; *US – Section 129*; and *US – Countervailing Measures*.

laws, it is necessary to be cognizant of their "multi-layered character," which may include statutory language as well as various other institutional and administrative elements.[46]

In *US – 1916 Act I & II*, the Panel expressed the view that the starting point for the determination of the meaning of a law is an analysis of the terms of the law. However, even if the text were to be clear on its face, panels should take into account the interpretation of the law by domestic courts or other authorities, in order to avoid developing an understanding of the law different from how it is actually understood and applied by the relevant Member. The Panel also noted that a failure to consider all the relevant aspects of a domestic law would be contrary to panels' obligation under DSU Article 11 to make an objective assessment of the facts of the case.[47] The Panel, in these two cases, took into account: (i) the text of the law at issue; (ii) its historical background and/or legislative history; and (iii) the relevant domestic case law. In addition to these three elements, four more were considered by other panels, namely: (iv) intention or object and purpose of the law;[48] (v) the context of the legal provision in question;[49] (vi) administrative criteria and practice;[50] and (vii) representations made before panels.[51]

It is not at all a perfect analogy, but simply to highlight the interpretative aspect of the determination of the content of national law it may be interesting to compare the above seven elements with the rules of treaty interpretation as contained in Articles 31 and 32 of the Vienna Convention on the Law of Treaties (VCLT). In parts that are relevant for purposes of such a comparison the Articles provide as follows:

Article 31: General rule of interpretation
1. A treaty shall be interpreted in good faith in accordance with the ordinary meaning to be given to the terms of the treaty in their context and in the light of its object and purpose . . .
3. There shall be taken into account, together with the context: . . . (b) any subsequent practice in the application of the treaty which establishes the agreement of the parties regarding its interpretation.

Article 32: Supplementary means of interpretation
Recourse may be had to supplementary means of interpretation, including the preparatory work of the treaty and the circumstances of its conclusion, in order

[46] Panel Report, *US – Section 301*, paras. 7.25–26.
[47] Panel Reports, *US – 1916 Act I*, para. 6.48; and *US – 1916 Act II*, para. 6.47.
[48] See, e.g., *US – Countervailing Measures*; and *US – Offset Act*.
[49] See, e.g., *US – Hot-Rolled Steel*; and *US – Section 129*.
[50] See, e.g., *India – Patent I & II*; *US – Section 301*; *US – Section 129*; and *US – Countervailing Measures*.
[51] See, e.g., *US – Superfund*; *US – Section 301*; *US – Section 211*; and *Canada – Pharmaceuticals*.

to confirm the meaning resulting from the application of article 31, or to determine the meaning when the interpretation according to article 31:
a. leaves the meaning ambiguous or obscure; or
b. leads to a result which is manifestly absurd or unreasonable.

Some correspondence between factors that are to be taken into account in interpreting national law and international treaty is identifiable. Thus, in both respects, at least the following four elements are common: (i) text/terms of the law/treaty; (ii) its context; (iii) object and purpose; and (iv) legislative history / preparatory work. In addition, administrative practice and judicial decisions under domestic law have some correspondence with "subsequent practice" mentioned in VCLT Article 31(3)(b).

The above by no means is a suggestion that the common elements have exactly the same meaning in both respects. For instance, context of a domestic legal provision has been understood as comprising related legal provisions appearing in the same or other relevant statutes,[52] whereas the VCLT defines context as comprising the entire text of the treaty (including its preamble and annexes) as well as any agreement or instrument related to the treaty that satisfies certain criteria.[53] Likewise, the significance of the elements also varies in respect of national law and international treaty. For instance, while preparatory work is only a supplementary means of interpretation in respect of treaties, in interpreting the domestic law of certain countries (e.g. US law) legislative history is much more vital. A further point that needs to be duly underscored is that the correspondence has not resulted due to any intentional application of the VCLT rules in respect of national law as well. Rather, it is fairly coincidental, because each particular national law has supposedly been – and, of course, ought to be – interpreted in accordance with the canons of interpretation of the country concerned. The differences no doubt are important, but so is the correspondence, which, as a minimum, demonstrates that, despite denials by panels and the AB, the determination of the content or meaning of national law involves an exercise in interpreting such law.

3.3 *Evaluation of various elements of national law*

This section has two main objects: first, to depict in fuller detail that national laws are indeed interpreted by WTO adjudicative organs; and second, and more importantly, to elucidate the rules of interpretation of national law that are gradually taking shape in the jurisprudence

[52] See, further, p. 231 below. [53] See VCLT Article 31(2).

of those organs. A convenient way to canvass both themes is to discuss how the seven elements noted in the preceding section have so far been treated in dispute settlement cases.

3.3.1 Text / statutory language

Certainly, the text or the terms are most crucial in interpreting any legal norm – be it national or international. Despite this importance, panels have not formulated any broad general principles as to how domestic legal texts should be evaluated. In *US – Section 301*, the Panel, as a corollary to its statement that it would not interpret national laws in the manner in which it would interpret the WTO agreements, observed that the same terms used both in the US law at issue and in WTO provisions did not necessarily have the same meaning.[54] Whatever may be the merits of this statement (other than preempting criticism that panels engage in interpretation of national laws), it is not highly probable that, if the domestic law at issue and the WTO provision concerned address the same subject-matter, a panel would attribute different meanings to the same or similar expression depending on where it appears. Indeed, except for the fact that, in respect of domestic laws, panels were cautious not to resort to dictionary meanings of words as they often do in respect of WTO texts,[55] in many instances it is not easy to find any noticeable difference in panels' treatment of domestic and WTO legal texts when they concern the same subject-matter.[56]

Sometimes it may be necessary to ascertain the meaning of words in a domestic legal text in the absence of any guidance from the Member that authored the text. In *US – Countervailing Measures*, the EC challenged a US law which dealt with the effect of a change of ownership of an enterprise through "an arm's length transaction" on prior subsidies received by that enterprise. The Panel needed to determine whether the expression "arm's-length transaction" as used in the US law included the concept of "fair market value" even though the law did not contain the latter expression. Accordingly, the Panel requested that the USA explain the meaning of both expressions as well as the differences between the two. The USA indicated that there was a great deal of confusion about these

[54] Panel Report, *US – Section 301*, para. 7.20.

[55] Cf., however, *India – Patent II*, where the Panel in interpreting certain rules of Indian law had recourse to *Black's Law Dictionary* (6th edn., 1990): see Panel Report, para. 7.49, footnote 119.

[56] See, e.g., Panel Reports, *US – 1916 Act I*, paras. 6.102–9; and *US – 1916 Act II*, paras. 6.115–22.

terms in the USA and that it was not in a position to reply. In the face of such inability of the USA to explain the meaning of the terms, the Panel concluded that, for the purposes of its findings, it would consider the concept of "arm's length transaction" as including the concept of "fair market value."[57]

As noted earlier, sometimes the meaning of the text can be either straightforward or undisputed by the parties, but sometimes the meaning can also be far from clear.[58] In the latter case, it is particularly necessary to have recourse to other means of interpretation such as domestic jurisprudence, legislative history, etc., to clarify the meaning of the text or to resolve textual ambiguities. Furthermore, sometimes by itself the text may seem WTO-incompatible, but interpreted in the light of other relevant means the law as a whole can be WTO-compatible.[59] The converse is equally possible. That is to say, a text can prima facie be WTO-compatible, but interpreted in the light of, say, domestic judicial decisions, it can be WTO-incompatible.[60]

3.3.2 Judicial decisions

The jurisprudence, or decisions, of domestic courts is one of the foremost means of interpretation of domestic law. The manner in which domestic jurisprudence is to be assessed has received some attention from both the PCIJ and the ICJ on a few occasions. In the *ELSI* case a Chamber of the ICJ observed as follows: "Where the determination of a question of municipal law is essential to the Court's decision in a case, the Court will have to weigh the jurisprudence of the municipal courts, and 'If this is uncertain or divided, it will rest with the Court to select the interpretation which it considers most in conformity with the law.'"[61]

While a number of WTO panels have referred to the above dictum,[62] the Panel in the *US – 1916 Act* cases gave the most detailed consideration

[57] Panel Report, *US – Countervailing Measures*, paras. 7.130–31.

[58] See above, p. 216. [59] See, e.g., Panel Report, *US – Section 301*, paras. 7.97, 7.131.

[60] See, e.g., Panel Report, *US – Countervailing Measures*, paras. 7.138, 7.157.

[61] *Elettronica Sicula S.p.A. (ELSI)*, ICJ Rep. 15 (1989) at 47 (para. 62) (citing *Brazilian Loans* case, PCIJ Ser. A No. 21 [1929] at 124). See also *Serbian Loans* case, PCIJ Ser. A No. 20 (1929) at 46.

[62] See, e.g., Panel Reports, *US – Section 301*, footnote 635; *US – 1916 Act I*, para. 6.53; *US – 1916 Act II*, para. 6.52; and *US – Countervailing Measures*, para. 7.124. Other cases in which panels examined or interpreted domestic judicial decisions include: *EC – Bananas*; *India – Patent I* (para. 7.37); *Canada – Pharmaceuticals* (para. 7.97); *US – Copyright Act* (paras. 6.135–44); *US – Shrimp 21.5* (paras. 5.108–11); and *US – Section 211* (footnotes 133, 152, 156). See also AB Reports, *US – Shrimp 21.5* (paras. 93–95); and *US – Section 211* (para. 98).

to various issues that arise in connection with the assessment of domestic case law. These cases concerned the WTO-compatibility of a US law. The Panel noted that in weighing the jurisprudence of the US courts interpreting that law it was necessary to have due regard to the hierarchy of decisions in the US judicial system. Thus, for instance, a circuit court of appeals decision must prevail over a district court decision. However, a rigid application of such an approach might be insufficient in some instances, for example when the decisions to be compared came from different circuits.[63] Therefore, before giving preference to one judgment against another belonging to a different circuit, it was necessary to ascertain whether the judgments concerned addressed the same issue at the same level of detail so as to ensure that a comparison could reasonably be made. Also, with respect to any given issue, more weight should be given to a final judgment than to an interim or interlocutory decision, because the latter does not definitively determine a cause of action, but only decides some intervening matter pertaining to the cause. Most interestingly, the Panel expressed the view that it was necessary to determine *which argumentation contained in domestic court decisions was more convincing*.[64] Such determination must be based not only on the quality of the reasoning, but also on what a panel perceives to be in line with the dominant interpretation of the law. Finally, a panel must not accept at face value statements made or words and terminologies used in court decisions that are not supported by sufficient *reasoning* or are not further elaborated. The Panel also noted that if, on the basis of the above, it could not come to a conclusion as to the most appropriate interpretation by domestic courts, it would accept the interpretation that favored the respondent, considering that the claimant was not able to establish its case.[65]

A further aspect of panels' evaluation of domestic judicial decisions is exemplified by *US – Shrimp 21.5*: namely, that decisions against which

[63] In this regard the Panel noted that the doctrine of *stare decisis* does not apply between judgments handed down in different US circuits.

[64] The Panel noted the practice of the US courts to the effect that, if a precedent is not binding, the weight afforded to it will depend on the persuasive value of its reasoning.

[65] It is worth noting that, after setting out the analytical framework, the Panel embarked on an analysis of the relevant US case law. Because of space constraints it is not possible here to discuss that analysis. But, if one flips through the thirty-seven or so long and heavily footnoted paragraphs in which the Panel examined US case law, it is difficult to resist the impression that the Panel's role was not so different from that of a domestic court addressing a plethora of arguments as to the meaning and persuasive authority of countless precedents that the bar had thrust upon it: see Panel Reports, *US – 1916 Act I*, paras. 6.52–59, 6.134–62; and *US – 1916 Act II*, paras. 6.51–58, 6.152–81.

appeals are pending may not readily be given determinative effect. This case concerned certain statutory guidelines issued by the USA with a view to complying with the recommendations of the DSB in the earlier *US – Shrimp* case. However, the part of the guidelines that ensured such compliance had been struck down in a judgment of the US Court of International Trade (CIT). Therefore, the claimant, Malaysia, argued that in this regard the judgment rather than the guidelines reflected the position in US law. This argument was rejected by both the Panel and the AB because the CIT judgment had been appealed to the relevant US court and, pending the outcome of the appeal, the rules as set out in the guidelines were to be regarded as still in effect.[66]

3.3.3 Legislative history

In the *US – 1916 Act* cases the Panel noted that, for US courts, legislative history is an important tool of statutory construction to which recourse is made to interpret a law, in accordance with the original intent of the US Congress, when the text of the law is not clear, as well as to confirm the clear meaning of a law. Since the Panel's task was to determine how the contested US law was understood within the US legal system, it must, "as US courts do, pay attention to the legislative history."[67] This makes it clear that the relevance as well as the weight to be attached to the legislative history would depend in each case on the rules of statutory construction of the Member that authored the law.

Another notable aspect of the *1916 Act* cases is that they concerned a law that was almost a century old. Consequently, the Panel, in addition to the legislative history, took into account other historical evidence such as legal monographs written around the time when the contested legislation was passed. This was done with a view to determining how the legal concepts of "antitrust" and "anti-dumping," which were vital for purposes of the Panel's decision, were understood in the United States at that time.[68]

In *US – Exports Restraints* an interesting issue arose as to whether a particular administrative document was merely a part of the legislative history or was an authoritative interpretation of the statute. The parties

[66] *US – Shrimp 21.5* (Panel Report, paras. 5.107–11, and AB Report, paras. 94–95).

[67] Panel Reports, *US – 1916 Act I*, para. 6.60; and *US – 1916 Act II*, para. 6.59. This statement, again, exemplifies that, contrary to the rhetoric that panels do not engage in the interpretation of domestic law, on occasion their task may not be very different from that of a domestic court.

[68] Panel Reports, *US – 1916 Act I*, paras. 6.122–33; and *US – 1916 Act II*, paras. 6.144–51.

had different views on this. However, the Panel was able to avoid explicitly addressing the issue, because the USA, while arguing that the document was merely "a type of legislative history," had conceded its superior authoritativeness over other types of legislative history.[69] Nonetheless, it demonstrates that the issues of interpretation that a panel may confront in determining the content of national law are not finite in number and scope.

As a final remark, it may be mentioned that panels and the AB have shown some reluctance to give much significance to broad general statements contained in the legislative history, especially when the statement cannot be reconciled with the text or judicial interpretation of the law.[70] However, such an approach, so far, has not resulted in any noticeable detraction from the overriding methodology that the weight to be attached to the legislative history should depend on the practice of the Member concerned. This is so because the statements that panels have refused to rely upon, arguably, would also have been rejected by relevant domestic courts as unpersuasive had they confronted circumstances similar to those confronted by the panels concerned.

3.3.4 Intention or object and purpose of the law

The question of whether and how far legislative intent or object and purpose of a domestic law is relevant in determining its meaning is not susceptible to a simple answer. Firstly, certain WTO provisions employ language that can be viewed as requiring a consideration of the intent of a domestic law in assessing its conformity with those provisions.[71] As a consequence, it may prove difficult to discuss the relevance and role of object and purpose as a means of interpretation of domestic law without treading on issues of substantive WTO law. It also raises the question of whether intent should be considered only when examining a national law under a WTO provision that makes it relevant, or whether it should be taken into account as a general tool of interpretation of national law and irrespective of the substantive provision concerned. Secondly, the Appellate Body has created further uncertainties by completely failing

[69] Panel Report, *US – Exports Restraints*, paras. 4.45–46, 8.97–98.

[70] See, e.g., Panel Reports, *Canada – Pharmaceuticals*, paras. 7.85–87, 7.95–99; and *US – FSC 21.5 I*, paras. 8.76–108, footnotes 197, 215; and AB Report, *US – FSC 21.5 I*, paras. 149–86. Cf. Panel Reports, *EC – Hormones I*, para. 8.22; *EC – Hormones II*, para. 8.25; *US – Copyright Act*, paras. 6.155–59, 6.212–19, 6.267–72; *US – Countervailing Measures*, paras. 7.139–42; and *US – Offset Act*, paras. 7.30, 7.40–41 (in these cases the Panels referred to legislative history with a view to confirming conclusions based on other evidence).

[71] See, e.g., GATT 1994, Article XX(g). Cf. AB Report, *US – Shrimp*, paras. 137–42.

to adopt a consistent approach. That is to say, in respect of the *same* substantive WTO provision, in some cases it took the view that legislative intent is not relevant,[72] while in others it espoused the opposite view and took legislative intent into account![73]

A further difficult question is what kind of materials can and should be relied upon in ascertaining the legislative intent. Rather than relying on any "extrinsic" material (e.g. legislative history, administrative documents, etc.) or on the stated purpose/s (e.g. purpose/s set out in the preamble) of legislation, the AB has shown a preference for ascertaining the intent or policy goals of a law on the basis of the law itself.[74] But, again, the AB has also determined the policy goals of a domestic law on the basis of its legislative history.[75]

A consideration of a few relevant cases may usefully illustrate the difficulties that exist and, at the same time, elucidate the significance of legislative intent in interpreting domestic law. Article III:1 of the GATT 1994, which is one of the most heavily litigated WTO provisions, requires Members not to apply their laws to imported or domestic products "*so as to afford protection*" to domestic production. In *Japan – Alcohol II* the complainants[76] claimed that a Japanese law violated Article III:1. Both Japan and one of the complainants (the United States) argued that, in order to determine whether a law falls within the terms "so as to afford protection," it was necessary to ascertain the aim of the law.[77] However, the Panel concluded otherwise.[78] On appeal, Japan argued that the Panel erred in disregarding the need to determine the aim of the Japanese law.[79] The Appellate Body rejected this argument on the following grounds:

[72] See, e.g., AB Reports, *Japan – Alcohol II*; and *Chile – Alcohol*.

[73] See, e.g., AB Report, *Canada – Periodicals*.

[74] See AB Reports, *EC – Hormones I & II*, para. 191; *US – Shrimp*, paras. 137–42; *Chile – Alcohol*, para. 62; and *US – Offset Act*, para. 259.

[75] See AB Report, *Canada – Periodicals*, at 30–32. Compared to the Appellate Body, panels have been much more consistent both in taking, where appropriate, legislative intent into account and in relying, for that purpose, not simply on the law itself, but also on other "extrinsic" evidence and on the stated purpose/s of the law: see, e.g., Panel Reports, *US – Section 129*, paras. 6.50–53; *US – Countervailing Measures*, paras. 7.145–46, 7.157; and *US – Offset Act*, paras. 7.40–41 (in these cases the Panels, in interpreting domestic laws, took their object and purpose into account). Cf. Panel Reports, *Japan – Alcohol II*; *Chile – Alcohol*; *Canada – Pharmaceuticals*, paras. 7.103–5; and *US – FSC 21.5 I*, footnote 197, para. 8.106 (in these cases the Panels either concluded that the legislative intent was not relevant or, after considering the objects and purpose of domestic laws, decided not to rely on them).

[76] There were three complainants in this case.

[77] Panel Report, *Japan – Alcohol II*, paras. 4.24–50, 4.69–71.

[78] Ibid. para. 6.33.

[79] AB Report, *Japan – Alcohol II*, at 3.

> This ["so as to afford protection"] is not an issue of intent. It is not necessary for a panel to sort through the many reasons legislators and regulators often have for what they do and weigh the relative significance of those reasons to establish legislative or regulatory intent . . . It is irrelevant that protectionism was not an intended objective if the particular . . . measure in question is nevertheless, to echo Article III:1, "*applied* to imported or domestic products so as to afford protection to domestic production."[80]

A different approach was adopted by the AB in the *Canada – Periodicals* case. In this case it turned directly to the policy objectives of a Canadian law in assessing the law under the language "so as to afford protection." And, for this purpose, it relied almost entirely on the legislative debate on the bill that later became the law that was being examined and other government documents and opinions of Canadian ministers, all of which preceded the enactment of the law and indicated that its policy objective was to protect Canadian periodicals from foreign competition.[81]

While the approach of not considering the legislative intent may seem appropriate in some cases, there could be circumstances in which it may be problematic to adhere strictly to that approach. For instance, if a law expressly states certain objectives that are unconnected with trade (e.g. fiscal reform), then it would be difficult to come to a conclusion that nonetheless the law affords protection to domestic production without considering how the stated objectives relate to the law itself. This difficulty was highlighted in *Chile – Alcohol*. The Chilean law that was at issue in this case had certain stated revenue, health and social purposes. This presented the Panel with a dilemma: on the one hand, *Japan – Alcohol II* provided a clear authority that it was not necessary to consider the aims of the law; on the other hand, given the Chilean argument that the stated purposes demonstrated that the law was not protective legislation, the Panel could not dispose of the matter without some consideration of those purposes. The Appellate Body's reliance in *Canada – Periodicals* on the policy objectives of the law posed additional difficulties.

The Panel sought to get out of the conundrum by noting that the statements that were relied upon by the AB in *Canada – Periodicals* were supportive of a finding of protective objectives. Thus, statements by a government revealing WTO-incompatible objectives of its legislation are probative, but self-serving comments by a government attempting to

[80] Ibid. 27–28 (italics in original).

[81] AB Report, *Canada – Periodicals*, at 30–32. Other cases in which the AB considered policy goals of domestic law include *US – Shrimp* (see AB Report, paras. 137–42) (this case concerned a different WTO provision, however, i.e. GATT 1994 Article XX[g]).

justify its laws are not. In this way the Panel reconciled the two divergent approaches of the Appellate Body, and proceeded to examine the stated purposes of the Chilean law. Eventually, the Panel found that the Chilean law could not achieve its stated objectives and as such there was a lack of rational relationship between the objectives and the law itself.[82] On appeal, Chile, relying on *Japan – Alcohol II*, argued that the Panel erred in considering Chile's legislative objectives.[83] However, the Appellate Body upheld the Panel's finding. It clarified that its view in *Japan – Alcohol II* only meant that the *subjective* intentions of individual legislators or regulators are not relevant; but from that it does not follow that the statutory purposes or objectives (of a Member's legislature and government as a whole), to the extent that they are given *objective* expression in the statute itself, are not pertinent. On the contrary, the "identification of a measure's objectives or purposes *as revealed or objectified in the measure itself*" is extremely relevant in evaluating its "design and architecture."[84]

US – Offset Act provides an example where the consideration of the object and purpose of a domestic law was not uneasily intertwined with the substantive WTO provision concerned.[85] In this case an issue before the Panel was whether the US law under consideration, i.e. the Continued Dumping and Subsidy Offset Act of 2000 (CDSOA), constituted a "specific action against dumping." The Panel concluded in the affirmative, and in support of its conclusion relied, inter alia, on the stated purpose of the legislation, as expressed in the "Findings of Congress" set forth in section 1002 of the CDSOA.[86] Thus, in this case, the Panel's reliance on the legislative intent was strictly within the parameters set by the AB in *Chile – Alcohol*. That is to say, reliance was placed not on any subjective intention of the legislators, but on the intent of the legislature as a whole, which was given objective expression in the statute itself. Nonetheless, the AB was somewhat critical about the Panel's approach. It observed, citing *Japan – Alcohol II*, that there was no need for the Panel to inquire into the legislative intent and to take that into account

[82] Panel Report, *Chile – Alcohol*, paras. 7.114–20, 7.146–54, 7.159.

[83] AB Report, *Chile – Alcohol*, para. 14.

[84] Ibid. paras. 62, 71. Notably, the view expressed here that the relevant objectives are those that can be ascertained from the statute itself is not in accord with the approach adopted by the AB in *Canada – Periodicals*.

[85] Other such examples include *Canada – Pharmaceuticals*; *US – FSC 21.5 I*; *US – Section 129*; and *US – Countervailing Measures*.

[86] Panel Report, *US – Offset Act*, paras. 7.40–41.

in its analysis, particularly when the text of the CDSOA provided sufficient information to permit the relevant analysis. However, the Appellate Body did not overturn the Panel's decision, because it relied on the purpose of the law simply as a confirmation and not as a basis for its conclusion.[87]

From the above, it is apparent that, in respect of the relevance of the object and purpose of domestic law, the AB has espoused different views at different times. Its approach is also characterized by cautiousness, stemming from concerns that an examination of the legislative intent might draw panels into an analysis that is ill-suited for them. This reflects, at least ostensibly, the approach adopted by the AB with regard to the interpretation of the WTO agreements. It is well known that, relying on Article 31 of the VCLT, the Appellate Body has adopted a textual approach to treaty interpretation, and rejected the "teleological" approach, by emphasizing that it is in the text, read in its context, that the object and purpose of the treaty must be sought.[88] However, given that the governing rule for the interpretation of the WTO agreements, i.e. VCLT Article 31, explicitly requires a treaty interpreter to take "object and purpose" into account, so far as WTO agreements are concerned, this element is not entirely irrelevant. By contrast, in the absence of any explicit provision, either in the WTO agreements or elsewhere, within the corpus of public international law in general, as to how domestic law should be interpreted, the question of the relevance of the object and purpose of domestic law is more precarious.

No doubt, there are reasons to be cautious. Panels are not most conveniently placed so as to have access to the intentions of the legislatures of now some 150 Member countries. Accordingly, care needs to be taken as to the type of materials that are relied upon for this purpose.[89] Also, turning too quickly to the legislative intent might open the door to a process of subjective interpretation of national law. These do not mean, however, that "object and purpose" cannot have any relevance in determining the content of domestic law. On the contrary, turning a blind eye to the object and purpose might, on occasion, be tantamount to ignoring the normative quality of domestic law. As most lawyers would

[87] AB Report, *US – Offset Act*, para. 259.

[88] See, e.g., AB Reports, *Japan –Alcohol II*, footnote 20; and *US – Shrimp*, para. 114. See also Lennard 2002, 22–29.

[89] It is worth noting that, even if object and purpose is considered separately, the analysis usually draws on other elements, e.g. legislative history, administrative documents or the text itself.

agree, the meanings of words constituting legal norms are not ascertained mechanically by mere recourse to dictionaries. It is no wonder that Article 31 of the VCLT calls for attributing the ordinary meaning to the terms of a treaty "*in the light of its object and purpose*" (italics added). There can be circumstances where the same is necessary for national laws.[90] Furthermore, WTO panels are not breaking new ground by considering the aims of domestic legislation. For instance, in the *Guardianship of Infants* case, the ICJ has determined the scope of a Swedish law on the basis of its intention or purpose.[91] Accordingly, while some caution is appropriate, the possibility of having regard to the legislative intent where the circumstances so require should not be foreclosed.

3.3.5 Context

To shed light on the meaning of a particular domestic legal provision, its context has also been taken into account by panels and the AB. Context, as already noted,[92] has been understood as comprising related legal provisions appearing in the same or other relevant statutes, which may include statutes outside the terms of reference of a panel.[93] Sometimes context can be quite useful in resolving textual ambiguities. In *US – Hot-Rolled Steel* the Panel needed to determine whether the contested provision of a US statute required the US authorities to consider the domestic industry *as a whole* or only *a particular segment* of the industry in determining injury for purposes of imposing anti-dumping measures. Although the provision itself referred only to a particular segment, the Panel, having read the provision in the "context" of the other parts of the US statute, concluded that it did allow an injury determination on the basis of the state of the industry as a whole.[94]

3.3.6 Administrative criteria and practice

Compared to judicial decisions, the assessment of administrative interpretation of domestic law could be less perplexing for panels, so far as

[90] For instance, in the *US – Section 129* case the Panel referred to the purpose or intent of the law in an abstract manner (i.e. without relying on legislative history, administrative documents, etc.) with a view to elucidating its meaning (see Panel Report, paras. 6.51–52, 6.75–76, 6.80, 6.90).

[91] *Guardianship of Infants* case, ICJ Rep. 55 (1958) at 65, 69.

[92] See above, p. 221.

[93] See AB Report, *US – Offset Act*, para. 212.

[94] Panel Report, *US – Hot-Rolled Steel*, paras. 7.196–98. See also AB Report, *US – Hot-Rolled Steel*, paras. 200–9. Other cases in which provisions of national law were interpreted in the light of their context include *US – Section 211* (see AB Report, paras. 94–95, 97) and *US – Section 129* (see Panel Report, para. 6.50).

uncertainty or confusion resulting from multiplicity of interpretations is concerned. That is to say, while, depending on the judicial structure of a Member, different courts (e.g. courts in different federal units) may interpret the same statutory language differently and thus make it problematic to assess the respective value of the judgments, it is more likely that there will be a single administrative interpretation of a statutory provision. But there is the difficulty that, unlike many final judicial decisions, administrative interpretations may be overruled by domestic courts.[95] This susceptibility of being overruled has also affected the degree of reliance placed by panels on administrative interpretations.

Panels may be required to consider administrative interpretation or criteria that are given formal expression in administrative documents,[96] as well as the practice of administrative agencies that demonstrates that the administration has a certain view as to the meaning of a law.[97] An example of the former is the US Statement of Administrative Action (SAA) that was adopted by the US administration and approved by the US Congress as an authoritative interpretation of the US implementing legislation for the WTO agreements. As to the latter (i.e. administrative practice), it is worth nothing that the practice of the administrative branch of a government may not, necessarily, be tied to a specific identifiable document. Rather, the administration may adopt certain criteria for the implementation of a domestic law even without having recourse to a formal document; and these criteria may demonstrate the meaning that is attributed to the law in question by the Member concerned. For instance, the anti-dumping or countervailing duty determinations made by the administrative agencies of a Member, in pursuance of its anti-dumping and countervailing duty laws, may demonstrate how those laws are understood by that Member.

In addition to administrative documents and practice, parties sought to rely on statements made by government officials in their official capacity. In the *1916 Act* cases, the Panel ruled that such statements could not be regarded as important and that they could be relevant merely to confirm other established evidence.[98] This makes good sense, because statements made by individual officials, albeit in the exercise of their

[95] Panel Reports, *US – 1916 Act I*, para. 6.52; and *US – 1916 Act II*, para. 6.51.

[96] See, e.g., *US – Section 301*; *US – Hot-Rolled Steel*; *US – Exports Restraints*; *US – Section 129*; and *US – Countervailing Measures*.

[97] See, e.g., *India – Patent I & II*; *US – Section 301*; *US – Exports Restraints*; and *US – Section 129*.

[98] Panel Reports, *US – 1916 Act I*, paras. 6.61–65; and *US – 1916 Act II*, paras. 6.60–62.

official duty, are quite unlikely to be treated by the domestic courts of most Members as authoritative interpretation of domestic laws.

With respect to panels' and the AB's treatment of administrative interpretation, the twin *India – Patent* cases have attracted the greatest amount of attention from all quarters. These cases concerned whether India had established the so-called "mailbox system," i.e. a system whereby applications for patents of pharmaceutical products could be filed and the novelty and priority of such applications could be preserved until such time as India would begin to grant patents for pharmaceutical products in accordance with the WTO TRIPS Agreement.

India claimed that it had established a mailbox system through "administrative instructions." According to India, these instructions directed the Patent Office to store applications for pharmaceutical product patents separately for future action, and not to refer them to an examiner until January 1, 2005. Although no record of these instructions was made available to the Panels, India submitted as evidence the response by the Indian Minister of Industry to a question posed in Parliament, which showed that, up to July 15, 1996 India had received 893 patent applications for pharmaceutical products, and that those would be referred for examination after January 1, 2005. This administrative practice of delaying referral of applications to patent examiners was being followed, notwithstanding that section 12 of the Indian Patent Act provided that a patent application should be referred to an examiner when the complete specification was filed, and section 15 provided for the rejection of product patent applications for pharmaceutical products. India, however, took the view that the administrative instructions and practice were not in conflict with the Patent Act. In support of this argument India relied, inter alia, on a constitutional provision concerning executive power, as well as on the fact that no Indian court had declared invalid the interpretation given to the Patent Act by the executive.

The Panels disagreed with the Indian administration's interpretation, and took the view that the administrative instructions and practice were in conflict with the Patent Act.[99] In rejecting the Indian interpretation, the Panels relied, inter alia, on the following factors. First, the relevant provisions of the Act were "mandatory" in nature and, as such, the administrative instructions and practice created legal insecurity by

[99] Panel Reports, *India – Patent I*, para. 7.37; and *India – Patent II*, para. 7.49.

requiring patent officials to ignore those provisions.[100] Second, even if mailbox applications were not examined and rejected by the Patent Office, there remained the possibility that, on an application by a competitor, an Indian court would declare the practice to be illegal because it contradicted the mandatory provisions of the Act.[101] Third, the administrative instructions were "unwritten and unpublished."[102]

On appeal from *India – Patent I*,[103] the Appellate Body agreed with the Panel that the relevant provisions of the Indian law were mandatory and was not persuaded that the "administrative instructions" would prevail over the contradictory mandatory provisions or would survive a legal challenge in Indian courts.[104]

These two cases are remarkable for the way in which they made it evident that it is a mere rhetoric that panels do not interpret national law. In these cases, in order to determine whether India had put in place a WTO-compatible mailbox system, the Panels and the Appellate Body had to address the purely municipal law issue of whether the administratively established mailbox system of India was valid under its domestic law. According to the Indian (albeit its administration's) interpretation of the Patent Act, it was. But the Panels as well as the Appellate Body rejected that interpretation and, on the basis of their own interpretation of the relevant texts of the Indian law, concluded that the administrative practice was in conflict with the Patent Act. This was highlighted by India in its submissions in *India – Patent II*. Since this case was heard after both the Panel and the AB reports were issued in *India – Patent I*, it was possible for India to question, although without any success, the propriety of the conclusions in those reports. These submissions bring into focus critical issues that concern and intertwiningly relate to both the question of standard of review of national law[105] and the notion that, as "facts," national law is not interpreted by international tribunals.[106] For instance, India submitted that the formulation of the Appellate Body that it (and also the Panel) was not interpreting Indian law, but rather was simply examining the same,[107] had "*disguised*"

100 Panel Reports, *India – Patent I*, para. 7.35; and *India – Patent II*, para. 7.43.
101 Panel Reports, *India – Patent I*, para. 7.37; and *India – Patent II*, para. 7.52.
102 Panel Reports, *India – Patent I*, para. 7.42; and *India – Patent II*, para. 7.56.
103 *India – Patent II* was not appealed. 104 AB Report, *India – Patent I*, paras. 69–70.
105 I.e., up to what point must panels accept a Member's description of its own law? See above, pp. 218–19.
106 See Panel Report, *India – Patent II*, paras. 4.11–16.
107 See AB Report, *India – Patent I*, para. 66 (part of it is quoted above at p. 216).

its approach to municipal law and "*misrepresented*" the issues that were before it.[108] India further noted that:

> The Appellate Body conducted what it called "an examination of the relevant aspects of Indian municipal law" and declared that it was not persuaded by the "explanations" given by India. In fact, the "examination" of Indian law had been an interpretation of that law and the "explanations" rejected had been the interpretations of that law by the Indian authorities.[109]

Compared to the *India – Patent* cases, the outcome was diametrically opposite in *US – Section 301*. In the latter case the Panel found that the contested provisions of a US law provided for matters that were inconsistent with the DSU. However, taking into account the interpretation of those provisions contained in an administrative document, i.e. the SAA (which was also confirmed in representations made by the USA before the Panel[110]), the Panel concluded that there was no violation of the DSU. Thus, administrative interpretation was given precedence over the text, in circumstances where there was significant difference between the two.[111] There are also a number of cases that can be placed between the two extremes of *India – Patent* and *US – Section 301*. For instance, in some cases panels relied on administrative documents or practice only to confirm or support their conclusion based on other evidence, e.g. the text of the law,[112] judicial decisions,[113] etc. Or, although the text was given precedence over administrative interpretation, the outcome, unlike *India – Patent*, was favorable for the Member whose law was in question, because it was the opposite party that sought to rely on administrative interpretation.[114]

3.3.7 Statements/representations made before panels

In a number of cases, submissions or statements made before panels by the Member whose domestic law was in question were relied upon in interpreting the law in a WTO-consistent manner. For this purpose, it is possible to distinguish between two types of submissions: first, submissions as to how the law in question should be interpreted by the

[108] Panel Report, *India – Patent II*, para. 4.14 (italics added).
[109] Ibid. para. 4.15. [110] This factor is discussed in the next section.
[111] Panel Report, *US – Section 301*, paras. 7.31–113, 7.131–36.
[112] See, e.g., Panel Reports, *US – Hot-Rolled Steel*, para. 7.198; and *US – Section 129*, paras. 6.35–40, 6.55–58, 6.93–123.
[113] See, e.g., Panel Report, *US – Countervailing Measures*, paras. 7.139–40, 7.143–47, 7.157.
[114] See, e.g., Panel Report, *US – Exports Restraints*, paras. 8.77–131.

panel; and second, representations or commitments as to how the Member concerned intends to interpret and apply the law. As already noted, mere acceptance by panels of the former type of submissions may not amount to "an objective assessment of the matter" as required by DSU Article 11.[115] However, with regard to the latter kind of statements, the situation can be different (or at least some panels considered it to be different). That is to say, where a respondent government voluntarily confirms before a panel that the law under examination would unfailingly be interpreted and applied in a WTO-consistent manner, the panel can possibly make a finding on that basis without compromising its obligations under DSU Article 11.

The principal case concerning this issue is *US – Section 301*.[116] In this case, in attributing a WTO-consistent interpretation to the contested US law, the Panel relied, as pointed out above, on the SAA and the US representations made before the Panel. These representations, the Panel noted, were made "*explicitly, officially, repeatedly and unconditionally*"[117] confirming that the USA would apply the law consistently with its obligations under the WTO DSU. Citing the *Nuclear Tests* cases,[118] the Panel observed that such "unilateral" statements should not be relied upon lightly – rather, they must be subjected to stringent criteria before being attributed any legal effect. The Panel thought it appropriate to rely on the US representations because they reflected official US policy and were solemnly made by representatives having full powers to make them with the intention that all WTO Members place reliance on them.[119]

Although the Panel referred to the *Nuclear Tests* cases, it is notable that those cases do not provide a perfect analogy, and the Panel acknowledged as much. First, in the *Nuclear Tests* cases the question was whether the "unilateral declarations" concerned had the effect of *creating* international legal obligations, and the ICJ had found that they had had that effect.[120] In contrast, in the context of a Member's representation

115 See above, p. 219.

116 However, it is not the first case in which a respondent government made commitments regarding the interpretation or application of a domestic law: see, e.g., GATT Panel Reports, *US – Superfund*, paras. 5.2.9–10; and *US – Tobacco*, para. 115. In addition to *US – Section 301*, WTO cases in which the respondent's commitments were relied upon in interpreting its law include *Canada – Pharmaceuticals* and *US – Section 211* (the latter case, however, is somewhat puzzling because reliance was placed not so much on a "formal" commitment, but rather on submissions regarding interpretation of the contested law: see Panel Report, paras. 4.197, 8.69, footnote 60).

117 Panel Report, *US – Section 301*, para. 7.115 (italics added).

118 ICJ Rep. 253, 457 (1974).

119 Panel Report, *US – Section 301*, paras. 7.118–25.

120 *Nuclear Tests* cases, n. 118 above, at 267–72, 472–77.

regarding the interpretation/application of domestic law, the question as to whether thereby new international obligations are *created* does not even arise, because the relevant obligations are already in existence as a result of the Member's acceptance of the WTO agreements. Second, although in *US – Section 301* the Panel described the US statements as being "unilateral," they can hardly be classed as "unilateral" in the sense of the *Nuclear Tests* cases. Unlike the declarations at issue in the latter cases, which were addressed to the general public, the representations in *US – Section 301* were made to an international judicial organ. There appears to be a general consensus that declarations made before international tribunals bind the party making them.[121] Thus, while attributing legal significance to the *Nuclear Tests* type of "unilateral declarations" may spur concerns for various reasons,[122] statements made before panels can more safely be regarded as binding.

However, it was right for the Panel in *US – Section 301* to exercise caution in relying on representations, in particular because, on that basis, it attributed an interpretation to the US law that differed from the *text* of the statute. Members' assurances can possibly be relied upon more readily when, as was the case in *Canada – Pharmaceuticals*, the reliance is placed simply to confirm conclusions based on other evidence.[123] It is worth mentioning that the Panels in both *US – Section 301* and *Canada – Pharmaceuticals* added a caveat that, should the undertakings given by the respondent Member be repudiated or proved wrong, their finding as to the meaning of the law would no longer be warranted.[124]

It is difficult to leave the present issue without saying a few words about the *India – Patent* cases. Although the Indian statements in these cases, arguably, were not as solemnly made as those of the USA in the *US – Section 301* case, they indubitably pertained to how India was implementing and would continue to implement its patent law. Moreover, compared to certain other cases where Members' statements were relied upon,[125] some of India's representations were very "formal" and showed a genuine intention to be bound. For instance, referring to the statement

[121] See *German Interests in Polish Upper Silesia*, PCIJ Ser. A No. 7 (1926) at 13; *Free Zones* case, PCIJ Ser. A/B No. 46 (1932) at 169–70. Cf. Bethlehem 2000, 180–81 (discussing the principle that pleading before an international tribunal is "an act of State").

[122] See Rubin 1977; and Franck 1975.

[123] Panel Report, *Canada – Pharmaceuticals*, para. 7.99.

[124] Panel Reports, *US – Section 301*, paras. 7.126, 7.136; and *Canada – Pharmaceuticals*, para. 7.99.

[125] See, e.g., Panel Reports, *Canada – Pharmaceuticals*, para. 7.99; and *US – Section 211*, paras. 4.197, 8.69.

of the Indian Minister of Industry in the Parliament, India submitted that that statement had put the Indian government under an "estoppel" in the sense that the government at no stage could perform any act in contravention of the position taken therein.[126] From this perspective the Panels' and the Appellate Body's refusal to rely on the Indian representations may seem rather strange. As India had put it, given that the correctness of the interpretation of its own law put forward by India could only be determined by its domestic courts, in the absence of a contrary decision by an Indian court, the Panels and the AB should have given India "the benefit of the doubt" on that interpretation.[127]

An argument that can be made in support of the outcome in the *India – Patent* cases is that in these cases the text of the law was found to be of a "mandatory" character, which, as the Panels concluded, meant that the commitment by the Indian administration was essentially a promise to act inconsistently with the terms of the statute. In contrast, the provision at issue in *US – Section 301* gave the executive a "discretion" over how to act and, as such, the relevant commitments could be carried out without contravening the terms of the law.[128] One may still wonder why, as a minimum, the Indian government's view could not have been accepted subject to a caveat similar to the ones adopted in *US – Section 301* and *Canada – Pharmaceuticals*[129] (i.e. by expressly noting that the finding concerned would no longer be warranted if the government's view were to be found wrong by an Indian court). It is not surprising that the *India – Patent* cases were criticized, inter alia, for their blatant failure to acknowledge that, in terms of "institutional strengths and weaknesses," domestic institutions are much better placed to interpret their own laws than the WTO panels and the Appellate Body.[130]

At any rate, it seems that Members' representations can be more readily relied upon where the text of the law is not unequivocal, in that it leaves some discretion with the domestic administering agencies as to how to act under the law.[131]

126 Panel Report, *India – Patent I*, para. 4.12. See also AB Report, *India – Patent I*, para. 60.
127 Panel Report, *India – Patent II*, paras. 4.13–14.
128 On the mandatory/discretionary distinction, see Chapter 8 below.
129 These two precedents, however, were not available at that time, as these cases were decided subsequent to the *India – Patent* cases.
130 Howse 2000, 62, 68; and Davey 2001, 92–93.
131 The same may be the case in respect of administrative interpretation discussed in the preceding section.

4 Appellate review of panels' findings regarding the interpretation/meaning of national law

As may be recalled from Chapter 4, under DSU Article 17.6 the jurisdiction of the Appellate Body is limited to questions of law, and findings of fact cannot be appealed.[132] The following two questions (concerning the assessment of facts and the qualification of facts in terms of the applicable law, which, it has been recognized by the AB, are questions of law) are most crucial for a proper understanding of the jurisdiction of the AB in respect of national law:

> [1] The consistency or inconsistency of a given fact or set of facts with the requirements of a given treaty provision is . . . a legal characterization issue. It is a legal question. [2] Whether or not a panel has made an objective assessment of the facts before it, as required by Article 11 of the DSU, is also a legal question which, if properly raised on appeal, would fall within the scope of appellate review.[133]

While the first of the above two questions is pretty straightforward, the second needs some further elaboration. Although the AB has acknowledged that the standard of "objective assessment of the facts" entails a question of law, it has put the threshold for interfering with a panel's factual findings on the ground of a violation of that standard at too high a level. Thus the appreciation of (i.e. determining the credibility and the weight to be ascribed to) the evidence submitted is "left to the discretion of a panel as the trier of facts."[134] And not every error in the appreciation of the evidence is to be treated as a failure to make an objective assessment of the facts. Rather, only "an egregious error that calls into question the good faith of a panel" can be so treated.[135] The AB has further exemplified that a panel can be said to have committed such an error only if it has wilfully disregarded, distorted or misrepresented the evidence,[136] or there is a gross negligence on its part amounting to bad faith,[137] or there is an error that goes to the very core of the integrity

[132] See above, Chapter 4, p. 106. [133] AB Report, *EC – Hormones I & II*, para. 132.

[134] Ibid. See also AB Reports, *Australia – Salmon*, para. 261; and *Korea – Alcohol*, para. 161.

[135] AB Reports, *EC – Hormones I & II*, para. 133; *EC – Poultry*, para. 133; *Australia – Salmon*, para. 264; *Korea – Alcohol*, paras. 162, 164; and *Japan – Agricultural Products II*, paras. 141–42.

[136] AB Reports, *EC – Hormones I & II*, para. 133; *Australia – Salmon*, para. 266; and *Korea – Alcohol*, para. 164.

[137] AB Report, *EC – Hormones I & II*, para. 138.

of the WTO dispute settlement process itself.[138] Clearly, as has rightly been commented, the Article 11 standard of "objective assessment" has been turned into "a blunt instrument" that hardly anyone will be able to use.[139]

Now, if the above principles are applied to findings on domestic law the likely position can be as follows. First, a panel's findings as to the *content/meaning* of a domestic law, being findings of fact based on an appreciation of the evidence submitted, will not be subject to appellate review unless the panel has committed "an egregious error." Second, and in contrast, it will appropriately be within the Appellate Body's jurisdiction to review whether or not the content of national law, *as established by the panel*, is WTO-consistent. However, as discussed below, this is not the position that the AB has taken.

Although in many cases the AB has reviewed panels' findings on national law, the question of the scope of such review has been explicitly raised in *US – Section 211*. This case concerned section 211 of the US Omnibus Appropriations Act of 1998. Before the panel the parties disagreed about the meaning of this section. The USA was of the view that it regulated ownership of trademarks; the EC, on the contrary, maintained that it did not regulate ownership and instead regulated the enjoyment of trademark rights. The Panel found the US view to be correct. While the disagreement continued on appeal, the USA also argued that the AB could not review this matter because it was a question of fact. However, the AB concluded otherwise and, accordingly, re-examined the matter and made its own finding that section 211 related to ownership.[140] Although, for reasons discussed below, this is a welcome development, the reasoning put forward by the AB in support of its conclusion is not entirely sound.

The Appellate Body did not re-examine the question because there was a violation of DSU Article 11. Indeed, neither of the parties made such an argument. Rather, the AB had thought that a review of the Panel's findings as to the meaning of section 211 was a part and parcel of its review of the WTO-compatibility of the section. In other words, the AB was of the view that, in order to determine whether section 211 violated the TRIPS provisions invoked, it was absolutely necessary for it to make a finding as to whether or not the section regulated ownership

[138] AB Reports, *EC – Poultry*, para. 133; *Australia – Salmon*, para. 265; and *Korea – Alcohol*, para. 163.

[139] Kuyper 2000, 317–18. See also Lugard 1998.

[140] AB Report, *US – Section 211*, paras. 107–21.

of trademarks.[141] That was not the case, however. The part of the analysis that related to whether section 211 regulated ownership was a "factual" matter. Thus, under the strict terms of DSU Article 17.6, the AB needed simply to review whether section 211, *given its meaning already established by the Panel* (i.e. it regulated ownership), was TRIPS-consistent or not.

Since the Appellate Body itself had already turned the Article 11 standard into an almost impossible-to-use "escape hatch," in order to entertain appeals regarding findings on the meaning of national law it had no other option but to mischaracterize this factual question as a legal question. While with reference to "ordinary" facts (i.e. events occurring in time and space) it is possible to conceive of important practical reasons that prompted the AB to put the Article 11 standard at too high a level, the same is not true for factual findings on national law. Given that under Article 17.6 the AB cannot solicit or consider fresh evidence, in respect of ordinary facts, readily admitting appeals on the ground of a violation of Article 11 would have made it necessary to remand the matter to the panel for re-assessment. But the AB was reluctant to embrace the power of remand, inter alia to ensure prompt settlement of disputes.[142] In contrast, even if the AB had entertained appeals regarding findings on national law without mischaracterizing them as questions of law, it would not have thereby created a problem of remand. That is to say, because of the "peculiarity" of domestic laws as facts – the determination of the content of which involves, largely, the construction of legal texts – in most cases the AB itself could have conducted the necessary re-assessment on the basis of the record of the case, and without any need for remand. Thus, with respect to national laws, the Article 11 standard could have been placed at a much lower level. However, it was not possible for the AB to do so, owing to its insistence from the very beginning that national laws are *merely* facts and, as such, its failure to recognize that, although facts, they are facts of an unusual type (one may even say "laws of a special kind"[143]).

At any rate, the Appellate Body has adopted the second best option, i.e. to review the meaning of a national law as part of its review of the WTO-compatibility of that law. In addition to the fact that this methodology is based on an incorrect premise, it is also possible to imagine circumstances in which it might be unworkable. This is exemplified by *US – Section 129* where, as discussed in Chapter 4, the Panel issued its ruling solely on the basis of its findings as to the content of the US

141 Ibid. paras. 100–6. 142 See Kuyper 2000, 310, 318. 143 Cf. Fentiman 1998, 287.

law in question; and issues relating to the interpretation of the WTO provisions invoked or the examination of the US law in the light of those provisions were not addressed.[144] Clearly, in such a case, the AB will find it extremely difficult to review the panel's findings regarding the content of the domestic law on the ground that it is a prerequisite for its review of the panel's assessment of the law in the light of the WTO obligations (the latter assessment being non-existent). Since *US – Section 129* was not appealed, the ingenuity to overcome this difficulty must await future litigation.

Why, nonetheless, is the preparedness shown by the AB to entertain appeals regarding findings on national law a welcome development? First, however imperfect, this is a notable step towards acknowledging the special nature of national laws as facts. Second, as a matter of legal policy, it is entirely advisable for the AB to reconsider issues of national law. Indeed, for the simple reason that international tribunals cannot take judicial notice of national laws, such laws do not lose their normative quality. Thus temptations to equate national law with ordinary facts must be avoided. In this context, one may also refer to many developed municipal legal systems in which, although foreign laws are formally treated as facts (i.e. judicial notice does not apply), in recognition of their legal character appeals are readily entertained from questions of foreign law.[145] At a minute level, the problems of establishing the content of national law by international tribunals and of foreign law by national courts have much in common. Accordingly, the viable solution to the problem devised by national legal systems can furnish an additional persuasive ground for the Appellate Body to allow appeals on questions of national law.

5 Concluding remarks

From the foregoing it is apparent that, so far as the determination of the content of national law is concerned, it is not at all unusual for a WTO panel to be presented with an array of arguments and materials that would have been presented to a domestic court had the matter been raised before the latter forum. Confronted with this challenging task, panels have made serious efforts to understand the law in its proper setting and to attribute due significance to different "elements" making up

[144] See above, Chapter 4, p. 104.

[145] See, e.g., Fentiman 1998, 201–2, 287 (discussing the position in English law).

the organic and normative life of the domestic law. It is notable that, in establishing the content of national law, issues of proof, unlike issues of interpretation, did not present much difficulty. Despite issues of interpretation being most crucial, panels and the AB were very prompt in referring to the proposition that international tribunals do not interpret national law. They did so, as pointed out earlier, because of the usefulness of the proposition for dealing with arguments by Members that they cannot and should not interpret national law.[146] These arguments, of course, raise policy issues that are rather important – namely, whether and how far reliance can be placed on the ability and expertise of panels and the AB to interpret national law. Thus, for panels and the AB, the proposition is a device to assure Members that they are not engaging in an exercise for which they are not most conveniently placed.

However, given that the practice is entirely at odds with the proposition, it is difficult not to wonder whether there could be a better way to address the policy issues that are at stake. Certainly, interpreting domestic law under the guise of a rhetoric suggesting the contrary is not most conducive for the development of a well-thought-out body of rules. On the contrary, acknowledging what is already the practice can make the process more transparent and give the parties the opportunity to explore and argue the full range of issues properly and adequately, which in turn can increase the quality of the decisions on the part of the panels. Such an approach will also enable panels to give more explicit consideration to the comparative institutional advantages enjoyed by domestic and international bodies in interpreting a national law in the particular context of a dispute. The development of a body of jurisprudence along these lines will eventually allow more confident predictions about how future issues of interpretation of national law would be resolved. It will also facilitate useful scrutiny and analysis of panels' interpretation of national law. Thus, in the long run, acknowledging the need to interpret national law can better address the concerns underlying its denial.

[146] See above, p. 217.

8 Mandatory and discretionary legislation

1 Introduction

In exercising their power of review, it is not unusual for judicial organs – whether domestic or international – to turn to analytical tools against which the legality of the contested measure can be usefully tested.[1] For instance, under the administrative law of many countries, it is quite common for domestic courts to test the legality of administrative acts with the aid of tools of review such as "proportionality," "legitimate expectations," etc.[2] As seen in Chapter 6, as a tool of review proportionality is also applied by international courts including WTO organs. It was also mentioned in that chapter that the distinction between mandatory and discretionary legislation is one of the prominent tools that WTO adjudicative bodies apply in reviewing the compatibility of national laws with the WTO obligations.[3] In this context, the shorthand expression "mandatory legislation" is used to refer to national legislation that *requires* the executive authority of a Member to act inconsistently with its WTO obligations; and the expression "discretionary legislation" is used to refer to legislation that *does not require* but gives the executive a *discretion* to act in a WTO-incompatible manner.[4]

According to this distinction (throughout this chapter the word "distinction" is used to refer to the distinction between mandatory and discretionary legislation), a mandatory law by itself violates WTO obligations even if there is no specific application of the law. By contrast,

[1] A more elaborate version of this chapter has been published in the *Journal of International Economic Law*: see Bhuiyan 2002. This chapter takes into account recent cases and academic works on the subject.

[2] See Thomas 2000. [3] See above, Chapter 6, p. 194.

[4] See, e.g., Panel Report, *US – Tobacco*, para. 118; and AB Report, *US – 1916 Act I & II*, para. 88.

a discretionary law cannot by itself amount to a violation of WTO obligations and a violation can occur only if the law is actually applied in a specific case and in a WTO-inconsistent manner. Put another way, in case of mandatory legislation a complainant government would have remedies both against the legislation per se[5] and its application, if any, while in case of discretionary legislation there would be a remedy only against any GATT-inconsistent application of the legislation.

The distinction is unique in two respects. First, it is only the WTO (and before it the GATT) adjudicative bodies that apply the distinction; that is to say, no other international courts and tribunals seem to make a distinction between mandatory and discretionary national laws for reviewing their international legal conformity. Second, within the WTO, the relevance of the distinction is limited to national *laws* only; that is to say, it is not relevant when the review is not about the compatibility of a law on its face but rather about the compatibility of a specific trade measure taken against specific products or countries.

The distinction, although originated under the GATT, has undergone some significant changes with the emergence of the WTO. Consequently, for a proper understanding of those changes as well as how the distinction evolved and what its present significance is, it may be useful to discuss briefly the relevant *acquis* of the GATT 1947.

2 The distinction under the GATT 1947

Initially, the distinction was applied not as a tool of review of national laws, but rather as a device to keep GATT's so-called "grandfather clause/rights" within tolerable limits. As may be recalled from Chapter 3, under the Protocol of Provisional Application (PPA) or other accession protocols by which countries joined the GATT 1947, each Contracting Party had the right to apply Part II of the GATT 1947 only to the extent that the obligations contained therein were not inconsistent with domestic legislation that pre-dated the PPA or the relevant accession protocol. In a 1949 Working Party Report it was concluded that a measure was permitted under the grandfather clause: "provided that the legislation on which . . . [the measure] is based is by its terms or expressed intent of a mandatory character – that is, it imposes on the executive authority requirements which cannot be modified by executive action."[6]

[5] As regards the circumstances in which a party may want to challenge legislation per se, see Chapter 4, pp. 101–2, above.

[6] Working Party Report, *Existing Measures*, para. 99.

This meant that a GATT-incompatible measure taken under preexisting legislation was allowed by the grandfather clause only if the legislation did not leave any discretion with the executive to ensure GATT-compatibility. This interpretation was followed and reaffirmed in subsequent GATT practice.[7]

To consider a concrete example, in *Thai – Cigarettes*, Thailand restricted the importation of cigarettes under its Tobacco Act of 1966, which provided that "the importation . . . of tobacco is prohibited except by license of the Director-General." Thailand claimed that the import restrictions were permitted because they were based on an Act that pre-dated the Thai Protocol of Accession of 1982. The Panel concluded that the Act merely gave the executive a discretion to violate GATT obligations by not granting import licenses. It therefore held that the import restrictions were not permissible under the grandfather clause.[8] Conversely (and hypothetically), had the Thai Act provided that "importation of tobacco is prohibited" without the qualification "except by license of the Director-General," import restrictions imposed under the law would have been treated as GATT-consistent. They would have been so treated because, in that situation, it would not have been within the power or discretion of the executive to remove the restrictions in question.

Given that the purpose of the grandfather clause was to make it possible for the governments to apply the substance of the GATT 1947 by executive action without legislative approval,[9] the distinction made good sense. To wit, because in the case of discretionary legislation the executive could ensure GATT-conformity, there would be no ground for deviating from the GATT.[10] By contrast, in the case of mandatory legislation only the legislature could ensure GATT-conformity and, accordingly, the incompatible measure would be permissible under the grandfather clause. Thus, the distinction had the effect of ensuring the maximum amount of compliance with the GATT obligations by the *executive* branch within the framework, and without violation or modification, of preexisting domestic laws.[11]

[7] See Working Party and Panel Reports, *Belgian Family Allowances*, para. 6; *US – Manufacturing Clause*, para. 35; *Canada – Alcohol I*, para. 4.28; *Norway – Apples*, paras. 5.6–7; *Thai – Cigarettes*, para. 83; *Canada – Alcohol II*, para. 5.9; and *US – Malt Beverages*, para. 5.44. It may be mentioned that a few early working party reports noted disagreement among delegations with regard to this interpretation: see, e.g., *German Import Restrictions I*, para. 14; and *German Import Restrictions II*, paras. 2, 14, 22.

[8] Panel Report, *Thai – Cigarettes*, paras. 82–83.

[9] See above, Chapter 3, pp. 52–53.

[10] Working Party Report, *German Import Restrictions I*, para. 12.

[11] See Doc. EPCT/TAC/PV/5 at 20, quoted in World Trade Organization 1995, 1075. It is worth noting that, of all the cases in which GATT working parties or panels were

While the distinction originated and attained authoritativeness in the context of the grandfather clause in the late 1940s and during the 1950s, about four decades later it was applied in an entirely different context, namely to test whether a national law by itself amounted to a violation of GATT obligations. In the 1987 *US – Superfund* case a GATT Panel was called upon to determine whether a tax measure contained in a US law, i.e. the Superfund Amendments and Reauthorization Act of 1986, was GATT-consistent or not. The US law provided that the tax measure would not enter into effect before January 1, 1989; and regulations implementing it had not been drafted or put into effect. The United States objected to an examination of the measure on this ground contending that the tax had no immediate effect on trade and therefore did not cause nullification or impairment of benefits within the meaning of Article XXIII of the GATT 1947.[12] Accordingly, the question before the Panel was whether the complainant governments could challenge the Superfund Act per se. It concluded that they could, and gave the following reasons for its conclusion:

> The Panel on "Japanese Measures on Imports of Leather" examined the contention of Japan that an import quota had not been filled and considered that
>
> > "the existence of a quantitative restriction should be presumed to cause nullification or impairment not only because of any effect it had had on the volume of trade but also for other reasons e.g. it would lead to increased transaction costs and would create uncertainties which could affect investment plans" (BISD 31S/113).
>
> The reasoning endorsed by the CONTRACTING PARTIES on that occasion applies also in the present case. The general prohibition of quantitative restrictions under Article XI, which the Panel on Japanese Measures on Imports of Leather examined, and the national treatment obligation of Article III, which Canada and the EEC invoked in the present case, have essentially the same rationale, namely to protect expectations of the contracting parties as to the competitive relationship between their products and those of the other contracting parties. Both articles are not only to protect current trade but also to create the predictability needed

asked to decide whether a law was mandatory or discretionary in the context of the grandfather clause, only in one case did a working party hold that the law at issue was mandatory: see Working Party Report, *Brazilian Internal Taxes*, para. 5. This case is from a very early period of the GATT and in this case the Working Party reached its conclusion solely on the basis of the contention of the government concerned. Later panels did not follow this approach and undertook an examination of national legislation in order to determine whether it was mandatory or discretionary. These panels generally took a restricted view of mandatory legislation. Such a view enabled the panels to require the contracting parties to ensure GATT-conformity in most cases, notwithstanding the grandfather clause: see, further, Bhuiyan 2002, 579–81.

12 Cf. Chapter 4, pp. 98–100, above.

to plan future trade. That objective could not be attained if contracting parties could not challenge existing legislation mandating actions at variance with the General Agreement until the administrative acts implementing it had actually been applied to their trade.[13]

Stated simply, the theory that the *Superfund* Panel developed in the above extract is that a claim can be brought against legislation itself, even in the absence of any specific application of the legislation, if the legislation is mandatory, *because mandatory legislation by itself affects the competitive relationship between products.* Applying this theory, the Panel found the US law to be GATT-consistent. Specifically, although the law provided for a GATT-inconsistent penalty tax, it granted the US tax authorities the regulatory power not to impose the penalty tax and to impose, instead of the penalty tax, a different tax that would be GATT-consistent. Hence, the US law was not mandatory (or, conversely, it was discretionary) and could not by itself constitute a violation of the GATT 1947.[14]

Thus, the distinction between mandatory and discretionary legislation was applied for the first time by the *Superfund* Panel to determine the GATT-compatibility of national legislation. The Panel also articulated the *raison d'être* of the distinction in this context: namely, mandatory law adversely affects competitive opportunities while discretionary law does not. Both the relevance and the *raison d'être* of the distinction as a yardstick for determining the "culpability" of national legislation, as put forward by the *Superfund* Panel, were affirmed by all subsequent GATT panels that were called upon to review the GATT-compatibility of national laws per se.[15]

It is apparent that the distinction served different purposes in the contexts of the grandfather clause and challenges to national legislation. In the former context, the distinction was not applied as a tool of review of national *laws*, but rather it was utilized in determining whether *specific* trade measures taken under national laws were permissible; and panels required the executive authorities of the respondent state to comply with the GATT obligations if the contested specific measure was taken under a preexisting domestic law that was *discretionary and not mandatory*. By contrast, in the context of challenges to national legislation, GATT-conformity was required in respect of legislation *itself*;

[13] Panel Report, *US – Superfund*, para. 5.2.2. [14] Ibid. para. 5.2.9.

[15] See Panel Reports, *EEC – Parts and Components*; *Thai – Cigarettes*; *US – Malt Beverages*; *US – Non-Rubber Footwear*; and *US – Tobacco*.

and this was required when the legislation was *mandatory and not discretionary*.[16]

As pointed out in Chapter 3, the WTO treaty does not contain any grandfather clause.[17] As a result, in relation to the grandfather clause, the distinction between mandatory and discretionary legislation has now a mere historic significance. Because of this limited significance, this issue is not treated any further in the present chapter.[18] Before embarking on the central issue that this chapter aims to address, namely the significance of the distinction under the WTO as a tool of review of national laws, the next section reverts to the point made at the beginning that, unlike GATT/WTO organs, international courts and tribunals in general do not seem to make a distinction between mandatory and discretionary national laws.

3 The distinction vis-à-vis international law in general

As explained in Chapter 2, hardly any instances can be found where the PCIJ or the ICJ has been called upon to review the compatibility of national laws with international obligations in a manner comparable to such review by GATT/WTO panels.[19] Thus, the PCIJ and the ICJ simply did not get enough opportunity to articulate any test as to the type of legislation that may by itself violate international obligations.[20] It was also mentioned in that chapter that, unlike the PCIJ or the ICJ,

[16] Thus it is no wonder that, in applying the distinction in respect of challenge to national legislation, the *Superfund* Panel did not refer to the jurisprudence concerning the grandfather clause. The different roles of the distinction in the two contexts also affected the way in which national laws were typified. This was so because, in respect of the grandfather clause, greater GATT-conformity warranted a restrictive definition of mandatory legislation, whereas in the context of challenge to national legislation, the situation was the opposite, and greater GATT-conformity required a broader definition of mandatory legislation: see, further, Bhuiyan 2002, 572–81, 586–88.

[17] See above, Chapter 3, pp. 54–55.

[18] For a more detailed account of the mandatory/discretionary distinction in the context of the grandfather clause (including an assessment of the question confronted by panels, during the early years of GATT, of whether it was within their competence to determine the mandatory/discretionary character of national legislation), see Bhuiyan 2002, 572–73, 577–81.

[19] See above, Chapter 2, pp. 39–40.

[20] For the lack of cases bearing directly on the point, a few words can perhaps be said about the *Arrest Warrant* case. In this case, as noted in Chapter 2, p. 39 above, the subject-matter of the dispute before the ICJ was not a domestic law, but rather a specific measure, i.e. an arrest warrant issued by a Belgian court against the foreign minister of the Congo. A Belgian argument was that the warrant did not violate the minister's diplomatic immunity because no so-called "Interpol Red Notice" was issued.

courts that exercise supervisory jurisdiction in respect of a particular treaty regime, such as the ECJ or the ECHR, have been called upon to review the compatibility of national laws with international obligations quite frequently. However, these courts also did not find it necessary to articulate any general rule – similar to the rule concerning mandatory and discretionary legislation in GATT/WTO jurisprudence – regarding the type of laws that are per se capable of violating international obligations.

Amongst the international courts and tribunals the European Court of Justice has, by far, dealt with the largest number of cases concerning challenge to national legislation. In such cases the approach adopted by the ECJ was to interpret the relevant EC obligation and then decide whether the particular piece of domestic legislation in question was contrary to the obligation as construed by it.[21]

The European Court of Human Rights has a settled case law, as pointed out earlier, to the effect that, in proceedings originating in an individual application, its task is not to rule *in abstracto* as to the compatibility of national law with the EHR Convention; rather it should confine itself, as far as possible, to an examination of the concrete case before it.[22] Nevertheless, in a number of cases, the ECHR has addressed, sometimes implicitly, the question of the compatibility of domestic law with the Convention. In those cases, the ECHR arrived at its conclusion as to such compatibility by interpreting the relevant provisions of the Convention and then evaluating the domestic laws at issue for their conformity with those provisions: a process in which the circumstances of particular

The ICJ, however, rejected this argument and held that the mere issuance and international circulation of the warrant infringed the immunity of the foreign minister, because they were *liable* to affect the minister's diplomatic activity. Thus, it was not relevant whether or not there was a significant *actual* interference with the minister's activity: ICJ Rep. 3 (2002) at 29–30 (para. 71). In the light of this decision, one may wonder whether the potential (adverse) effects of a national *law* in respect of the rights, benefits or privileges that the relevant international rules seek to protect could be a relevant test for determining its international legal conformity.

21 See, e.g., Case 167–73, *Commission* v. *France* [1974] ECR 359; Case 104/86, *Commission* v. *Italy* [1988] ECR 1799; Case C-58/99, *Commission* v. *Italy* [2000] ECR I-3811; Case C-264/99, *Commission* v. *Italy* [2000] ECR I-4417; Case C-160/99, *Commission* v. *France* [2000] ECR I-6137; Case C-162/99, *Commission* v. *Italy* [2001] ECR I-541; Case C-265/99, *Commission* v. *France* [2001] ECR I-2305; Case C-159/99, *Commission* v. *Italy* [2001] ECR I-4007; Case C-283/99, *Commission* v. *Italy* [2001] ECR I-4363; Case C-40/00, *Commission* v. *France* [2001] ECR I-4539; Case C-70/99, *Commission* v. *Portugal* [2001] ECR I-4845; and Case C-78/00, *Commission* v. *Italy* [2001] ECR I-8195.

22 See above, Chapter 2, p. 41.

cases and the specific application of the laws, if any, provided a useful background.[23]

Thus, the only broad conclusion that can possibly be drawn from the practice in other international forums is that the question as to whether a law, which was prima facie incompatible with an international obligation, by itself violated that obligation was addressed on a case by case basis. The answer depended on the content and interpretation of the relevant obligation as well as on the circumstances of each particular case.[24]

4 The distinction under the WTO

4.1 *General remarks*

In addition to the extinction of the grandfather clause, the distinction between mandatory and discretionary legislation has undergone changes under the WTO in other important respects. First and foremost, Article XVI:4 of the WTO Agreement has introduced a rather far-reaching obligation for Members to ensure the conformity of their "*laws, regulations and administrative procedures*" with the obligations under the WTO treaty. As pointed out in Chapter 3, a question regarding Article XVI:4 that attracted, and continues to attract, much attention is whether the article has any implications for the mandatory/discretionary distinction. Does Article XVI:4 require WTO-conformity of discretionary, in addition to mandatory, laws?[25] Although on a few occasions this question has been raised before panels and the AB, so far they have been able to avoid addressing it. Thus, even twelve years after the entry into force of the WTO treaty, the question remains wide open.

Second, apart from the issue of any possible direct implications of Article XVI:4 for the mandatory/discretionary distinction, there is the question of whether the article has indirectly affected the distinction because of its requirement to ensure WTO-conformity of not only national *laws* but also *administrative procedures*. As must be apparent from

[23] See, e.g., *Luedicke* v. *Germany*, ECHR Ser. A No. 29 (1978); *Marckx* v. *Belgium*, ECHR Ser. A No. 31 (1979); *Dudgeon* v. *United Kingdom*, ECHR Ser. A No. 45 (1981); *Abdulaziz* v. *United Kingdom*, ECHR Ser. A No. 94 (1985); *Norris* v. *Ireland*, ECHR Ser. A No. 142 (1988); *Modinos* v. *Cyprus*, ECHR Ser. A No. 259 (1993); *Ahmed* v. *United Kingdom*, 1998-VI ECHR Rep. 2356; *Rekvenyi* v. *Hungary*, 1999-III ECHR Rep. 867; *Hashman* v. *United Kingdom*, 1999-VIII ECHR Rep. 4; and *SBC* v. *United Kingdom*, 34 EHRR 619 (2002).

[24] For a more elaborate analysis of this issue, see Bhuiyan 2002, 581–84.

[25] See above, Chapter 3, pp. 60–62.

the preceding discussions, the criterion on the basis of which national laws are characterized as discretionary or mandatory is whether or not the *administrative authorities* have discretion to ensure conformity. When the administration has such discretion, the law is discretionary, and a discretionary law cannot be found to be WTO-incompatible. As far as administrative procedures are concerned, the administration can always ensure WTO-conformity, because, if the procedures are not in compliance, the administration itself can modify the procedures without taking the matter to the legislature. Given this ability of the administration to ensure compliance, should administrative procedures, like discretionary legislation, be exempted from WTO-incompatibility? Certainly, they cannot be so exempted, because that would result in reading the requirement to ensure WTO-conformity of "administrative procedures" out of Article XVI:4. Thus, as far as administrative procedures are concerned, discretion enjoyed by the administration cannot be a ground for WTO-compatibility. Hence, the dilemma is whether the same should be the case in respect of discretionary legislation – that is to say, whether such legislation is no longer to be treated as WTO-compatible simply for the existence of administrative discretion. While in a number of cases WTO panels and the AB have struggled in getting to grips with this difficulty,[26] there is in fact a simple solution.

The difficulty arises, in the first place, because of attempts to apply the mandatory/discretionary distinction in respect of administrative procedures. It is, however, entirely unnecessary to make such attempts. In other words, the distinction should be considered relevant only when the review concerns national legislation; and, by contrast, it should not be regarded as having any bearing in respect of administrative procedures. This, of course, would mean that "administrative discretion" would be a ground for WTO-compatibility in respect of legislation but not in respect of administrative procedures. While, apparently, this solution may seem somewhat strange, in reality it is not. It would result in greater deference to Members' legislation than to administrative procedures; and treating or reviewing legislative measures less severely than administrative measures makes perfect sense. As far as the domestic legal systems of Members are concerned, legislative and administrative measures do not serve the same purpose, nor are they adopted through the same procedure. It is almost a matter of common sense that a finding of WTO-incompatibility would have entirely different implications for a

[26] See, e.g., *US – Steel Plate*; *US – Countervailing Measures*; and *US – CRCS Sunset Review*.

respondent Member depending on whether it relates to legislation or to administrative measures. There would be much greater resistance by the Member when the finding relates to legislation; and, accordingly, more deference needs to be shown in respect of legislation. Thus it is not difficult to rationalize the application of the mandatory/discretionary distinction in respect of legislation only.[27] But, at any rate, the introduction of the requirement to ensure WTO-conformity of administrative procedures has added a new shade to the understanding of the mandatory/discretionary distinction.

Third, the decision of the Panel in the *US – Section 301* case has created a further dent in the mandatory/discretionary distinction. In this case the Panel in effect held that under certain circumstances discretionary legislation can violate WTO obligations. This ruling was made not on the basis of Article XVI:4, but rather on the basis of the specific WTO obligation that was at issue, namely, DSU Article 23. That is to say, it was held that DSU Article 23 could be violated by discretionary legislation. This ruling has not supplanted the distinction, because the distinction would continue to apply in respect of *all* WTO provisions *other than* DSU Article 23, unless and until a similar ruling is made by a panel or the AB in respect of any other WTO provision/s (and no such ruling has yet been made[28]). But, certainly, the *US – Section 301* case has created the possibility that discretionary legislation may violate WTO obligations.

4.2 *The jurisprudence*

This section intends to discuss the fundamental features of the WTO jurisprudence on mandatory/discretionary legislation. However, because of space constraints it is not possible to assess how the issue has been decided in each individual case.[29] Accordingly, instead of a case by case evaluation, the discussion focuses on the nature and the extent of the continuing relevance of the distinction under the WTO.

Until *US – Section 301*, all WTO panels that confronted the mandatory/discretionary issue fully endorsed both the distinction and its rationale, i.e. mandatory legislation affects competitive opportunities between

[27] Notably, in the recent *US – CRCS Sunset Review* case, the Appellate Body has also expressed a similar view: see AB Report, paras. 73–101. See also Naiki 2004, 61–70.

[28] See, for instance, the cases cited in n. 44 below.

[29] Analyses of some of the individual cases (including cases decided under the GATT 1947) can be found elsewhere, in particular in: Bhuiyan 2002; Sim 2003; Davies 2004; and Naiki 2004.

products while discretionary legislation does not.[30] The Appellate Body confronted the mandatory/discretionary issue for the first time in the *US – 1916 Act* cases. The earlier cases in which the issue arose before panels either were not appealed or, if appealed, no question was raised before the AB about the distinction. (It is worth noting that the *US – Section 301* case was not appealed.) The AB's decision in the *US – 1916 Act* cases is an endorsement of the distinction, because the AB applied the distinction to determine the WTO-compatibility of the contested US legislation. Thus, in respect of the continuing significance of the distinction, the *Section 301* and *1916 Act* cases are particularly important. Consequently, these cases are discussed in some detail in the next few paragraphs. This discussion is followed by a general assessment of the cases decided subsequent to *Section 301* and *1916 Act.*

In *US – Section 301* the EC challenged sections 301–10 of the United States Trade Act of 1974. The EC made a number of claims regarding the WTO-inconsistency of these sections. For purposes of explaining the decision of the Panel on the question of mandatory/discretionary legislation, it may suffice to discuss the factual aspects of one such claim and the Panel's decision thereon.

As regards section 304, the EC argued that the section mandated the United States Trade Representative (USTR) to make a "unilateral" determination as to whether another WTO Member had violated US rights under the WTO agreements within eighteen months after the initiation of an investigation under section 302, a date that normally coincided with the date of the request for consultations under the WTO DSU. According to the EC, it could take longer than the eighteen months from the date of the request for consultations for the completion of the relevant DSU procedure to establish whether a violation of the WTO agreements had occurred. Thus, under section 304, the USTR was in effect required to make a determination irrespective of and prior to the adoption of a panel or Appellate Body finding on the matter. Therefore, the section violated Article 23.2(a) of the DSU, which provides that such determinations should be made in accordance with the relevant DSU procedure.

The United States formulated its defense on the basis of the mandatory/discretionary distinction. According to the USA, the distinction was fully applicable under the WTO and consequently only legislation

[30] See Panel Reports, *India Patent I & II*; *Argentina – Textiles*, para. 6.46; *US – DRAMS*; *Canada – Aircraft*, paras. 9.124, 9.208; and *Turkey – Textiles*, para. 9.37.

mandating a WTO-inconsistency or precluding WTO-consistency could violate WTO obligations. It argued that, even though section 304 mandated the USTR to make a determination at the end of the eighteen-month period, it did not mandate the USTR to make a determination that US rights under the WTO agreements had been denied ("determination of inconsistency"), and the USTR enjoyed full discretion as to the content of the determination. In the US view, the USTR had the discretion to make a number of determinations, which would be WTO-consistent: namely, that no violation had occurred; that no violation had been confirmed by the WTO DSB (Dispute Settlement Body); that a violation would be confirmed on the date the DSB adopted panel or Appellate Body findings; or that the ongoing investigation must be terminated. Thus, on the basis of the GATT/WTO jurisprudence on mandatory and discretionary legislation, section 304, which did not preclude the USA from acting consistently with Article 23.2(a), could not by itself be regarded as WTO-inconsistent.

On the question of mandatory/discretionary legislation, the EC argued that it would no longer be correct to rely on the distinction along the lines followed by the GATT practice. Rather it was necessary to distinguish between:

> (a) domestic law that is merely meant to transfer decision-making authority from one constitutional body (most often the Parliament) to another constitutional body (most often the executive authorities) within specified parameters, and
> (b) domestic law that does not preclude the executive authorities from acting consistently with WTO law but that is – by its design, structure and architecture – manifestly intended to encourage violations of WTO law or is otherwise biased against WTO-consistent action.[31]

The EC described the first type of legislation as "genuinely discretionary" and the second type as "not genuinely discretionary," to which category, according to the EC, section 304 belonged. The EC argued that, in the context of the WTO, such a law by itself should be regarded as WTO-inconsistent.

The Panel found that, since the relevant DSU procedure could take longer than eighteen months, the statutory language of section 304 mandated the USTR to make a unilateral determination prior to the completion of the DSU proceedings. However, it also found that, even though the USTR was required to make a determination within the

[31] Panel Report, *US – Section 301*, para. 4.250.

eighteen-month time frame, section 304 did not require the USTR to make a *determination of inconsistency* before the exhaustion of the DSU proceedings. Thus, the USTR had wide discretion as to the content of the determination.

From the above finding it could have followed, as argued by the USA, that, since section 304 left the discretion either to violate or not to violate WTO obligations with the USTR, it was discretionary legislation, and in accordance with the established practice it could not be challenged before the WTO. However, the Panel did not take such a simplistic view of the matter. Instead, the Panel began its analysis by finding that Article 23 could be violated either by an ad hoc, specific action in a given dispute or by a measure of general applicability, e.g. legislation or regulations.[32] The Panel considered that the question before it was whether section 304 could constitute a breach of the latter kind. In this connection the Panel noted the opposing arguments of the parties as to the type of legislation that could violate WTO obligations and observed that:

> We do not accept the legal logic that there has to be one fast and hard rule covering all domestic legislation. After all, is it so implausible that the framers of the WTO Agreement, in their wisdom, would have crafted some obligations which would render illegal even discretionary legislation and crafted other obligations prohibiting only mandatory legislation? Whether or not Section 304 violates Article 23 depends, thus, first and foremost on the precise obligations contained in Article 23 . . . since Article 23 may prohibit legislation with certain discretionary elements . . . the very fact of having in the legislation such discretion could, in effect, preclude WTO consistency.[33]

The Panel then proceeded to interpret Article 23.2(a) in accordance with the customary rules of treaty interpretation as contained in Article 31 of the VCLT. The Panel concluded that Article 23.2(a), thus interpreted, prohibited the type of legislation that was at issue before it. Accordingly, it held that the statutory language of section 304 constituted a prima facie violation of Article 23.2(a). However, later the Panel found that this prima facie violation was removed by the USA through commitments made in an administrative document and to the Panel that section 304 would not be applied in contravention of the DSU.[34] Therefore, although in the end the Panel upheld the validity of section 304, on the issue of mandatory/discretionary legislation it arrived at a solution

[32] Ibid. para. 7.46. [33] Ibid. paras. 7.53–54. [34] Cf. Chapter 7, pp. 235–37 above.

similar to that suggested by the EC, albeit through an altogether different methodology.

The Panel, however, expressly stated that it did not overturn "the classical test in the preexisting jurisprudence that *only* legislation mandating a WTO-inconsistency or precluding WTO-consistency, could, as such, violate WTO provisions."[35] But does this statement contradict the Panel's finding regarding section 304, which was not a mandatory but a discretionary provision? Paradoxically, the answer can be both in the affirmative and in the negative. For a proper understanding of the scope of the Panel's finding in the *Section 301* case, two limbs of the mandatory/discretionary rule need to be distinguished. One limb of the rule is that a mandatory law will *always* be WTO-inconsistent, and the other limb of the rule is that a discretionary law will *never* be WTO-inconsistent. While the first limb of the rule has remained entirely unaffected by the Panel's finding, the second limb has not. In other words, the Panel's finding that, despite its discretionary character, section 304 constituted a prima facie violation of the DSU is a clear departure from the second limb of the rule.

Turning now to the *US – 1916 Act* cases, these cases concerned Title VIII of the United States Revenue Act of 1916. The complainants, the EC and Japan, claimed that this US law violated the WTO Anti-Dumping Agreement (ADA), because, in contravention of that agreement, the law provided for civil and criminal proceedings against dumping. (The ADA limits the permissible remedies against dumping to definitive anti-dumping duties, provisional measures and price undertakings.[36]) One of the principal US defenses was that the Act was discretionary legislation and, hence, could not, by itself, amount to a breach. According to the USA, the Act was discretionary because, firstly, US courts had in the past interpreted or could in the future interpret the Act in a WTO-consistent manner, and, secondly, the US Department of Justice had discretion to initiate or not to initiate criminal proceedings. Japan argued that the Act was mandatory. Furthermore, it contended that the obligation contained in Article XVI:4 of the WTO Agreement would apply in the dispute, rather than the mandatory/non-mandatory distinction. According to the EC the legislation was not discretionary. It also argued that even though the distinction continued to be significant, Article XVI:4 had reduced the required degree of mandatoriness for actionability.

[35] Panel Report, *US – Section 301*, para. 7.54 (italics added). [36] See ADA, Articles 7–9.

The Panel concluded that the question of whether the Act had been or could be interpreted by the US courts in a WTO-consistent manner was simply a question of ascertaining the meaning of the law. Furthermore, the discretion enjoyed by the Department of Justice to initiate a case did not make the Act non-mandatory.[37] The Panel, therefore, held that the Act violated the ADA. Since the Panel found that the Act was not discretionary legislation, it did not find it necessary to address the arguments of the parties about the impact of Article XVI:4 of the WTO Agreement on the application of the distinction.[38]

On appeal, the Appellate Body recognized that: "the concept of mandatory as distinguished from discretionary legislation was developed by a number of GATT panels as a threshold consideration in determining when legislation as such – rather than a specific application of that legislation – was inconsistent with a Contracting Party's GATT 1947 obligations."[39] According to the AB the relevant discretion, for purposes of distinguishing between mandatory and discretionary legislation, was a discretion accorded to the *executive*. With regard to the civil actions that *private parties* could bring, it noted that there was no relevant discretion vested in the executive. With regard to the criminal proceedings, it concluded that the discretion enjoyed by the Department of Justice was not of such a nature or breadth as to transform the Act into discretionary legislation. The Appellate Body, therefore, agreed with the Panel that the Act was mandatory.[40]

The question of the continued relevance of the distinction for claims brought under the ADA arose before the Appellate Body in the context of a US contention. The USA argued that the Panel wrongly concluded that, since Article 18.4 of the ADA[41] required each Member to ensure the conformity of its laws with the ADA, the notion of mandatory/non-mandatory legislation was no longer relevant in determining whether the Panel could review the WTO-conformity of the US Act.[42] The Appellate Body found that it was not necessary to address the US contention for the following reasons:

[37] Panel Reports, *US – 1916 Act I*, paras. 6.84, 6.169; and *US – 1916 Act II*, paras. 6.97, 6.191.

[38] See Panel Reports, *US – 1916 Act I*, footnote 425; and *US – 1916 Act II*, footnote 553.

[39] AB Report, *US 1916 Act I & II*, para. 88. [40] Ibid. paras. 89–91.

[41] ADA Article 18.4 is a provision that mirrors Article XVI:4 of the WTO Agreement, but is applicable only in respect of the ADA: see above, Chapter 3, p. 55.

[42] Panel Report, *US – 1916 Act II*, para. 6.189.

answering the question of the continuing relevance of the distinction between mandatory and discretionary legislation for claims brought under the Anti-Dumping Agreement would have no impact upon the outcome of these appeals, because the 1916 Act is clearly not discretionary legislation, as that term has been understood for purposes of distinguishing between mandatory and discretionary legislation. Therefore, we do not find it necessary to consider, in these cases, whether Article 18.4, or any other provision of the Anti-Dumping Agreement, has supplanted or modified the distinction between mandatory and discretionary legislation.[43]

Thus, the AB did not express any view on the implications of ADA Article 18.4 – or, for that matter, on the implications of the similarly worded Article XVI:4 of the WTO Agreement – for the mandatory/discretionary distinction. Nonetheless, the *US – 1916 Act* cases are important, because the AB, as seen above, *applied* the distinction with a view to determining whether the contested US legislation was WTO-consistent or not. This, of course, is an endorsement of the distinction without foreclosing the more difficult question of the implications of Article XVI:4.

Subsequent to the *1916 Act* cases, the issue of mandatory/discretionary legislation arose in quite a large number of cases.[44] In many of those cases the decision of the AB in the *1916 Act* cases has been cited as the authority for the applicability of the distinction in reviewing national legislation per se.[45] In some instances reference has been made, without expressing any approval or disapproval, to the decision of the Panel, in the *US – Section 301* case, that discretionary legislation may violate WTO obligations.[46] Another notable aspect of the recent cases is the difficulty that arose in some instances because of misunderstandings about the relevance of the distinction when the subject-matter of the review is not

[43] AB Report, *US 1916 Act I & II*, para. 99.

[44] See, e.g., *US – Hot-Rolled Steel*; *US – Exports Restraints*; *Brazil – Aircraft 21.5 II*; *US – Section 211*; *India – Autos*; *Canada – Regional Aircraft*; *US – Steel Plate*; *US – Carbon Steel*; *US – Section 129*; *US – Countervailing Measures*; *US – Offset Act*; *US – Softwood Lumber III*; *US – CRCS Sunset Review*; *Canada – Wheat*; *Korea – Commercial Vessels*; *US – Upland Cotton*; *Mexico – Rice*; and *US – Zeroing*.

[45] See, e.g., Panel Reports, *US – Hot-Rolled Steel*; *US – Exports Restraints*; *Brazil – Aircraft 21.5 II*; *US – Section 211*; *Canada – Regional Aircraft*; *US – Steel Plate*; *US – Section 129*; *US – Countervailing Measures*; *US – Softwood Lumber III*; and *US – CRCS Sunset Review*; and AB Report, *US Section 211*.

[46] See, e.g., Panel Reports, *US Exports Restraints*; *Brazil – Aircraft 21.5 II*; *Canada – Regional Aircraft*; and *US – Countervailing Measures*; and AB Reports, *US – 1916 Act I & II*; and *US – Countervailing Measures*.

legislation but "administrative procedures."[47] Perhaps the most significant aspect of the post-*Section 301* cases is that the path opened by the *Section 301* Panel has not been followed by any other panel or the AB. That is to say, there is no other instance in which a discretionary law was found to be WTO-incompatible. Thus, on the whole, the mandatory/discretionary doctrine does not seem to be losing ground under the WTO.[48]

Indeed, there are important reasons for not overthrowing the doctrine. The doctrine is now about twenty years old. Accordingly, if the AB suddenly dismantles the doctrine, it would not be unreasonable to criticize the AB for being unpredictable and for creating legal insecurity by overruling a long line of GATT/WTO decisions. The demands of "*stare decisis*"[49] are, of course, not hollow, because the doctrine has a certain usefulness in determining the WTO-compatibility of national legislation. The limb of the doctrine according to which a mandatory law – i.e. a law that *requires* the executive to act inconsistently with the WTO obligations – by itself amounts to a breach is entirely sound. The other limb, according to which a discretionary law cannot be held to be WTO-inconsistent, may, in some rare instances, be problematic. That is to say, there could be some very rare cases where, notwithstanding administrative discretion, the law might be so egregiously irreconcilable with the WTO obligations that a "mechanistic"[50] application of the second limb of the doctrine would fly in the face of effective international supervision. Given that, in the *Section 301* case, the Panel has created the possibility of finding discretionary legislation WTO-inconsistent, the doctrine seems to have evolved into an ideal state. However, because the Panel in the *Section 301* case has made a departure from the earlier jurisprudence, it may be useful to consider, in slightly more detail, the justifications for treating – albeit rarely – discretionary legislation as WTO-incompatible.

5 Justifications for treating some discretionary laws as WTO-inconsistent

The justification put forward by the Panel in *US – Section 301* for widening the scope of reviewable measures to include discretionary legislation took the form of treaty interpretation in accordance with VCLT Article 31. This Article provides that a treaty be interpreted in good

[47] See above, pp. 251–53. [48] See Naiki 2004, 61, 70.
[49] See, generally, Bhala 1999a, 1999b and 2001.
[50] Cf. AB Report, *US CRCS Sunset Review*, para. 93.

faith in accordance with the ordinary meaning to be given to the terms of the treaty in their context and in the light of its object and purpose.[51] The Panel stated that text, context, and object and purpose correspond to well-established textual, systemic and teleological methodologies of treaty interpretation.[52] Accordingly, it arrived at its conclusion that DSU Article 23 prohibits discretionary legislation through a rigorous process of textual, systemic and teleological interpretation of the article.[53]

In addition to the above, it is possible to conceive of other justifications. First, as discussed earlier, the rationale for the principle that mandatory legislation can be WTO-inconsistent is that such legislation adversely affects competitive opportunities in trade.[54] Arguably, this rationale can be taken into account even in respect of challenges against some discretionary laws. It is remarkable that panels have consistently applied this rationale in respect of mandatory legislation, while declining to apply it to legislation containing discretionary elements even in a most tenuous way. For instance, the *Superfund* Panel noted that "it is *regrettable* that the Superfund Act explicitly directs the United States tax authorities to impose a tax inconsistent with the national treatment principle."[55] Nevertheless, the Panel upheld the validity of the law on the basis that the Act left open the possibility of avoiding a discriminatory tax by issuing regulations which, at the time of the Panel proceedings, had not yet been issued.[56] Perhaps implicit in the *Superfund* Panel's regret was the assumption that the discretionary law at issue might affect competitive relationship and predictability as was so adeptly elaborated by itself in the context of mandatory legislation.

In certain circumstances it may not be accurate to assume that the competitive relationship will not be affected or decisions of economic operators will not be influenced by discretionary legislation.[57] In other words, some discretionary laws may cause a "chilling effect" on the market and on the economic activities of individuals. These laws should be regarded as WTO-inconsistent on the basis of the rationale for sustaining challenges against mandatory legislation. From this perspective the decision in the *Section 301* case can be regarded as resting on the rationale articulated in prior GATT/WTO cases.

[51] The relevant part of VCLT Article 31 is quoted in Chapter 7, p. 220 above.
[52] Panel Report, *US – Section 301*, para. 7.22. [53] Ibid. paras. 7.58–97.
[54] See above, p. 248. [55] Panel Report, *US – Superfund*, para. 5.2.9 (italics added).
[56] Ibid.
[57] Cf. US response to third-party submission by Hong Kong in *US – Section 301*: Panel Report, paras. 4.276–84. See Davey 2001, 103.

Second, in reaching its conclusion, the *Section 301* Panel employed a methodology that, in essence, is the same as the methodology employed by earlier panels – namely, to construe the GATT/WTO provision at issue. Although the earlier panels referred to competitive relationship, they readily found a *textual basis* for the same. For instance, the *Superfund* Panel noted that the rationale of *Article III* is "to protect expectations of the contracting parties as to the competitive relationship between their product and those of other contracting parties."[58] Similarly, in *EEC – Parts and Components* the Panel noted that *the GATT obligations which were at issue* prohibited certain measures but not legislation under which such measures could be imposed.[59] In the WTO context, it may also be argued that Article XVI:4 of the WTO Agreement should be regarded as providing an additional textual basis for allowing challenges against *some* discretionary laws.[60]

Third, as pointed out earlier, in the field of non-WTO international law the question of the consistency of domestic laws with international obligations is addressed by interpreting the relevant obligation and without recourse to any general rule like the distinction between mandatory and discretionary legislation. Thus, if a panel were to find on the basis of its interpretation of the relevant WTO obligation that the national law at issue, notwithstanding its discretionary elements, is prohibited by that obligation, its decision can be defended as being one which does not fall beyond the parameters of the practice under international law in general. Moreover, even in WTO jurisprudence, there are cases in which it was not necessary to refer to the mandatory/discretionary distinction, in order to determine the WTO-compatibility of national legislation.[61]

6 Implications of bringing discretionary laws under WTO discipline

A suggestion of allowing WTO claims against some discretionary laws needs to take into account its possible implications. A few such implications are discussed below.

[58] Panel Report, *US – Superfund*, para. 5.2.2. Cf. the Panel's observation in *US – Section 301* that, even though Article III:2 would not, on its face, seem to prohibit legislation per se, in *US – Superfund* it was read as a promise not only to abstain from imposing discriminatory taxes, but also not to enact legislation with that effect: Panel Report, para. 7.82.

[59] Panel Report, *EEC – Parts and Components*, para. 5.25.

[60] Cf. third-party submission by Brazil in *US – Section 301*: Panel Report, para. 5.16.

[61] See, e.g., *Canada – Periodicals*; *US – FSC*; and *US – Copyright Act*.

6.1 *"The sovereignty debate"*

Any institutional structure put in place by an international treaty is apt to raise some sovereignty concerns in one way or another.[62] Sovereignty concerns may arise not only from broad institutional issues but also from more specific and minute rules, which evince the potential of removing power from the national level to the international plane. With regard to the widening of the scope of reviewable measures, it is possible to discern certain sovereignty concerns, some of which were raised in the *US – Section 301* case itself. One such concern relates simply to feasibility. That is to say, since many Members may have legislation enabling them to act inconsistently with the WTO obligations while not mandating such action, how far would it be reasonable to require each Member, as the USA put it, "to make the WTO Agreement pre-eminent in its legal order"?[63] It has also been suggested that there could be circumstances in which it might be politically necessary to have laws on the statute books authorizing WTO-inconsistent actions, even though it might not be necessary to apply those laws.[64]

Perhaps the pragmatic reply to these concerns is that not every piece of discretionary legislation would ever be subject to challenge before the WTO, or, if challenged, would be found WTO-inconsistent. Only legislation which, to use the rationale of the GATT/WTO cases, tends to affect adversely the competitive opportunities and thus increases the risk premium in international trade would be susceptible to such challenge or finding. Besides, Members will have some latitude, in that the standard required is, as indicated by the Appellate Body, that of providing a sound legal basis to ensure compliance with the WTO obligations and not of removing every reasonable doubt regarding the WTO-compatibility of domestic law.[65] Furthermore, not each and every article contained in the WTO agreements needs to be construed as prohibiting discretionary legislation.[66]

It was asserted that making discretionary laws amenable to challenge before the WTO would entail interference with the sovereign power to legislate on matters relating to relationship with non-WTO Members and with respect to Members on matters not subject to the WTO

[62] See, generally, Jackson 1997c and 2003; Barfield 2001; Raustiala 2003; and Sarooshi 2005.

[63] Panel Report, *US – Section 301*, para. 4.181.

[64] See Davey 2001, 103.

[65] AB Report, *India – Patent I*, paras. 57, 70. Cf. Chapter 6, pp. 193–94 above.

[66] Recall, for instance, that in none of the cases decided subsequent to *US – Section 301* was a WTO provision construed as prohibiting discretionary legislation.

agreements.[67] It is difficult to imagine why appropriately worded laws could not be drafted to preserve sovereign rights in these spheres.

6.2 *Rule orientation*

It is quite well known in trade law circles that, historically, the GATT had evolved from a power-oriented to a rule-oriented system and that, compared to the GATT, the WTO is much more rule-oriented.[68] From this perspective, bringing some discretionary laws within the WTO discipline can be regarded as a further development towards rule orientation. On occasion, the mere existence of a discretionary law in the statute books of a WTO Member may influence other Members as well as private actors to modify their policies and practice. As the Panel in the *Section 301* case put it, the threat of prohibited conduct may enable a Member "to exert undue leverage on other Members."[69] Requiring WTO-consistency of some discretionary laws may prevent the possibility of such undue leverage and increase the rule-orientation of the WTO.

6.3 *Individual rights*

The reference by all the panels, starting with the Panel on *US – Superfund*, which dealt with the issue of mandatory/discretionary legislation to the protection of the competitive relationship as the underlying rationale of their decisions is, in essence, a reference to the guarantee of secure market conditions for individual economic activity. Some of the panels explicitly referred to the influence of measures on the decisions of economic operators. In *US – Section 301* this theme occupied a central place in the Panel's interpretation of DSU Article 23 in accordance with the VCLT.[70] It is possible to imagine circumstances in which discretionary powers could be used for the benefit of "rent-seeking" interest groups. Thus, in order to protect individual rights and to promote good governance at domestic levels it may be useful to assert international supervision in respect of – some would say, to "constitutionalize"[71] – some discretionary trade policy powers.

6.4 *Distinguishing between different kinds of discretionary legislation*

Once it is accepted that discretionary legislation may violate WTO obligations, the question of drawing distinctions between different types of

[67] See US submissions in *US – Section 301*: Panel Report, paras. 4.283–84.
[68] See, e.g., Long 1987, 61–88; Jackson 1997a, 109–11; and Hilf 2001.
[69] Panel Report, *US – Section 301*, para. 7.89. [70] See ibid. paras. 7.71–91.
[71] See Petersmann 1997a, 1–57, and 1998b.

legislation becomes crucial, inasmuch as finding all discretionary laws WTO-incompatible will not be appropriate. The Panel on *US – Section 301* thought that it was not necessary to decide "which type of legislation, *in abstract*, is capable of violating WTO obligations"[72] to resolve the dispute. Thus it did not address the question of distinguishing between different types of discretionary legislation and it may appear from the Panel's analysis that this issue will not have to be addressed in future either.

However, this issue may indeed come before future panels, not least owing to the expansion of the scope of reviewable measures in *US – Section 301*. If future panels adopt the methodology employed in *US – Section 301*, they will construe the WTO provision at issue to find out whether the type of discretionary legislation under challenge is prohibited by that provision. In this context, these panels may have to address the issue of drawing distinctions in two different settings. Firstly, if a provision in respect of which the question of mandatory/discretionary legislation has been addressed previously, e.g. Article III of the GATT 1994, is at issue, a panel may have to reconcile the earlier jurisprudence with *US – Section 301*. In so doing, the panel may need to decide whether the contested discretionary law should at all be regarded as prohibited. Secondly, even in construing new Uruguay Round provisions, a panel may have to satisfy itself whether, notwithstanding discretionary elements, a particular legislation should be regarded as prohibited by the provision at issue.

The EC made interesting submissions before the *Section 301* Panel as to how it may be possible to draw distinctions among discretionary laws, and the USA took the position that no such distinctions could lawfully be made and that any attempt to do so would lead to "substantial unpredictability."[73] As the Panel did not address those submissions, any clarification must await future litigation. One point needs to be made though: since the widening of the scope of reviewable laws shifts powers to the WTO dispute settlement system, in that the panels will have the leeway to determine whether a particular piece of discretionary legislation violates a WTO obligation, the panels and the AB will have to develop a nuanced approach to balance this shift of power and other important objectives (e.g., rule orientation, individual rights, etc.).

[72] Panel Report, *US – Section 301*, para. 7.53 (italics in original).
[73] For submissions by the EC and the USA on this point, see ibid. paras. 4.250–90.

7 Techniques of avoiding unreasonable intrusion

7.1 *General remarks*

Recognizing the desirability of subjecting some discretionary laws to WTO discipline, in order to better protect international rule of law and individual rights, does not lessen the importance of an appropriately deferential standard of review in respect of legislative acts of Members. With regard to the WTO dispute settlement system generally, it has been suggested that the panels and the Appellate Body should consider using traditional judicial techniques to avoid unwarranted decisions.[74] Aside from techniques relevant to the dispute settlement system generally, certain approaches that are particularly relevant in avoiding intrusive decisions by panels in respect of Members' discretionary legislation may merit consideration. The *Section 301* Panel has employed, explicitly or implicitly, three such techniques, which are discussed below.

7.2 *Case by case analysis*

Since drawing appropriate distinctions between different types of discretionary laws could be significant in avoiding intrusive decisions by the panels, care needs to be taken to avoid any generalized approach. Thus, the question of whether discretionary legislation violates WTO obligations should be decided on a case by case basis. The Panel on *US – Section 301* also endorsed such an approach: "Construing a WTO obligation as prohibiting a domestic law that 'merely' exposes Members and individual operators to risk of WTO inconsistent action should not be done lightly. It depends on the specific obligation at issue, the measure under consideration and the specific circumstances of each case."[75]

7.3 *Non-statutory elements*

The obligation of Members to bring their laws into conformity with the WTO treaty, important as it is, should be enforced in the least intrusive way possible. This obligation can be fulfilled under the different legal systems of Members (now some 150 legal systems) in very many ways.[76] It is important to be cognizant of the "multi-layered character" of many modern, complex, economic and regulatory laws, which comprise not

[74] Professor William Davey considered a number of such techniques, which he termed "issue-avoidance techniques," available in US and international law, and recommended that the WTO system should make more use of three such techniques: mootness, ripeness and the exercise of judicial economy. See Davey 2001, 96–110.

[75] Panel Report, *US – Section 301*, para. 7.93.

[76] Cf. Chapter 6, p. 194 above.

simply a statutory text but, in addition, different other institutional and administrative elements.[77] In the *Section 301* case, the Panel, after having found that the US statute prima facie violated DSU Article 23, went on to consider whether the violation had been lawfully and effectively removed by other factors. Eventually, on the basis of the US Statement of Administrative Action and the US commitments made to the Panel, it was concluded that the violation had been so removed.[78] Thus, should there be any criteria adopted by the respondent Member for administering a particular piece of discretionary legislation, a panel can take those into account in reaching its conclusion as to whether the law violates the WTO obligation at issue.[79]

7.4 *Mootness*

A dispute is regarded as moot where an event, occurring subsequent to the commencement of a case, effectively resolves the dispute. The International Court of Justice has recognized that events subsequent to the filing of an application may render the application "without object."[80] A case may be rendered without object, inter alia, when a respondent state makes a binding statement to the effect that it will comply with its international obligations.[81] An elaborate survey of the issue of mootness in the context of the WTO dispute settlement generally is not warranted here.[82] However, noting whether panels, with a view to avoiding difficult issues relating to discretionary legislation, should attribute legally binding effect to statements made before them by the respondent governments is not beside the point.

It may not be unusual for a respondent Member to state voluntarily before a panel that the contested discretionary legislation would unfailingly be applied in a WTO-consistent manner.[83] As discussed in the last chapter, an advantage of attributing legal significance to such a statement is that there appears to be a general consensus that declarations made before international tribunals bind the party making them.[84] Also, if a respondent government declares before a panel (or otherwise?) that

[77] See above, Chapter 7, pp. 219–20. [78] Panel Report, *US – Section 301*, paras. 7.98–136.

[79] See, generally, Chapter 7, pp. 231–35 above.

[80] *Lockerbie* case, ICJ Rep. 115 (1998) at 131 (para. 45); and *Border and Transborder Armed Actions*, ICJ Rep. 69 (1988) at 95 (para. 66).

[81] *Nuclear Tests* cases, ICJ Rep. 253, 457 (1974) at 267–72, 472–77.

[82] See, generally, Panel Report, *Indonesia – Autos*, para. 14.9, footnote 642 and the cases cited there. See also Davey 2001, 99–101.

[83] Cf. Chapter 7, n. 116 above. [84] See above, Chapter 7, p. 237.

it will apply its discretionary legislation in a WTO-consistent manner, the panel, from a pragmatic point of view, may feel encouraged to interpret definitively the legally binding character of the declaration so as to preclude the possibility that the government might later claim that it is not bound by its statement and may enforce the law in a WTO-inconsistent manner. Despite elaborate discussion of the circumstances in which and the reasons why discretionary legislation may violate WTO obligations, in essence this was the "expedient" that the Panel adopted in *US – Section 301* in coming to its eventual conclusion.[85]

8 Concluding remarks

Exempting all discretionary laws from WTO-incompatibility is not satisfactory because it is possible to imagine negative trade effects generated by laws that permit, but do not mandate, WTO-inconsistent measures. To ensure effectiveness of WTO rules and supervision it may be necessary, albeit on rare occasions, to treat discretionary laws as WTO-incompatible. Furthermore, in some cases, strong political incentives may exist to use discretionary authority under domestic laws for the benefit of "rent-seeking" interest groups. Thus, in appropriate circumstances, rulings against discretionary laws may also promote good governance at the domestic level.

It was suggested by the EC that the DSU should be amended to eliminate the distinction between mandatory and discretionary legislation, so that WTO-incompatibility of discretionary legislation could be established through the DSU procedures.[86] *US – Section 301* could be considered as having partly achieved that result without the need to amend the DSU. Nevertheless, the distinction continued – and will probably continue – to be relevant under the WTO. Indeed, in the *Section 301* case itself, no departure has been made from the part of the doctrine according to which a mandatory law is to be held WTO-inconsistent; and this part also seems entirely sound. Thus, it is not surprising that, in cases decided subsequent to *Section 301*, where national legislation was

[85] Indeed, the eventual conclusion of the *Section 301* Panel aptly demonstrates that, notwithstanding the end of the GATT era of "diplomat's jurisprudence," at times pragmatic decision-making may still be useful. On GATT's "diplomat's jurisprudence," see Hudec 1999, 17–76.

[86] See Review of the Dispute Settlement Understanding, Non-Paper by the European Communities (October, 1998), referenced in Panel Report, *US – Section 301*, footnotes 126, 132, 220, 269.

challenged as such, panels still wanted to find out whether the contested legislation was mandatory or discretionary. It is also very likely that future panels will adopt the same approach. Although whether a law is WTO-incompatible is to depend on the WTO provision at issue (which is to be construed in accordance with the VCLT), in the case of mandatory legislation a finding of violation can be made quite easily. In respect of discretionary legislation, although after *US – Section 301* it is apparent that certain discretionary laws may violate WTO obligations, the issue of how it may be possible to distinguish between different discretionary laws must await future litigation.

9 Conclusion

The tremendous growth of international law and the sharp increase in the number of international courts and tribunals during the second half of the twentieth century have led to many new features and avenues of interaction between national and international legal norms. In this context it is notable that, in the nineteenth and early twentieth centuries, critical analyses of the relationship between national and international law focused primarily on the theoretical debate known as monist–dualist controversy and on the position of international law in national legal systems. The latter concerned issues such as whether, to what extent and in what manner municipal courts in various countries make reference to or do apply rules of international law. Nowadays the questions of whether and how international courts and tribunals refer to, assess or apply rules of national law have become equally important.

Consider, for instance, the issue of the *application* of national law rules by international courts and tribunals. As may be recalled from Chapter 4, there are cases decided by the Permanent Court of International Justice where, instead of international law, a particular municipal law was applied by that Court as the applicable substantive law.[1] However, the most fascinating jurisprudence and academic discourse concerning the application of national law by international courts and tribunals have come into existence not in the context of dispute settlement by the PCIJ or its successor, the ICJ. Rather, such jurisprudence and academic discourse have emerged in the context of arbitration of disputes between states and foreign companies under state contracts (commonly referred to as mixed arbitrations), largely a late twentieth-century

[1] See above, Chapter 4, p. 103.

development.[2] As is well known, state contracts (i.e. contracts between a state and a private individual or corporate entity) often contain choice of law clauses subjecting the contracts either to the law of the state party or to a "hybrid" system of law, that is to say, to a combination of national and international law.[3] Accordingly, in adjudicating disputes arising out of state contracts, the arbitral tribunal necessarily confronts issues concerning the extent to which and the manner in which rules of the relevant national legal system are to be applied.[4] These intriguing issues have also attracted a considerable amount of critical attention leading to an ever increasing body of scholarly analysis on the interaction between national and international law rules in the context of mixed arbitrations.[5]

As explained earlier, WTO dispute settlement organs are unlikely to confront disputes where they may be required to *apply* national law as part of the applicable substantive law.[6] Rather, they confront issues of national law when called upon to *review* the WTO-compatibility of national laws. And, of course, issues of national law can also be important in cases where the review concerns other national measures, such as administrative or judicial decisions, because such decisions are often taken in pursuance of a law.[7] In this respect, WTO organs have already generated a significant body of jurisprudence. This is not to suggest that there does not exist a certain degree of commonality in international tribunals' assessment of national law, whether undertaken for purposes of applying or reviewing the law in question.

It may be recalled from Chapter 4 that, in some measure, the review of national laws by WTO bodies resembles the review of constitutionality

[2] Cf. also Chapter 6, n. 25, above, regarding the application of national law by NAFTA Chapter 19 bi-national panels.

[3] Even in the absence of an explicit choice of law clause, state contracts are often regarded as governed by a combination of national and international law: cf., for instance, Convention on the Settlement of Investment Disputes between States and Nationals of Other States 1965, Article 42(1).

[4] See, e.g., *Sapphire International Petroleums Ltd.* v. *National Iranian Oil Co.*, 35 ILR 136 (1963); *BP* v. *Libya*, 53 ILR 297 (1974); *Texaco* v. *Libya*, 53 ILR 389 (1977); and *LIAMCO* v. *Libya*, 62 ILR 140 (1977). It may be noted that, in addition to the question of the proper law of state contracts, there is another question as to whether in mixed arbitrations the arbitral process itself is to be governed by international law or the municipal law of the "seat" of the arbitration: see, generally, Toope 1990, ch. 2; and Redfern & Hunter 1999, 78–93.

[5] See, for instance, Mann 1959; Jennings 1961; Lalive 1964; Luzzatto 1977; Lew 1978; Delaume 1981; Greenwood 1982; Toope 1990, ch. 3; and Redfern & Hunter 1999, 93–134.

[6] See above, Chapter 4, pp. 103–4.

[7] See above, Chapter 1, p. 10.

of national laws by national supreme or constitutional courts.[8] As is well known, under national legal systems it is not uncommon for a supreme or constitutional court to possess and exercise the power to review the constitutionality of laws enacted by the legislature.[9] Such review by domestic courts is intended to ensure that constitutional norms and guarantees are not transgressed by the legislature, whether intentionally or by mere accident. Of course, the review of national laws by WTO bodies is not intended to check their constitutionality under national constitutions. Rather, the purpose of this review is to determine whether a contested national law transgresses the limits set by the WTO treaty. Nonetheless, the similarity between review by a domestic supreme or constitutional court and review by a WTO adjudicative organ lies in the fact that in both instances a judicial body reviews whether a law violates some superior legal norms – constitutional in one case and international in another.[10]

In a domestic context, the power of judicial review of legislation has its historical origin in *Marbury* v. *Madison*.[11] As will be seen, the analogy is not at all a perfect one, yet it is interesting to read a few sentences from the decision of Chief Justice Marshall in *Marbury* v. *Madison*. And, by way of thought experiment, let us do so by replacing Justice Marshall's references to the US Constitution and the US legislature with the WTO treaty and WTO Members, respectively:

> The powers of [Members] are defined and limited; and that those limits may not be mistaken or forgotten, the [WTO treaty] is written. To what purpose are powers limited, and to what purpose is that limitation committed to writing; if these limits may, at any time, be passed by those intended to be restrained? . . . It is a proposition too plain to be contested, that the [WTO treaty] controls any legislative act [of a Member] repugnant to it; or, that [a Member] may alter the [treaty] by [a unilateral] act. Between these alternatives there is no middle

[8] See above, Chapter 4, pp. 86–87.

[9] It may be mentioned parenthetically that, in a domestic context, in addition to legislative measures, the power of judicial review is exercised in respect of administrative measures. The grounds of review are often wider in respect of administrative measures, which can be reviewed for constitutionality as well as for the violation of basic principles of justice. For obvious reasons, the present comparison is with judicial review of legislative measures.

[10] See above, Chapter 4, pp. 86–87. Cf., however, Chapter 6, pp. 161–62 above (pointing out that, as far as *specific* techniques or criteria of review are concerned, international and national methods of review can, should and do vary in important respects).

[11] 1 Cranch 137 (1803).

> ground. The [WTO treaty] is either a superior, paramount law, unchangeable by [a Member unilaterally], or it is . . . alterable when [a Member] shall please to alter it . . . Certainly all those who have framed [the WTO treaty] contemplate . . . that an act of [a Member's] legislature repugnant to the [treaty is impermissible].[12]

The theory that Justice Marshall has put forward as the basis for the power to review the constitutionality of legislative acts has some resonance in the context of the review of the WTO-compatibility of national legislation.

The power of "judicial review"[13] of national measures was not unknown to international law before the WTO. Both the European Court of Human Rights and the European Court of Justice had already been exercising this power for a number of decades when the WTO came into existence in 1995. Yet, what make the WTO unique are its nearly universal compulsory jurisdiction and the increasing frequency with which it is called upon to review national measures and laws.[14] Even though the ECHR is an organ of public international law, like national courts it has a limited geographical jurisdiction confined to Europe, which as a continent has achieved a degree of cohesion that is impossible to find in other parts of the world.

The major contribution of the WTO jurisprudence on national law is in the review context. An obvious example is the WTO's increasing body

[12] Ibid. 176–77.

[13] In order to avoid any possible confusion, it is worth pointing out that here the expression "judicial review" is not used in the sense in which it is popularly used in the public international law context. The popular sense has its origin in the *Lockerbie* case, Provisional Measures, ICJ Rep. 3 (1992), Preliminary Objections, ICJ Rep. 9, 115 (1998). In that case, during the pendency before the ICJ of a request by Libya for provisional measures, the UN Security Council adopted a resolution taking actions which, in essence, the Libyan request was designed to prevent. This gave rise to the questions of whether the Security Council resolution was legal and whether the ICJ, for purposes of dealing with the Libyan request, should address the legality of that resolution. Although at the provisional measures stage the ICJ managed to avoid addressing these questions explicitly, the debate about whether the ICJ can and should "judicially review" the Security Council gained momentum: see, for instance, Franck 1992; R. F. Kennedy 1993; Gowlland-Debbas 1994; Roberts 1995; Alvarez 1996; and D'Angelo 2000. Thus, the popular notion of judicial review in international law is concerned with the question of the possibility of review of an *international* political body by an international court. By contrast, for present purposes, the expression "judicial review" is used not to refer to the review of one international body by another international body but rather to the review of a *national* (legislative) body by an international (e.g. a WTO) organ.

[14] See above, Chapter 1, pp. 7–10.

of jurisprudence on standard of review. As explained in Chapter 6, this body of jurisprudence has dealt with many intricate issues of proper balance between effective international supervision and preservation of national regulatory competence in the WTO setting, but there is much to be learnt from it even in the wider context of international dispute settlement in general.[15]

As already noted, in some respects the national law issues that international tribunals need to address are rather similar, irrespective of whether they arise in the context of applying or reviewing national law rules. Thus, for instance, in both these contexts, an international tribunal needs to determine the content or meaning of the relevant national law rules that are to be applied or reviewed. In this regard, the practice of international tribunals is generally described under the formulaic principle that national laws are facts before international courts and tribunals. As discussed in Chapters 2 and 7, this principle has a number of different dimensions. While some aspects of the principle make good sense, the suggestion that is often made that an international tribunal does not interpret national laws because they are merely facts is untenable.[16]

The preceding remark leads to a broader issue that needs to be underscored. The preoccupation of the nineteenth- and early twentieth-century analyses of the relation between national and international law with theoretical issues has been noted. Happily, the focus has long since shifted from theory to practice. Yet, as far as the position of national law in international law is concerned, there is a general tendency to set out the practice with reference to a few formulaic principles. Examples will include principles such as: national laws cannot be relied upon to avoid international obligations; national laws are facts; international tribunals do not interpret national laws; etc. Because of the over-reliance on formulas, many finer dimensions of the process of interaction between national and international law have escaped careful scrutiny, both judicial and scholarly. This work has sought to extend the enquiry beyond well-known formulas and to address a wider range of issues. A summary of some of the key findings made in various chapters of this book is set out below.

As an obvious starting point, Chapter 2 looked at how national law is treated in international law in general. In this regard a fundamental international law principle is that national laws cannot be relied

[15] See above, Chapter 6, pp. 150–53. [16] See, generally, Chapter 7 above.

upon to avoid international obligations. While this principle does not address the question of whether there exists any *positive* obligation to *implement* international law commitments in domestic law, many international treaties, including the WTO treaty, contain express provision on implementation. There is a further issue as to whether a prima facie incompatible national law can by itself violate international obligations. As far as practice is concerned, the PCIJ/ICJ has seldom been called upon to review the international legal conformity of national laws. By contrast, such review forms a regular part of the business of the courts that exercise supervisory jurisdiction in respect of a particular treaty regime, such as the ECJ, the ECHR and the WTO bodies.

The WTO dimensions of the two central issues of Chapter 2 singled out in the preceding paragraph, i.e. obligations regarding implementation and competence of international adjudicative bodies over domestic law, were discussed in the next two chapters. Chapter 3 examined the overarching systemic framework that the WTO treaty establishes concerning the relationship between WTO law and national law. The most significant aspect of this systemic framework is the obligation to ensure conformity of domestic laws with the WTO agreements. This obligation is more rigorous than the implementation obligations under many contemporary international treaties. There is, however, one gap in the WTO treaty regarding implementation. Certain WTO agreements contain provisions that purport to qualify the obligations of the territorial units of federal states to implement and observe WTO commitments. Then again, most of these "federal clauses," as explained in Chapter 3, are devoid of any real meaning. In addition to the obligation to ensure WTO-compatibility of national laws, there are other systemic WTO obligations regarding national law, namely those providing guarantees of transparency, fair and equitable administration of national laws, and availability of domestic legal remedies.

Chapter 4 examined the adjudicative competence of WTO dispute settlement organs regarding national measures, including laws, and the functions that those organs may need to perform in adjudicating disputes concerning such measures or laws. It also discussed WTO remedies and the mechanism for the enforcement of dispute settlement recommendations and rulings, with a view to explaining whether an adverse WTO ruling can effectively lead to changes in national measures including laws. As regards the latter, it is worth recalling that the WTO has one of the most effective mechanisms in international law for the enforcement of "judgments."

Part II took up national law issues that arise before WTO dispute settlement bodies. Chapter 5 discussed the problem of characterization, i.e. typifying national laws for purposes of determining whether WTO rules are applicable and, if so, which particular rules are to apply. This problem is not unique to the WTO. For instance, the problem that underlies the ECHR's doctrine of autonomous concepts is that of characterization of rules of national law or national legal institutions. Characterization can be a useful tool of deference to national regulatory competence. It can also be utilized in ensuring that disputes that appropriately belong to one international forum are not forced into another. The deferential objectives of characterization need to be balanced against effective international supervision, however. Thus, an international tribunal may depart from the characterization accorded by a state to its own law where acceptance of that characterization would endanger the effectiveness of the relevant international rules.

One of the thorniest issues of WTO dispute settlement, namely that of the standard of review, was examined in Chapter 6. Put simply, this involves the manner in which panels and the Appellate Body should *review* Members' measures for their conformity with the WTO obligations. The problem of standard of review, of course, is not confined to the WTO. Rather, it arises whenever an international tribunal is called upon to *review* the conformity of national measures with international obligations. Thus, for instance, in different ways, it is confronted by NAFTA dispute settlement bodies, the ECJ and the ECHR. In important respects, the ECHR's well-known doctrine of margin of appreciation concerns standard of review. The international, EC/EU or European human rights law concepts of proportionality and subsidiarity have elements that bear directly on it. In the WTO context, academic discourse often confuses issues of standard of review with those of treaty interpretation. Treaty interpretation and standard of review, however, are discrete matters. In large measure the confusion has resulted from attempts to understand and explain the problem of standard of review in WTO dispute settlement in the light of the *Chevron* doctrine of US administrative law. But the *Chevron* doctrine, being a doctrine of municipal law, can barely provide an appropriate analogy. Indeed, if one were to look for analogous concepts or doctrines, attention should be directed, in the first instance, to concepts and doctrines applied by international tribunals in reviewing national measures,[17] rather than to concepts of

[17] E.g. margin of appreciation, proportionality, subsidiarity.

municipal law. For a proper understanding of the problem of standard of review, its context-dependent nature should also be borne in mind. Because the standards, criteria or benchmarks of review can vary for numerous reasons, extrapolating specific standards or criteria of review from their particular context may give an entirely inaccurate picture of their relevance and significance.

As part of their review of a national law, WTO adjudicative bodies need to determine its content or meaning. This involves *proof* and *interpretation* of national law. Proof is the process whereby the necessary evidence – such as text of legislation, evidence on pertinent legislative history, judicial decisions, etc. – on the relevant national law issue is gathered. Interpretation is the process of construing the evidential materials to determine what is it that the national law provides on the particular issue/s that are at stake. Both of these aspects of the establishment of the content of national law were examined in Chapter 7. It is notable that WTO panels have always been able to determine national law issues on the basis of party-led *documentary evidence*. Thus proof of national law does not usually necessitate recourse to such method of proof as examination of witness or expert testimony.[18] Unlike the question of proof, the question of interpretation is less straightforward. Or, to be exact, this question has unnecessarily been shrouded in confusion through assertions made by panels and the AB that they do not interpret national laws. These assertions, however, are entirely at odds with the actual practice. Because the content of national law is established by panels as facts, there is a further critical question as to whether appeals can be made from panels' findings. The Appellate Body has shown the preparedness to entertain appeals on the ground that a review of a panel's findings regarding the meaning of a national law is a part and parcel of the appellate review of the WTO-compatibility of that national law. Although this ground is not entirely sound, as a matter of legal policy it is advisable for the AB to reconsider issues of national law.

It is possible to identify a number of tools that are applied in determining the WTO-compatibility of national measures/laws. While some of these were discussed in Chapter 6,[19] a tool of review *sui generis* to the WTO, namely the doctrine of mandatory and discretionary legislation, was examined in Chapter 8. This doctrine has two limbs. According to

[18] Cf. *Japan – Film*, where recourse to experts was made to resolve translation issues.

[19] E.g. reasoned and adequate explanation of decisions by domestic authorities, proportionality, transparency.

the first limb a mandatory domestic law, by itself, violates WTO obligations. And according to the other limb, a discretionary law does not, by itself, amount to a violation. While the first limb is entirely sound, in some rare cases a mechanistic application of the second limb could be problematic. That is to say, some discretionary laws could cause a serious chilling effect on the market and, accordingly, it may not be appropriate to treat such discretionary laws as WTO-consistent. There are, however, important reasons for which the Appellate Body should not overthrow the doctrine. Firstly, the usefulness of the mandatory limb of the doctrine can hardly be questioned. Secondly, the discretionary limb can also be quite useful in most cases, i.e. in cases other than those concerning discretionary laws that cause a serious chilling effect on the market.

Thematically, the work has developed two different but related strands. Firstly, it explained and critically evaluated the treatment of national law in the WTO treaty and by the WTO dispute settlement organs. Secondly, it analyzed WTO dispute settlement organs' review of the legality, i.e. WTO-compatibility, of national laws: Part I has elucidated the foundational aspect of this review, by explaining the approach of international courts and tribunals in general to national law (Chapter 2), the nature of the WTO obligations regarding national law (Chapter 3) and the key features of the WTO dispute settlement mechanism (Chapter 4). Part II then examined different dimensions of the actual process of review of the legality of national laws by the WTO dispute settlement bodies (Chapters 5 through 8).

Since some comparison has been made earlier between WTO review and domestic constitutional review, to avoid confusion it is necessary to point out their most fundamental differences as well. Typically, a finding by a domestic supreme or constitutional court that a law is unconstitutional will mean that the law is "void." An unconstitutional law will therefore cease to bind any court or individual. By contrast, a WTO organ cannot declare a domestic law "void." It can simply make a finding that the contested national law is WTO-inconsistent. Despite such a finding, the law will usually remain effective within the Member's domestic legal system, unless the Member itself chooses to repeal or amend the inconsistent law or there is some other domestic mechanism that addresses the issue. Thus, there is a stark contrast between the consequences of a finding of WTO-incompatibility by a WTO organ and a finding of unconstitutionality by a domestic court.

Nevertheless, the very facts that the WTO adjudicative organs have the authority to review the legality of national legislation, and that they are called upon to conduct such review so often that it has become a regular part of their business, are reason enough for one to pause and think seriously about the basis, necessity, limits and mode of the review. While a domestic constitutional court can strike down laws, there are many safeguards and checks and balances that create and sustain public confidence in its power to do so.

The thought that three panel or Appellate Body members – "faceless foreign judges," as they are occasionally called by critics – sitting at the WTO Secretariat in Geneva can pass "judgments" about the legality of the laws enacted by 150 countries of the world may be startling not only to the public at large, but even to well-informed professionals, including lawyers. The astonishment could be even greater if one is mindful that these 150 countries belong to different levels of economic development and shades of political and social orientation. Because of the wide differences between Members, unlike a national constitutional court, a WTO adjudicative organ can barely have a deep understanding of the economic, social and other realities of life of the people who may be affected by its decision.

No doubt, the exercise of the power of judicial review on a global scale, which, in a rudimentary form, is visible at the WTO, raises much more difficult issues than the exercise of that power within regions or nations. It is, however, difficult to imagine that the present-day global economic interdependence could be managed without centralized institutions, which have vital roles to play.[20] Thus, there is a need both for an institution like the WTO and for an effective mechanism to resolve disputes among trading nations. And to ensure that international rules on trade are not evaded by means of domestic legislation, the dispute settlement mechanism needs to have the authority to determine the conformity of domestic laws with those rules. But there is equally a need to be vigilant against overreaching by an international institution as powerful as the WTO. In so far as the review of national legislation by the WTO adjudicative organs is concerned, there is a constant need not only to understand the basis, necessity and limits of that review, but also to scrutinize how that review is conducted in real cases. By examining the obligations that Members have assumed under the WTO treaty in respect of their national law (Part I) and the treatment of national law in WTO dispute settlement (Part II), the present work has made an endeavor to that end.

[20] Cf. Chapter 6, p. 167 above.

Finally, it is necessary to say a few words about the values that are at stake as regards the treatment of national law by international tribunals. The determination of national law issues by international tribunals of course raises the question of proper allocation of power between national and international levels. In adjudicating disputes regarding the WTO-compatibility of national measures and laws, it is vital for WTO bodies to strike an appropriate balance between national regulatory competence and international obligations. Confronted with a domestic regulatory measure, the validity of which is challenged before it, an international adjudicative body must embark on its task by trying to understand who is better placed to make the decision/s underlying the regulatory measure: is it the international judge or the national authority? Decision-making closer to the constituencies affected is important not only for reasons of democratic accountability and legitimacy but also as a check and balance against centralized power.

A number of other important values flow directly from the value of proper allocation of power. The significance of the value of deference to national authorities, in preserving national regulatory competence, can hardly be overemphasized. It is therefore no wonder that in the preceding pages of this book repeated references have been made to deference. For instance, in discussing the problem of characterization (Chapter 5), it has been stressed that a mischaracterization by WTO organs of national laws and regulations dealing with non-WTO subjects as trade measures, thereby granting the WTO jurisdiction over them, would amount to a grave encroachment on the legislative freedom of Members. In contrarst, in appropriate cases WTO panels and the Appellate Body (as well as other international tribunals) may defer to the national regulatory competence by characterizing the laws and regulations at stake as falling outside the sphere of international norms over which they have jurisdiction. Likewise, deference to matters of fact as well as law put forward by the respondent party to a dispute not only lies at the heart of the problem of standard of review in WTO dispute settlement, but also is central to the question of standard of review in international dispute settlement in general (Chapter 6). In this context, recall that the ECHR standard of review doctrine, i.e. the doctrine of margin of appreciation, has been described as "a doctrine of deference in the exercise of judicial review."[21] The determination of the meaning or content of national law as facts also raises critical issues of deference. As shown in Chapter 7, the

[21] See above, Chapter 6, n. 79.

establishment of the content of national law necessarily involves interpretation of national law. And in this regard a crucial methodological question is how far an international tribunal should accept (i.e. *defer* to) the interpretation or meaning attributed by the respondent state to its own laws, either internally by various governmental organs (e.g. courts and administrative bodies) or in the context of submissions before the tribunal.

A further value fundamental in ensuring proper balance between international obligations and national regulatory decisions is flexibility.[22] An international tribunal adjudicating disputes between states must retain a certain flexibility in its process and in its application of substantive rules, both for a successful resolution of the particular dispute under adjudication and for fostering a sustained support from the participant states for the adjudicative process. Given that the authority of international adjudicative organs rests on the relatively fragile foundations of the consent of "sovereign" nations, a lack of flexibility to accommodate the diverse points of view of various nations can lead not merely to antipathy but even to disintegration of the adjudicative process. In the WTO context, it has been noted earlier that in some circumstances an intrusive review of a national measure or law might entail a damaging confrontation between a panel and the respondent WTO Member over their respective spheres of authority, while in others conducting a lax review might empty the rights of the complainant, which again is a WTO Member, of real meaning. The task no doubt is a very delicate one; and this, by itself, calls for a certain amount of flexibility.

Apart from the generalized dimension of flexibility, various specific facets of flexibility have also been underscored in the preceding pages. Thus, in characterizing rules of national law, in some instances it may be appropriate to attribute to a rule the characterization of the legal system to which the rule belongs, while in others it may be necessary to attribute an autonomous characterization. Then again, cautions have been expressed as regards taking the process of autonomous characterization too far, such that the resulting characterization, although philosophically valid, is devoid of any basis in law and reality. A central argument developed in Chapter 6 concerned the context-dependent nature of the problem of standard of review. It has been pointed out time and

[22] Cf. de Búrca & Scott 2000 (this volume contains a set of interesting articles on the role of flexibility in the EU legal order).

again and has been illustrated by considering numerous practical examples that a particular standard of review is not apposite in reviewing every national measure, nor is the same standard appropriate in resolving every issue in the course of such review. Rather, the benchmark of intensity, rigor, thoroughness or severity of review ought to vary for a number of reasons, and so should the standard of review. Furthermore, in respect of the inter-relation between treaty interpretation and standard of review, it has been argued that WTO panels and the AB should remain true to a single and coherent interpretation of treaty provisions. Yet, the single interpretation should be wide and flexible enough to accommodate different national measures taken by different Members in different circumstances. In respect of interpretation of national laws, which has been one of the main themes of Chapter 7, the importance of reasoned judgments on a flexible case by case basis has been duly highlighted. Likewise, in Chapter 8 it has been argued that a case by case approach can be one of the techniques of avoiding intrusive decisions by panels in respect of Members' discretionary laws.

While on the one hand proper allocation of power entails that there should not be a usurpation of legitimate national authority by an international tribunal, on the other hand it requires that the effectiveness of both the international rules and the associated mechanism – if there is one – of international supervision are ensured. Indeed, this work has illustrated that, in respect of the relationship between WTO law and national law, the policy objective of effectiveness of international rules and supervision has both a constitutive and an evaluative role.

The general international law principle that national laws cannot be relied upon to avoid international obligations serves no other purpose than ensuring effectiveness of international obligations by preventing their evasion by means of domestic legislation. Through its systemic obligations regarding national law and its powerful dispute settlement system, the WTO treaty, however, goes much further than this general international law principle in ensuring effectiveness of the WTO obligations. For instance, systemic obligations ensure effectiveness of the WTO treaty in the domestic legal systems of WTO Members through international guarantees of "supremacy" of WTO law, as well as guarantees of transparency, fairness and judicial protection in favor of individuals. Effectiveness is a major hallmark of WTO dispute settlement. It is an attribute of the dispute settlement mechanism itself. In addition, through its contribution to resolution of disputes between parties, the dispute settlement system contributes significantly to the promotion of free trade and to the effectiveness of the WTO legal system as a whole. Chapters 3 and 4, devoted, respectively, to systemic obligations and dispute settlement, have explored these constitutive dimensions of effectiveness in respect of the relationship between WTO law and national law.

The evaluative function of effectiveness has been a recurring theme of Part II of this book. In Chapter 5 it has been seen that the entire approach of international tribunals towards the issue of characterization of rules of national law or national legal institutions is conditioned by a concern to ensure the effectiveness of international rules and supervision. Thus the concept of autonomous characterization has been developed by the ECHR to prevent the risk, in certain circumstances, of subordinating the operation of the Convention rights to the "sovereign will" of the contracting states. WTO organs also take the view that, if a domestic law characterization is regarded as providing the required connection for the applicability of WTO rules, then, in various instances, Members will be able to determine themselves whether, and if so which, WTO rules are to apply to their measures. In respect of standard of review it has been stressed in Chapter 6 that, from a policy point of view, it is of utmost importance that the benchmark of the rigor or thoroughness of review be tuned so as to avoid sacrificing the effectiveness of international adjudication, while ensuring proper deference to national authorities. Consequently, the ultimate authority to interpret the WTO treaty must rest with the WTO judiciary and not individual Members; and some control ought to be retained by the WTO judiciary over legal characterization issues (i.e. applying the law to the facts and determining the conformity of the facts with the law) as well. However, considerable deference may be accorded to national authorities on matters of fact. A key argument in Chapter 8 has been that a mechanistic application of the second limb of the mandatory/discretionary doctrine, according to which a discretionary law cannot violate WTO obligations, can fly in the face of effective international supervision. Accordingly, it has been suggested that a departure from that limb is justifiable in those very rare cases where, notwithstanding administrative discretion, the contested law is egregiously irreconcilable with the WTO obligations.

Like effectiveness, the policy objective of good governance at the domestic level also has constitutive and evaluative roles in respect of the relationship between WTO law and national law. The constitutive function of good governance has a number of different facets. First, a key object of the systemic obligations regarding availability of domestic remedies, and transparency and fairness in the adoption and administration of domestic laws and regulations, is to further good governance within national legal systems. Second, the guarantees of non-discrimination, substantive equality, proportionality, non-arbitrariness, non-abuse of domestic trade and foreign policy power contained in various substantive WTO obligations promote good governance in important ways. Third, WTO dispute settlement, which often operates as a further layer of judicial review of national laws and administrative measures, promotes good governance by acting as a check on national legislators and executives and by providing guarantees of rule of law. Chapters 3 and 4 have elaborated these constitutive features of good governance.

As seen in Chapter 6, standard of review is a crucial part of the system of checks and balances in governance, helping to ensure the accountability of decision-makers. It functions to allocate decision-making authority and resources in an efficient fashion among different branches and levels of governance. Thus, in essence, standard of review is concerned with good governance. It is therefore only natural that good governance would have important evaluative functions in respect of the review of the WTO-compatibility of national laws and measures. From the perspective of good governance, the overriding authority to interpret the WTO treaty should belong the WTO adjudicative organs, because those organs are accountable to the WTO membership and have comparative institutional advantages over individual Members in respect of treaty interpretation. By contrast, national authorities enjoy institutional advantages over international courts in respect of fact-finding or fact-assessment exercises. In respect of legal characterization, the institutional advantages of international courts and national authorities are relatively equipoised. Consequently, an international court should accord considerable deference to national authorities on matters of fact, while also according some deference on matters of legal characterization.

Good governance acts as a specific tool of review in respect of questions of both fact and legal characterization. For instance, factual decisions made by domestic authorities are often assessed on the basis of standards of review that focus on the governance processes that underpin their adoption. These standards of review promote good governance by making deliberative, transparent and rational decision- and rule-making relevant for the review of the legality of national measures. Good governance becomes relevant for legal characterization when the WTO provision under which the characterization is made incorporates elements of good governance (e.g. non-discrimination; proportionality;

non-arbitrariness; transparency; fair and equitable administration of laws; procedural fairness and due process; opportunity to be heard; providing formal, written and reasoned decisions; availability of review or appeal procedures; etc.). The Appellate Body has also demonstrated the innovativeness to extrapolate far-reaching good governance-spirited standards of review – such as standards condemning "unilateralism" and promoting deliberative decision- and rule-making – from relatively plain treaty language. It has been argued in Chapter 6 that, although in a variety of contexts good governance already functions as an important evaluative tool of review, its full potential as a standard of review is yet to be realized.

This work, of course, does not take the view that good governance is something that can be imposed in a truly effective and wholesome manner from the above. Efforts to ensure good governance in trade policy making and implementation must in the first place come from nation-states themselves who are WTO Members. However, the WTO process, including its dispute settlement, can make a useful contribution in that direction. It is therefore no wonder that criticisms about the "fairness" of the current state of trade liberalization under the WTO – for not having free or freer trade in agricultural products, for instance – also recognize the beneficial effects of the guarantees of "rule of law" that come from the WTO and its dispute settlement mechanism.[23]

The concluding prescription must be that the assessment and review of national measures and laws by international tribunals in general, and by the WTO bodies in particular, should be based upon an integrated understanding of the above-noted underlying values and policy objectives, as well as their interactions. An integrated grasp of those values, policy objectives and their interactions is vital both for furthering the international rule of law by exposing questionable national measures and for bolstering support for the international adjudicative process by showing due and necessary restraint in respect of rightful national decisions.

[23] See Stiglitz & Charlton 2005, 75.

References

Abbott, R. (1993), "GATT and the Trade Policy Review Mechanism: Further Reflections on Earlier Reflections," 27(3) JWT 117.

Abi-Saab, G. (2005), "The WTO Dispute Settlement and General International Law," in R. Yerxa & B. Wilson (eds.), *Key Issues in WTO Dispute Settlement: The First Ten Years* (Cambridge: Cambridge University Press) 7.

Akakwam, P. A. (1996), "The Standard of Review in the 1994 Antidumping Code: Circumscribing the Role of GATT Panels in Reviewing National Antidumping Determinations," 5 *Minnesota Journal of Global Trade* 277.

Alston, P. (2002), "Resisting the Merger and Acquisition of Human Rights by Trade Law: A Reply to Petersmann," 13 EJIL 815.

Alvarez, J. E. (1996), "Judging the Security Council," 90 AJIL 1.

(2002), "The WTO as Linkage Machine," 96 AJIL 146.

Amerasinghe, C. F. (2004), *Local Remedies in International Law* (Cambridge: Cambridge University Press).

Anderson, K. (2002), "Peculiarities of Retaliation in WTO Dispute Settlement," 1 *World Trade Review* 123.

Applebaum, H. M. & Schlitt, L. M. (1995), *The GATT, the WTO and the Uruguay Round Agreements Act: Understanding the Fundamental Changes* (New York: Practising Law Institute).

Appleton, A. E. (1999), "Shrimp/Turtle: Untangling the Nets," 2(3) JIEL 477.

Arai-Takahashi, Y. (2002), *The Margin of Appreciation Doctrine and the Principle of Proportionality in the Jurisprudence of the ECHR* (Antwerp, Oxford, New York: Intersentia).

Aust, A. (2000), *Modern Treaty Law and Practice* (Cambridge: Cambridge University Press).

Bacchus, J. (2002), "Table Talk: Around the Table of the Appellate Body of the World Trade Organization," 35(4) *Vanderbilt Journal of Transnational Law* 1021.

(2003), "The Appeals of Trade: The Making of an Old GATT Hand," address by James Bacchus, Chairman, Appellate Body, World Trade Organization, Geneva, Switzerland, to the International Trade Law Conference of the

American Bar Association, Georgetown University Law School, Washington, DC (January 31).

(2004), "A Few Thoughts on Legitimacy, Democracy, and the WTO," 7(3) JIEL 667.

Barfield, C. E. (2001), *Free Trade, Sovereignty, Democracy: The Future of the World Trade Organization* (Washington: AEI Press).

Bartels, L. (2001), "Applicable Law in WTO Dispute Settlement Proceedings," 35(3) JWT 499.

(2005), "The Appellate Body Report in *European Communities – Conditions for the Granting of Tariff Preferences to Developing Countries* and its Implications for Conditionality in GSP Programmes," in T. Cottier, J. Pauwelyn & E. Bürgi Bonanomi (eds.), *Human Rights and International Trade* (Oxford: Oxford University Press) 463.

Beckett, W. E. (1934), "The Question of Classification ('Qualification') in Private International Law," 15 BYIL 46.

Becroft, R. (2006), "The Standard of Review Strikes Back: The *US – Korea DRAMS* Appeal," 9(1) JIEL 207.

Bedjaoui, M. (2000), "Expediency in the Decisions of the International Court of Justice," 71 BYIL 1.

Bello, J. H. (1996), "The WTO Dispute Settlement Understanding: Less Is More," 90 AJIL 416.

Bernhardt, R. (1993), "The Convention and Domestic Law," in R. St. J. Macdonald, F. Matscher & H. Petzold (eds.), *The European System for the Protection of Human Rights* (Dordrecht, Boston, London: Martinus Nijhoff Publishers) 25.

Bethlehem, D. (1998), "International Law, European Community Law, National Law: Three Systems in Search of a Framework," in M. Koskenniemi (ed.), *International Law Aspects of the European Union* (The Hague, London, Boston: Kluwer Law International) 169.

(2000), "Submissions on Points of Fact and Law: Written and Oral Pleadings Before the International Court of Justice," in F. Weiss (ed.), *Improving WTO Dispute Settlement Procedures: Issues and Lessons from the Practice of Other International Courts and Tribunals* (London: Cameron May) 175.

Beviglia Zampetti, A. (2003), "Democratic Legitimacy in the World Trade Organization: The Justice Dimension," 37(1) JWT 105.

Bhagwati, J. (2002), "The Question of Linkage," 96 AJIL 126.

(2004), *In Defense of Globalization* (Oxford: Oxford University Press).

Bhagwati, J. & Patrick, H. T. (eds.) (1991), *Aggressive Unilateralism: America's 301 Trade Policy and the World Trading System* (New York: Harvester Wheatsheaf).

Bhala, R. (1999a), "The Myth about Stare Decisis and International Trade Law (Part One of a Trilogy)," 14 *American University International Law Review* 845.

(1999b), "The Precedent Setters: De Facto Stare Decisis in WTO Adjudication (Part Two of a Trilogy)," 9 *Florida State University Journal of Transnational Law and Policy* 1.

(2001), "The Power of the Past: Towards De Jure Stare Decisis in WTO Adjudication (Part Three of a Trilogy)," 33 *George Washington International Law Review* 873.

Bhuiyan, S. (2002), "Mandatory and Discretionary Legislation: The Continued Relevance of the Distinction under the WTO," 5(3) JIEL 571.

(2004), "Unreal Federal Clauses of the World Trade Organization Treaty: A Case for Removing the 'Apparent' Limitations on Implementation and Observance of World Trade Organization Commitments at Sub-national Levels," 38(1) JWT 123.

Bierman, L., Fraser, D. R. & Kolari, J. W. (1996), "The General Agreement on Tariffs and Trade: World Trade from a Market Perspective," 17 *University of Pennsylvania Journal of International Economic Law* 821.

Blackhurst, R. (1991), "Strengthening GATT Surveillance of Trade-Related Policies," in E.-U. Petersmann & M. Hilf (eds.), *The New GATT Round of Multilateral Trade Negotiations: Legal and Economic Problems* (2nd edn.; Deventer, Boston: Kluwer Law and Taxation Publishers) 123.

Bloche, M. G. (2002), "WTO Deference to National Health Policy: Toward an Interpretive Principle," 5(4) JIEL 825.

Bourgeois, J. H. J. (1998), "WTO Dispute Settlement in the Field of Anti-Dumping Law," 1(2) JIEL 259.

(2000a), "The European Court of Justice and the WTO: Problems and Challenges," in J. H. H. Weiler (ed.), *The EU, the WTO, and the NAFTA: Towards a Common Law of International Trade?* (Oxford: Oxford University Press) 71.

(2000b), "'Subsidiarity' in the WTO Context from a Legal Perspective," in M. Bronckers, & R. Quick (eds.), *New Directions in International Economic Law: Essays in Honour of John H. Jackson* (The Hague, London, Boston: Kluwer Law International) 35.

Bridge, J. (1984), "Procedural Aspects of the Enforcement of European Community Law through the Legal Systems of the Member States," 9 *European Law Review* 28.

Bronckers, M. & McNelis, N. (2000), "Fact and Law in Pleadings Before the WTO Appellate Body," in F. Weiss (ed.), *Improving WTO Dispute Settlement Procedures: Issues and Lessons from the Practice of Other International Courts and Tribunals* (London: Cameron May) 321.

Bronckers, M. & Quick, R. (eds.) (2000), *New Directions in International Economic Law: Essays in Honour of John H. Jackson* (The Hague, London, Boston: Kluwer Law International).

Brownlie, I. (1998), *Principles of Public International Law* (5th edn.; Oxford: Oxford University Press).

Cameron, J. & Campbell, K. (eds.) (1998), *Dispute Resolution in the World Trade Organisation* (London: Cameron May).

Cameron, J. & Gray, K. R. (2001), "Principles of International Law in the WTO Dispute Settlement Body," 50 *International and Comparative Law Quarterly* 248.

Cameron, J. & Orava, S. J. (2000), "GATT/WTO Panels Between Recording and Finding Facts: Issues of Due Process, Evidence, Burden of Proof, and Standard of Review in GATT/WTO Dispute Settlement," in F. Weiss (ed.), *Improving WTO Dispute Settlement Procedures: Issues and Lessons from the Practice of Other International Courts and Tribunals* (London: Cameron May) 195.

Cannizzaro, E. (2001), "The Role of Proportionality in the Law of International Countermeasures," 12 EJIL 889.

Carmody, C. (2002), "Remedies and Conformity under the WTO Agreement," 5(2) JIEL 307.

Carozza, P. G. (2003), "Subsidiarity as a Structural Principle of International Human Rights Law," 97 AJIL 38.

Cass, D. Z. (2001), "The 'Constitutionalization' of International Trade Law: Judicial Norm-Generation as the Engine of Constitutional Development in International Trade," 12(1) EJIL 39.

(2005), *The Constitutionalization of the World Trade Organization: Legitimacy, Democracy, and Community in the International Trading System* (Oxford: Oxford University Press).

Cassese, A. (2001), *International Law* (Oxford: Oxford University Press).

Charnovitz, S. (2001), "Rethinking WTO Trade Sanctions," 95 AJIL 792.

Chayes, A. & Chayes, A. H. (1995), *The New Sovereignty: Compliance with International Regulatory Agreements* (Cambridge, MA: Harvard University Press).

Cheng, B. (1987), *General Principles of Law as Applied by International Courts and Tribunals* [1953] (reprinted, Cambridge: Grotius Publications Limited).

Cho, S.-J. (1998), "GATT Non-Violation Issues in the WTO Framework: Are They the Achilles' Heel of the Dispute Settlement Process?" 39 *Harvard International Law Journal* 311.

(2004), "A Bridge Too Far: The Fall of the Fifth WTO Ministerial Conference in Cancún and the Future of Trade Constitution," 7(2) JIEL 219.

Christoforou, T. (2000), "WTO Panels in the Face of Scientific Uncertainty," in F. Weiss (ed.), *Improving WTO Dispute Settlement Procedures: Issues and Lessons from the Practice of Other International Courts and Tribunals* (London: Cameron May) 243.

Clarkson, C. M. V. & Hill, J. (1997), *Jaffey on the Conflict of Laws* (London, Edinburgh, Dublin: Butterworths).

Clayton, R. & Tomlinson, H. (2000), *The Law of Human Rights* (Oxford: Oxford University Press).

Collier, J. & Lowe, V. (1999), *The Settlement of Disputes in International Law: Institutions and Procedures* (Oxford: Oxford University Press).

Collins, L. (ed.) (2000), *Dicey and Morris on the Conflict of Laws* (13th edn.; London: Sweet & Maxwell).

Cottier, T. & Schefer, K. N. (1997), "Non-Violation Complaints in WTO/GATT Dispute Settlement: Past, Present and Future," in E.-U. Petersmann (ed.), *International Trade Law and the GATT/WTO Dispute Settlement System* (London, The Hague, Boston: Kluwer Law International) 143.

(1998), "The Relationship Between World Trade Organization Law, National and Regional Law," 1(1) JIEL 83.

Cottier, T., Pauwelyn, J. & Bürgi Bonanomi, E. (eds.) (2005), *Human Rights and International Trade* (Oxford: Oxford University Press).

Craig, P. (2001), "Constitutions, Constitutionalism, and the European Union," 7(2) *European Law Journal* 125.

Craig, P. & de Búrca, G. (1998), *EU Law: Text, Cases, and Materials* (Oxford: Oxford University Press).

Crawford, J. (2002), *The International Law Commission's Articles on State Responsibility: Introduction, Text and Commentaries* (Cambridge: Cambridge University Press).

Croley, S. P. & Jackson, J. H. (1996), "WTO Dispute Procedures, Standard of Review, and Deference to National Governments," 90 AJIL 193.

Croome, J. (1999), *Reshaping the World Trading System: A History of the Uruguay Round* (The Hague, London, Boston: Kluwer Law International).

Cunningham, R. O. & Cribb, T. H. (2003), "Dispute Settlement Through the Lens of 'Free Flow of Trade': A Review of WTO Dispute Settlement of US Anti-Dumping and Countervailing Duty Measures," 6(1) JIEL 155.

D'Angelo, D. (2000), "The 'Check' on International Peace and Security Maintenance: The International Court of Justice and Judicial Review of Security Council Resolutions," 23 *Suffolk Transnational Law Review* 561.

Davey, W. J. (2001), "Has the WTO Dispute Settlement System Exceeded its Authority? A Consideration of Deference Shown by the System to Member Government Decisions and its Use of Issue-Avoidance Techniques," 4(1) JIEL 79.

(2006), "The WTO: Looking Forwards," 9(1) JIEL 3.

Davey, W. J. & Morrison, P. (1997), *Dispute Resolution in the World Trade Organization: Proceedings of the Second Annual Conference on Dispute Resolution in the World Trade Organization* (Geneva: WTO).

Davies, A. (2004), "Mandatory and Discretionary Legislation in WTO Law: A Distinction Worth Preserving?" 31(3) *Legal Issues of Economic Integration* 185.

de Búrca, G. & Scott, J. (eds.) (2000), *Constitutional Change in the EU: From Uniformity to Flexibility?* (Oxford: Hart Publishing).

(eds.) (2001), *The EU and the WTO: Legal and Constitutional Issues* (Oxford: Hart Publishing).

Delaume, G. R. (1981), "State Contracts and Transnational Arbitration," 75 AJIL 784.

Denza, E. (2003), "The Relationship Between International and National Law," in M. D. Evans (ed.), *International Law* (Oxford: Oxford University Press) 415.

Desmedt, A. (2001), "Proportionality in WTO Law," 4(3) JIEL 441.

Desmedt, G. A. (1998), "Hormones: 'Objective Assessment' and (or as) Standard of Review," 1(4) JIEL 695.

Dunoff, J. L. (1992), "Reconciling International Trade with Preservation of the Global Commons: Can We Prosper and Protect?" 49 *Washington and Lee Law Review* 1407.

(2006), "Constitutional Conceits: The WTO's 'Constitution' and the Discipline of International Law," 17(3) EJIL 647.

Durling, J. P. (2003), "Deference, But Only When Due: WTO Review of Anti-Dumping Measures," 6(1) JIEL 125.

Durling, J. P. & Hardin, D. (2005), "Amicus Curiae Participation in WTO Dispute Settlement: Reflections on the Past Decade," in R. Yerxa & B. Wilson (eds.), *Key Issues in WTO Dispute Settlement: The First Ten Years* (Cambridge: Cambridge University Press) 221.

Eeckhout, P. (1997), "The Domestic Legal Status of the WTO Agreement: Interconnecting Legal Systems," 34(1) *Common Market Law Review* 11.

(2002), "Judicial Enforcement of WTO Law in the European Union: Some Further Reflections," 5(1) JIEL 91.

Ehlermann, C.-D. (2002), "Six Years on the Bench of the 'World Trade Court': Some Personal Experiences as Member of the Appellate Body of the World Trade Organization," 36(4) JWT 605.

(2003), "Reflections on the Appellate Body of the WTO," 6(3) JIEL 695.

Ehlermann, C.-D. & Lockhart, N. (2004), "Standard of Review in WTO Law," 7(3) JIEL 491.

Eisenmann, P. M. (ed.) (1996), *The Integration of International and European Community Law into the National Legal Order* (Deventer: Kluwer Law International).

Eissen, M.-A. (1993), "The Principle of Proportionality in the Case-Law of the European Court of Human Rights," in R. St. J. Macdonald, F. Matscher & H. Petzold (eds.), *The European System for the Protection of Human Rights* (Dordrecht, Boston, London: Martinus Nijhoff Publishers) 125.

Ellis, E. (ed.) (1999), *The Principle of Proportionality in the Laws of Europe* (Oxford: Hart).

Emiliou, N. (1996), *The Principle of Proportionality in European Law: A Comparative Study* (London, The Hague, Boston: Kluwer Law International).

Estella, A. (2002), *The EU Principle of Subsidiarity and its Critique* (Oxford: Oxford University Press).

Esty, D. C. (2002), "The World Trade Organization's Legitimacy Crisis," 1(1) *World Trade Review* 7.

(2006), "Good Governance at the Supranational Scale: Globalizing Administrative Law," 115 *Yale Law Journal* 1490.

Fentiman, R. (1998), *Foreign Law in English Courts: Pleading, Proof and Choice of Law* (Oxford: Oxford University Press).

Finger, J. M. (2005), "The Future of the World Trade Organization: Addressing Institutional Challenges in the New Millennium – A Review," 39(4) JWT 795.

Fitzmaurice, G. (1957), "The General Principles of International Law Considered from the Standpoint of the Rule of Law," 92 *Recueil des Cours* (II).

(1959), "The Law and Procedure of the International Court of Justice, 1954–9: General Principles and Sources of International Law," 35 BYIL 183.

Franck, T. M. (1975), "Word Made Law: The Decision of the ICJ in the Nuclear Test Cases," 69 AJIL 612.

(1992), "The 'Powers of Appreciation': Who Is the Ultimate Guardian of UN Legality?" 86 AJIL 519.

Fukunaga, Y. (2006), "Securing Compliance through the WTO Dispute Settlement System: Implementation of DSB Recommendations," 9(2) JIEL 383.

Gaja, G. (1992), "Positivism and Dualism in Dionisio Anzilotti," 3(1) EJIL 123.

Gantz, D. A. (2000), "Government-to-Government Dispute Resolution under NAFTA's Chapter 20: A Commentary on the Process," 11 *American Review of International Arbitration* 481.

GAO (2003), *World Trade Organization: Standard of Review and Impact of Trade Remedy Rulings* (Washington, DC: United States General Accounting Office, July), available at the GAO website, www.gao.gov.

Garcia-Rubio, M. (2001), *On the Application of Customary Rules of State Responsibility by the WTO Dispute Settlement Organs: A General International Law Perspective* (Geneva: Institut Universitaire de Hautes Etudes Internationales).

Gardam, J. G. (1993), "Proportionality and Force in International Law," 87 AJIL 391.

Gathii, J. T. (2001), "Re-characterizing the Social in the Constitutionalization of the WTO: A Preliminary Analysis," 7 *Widener Law Symposium Journal* 137.

Gerhart, P. M. (2003), "The Two Constitutional Visions of the World Trade Organization," 24 *University of Pennsylvania Journal of International Economic Law* 1.

Goh, G. (2006), "Tipping the Apple Cart: The Limits of Science and Law in the SPS Agreement after *Japan – Apples*," 40(4) JWT 655.

Goh, G. & Ziegler, A. R. (2003), "Retrospective Remedies in the WTO after *Automotive Leather*," 6(3) JIEL 545.

Gomula, J. (1999), "The Standard of Review of Article 17.6 of the Anti-Dumping Agreement and the Problem of Its Extension to other WTO Agreements," in P. Mengozzi (ed.), *International Trade Law on the 50th Anniversary of the Multilateral Trade System* (Milan: Dott. A. Giuffre Editore) 577.

Gonzalez, J. P. (1995), "The Principle of Subsidiarity (A Guide for Lawyers with a Particular Community Orientation)," 20(4) *European Law Review* 355.

Gowlland-Debbas, V. (1994), "The Relationship Between the International Court of Justice and the Security Council in the Light of the *Lockerbie* Case," 88 AJIL 643.

Grane, P. (2001), "Remedies under WTO Law," 4(4) JIEL 755.

Gray, C. (1987), *Judicial Remedies in International Law* (Oxford: Clarendon Press).

(1996), "Bosnia and Herzegovina: Civil War or Inter-State Conflict? Characterization and Consequences," 67 BYIL 155.

(2000), "Types of Remedies in ICJ Cases: Lessons for the WTO?" in F. Weiss (ed.), *Improving WTO Dispute Settlement Procedures: Issues and Lessons from the Practice of Other International Courts and Tribunals* (London: Cameron May) 401.

Greenwood, C. (1982), "State Contracts in International Law: The Libyan Oil Arbitrations," 53 BYIL 27.

Griller, S. (2000), "Judicial Enforceability of WTO Law in the European Union," 3(3) JIEL 441.

Guruswamy, L. D. (1998), "Should UNCLOS or GATT/WTO Decide Trade and Environment Disputes?" 7 *Minnesota Journal of Global Trade* 287.

Habermas, J. (1984), *The Theory of Communicative Action: Reason and the Rationalization of Society*, trans. T. McCarthy (Cambridge: Polity).

(1996), *Between Facts and Norms: Contributions to a Discourse Theory of Law and Democracy*, trans. W. Rehg (Cambridge, MA: MIT Press).

Hansen, M. & Vermulst, E. (1989), "The GATT Protocol of Provisional Application: A Dying Grandfather?" 27(2) *Columbia Journal of Transnational Law* 263.

Hansen, P. I. (1999), "Transparency, Standards of Review, and the Use of Trade Measures to Protect the Global Environment," 39 *Virginia Journal of International Law* 1017.

Harris, D. J. (1998), *Cases and Materials on International Law* (5th edn.; London: Sweet & Maxwell).

Harris, D. J., O'Boyle, M. & Warbrick, C. (1995), *Law of the European Convention on Human Rights* (London, Dublin, Edinburgh: Butterworths).

Helfer, L. R. (1999), "Forum Shopping for Human Rights," 148 *University of Pennsylvania Law Review* 285.

Henkin, L. (1979), *How Nations Behave: Law and Foreign Policy* (New York: Columbia University Press).

(1996), *Foreign Affairs and the United States Constitution* (Oxford: Clarendon Press).

Higgins, D. R. (2000), "Dualism in the Face of a Changing Legal Culture," in M. Andenas & D. Fairgrieve (eds.), *Judicial Review in International Perspective: Liber Amicorum in Honour of Lord Slynn of Hadley* (The Hague, London, Boston: Kluwer Law International) 9.

Hilf, M. (1997), "The Role of National Courts in International Trade Relations," 18 *Michigan Journal of International Law* 321.

(2001), "Power, Rules and Principles – Which Orientation for WTO/GATT Law?" 4(1) JIEL 111.

Hilf, M. & Petersmann, E.-U. (eds.) (1993), *National Constitutions and International Economic law* (Deventer: Kluwer Law and Taxation Publishers).

Holmes, P. (2001), "The WTO and the EU: Some Constitutional Comparisons," in G. de Búrca & J. Scott (eds.), *The EU and the WTO: Legal and Constitutional Issues* (Oxford: Hart Publishing) 59.

Horlick, G. N. (2002), "Problems with the Compliance Structure of the WTO Dispute Resolution Process," in D. L. M. Kennedy & J. D. Southwick (eds.), *The Political Economy of International Trade Law: Essays in Honor of Robert E. Hudec* (Cambridge: Cambridge University Press) 636.

Horlick, G. N. & Clarke, P. A. (1997), "Standards for Panels Reviewing Anti-dumping Determinations under the GATT and WTO," in E.-U.

Petersmann (ed.), *International Trade Law and the GATT/WTO Dispute Settlement System* (London, The Hague, Boston: Kluwer Law International) 313.

Horn, H. & Mavroidis, P. C. (2004), "Still Hazy after All These Years: The Interpretation of National Treatment in the GATT/WTO Case-law on Tax Discrimination," 15(1) EJIL 39.

Howse, R. (2000), "Adjudicative Legitimacy and Treaty Interpretation in International Trade Law: The Early Years of WTO Jurisprudence," in J. H. H. Weiler (ed.), *The EU, the WTO and the NAFTA: Towards a Common Law of International Trade?* (Oxford: Oxford University Press) 35.

Howse, R. & Nicolaidis, K. (2001), "Legitimacy and Global Governance: Why Constitutionalizing the WTO Is a Step Too Far," in R. B. Porter, P. Sauvé, A. Subramanian & A. Beviglia Zampetti (eds.), *Efficiency, Equity, and Legitimacy: The Multilateral Trading System at the Millennium* (Washington, DC: Brookings Institution Press) 227.

(2003), "Legitimacy through 'Higher Law'? Why Constitutionalizing the WTO Is a Step Too Far," in T. Cottier & P. C. Mavroidis (eds.), *The Role of the Judge in International Trade Regulation: Experience and Lessons for the WTO* (Ann Arbor, MI: University of Michigan Press) 307.

Hu, J. (2004), "The Role of International Law in the Development of WTO Law," 7(1) JIEL 143.

Hudec, R. E. (1993), *Enforcing International Trade Law: The Evolution of the Modern GATT Legal System* (Salem, NH: Butterworth Legal Publishers).

(1998), "GATT/WTO Constraints on National Regulation: Requiem for an 'Aim and Effects' Test," 32 *International Lawyer* 619.

(1999), *Essays on the Nature of International Trade Law* (London: Cameron May).

(2000a), "Broadening the Scope of Remedies in WTO Dispute Settlement," in F. Weiss (ed.), *Improving WTO Dispute Settlement Procedures: Issues and Lessons from the Practice of Other International Courts and Tribunals* (London: Cameron May) 369.

(2000b), "The Product–Process Doctrine in GATT/WTO Jurisprudence," in M. Bronckers & R. Quick (eds.), *New Directions in International Economic Law: Essays in Honour of John H. Jackson* (The Hague, London, Boston: Kluwer Law International) 187.

(2003), "Industrial Subsidies: Tax Treatment of 'Foreign Sales Corporations,'" in E.-U. Petersmann & M. A. Pollack (eds.), *Transatlantic Economic Disputes: The EU, the US, and the WTO* (Oxford: Oxford University Press) 175.

Hudec, R. E., Kennedy, D. L. M. & Sgarbossa, M. (1993), "A Statistical Profile of GATT Dispute Settlement Cases: 1948–1989," 2 *Minnesota Journal of Global Trade* 1 (1993).

Hughes, L. (1998), "Limiting the Jurisdiction of Dispute Settlement Panels: The WTO Appellate Body Beef Hormone Decision," 10 *Georgetown International Environmental Law Review* 915.

Hughes, V. (2005), "Special Challenges at the Appellate Stage: A Case Study," in R. Yerxa & B. Wilson (eds.), *Key Issues in WTO Dispute Settlement: The First Ten Years* (Cambridge: Cambridge University Press) 80.

Hurst, D. R. (1998), "Hormones: European Communities – Measures Affecting Meat and Meat Products," 9(1) EJIL 182, text available at the EJIL website, www.ejil.org.

Iwasawa, Y. (2000), "WTO Dispute Settlement and Japan," in M. Bronckers & R. Quick (eds.), *New Directions in International Economic Law: Essays in Honour of John H. Jackson* (The Hague, London, Boston: Kluwer Law International) 473.

(2002), "WTO Dispute Settlement as Judicial Supervision," 5(2) JIEL 287.

Jackson, J. H. (1969), *World Trade and the Law of GATT* (Indianapolis: Bobbs-Merrill).

(1978), "The Jurisprudence of International Trade: The DISC Case in GATT," 72 AJIL 747.

(1992), "Status of Treaties in Domestic Legal Systems: A Policy Analysis," 86 AJIL 310.

(1997a), *The World Trading System: Law and Policy of International Economic Relations* (2nd edn.; Cambridge, MA, London: MIT Press).

(1997b), "The WTO Dispute Settlement Understanding – Misunderstandings on the Nature of Legal Obligation," 91 AJIL 60.

(1997c), "The Great 1994 Sovereignty Debate: United States Acceptance and Implementation of the Uruguay Round Results," 36 *Columbia Journal of Transnational Law* 157.

(1998), *The World Trade Organization: Constitution and Jurisprudence* (London: Royal Institute of International Affairs).

(2001), "The WTO 'Constitution' and Proposed Reforms: Seven 'Mantras' Revisited," 4(1) JIEL 67.

(2002), "Sovereignty, Subsidiarity, and Separation of Powers: The High-Wire Balancing Act of Globalization," in D. L. M. Kennedy & J. D. Southwick (eds.), *The Political Economy of International Trade Law: Essays in Honor of Robert E. Hudec* (Cambridge: Cambridge University Press) 13.

(2003), "Sovereignty-Modern: A New Approach to an Outdated Concept," 97 AJIL 782.

(2004), "International Law Status of WTO Dispute Settlement Reports: Obligation to Comply or Option to 'Buy Out'?" 98 AJIL 109.

(2006), *Sovereignty, the WTO and Changing Fundamentals of International Law* (Cambridge: Cambridge University Press).

Jackson, J. H., Davey, W. J. & Sykes, A. O. (1995), *Legal Problems of International Economic Relations* (St. Paul, MN: West Group).

Jackson, J. H. & Sykes, A. O. (eds.) (1997), *Implementing the Uruguay Round* (Oxford: Clarendon Press).

Jacobs, F. & Roberts, S. (eds.) (1987), *The Effects of Treaties in Domestic Law* (London: Sweet & Maxwell).

Jenks, C. W. (1938), "The Interpretational and Application of Municipal Law by the Permanent Court of International Justice," 19 BYIL 67.

(1964), *The Prospects of International Adjudication* (London: Stevens & Sons Limited).

Jennings, R. (1961), "State Contracts in International Law," 37 BYIL 156.
Jennings, R. & Watts, A. (eds.) (1992), *Oppenheim's International Law*, vol. I (9th edn.; Harlow: Longman).
Joergens, K. J. (1999), "True Appellate Procedure or Only a Two-Stage Process? A Comparative View of the Appellate Body under the WTO Dispute Settlement Understanding," 30 *Law and Policy in International Business* 193.
Joerges, C., Sand, I.-J. & Teubner, G. (eds.) (2004), *Transnational Governance and Constitutionalism* (Oxford: Hart Publishing).
Jürgensen, T. (2005), "Crime and Punishment: Retaliation under the World Trade Organization Dispute Settlement System," 39(2) JWT 327.
Kazazi, M. (1996), *Burden of Proof and Related Issues: A Study on Evidence Before International Tribunals* (The Hague, London, Boston: Kluwer Law International).
Kearns, J. E. & Charnovitz, S. (2002), "Adjudicating Compliance in the WTO: A Review of DSU Article 21.5," 5(2) JIEL 331.
Kelly, J. P. (2001), "The WTO and Global Governance: The Case for Contractual Treaty Regimes," 7 *Widener Law Symposium Journal* 109.
(2002), "Judicial Activism at the World Trade Organization: Developing Principles of Self-Restraint," 22 *Northwestern Journal of International Law and Business* 353.
Kelsen, H. (1949), *General Theory of Law and State* [1945], trans. A. Wedberg (Cambridge, MA: Harvard University Press).
(1966), *Principles of International Law*, rev. & ed. R. W. Tucker (2nd edn.; New York, London: Holt, Rinehart and Winston).
Kennedy, D. (1994), "The International Style in Postwar Law and Policy," *Utah Law Review* 7.
Kennedy, D. L. M. & Southwick, J. D. (2002), *The Political Economy of International Trade Law: Essays in Honor of Robert E. Hudec* (Cambridge: Cambridge University Press).
Kennedy, R. F. (1993), "*Libya v. United States*: The International Court of Justice and the Power of Judicial Review," 33 *Virginia Journal of International Law* 899.
Keyser, P. D. (2001), "Exploring WTO Dispute Settlement in *US Anti-Dumping Act 1916*: An Easy Case?" Jean Monnet Working Paper 11/01, available at www.jeanmonnetprogram.org.
Kingsbury, B. (1999), "Is the Proliferation of International Courts and Tribunals a Systemic Problem?" 31 *New York University Journal of International Law and Politics* 679.
Koh, H. H. (1997), "Why Do Nations Obey International Law?" 106 *Yale Law Journal* 2599.
Krajewski, M. (2001), "Democratic Legitimacy and Constitutional Perspectives of WTO Law," 35(1) JWT 167.
Krisch, N. & Kingsbury, B. (2006), "Global Governance and Global Administrative Law in the International Legal Order," 17(1) EJIL 1.

Kuilwijk, K. J. (1997), "Castro's Cuba and the US Helms-Burton Act: An Interpretation of the GATT Security Exemption," 31(3) JWT 49.

Kuyper, P. J. (1994), "The Law of GATT as a Special Field of International Law: Ignorance, Further Refinement or Self-Contained System of International Law?" 25 *Netherlands Yearbook of International Law* 227.

(1995), "The New WTO Dispute Settlement System: The Impact on the Community," in J. H. J. Bourgeois, F. Berrod & E. G. Fournier (eds.), *The Uruguay Round Results: A European Lawyers' Perspective* (Brussels: European Interuniversity Press) 87.

(1997), "Remedies and Retaliation in the WTO: Are They Likely to be Effective? The State Perspective and the Company Perspective," 91 *American Society of International Law Proceedings* 282.

(2000), "The Appellate Body and the Facts," in M. Bronckers & R. Quick (eds.), *New Directions in International Economic Law: Essays in Honour of John H. Jackson* (The Hague, London, Boston: Kluwer Law International) 309.

Lacarte, J. A. (2004), "Transparency, Public Debate and Participation by NGOs in the WTO: A WTO Perspective," 7(3) JIEL 683.

Lalive, J.-F. (1964), "Contracts Between a State or a State Agency and a Foreign Company," 13 *International and Comparative Law Quarterly* 987.

Lamy, P. (2006), Statement by Pascal Lamy, Director-General of the WTO, before the European Parliament Committee on International Trade, Brussels (October 17), available in the news archives of the WTO, www.wto.org.

Lauterpacht, H. (1950), *International Law and Human Rights* (London: Stevens & Sons Limited).

(1975), "Is International Law Part of the Law of England?" 25 *Transactions of the Grotius Society* 51 [1939], reprinted in E. Lauterpacht (ed.), *International Law: Being the Collected Papers of Hersch Lauterpacht*, vol. II (Cambridge: Cambridge University Press) 537.

Lauwaars, R. H. (2000), "Interpretations of International Agreements by National Courts: An EC View," in M. Bronckers & R. Quick (eds.), *New Directions in International Economic Law: Essays in Honour of John H. Jackson* (The Hague, London, Boston: Kluwer Law International) 509.

Lavender, N. (1997), "The Problem of the Margin of Appreciation," 2 *European Human Rights Law Review* 380.

Leitner, K. & Lester, S. (2007), "WTO Dispute Settlement 1995–2006: A Statistical Analysis," 10(1) JIEL 165.

Lennard, M. (2002), "Navigating by the Stars: Interpreting the WTO Agreements," 5(1) JIEL 17.

Lester, Lord (1998), "Universality versus Subsidiarity: A Reply," 3(1) *European Human Rights Law Review* 73.

Lester, S. N. (2001), "WTO Panel and the Appellate Body Interpretations of the WTO Agreement in US Law," 35(3) JWT 521.

Letsas, G. (2004), "The Truth in Autonomous Concepts: How to Interpret the ECHR," 15(2) EJIL 279.

Lew, J. D. M. (1978), *Applicable Law in International Commercial Arbitration: A Study in Commercial Arbitration Awards* (Dobbs Ferry, NY: Oceana Publications).

Lewis, C. (1996), *Remedies and the Enforcement of European Community Law* (London: Sweet & Maxwell).

Lindroos, A. & Mehling, M. (2005), "Dispelling the Chimera of 'Self-Contained Regimes': International Law and the WTO," 16 EJIL 857.

Long, O. (1987), *Law and its Limitations in the GATT Multilateral Trade System* (London, Dordrecht, Boston: Graham & Trotman, Martinus Nijhoff).

Louis, J.-V. (2000), "Some Reflections on the Implementation of WTO Rules in the European Community Legal Order," in M. Bronckers & R. Quick (eds.), *New Directions in International Economic Law: Essays in Honour of John H. Jackson* (The Hague, London, Boston: Kluwer Law International) 493.

Lowenfeld, A. F. (1991), "Binational Dispute Settlement under Chapter 19 of the Canada – United States Free Trade Agreement: An Interim Appraisal," 24 *New York University Journal of International Law and Politics* 269.

(2002), *International Economic Law* (Oxford: Oxford University Press).

Lugard, M. (1998), "Scope of Appellate Review: Objective Assessment of the Facts and Issues of Law," 1(2) JIEL 323.

Luzzatto, R. (1977), "International Commercial Arbitration and the Municipal Law of States," 157 *Recueil des Cours* (IV).

Macdonald, R. St. J. (1993), "The Margin of Appreciation," in R. St. J. Macdonald, F. Matscher & H. Petzold (eds.), *The European System for the Protection of Human Rights* (Dordrecht, Boston, London: Martinus Nijhoff Publishers) 83.

Magnus, J. (2005), "Compliance with WTO Dispute Settlement Decisions: Is There a Crisis?" in R. Yerxa & B. Wilson (eds.), *Key Issues in WTO Dispute Settlement: The First Ten Years* (Cambridge: Cambridge University Press) 242.

Mahoney, P. (1997), "Universality versus Subsidiarity in the Strasbourg Case Law on Free Speech: Explaining Some Recent Judgments," 2(4) *European Human Rights Law Review* 364.

Malanczuk, P. (1997), *Akehurst's Modern Introduction to International Law* (7th edn.; London, New York: Routledge).

Mann, F. A. (1959), "The Proper Law of Contracts Concluded by International Persons," 35 BYIL 34.

Marceau, G. (1995), "Transition from GATT to WTO: A Most Pragmatic Operation," 29(4) JWT 147.

(1999), "A Call for Coherence in International Law: Praises for the Prohibition Against 'Clinical Isolation' in WTO Dispute Settlement," 33 JWT 5.

(2001), "Conflicts of Norms and Conflicts of Jurisdictions: The Relationship between the WTO Agreement and MEAs and other Treaties," 35(6) JWT 1081.

(2002), "WTO Dispute Settlement and Human Rights," 13 EJIL 753.

Marceau, G. & Trachtman, J. P. (2002), "The Technical Barriers to Trade Agreement, the Sanitary and Phytosanitary Measures Agreement, and the General Agreement on Tariffs and Trade: A Map of the World Trade Organization Law of Domestic Regulation of Goods," 36(5) JWT 811.

Martha, R. S. J. (1996), "World Trade Dispute Settlement and the Exhaustion of Local Remedies Rule," 30(4) JWT 107.

Matsushita, M., Schoenbaum, T. J. & Mavroidis, P. C. (2003), *The World Trade Organization: Law, Practice, and Policy* (Oxford: Oxford University Press).

Mavroidis, P. C. (1992), "Surveillance Schemes: The GATT's New Trade Policy Review Mechanism," 13 *Michigan Journal of International Law* 374.

McCrudden, C. & Gross, S. G. (2006), "WTO Government Procurement Rules and the Local Dynamics of Procurement Policies: A Malaysian Case Study," 17 EJIL 151.

McGivern, B. (2005), "Implementation of Panel and Appellate Body Rulings: An Overview," in R. Yerxa & B. Wilson (eds.), *Key Issues in WTO Dispute Settlement: The First Ten Years* (Cambridge: Cambridge University Press) 98.

McNair, Lord (1961), *The Law of Treaties* (Oxford: Clarendon Press).

McNelis, N. (2001), "The Role of the Judge in the EU and WTO: Lessons from the *BSE* and *Hormones* Cases," 4(1) JIEL 189.

McRae, D. (1998), "The Emerging Appellate Jurisdiction in International Trade Law," in J. Cameron & K. Campbell (eds.), *Dispute Resolution in the World Trade Organisation* (London: Cameron May) 98.

(2000), "GATT Article XX and the WTO Appellate Body," in M. Bronckers & R. Quick (eds.), *New Directions in International Economic Law: Essays in Honour of John H. Jackson* (The Hague, London, Boston: Kluwer Law International) 219.

(2004), "What is the Future of WTO Dispute Settlement?" 7(1) JIEL 3.

Mercury, J. M. (1995), "Chapter 19 of the United States – Canada Free Trade Agreement 1989–95: A Check on Administered Protection?" 15 *Northwestern Journal of International Law and Business* 525.

Mitchell, A. (2005), "Due Process in WTO Disputes," in R. Yerxa & B. Wilson (eds.), *Key Issues in WTO Dispute Settlement: The First Ten Years* (Cambridge: Cambridge University Press) 144.

Monnier, P. (2001), "The Time to Comply with an Adverse WTO Ruling: Promptness within Reason," 35(5) JWT 825.

Monroe, B. R. (2003), "WTO Dispute Settlement Procedure Bibliography," 6(3) JIEL 745.

Montaguti, E. & Lugard, M. (2000), "The GATT 1994 and Other Annex 1A Agreements: Four Different Relationships?" 3(3) JIEL 473.

Moore, J. B. (1898), *History and Digest of the International Arbitrations to Which the United States Has Been a Party*, vol. I (Washington: Government Printing Office).

Moore, M. (2002), "Foreword by the Director-General of the WTO," 1(1) *World Trade Review* 3.

Moore, P. M. (1996), "The Decisions Bridging the GATT 1947 and the WTO Agreement," 90 AJIL 317.

Morgenstern, F. (1950), "Judicial Practice and the Supremacy of International Law," 27 BYIL 42.

Morris, J. H. C. & McClean, D. (2000), *The Conflict of Laws* (5th edn.; London: Sweet & Maxwell).

Morrisson, C. C. Jr. (1973), "Margin of Appreciation in European Human Rights Law," 6 *Revue des Droits de l'Homme (Human Rights Journal)* 263.

Moyer, H. E. (1993), "Chapter 19 of the NAFTA: Binational Panels as the Trade Courts of Last Resort," 27 *International Lawyer* 707.

Mueller-Holyst, B. (2005), "The Role of the Dispute Settlement Body in the Dispute Settlement Process," in R. Yerxa & B. Wilson (eds.), *Key Issues in WTO Dispute Settlement: The First Ten Years* (Cambridge: Cambridge University Press) 25.

Murphy, S. D. (1999), "Contemporary Practice of the United States Relating to International Law," 93 AJIL 879.

Naiki, Y. (2004), "The Mandatory/Discretionary Doctrine in WTO Law: The *US – Section 301* Case and its Aftermath," 7(1) JIEL 23.

North, P. & Fawcett, J. J. (1999), *Cheshire and North's Private International Law* (13th edn.; London, Edinburgh, Dublin: Butterworths).

O'Connor, S. D. (2001), "Altered States: Federalism and Devolution at the 'Real' Turn of the Millennium," 60(3) *Cambridge Law Journal* 493.

O'Donnell, T. A. (1982), "The Margin of Appreciation Doctrine: Standards in the Jurisprudence of the European Court of Human Rights," 4(4) *Human Rights Quarterly* 474.

Odell, J. S. (2005), "Chairing a WTO Negotiation," 8(2) JIEL 425.

Oesch, M. (2003a), "Standards of Review in WTO Dispute Resolution," 6(3) JIEL 635.

(2003b), *Standards of Review in WTO Dispute Resolution* (Oxford: Oxford University Press).

Ohlhoff, S. & Schloemann, H. L. (1998), "Rational Allocation of Disputes and 'Constitutionalisation': Forum Choice as an Issue of Competence," in J. Cameron & K. Campbell (eds.), *Dispute Resolution in the World Trade Organisation* (London: Cameron May) 302.

Oppenheimer, A. (1994), *The Relationship Between European Community Law and National Law: The Cases* (Cambridge: Cambridge University Press).

Orrego Vicuña, F. (2004), *International Dispute Settlement in an Evolving Global Society: Constitutionalization, Accessibility, Privatization* (Cambridge: Cambridge University Press).

Pager, S. (2003), "Strictness and Subsidiarity: An Institutional Perspective on Affirmative Action at the European Court of Justice," 26 *Boston College International and Comparative Law Review* 35.

Palmeter, D. & Alexandrov, S. A. (2002), "Inducing Compliance in WTO Dispute Settlement," in D. L. M. Kennedy & J. D. Southwick (eds.), *The Political Economy of International Trade Law: Essays in Honor of Robert E. Hudec* (Cambridge: Cambridge University Press) 646.

Palmeter, D. & Mavroidis, P. C. (1998), "The WTO Legal System: Sources of Law," 92 AJIL 398.

(2004), *Dispute Settlement in the World Trade Organization: Practice and Procedure* (Cambridge: Cambridge University Press).

Pan, E. J. (1999), "Assessing the NAFTA Chapter 19 Binational Panel System: An Experiment in International Adjudication," 40 *Harvard International Law Journal* 379.

Pauwelyn, J. (1998), "Evidence, Proof and Persuasion in WTO Dispute Settlement: Who Bears the Burden?" 1(2) JIEL 227.

(1999), "The WTO Agreement on Sanitary and Phytosanitary (SPS) Measures as Applied in the First Three SPS Disputes," 2(4) JIEL 641.

(2000), "Enforcement and Countermeasures in the WTO: Rules Are Rules – Toward a More Collective Approach," 94 AJIL 335.

(2001), "The Role of Public International Law in the WTO: How Far Can We Go?" 95 AJIL 535.

(2002a), "The Use of Experts in WTO Dispute Settlement," 51 *International and Comparative Law Quarterly* 325.

(2002b), "Cross-Agreement Complaints Before the Appellate Body: A Case Study of the *EC-Asbestos* Dispute," 1 *World Trade Review* 63.

(2003a), *Conflict of Norms in Public International Law: How WTO Law Relates to other Rules of International Law* (Cambridge: Cambridge University Press).

(2003b), "How to Win a World Trade Organization Dispute Based on Non-World Trade Organization Law?" 37(6) JWT 997.

(2006), "Adding Sweeteners to Softwood Lumber: The WTO–NAFTA 'Spaghetti Bowl' is Cooking," 9(1) JIEL 197.

Pescatore, P. (1991 – loose-leaf), "Drafting and Analyzing Decisions on Dispute Settlement," in P. Pescatore, W. J. Davey & A. F. Lowenfeld, *Handbook of WTO/GATT Dispute Settlement* (New York: Transnational Juris Publications – loose-leaf) 3.

Petersmann, E.-U. (1997a), *The GATT/WTO Dispute Settlement System: International Law, International Organizations and Dispute Settlement* (London, The Hague, Boston: Kluwer Law International).

(1997b) (ed.), *International Trade Law and the GATT/WTO Dispute Settlement System* (London, The Hague, Boston: Kluwer Law International).

(1997c), "Constitutionalism and International Organizations," 17 *Northwestern Journal of International Law and Business* 398.

(1998a), "How to Constitutionalize International Law and Foreign Policy for the Benefit of Civil Society?' 20 *Michigan Journal of International Law* 1.

(1998b), "From the Hobbesian International Law of Coexistence to Modern Integration Law: The WTO Dispute Settlement System," 1(2) JIEL 175.

(1999), "Constitutionalism and International Adjudication: How to Constitutionalize the UN Dispute Settlement System?" 31 *New York University Journal of International Law and Politics* 753.

(2001), "European and International Constitutional Law: Time for Promoting 'Cosmopolitan Democracy' in the WTO," in G. de Búrca & J. Scott (eds.), *The EU and the WTO: Legal and Constitutional Issues* (Oxford: Hart Publishing) 81.

(2002a), "Time for a United Nations 'Global Compact' for Integrating Human Rights into the Law of Worldwide Organizations: Lessons from European Integration," 13 EJIL 621.

(2002b), "Taking Human Dignity, Poverty and Empowerment of Individuals More Seriously: Rejoinder to Alston," 13 EJIL 845.

Petzold, H. (1993), "The Convention and the Principle of Subsidiarity," in R. St. J. Macdonald, F. Matscher & H. Petzold (eds.), *The European System for the Protection of Human Rights* (Dordrecht, Boston, London: Martinus Nijhoff Publishers) 41.

Pippin, K. J. (1999), "An Examination of the Developments in Chapter 19 Antidumping Decisions under the North American Free Trade Agreement (NAFTA): The Implications and Suggestions for Reform for the Next Century Based on the Experience of NAFTA after the First Five Years," 21 *Michigan Journal of International Law* 101.

Puckett, A. L. & Reynolds, W. L. (1996), "Rules, Sanctions and Enforcement under Section 301: At Odds with the WTO?" 90 AJIL 675.

Quick, R. & Blüthner, A. (1999), "Has the Appellate Body Erred? An Appraisal and Criticism of the Ruling in the WTO Hormones Case," 2(4) JIEL 603.

Qureshi, A. H. (1990), "The New GATT Trade Policy Review Mechanism: An Exercise in Transparency or 'Enforcement'?" 24(3) JWT 147.

(1992), "Some Reflections on the GATT TPRM, in the Light of the Trade Policy Review of the European Communities: A Legal Perspective," 26(6) JWT 103.

(1996), *The World Trade Organization: Implementing International Trade Norms* (Manchester, New York: Manchester University Press).

Qureshi, A. H. & Grynberg, R. (2002), "United States Tax Subsidies Under Domestic International Sales Corporation, Foreign Sales Corporation and Extraterritorial Income Exclusion Act Legislation within the Framework of the World Trade Organization," 36(5) JWT 979.

Rabel, E. (1945), *The Conflict of Laws: A Comparative Study*, vol. I (Ann Arbor: University of Michigan Press).

Raustiala, K. (2003), "Rethinking the Sovereignty Debate in International Economic Law," 6(4) JIEL 841.

Redfern, A. & Hunter, M. (1999), *Law and Practice of International Commercial Arbitration* (London: Sweet & Maxwell).

Renouf, Y. (2005), "A Brief Introduction to Countermeasures in the WTO Dispute Settlement System," in R. Yerxa & B. Wilson (eds.), *Key Issues in WTO Dispute Settlement: The First Ten Years* (Cambridge: Cambridge University Press) 110.

Roberts, K. (1995), "Second-Guessing the Security Council: The International Court of Justice and its Powers of Judicial Review," 7 *Pace International Law Review* 281.

Roessler, F. (1985), "The Provisional Application of the GATT: Note on the Report of the GATT Panel on the 'Manufacturing Clause' in the US Copyright Legislation," 19(3) JWT 289.

(2000), "The Institutional Balance between the Judicial and the Political Organs of the WTO," in M. Bronckers & R. Quick (eds.), *New Directions in International Economic Law: Essays in Honour of John H. Jackson* (The Hague, London, Boston: Kluwer Law International) 325.

Romano, C. (2001), "The *Southern Bluefin Tuna* Dispute: Hints of a World to Come . . . Like It or Not," 32 *Ocean Development & International Law* 313.

Rosas, A. (2001), "Implementation and Enforcement of WTO Dispute Settlement Findings: An EU Perspective," 4(1) JIEL 131.

Rosenne, S. (1997), *The Law and Practice of the International Court, 1920–1996*, vol. III (3rd edn.; The Hague, Boston, London: Martinus Nijhoff Publishers).

Rubin, A. P. (1977), "The International Legal Effects of Unilateral Declarations," 71 AJIL 1.

Ryssdall, R. (1996), "The Coming of Age of the European Convention on Human Rights," 1(1) *European Human Rights Law Review* 18.

Sacerdoti, G. (1997), "Appeal and Judicial Review in International Arbitration and Adjudication: The Case of the WTO Appellate Review," in E.-U. Petersmann (ed.), *International Trade Law and the GATT/WTO Dispute Settlement System* (London, The Hague, Boston: Kluwer Law International) 245.

Sampson, G. P. (2001), *The Role of the World Trade Organization in Global Governance* (Tokyo: United Nations University Press).

Sands, P., Mackenzie, R. & Shany, Y. (eds.) (1999), *Manual on International Courts and Tribunals* (London: Butterworths).

Sarooshi, D. (2005), *International Organizations and Their Exercise of Sovereign Powers* (Oxford: Oxford University Press).

Sauvé, P. & Zampetti, A. B. (2000), "Subsidiarity Perspectives on the New Trade Agenda," 3(1) JIEL 83.

Schaefer, M. (1997), "Are Private Remedies in Domestic Courts Essential for International Trade Agreements to Perform Constitutional Functions with Respect to Sub-Federal Governments?" 17 *Northwestern Journal of International Law and Business* 609.

(1998), "Section 301 and the World Trade Organization: A Largely Peaceful Coexistence To Date," 1(1) JIEL 156.

(2000), "US States, Sub-Federal Rules, and the World Trading System," in M. Bronckers & R. Quick (eds.), *New Directions in International Economic Law: Essays in Honour of John H. Jackson* (The Hague, London, Boston: Kluwer Law International) 525.

Schloemann, H. L. & Ohlhoff, S. (1999), "'Constitutionalization' and Dispute Settlement in the WTO: National Security as an Issue of Competence," 93 AJIL 424.

Schwartz, W. F. & Sykes, A. O. (2002), "The Economic Structure of Renegotiation and Dispute Resolution in the World Trade Organization," 31 *Journal of Legal Studies* S179.

Schwebel, S. M. (2000), "The Proliferation of International Tribunals: Threat or Promise?" in M. Andenas & D. Fairgrieve (eds.), *Judicial Review in*

International Perspective: Liber Amicorum in Honour of Lord Slynn of Hadley (The Hague, London, Boston: Kluwer Law International) 3.

Scott, J. (2004), "International Trade and Environmental Governance: Relating Rules (and Standards) in the EU and the WTO," 15(2) EJIL 307.

Shaffer, G. (2004), "Parliamentary Oversight of WTO Rule-Making: The Political, Normative, and Practical Contexts," 7(3) JIEL 629.

Shany, Y. (2003), *The Competing Jurisdictions of International Courts and Tribunals* (Oxford: Oxford University Press).

(2005), "Toward a General Margin of Appreciation Doctrine in International Law?" 16 EJIL 907.

Shaw, M. N. (1997), *International Law* (4th edn.; Cambridge: Cambridge University Press).

Shearer, I. A. (1994), *Starke's International Law* (11th edn.; London: Butterworths).

Sher, M. (2003), "Chapter 20 Dispute Resolution under NAFTA: Fact or Fiction?" 35 *George Washington International Law Review* 1001.

Shoyer, A. W. & Solovy, E. M. (2000), "The Process and Procedure of Litigating at the World Trade Organization: A Review of the Work of the Appellate Body," 31 *Law and Policy in International Business* 677.

Sim, K. K. (2003), "Rethinking the Mandatory/Discretionary Legislation Distinction in WTO Jurisprudence," 2(1) *World Trade Review* 33.

Sinclair, I. (1984), *The Vienna Convention on the Law of Treaties* (Manchester: Manchester University Press).

Singh, R., Hunt, M. & Demetriou, M. (1999), "Current Topic: Is there a Role for the 'Margin of Appreciation' in National Law after the Human Rights Act?" 4 *European Human Rights Law Review* 15.

Skouteris, T. (1999), "Customary Rules of Interpretation of Public International Law and Interpretative Practices in the WTO Dispute Settlement System," in P. Mengozzi (ed.), *International Trade Law on the 50th Anniversary of the Multilateral Trade System* (Milan: Dott. A. Giuffre Editore) 113.

Smith, J. M. (2003), "WTO Dispute Settlement: The Politics of Procedure in Appellate Body Rulings," 2 *World Trade Review* 65.

Spamann, H. (2004), "Standard of Review for World Trade Organization Panels in Trade Remedy Cases: A Critical Analysis," 38(3) JWT 509.

(2006), "The Myth of 'Rebalancing' Retaliation in WTO Dispute Settlement Practice," 9(1) JIEL 31.

Spiermann, O. (1999), "The Other Side of the Story: An Unpopular Essay on the Making of the European Community Legal Order," 10(4) EJIL 763.

Staker, C. (1987), "Public International Law and the *Lex Situs* Rule in Property Conflicts and Foreign Expropriations," 58 BYIL 151.

Starke, J. G. (1936), "Monism and Dualism in the Theory of International Law," 17 BYIL 66.

Steger, D. P. (2002), "The Appellate Body and its Contribution to WTO Dispute Settlement," in D. L. M. Kennedy & J. D. Southwick (eds.), *The Political Economy of International Trade Law: Essays in Honor of Robert E. Hudec* (Cambridge: Cambridge University Press) 482.

Stehmann, O. (2000), "Foreign Sales Corporations under the WTO: The Panel Ruling on US Export Subsidies," 34(3) JWT 127.

Stewart, R. B. (1992), "International Trade and Environment: Lessons from the Federal Experience," 49 *Washington and Lee Law Review* 1329.

Stewart, T. P. (ed.) (1993), *The GATT Uruguay Round: A Negotiating History (1986–1992)*, vols. I–IV (Deventer: Kluwer Law and Taxation Publishers).

(ed.) (1996), *The World Trade Organization: The Multilateral Trade Framework for the 21st Century and US Implementing Legislation* (Chicago, IL: American Bar Association).

Stewart, T. P. & Johanson, D. S. (1999), "The WTO Beef Hormone Dispute: An Analysis of the Appellate Body Decision," 5 *UC Davis Journal of International Law and Policy* 219.

Stiglitz, J. E. & Charlton, A. (2005), *Fair Trade for All: How Trade Can Promote Development* (Oxford: Oxford University Press).

Stuart, A. W. (1992), "'I Tell Ya I Don't Get No Respect!': The Policies Underlying Standards of Review in US Courts as a Basis for Deference to Municipal Determinations in GATT Panel Appeals," 23 *Law and Policy in International Business* 749.

Sutherland, P., Bhagwati, J., Botchwey, K. *et al.* (2004), *The Future of the WTO: Addressing Institutional Challenges in the New Millennium* (Report by the Consultative Board to the Director-General Supachai Panitchpakdi) (Geneva: WTO).

Swaine, E. T. (2000), "Subsidiarity and Self-Interest: Federalism at the European Court of Justice," 41 *Harvard International Law Journal* 1.

Sykes, A. O. (2000), "The Remedy for Breach of Obligations under the WTO Dispute Settlement Understanding: Damages or Specific Performance?" in M. Bronckers & R. Quick (eds.), *New Directions in International Economic Law: Essays in Honour of John H. Jackson* (The Hague, London, Boston: Kluwer Law International) 347.

Tarullo, D. K. (2002), "The Hidden Costs of International Dispute Settlement: WTO Review of Domestic Anti-Dumping Decisions," 34 *Law and Policy in International Business* 109.

(2003), "Paved with Good Intentions: The Dynamic Effects of WTO Review of Anti-Dumping Action," 2 *World Trade Review* 373.

Thomas, R. (2000), *Legitimate Expectations and Proportionality in Administrative Law* (Oxford: Hart Publishing).

Toope, S. J. (1990), *Mixed International Arbitration: Studies in Arbitration Between States and Private Persons* (Cambridge: Grotius Publications Limited).

Toth, A. G. (1994), "Is Subsidiarity Justiciable?" 19 *European Law Review* 268.

Trachtman, J. P. (1998), "Trade and . . . Problems, Cost–Benefit Analysis and Subsidiarity," 9(1) EJIL 32.

(1999), "The Domain of WTO Dispute Resolution," 40(2) *Harvard International Law Journal* 333.

(2006), "The Constitutions of the WTO," 17(3) EJIL 623.

Trebilcock, M. & Howse, R. (1999), *The Regulation of International Trade* (2nd edn.; London and New York: Routledge).

Trebilcock, M. & Soloway, J. (2002), "International Trade Policy and Domestic Food Safety Regulation: The Case for Substantial Deference by the WTO Dispute Settlement Body under the SPS Agreement," in D. L. M. Kennedy & J. D. Southwick (eds.), *The Political Economy of International Trade Law: Essays in Honor of Robert E. Hudec* (Cambridge: Cambridge University Press) 537.

Trumble, W. R. & Stevenson, A. J. (eds.) (2002), *Shorter Oxford English Dictionary on Historical Principles* (5th edn.; Oxford: Oxford University Press).

United Nations (1983), *United Nations Convention on the Law of the Sea* (New York: United Nations).

Valles, C. M. & McGivern, B. P. (2000), "The Right to Retaliate under the WTO Agreement: The 'Sequencing' Problem," 34(2) JWT 63.

Van den Bossche, P. (2000), "Appellate Review in WTO Dispute Settlement," in F. Weiss (ed.), *Improving WTO Dispute Settlement Procedures: Issues and Lessons from the Practice of Other International Courts and Tribunals* (London: Cameron May) 305.

(2005a), *The Law and Policy of the World Trade Organization: Text, Cases and Materials* (Cambridge: Cambridge University Press).

(2005b), "The Making of the 'World Trade Court': The Origins and Development of the Appellate Body of the World Trade Organization," in R. Yerxa & B. Wilson (eds.), *Key Issues in WTO Dispute Settlement: The First Ten Years* (Cambridge: Cambridge University Press) 63.

Van den Bossche, P. & Alexovicová, I. (2005), "Effective Global Economic Governance by the World Trade Organization," 8(3) JIEL 667.

Van Panhuys, J. H. F. (1964), "Relations and Interactions Between International and National Scenes of Law," 112 *Recueil des Cours* (II).

Vázquez, C. M. (2004), "Judicial Review in the United States and in the WTO: Some Similarities and Differences," 36 *George Washington International Law Review* 587.

Verhoosel, G. (2002), *National Treatment and WTO Dispute Settlement, Adjudicating the Boundaries of Regulatory Autonomy* (Oxford: Hart Publishing).

Vermulst, E. (1999), "The Functioning of the Appellate Body after Four Years: Towards Rule Integrity," 33(2) JWT 1.

Vermulst, E. & Graafsma, F. (2002), *WTO Disputes: Anti-Dumping, Subsidies and Safeguards* (London: Cameron May).

Vervaele, J. A. E., Betlem, G., de Lange, R. & Veldman, A. G. (eds.) (1999), *Compliance and Enforcement of European Community Law* (The Hague, London, Boston: Kluwer Law International).

Villalpando, S. M. (2002), "Attribution of Conduct to the State: How the Rules of State Responsibility May be Applied within the WTO Dispute Settlement System," 5(2) JIEL 393.

Voon, T. & Yanovich, A. (2006), "The Facts Aside: The Limitation of World Trade Organization Appeals to Issues of Law," 40(2) JWT 239.

Waincymer, J. (2002), *WTO Litigation: Procedural Aspects of Formal Dispute Settlement* (London: Cameron May).

Walker, N. (2001), "The EU and the WTO: Constitutionalism in a New Key," in G. de Búrca & J. Scott (eds.), *The EU and the WTO: Legal and Constitutional Issues* (Oxford: Hart Publishing) 31.

Walker, V. R. (1998), "Keeping the WTO from Becoming the 'World Trans-Science Organization': Scientific Uncertainty, Science Policy, and Factfinding in the Growth Hormones Dispute," 31 *Cornell International Law Journal* 251.

Weatherill, S. & Beaumont, P. (1999), *EU Law* (London: Penguin Books).

Wehberg, H. (1959), "Pacta Sunt Servanda," 53 AJIL 775.

Weiler, J. H. H. (1991), "The Transformation of Europe," 100 *Yale Law Journal* 2403.

(2000a), "Cain and Abel – Convergence and Divergence in International Trade Law," in J. H. H. Weiler (ed.), *The EU, the WTO, and the NAFTA: Towards a Common Law of International Trade?* (Oxford: Oxford University Press) 1.

(2000b), "Epilogue: Towards a Common Law of International Trade," in J. H. H. Weiler (ed.), *The EU, the WTO, and the NAFTA: Towards a Common Law of International Trade?* (Oxford: Oxford University Press) 201.

(2001), "The Rule of Lawyers and the Ethos of Diplomats: Reflections on the Internal and External Legitimacy of WTO Dispute Settlement," 35(2) JWT 191.

Weiler, T. J. (1995), "Curial Deference and NAFTA Chapter 19 Panels: Is What is Good for the Goose, Good for the Gander?" 1 *Journal of International Legal Studies* 83.

Weiss, E. B. (2000), "Strengthening National Compliance with Trade Law: Insights from Environment," in M. Bronckers & R. Quick (eds.), *New Directions in International Economic Law: Essays in Honour of John H. Jackson* (The Hague, London, Boston: Kluwer Law International) 457.

Weiss, F. (ed.) (2000), *Improving WTO Dispute Settlement Procedures: Issues and Lessons from the Practice of Other International Courts and Tribunals* (London: Cameron May).

Williams, B. G. (1999), "Non-Violation Complaints in the WTO System," in P. Mengozzi (ed.), *International Trade Law on the 50th Anniversary of the Multilateral Trade System* (Milan: Dott. A. Giuffre Editore) 675.

Winham, G. R. (1998), "NAFTA Chapter 19 and the Development of International Administrative Law: Applications in Antidumping and Competition Law," 32(1) JWT 65.

Wirth, D. A. (1998), "European Communities – Measures Concerning Meat and Meat Products," 92 AJIL 755.

Wolfe, R. (2005), "Decision-Making and Transparency in the 'Medieval' WTO: Does the Sutherland Report Have the Right Prescription?" 8(3) JIEL 631.

Wolff, M. (1950), *Private International Law* (2nd edn.; Oxford: Clarendon Press).

World Trade Organization (1994), *The Results of the Uruguay Round of Multilateral Trade Negotiations: The Legal Texts* (Geneva: GATT Secretariat).

(1995), *Analytical Index: Guide to GATT Law and Practice* (Geneva: World Trade Organization).

(2001), *The WTO Dispute Settlement Procedures: A Collection of the Relevant Legal Texts* (Cambridge: Cambridge University Press).

(2006), *International Trade Statistics 2006* (Geneva: WTO).

Yamane, H. (1998), "The WTO Dispute Settlement Mechanism and Japanese Traders," 1(4) JIEL 683.

Yanovich, A. & Voon, T. (2005), "What is the Measure at Issue?" in A. D. Mitchell (ed.), *Challenges and Prospects for the WTO* (London: Cameron May).

Yerxa, R. & Wilson, B. (eds.) (2005), *Key Issues in WTO Dispute Settlement: The First Ten Years* (Cambridge: Cambridge University Press).

Zdouc, W. (2005), "The Reasonable Period of Time for Compliance with the Rulings and Recommendations Adopted by the WTO Dispute Settlement Body," in R. Yerxa & B. Wilson (eds.), *Key Issues in WTO Dispute Settlement: The First Ten Years* (Cambridge: Cambridge University Press) 88.

Zhang, X. (2003), "Direct Effect of the WTO Agreements: National Survey," 9(2) *International Trade Law and Regulation* 35.

Zleptnig, S. (2002), "The Standard of Review in WTO Law: An Analysis of Law, Legitimacy and the Distribution of Legal and Political Authority," 13(5) *European Business Law Review* 427.

Zoellner, C.-S. (2006), "Transparency: An Analysis of an Evolving Fundamental Principle in International Economic Law," 27 *Michigan Journal of International Law* 579.

Zonnekeyn, G. A. (1999), "The Legal Status of WTO Panel Reports in the EC Legal Order," 2(4) JIEL 713.

Index

www.ingramcontent.com/pod-product-compliance
Lightning Source LLC
LaVergne TN
LVHW090306210926
848480LV00001B/155

* 9 7 8 0 5 2 1 1 7 5 3 4 0 *